Tourism Development
Principles and Practices

Tourism Development
Principles and Practices

Fourth Revised Edition

A.K. Bhatia

STERLING

STERLING PUBLISHERS (P) LTD.
Regd. Office: A1/256 Safdarjung Enclave,
New Delhi-110029. Cin: U22110DL1964PTC211907
Phone: +91 82877 98380
E-mail: mail@sterlingpublishers.in
www.sterlingpublishers.in

Tourism Development: Principles and Practices

ISBN 978 93 862 4562 5
First Edition 1983
Second Revised Edition 2002
Third Revised Edition 2009
Fourth Revised Edition 2019

Printed and Published in India by

Sterling Publishers Pvt. Ltd.,
Plot No. 13, Ecotech-III, Greater Noida - 201306, U. P. India

To My Loving Parents

Who lived a life of excellence with unwavering compassion and love for their family. Integrity an honour had been their strength.

Their life was a blessing, their memory a treasure. They are loved beyond words and missed beyond measure. We miss them in every moment of our lives – with deepest love, greatest pride and honour. Their absence is felt deeply in our hearts. We continue to seek their blessings and affection.

To My Loving Wife

It has been almost four years that you left for heavenly abode and there has not been a single day that I have not missed your presence in my life. You may be gone from this world, but you are forever alive in my heart.

Acknowledgements

No published work is completely the work of the author or authors whose names are listed on the title page of the book. The unnamed authors as also research scholars and academicians of this book are legion as they are the ones who have done the pioneering work in explaining the complex tourism phenomenon in its various manifestations. In the first place my special thanks go to them from whom I have derived great inspiration. It is these pioneers who must be credited with whatever merit this book may have. My special thanks go first to them. On the other hand all the weaknesses and shortcomings of the book are solely the responsibility of the author.

Sincere thanks are extended to several international travel and tourism organisations and associations especially the UN World Tourism Organisation whose various reports and publications have immensely helped in shaping the present revised and enlarged version of the edition. The contributions of these organisations have been invaluable and for that I am deeply grateful.

My understanding of the complex subject of tourism and the knowledge have been influenced and shaped by my work in the Central Ministry of Tourism, Government of India. The manifold opportunities of work experience not only at the headquarters establishment but various overseas tourist-offices provided by the department proved to be quite invaluable in the writing of this book. I owe a debt of gratitude to my former Ministry of Tourism for providing me an opportunity to pursue a profession which I have always cherished.

My thanks and gratitude, as also appreciation, to all the professionals and organisations in the field and eminent persons in the travel industry in Belgium, France and Switzerland whose in-depth knowledge and experience proved to be of great value in explaining various facets of tourism.

My sincere thanks to Sterling for reorganising the entire manuscript of the book on computer. Thanks are also due to Priyanka Sah.

Finally, my special thanks to my wife Kamla who is no more, for encouraging me not only to complete the revised edition of the book but also assisting me in the final preparation of the manuscript for publication. Her assistance in editing the draft manuscript has proved be to quite invaluable.

Preface to the Fourth Edition

Preparing the fourth revised edition of this book has been a difficult exercise as it involved many different tasks and considerations. The very first concern has been in bringing the material up-to-date as tourism continues to grow rapidly. Since the first edition of the book was prepared almost two decades ago, there have been several changes in the nature and scope of the tourism phenomenon. The present edition, while updating the material, has also retained the material of the earlier work. This edition also incorporates several new topics which are as a result of new developments in the field of tourism.

Tourism today is one of the world's fastest growing and oldest industries. With the advent of industrialisation, people started moving in large numbers to places away from their usual places of residence and work with a view to seek change. This trend continued until tourism became a mass phenomenon. This phenomenon is a visible result of the great technological developments which have changed the social, demographic and political geography of the world since the nineteenth century. In the beginning the railways were responsible for opening up the continents—carrying people, material and food. This made possible the formation of great nineteenth century industrial towns and cities. Then came steamships, making it possible for people to cross continents to be qualified as international travellers. This was followed by the invention and introduction of the motor car which gave great freedom of mobility to people. Finally, it was the aeroplane which, when linked with rising affluence, coupled with free time and motivation, led to an entire new concept—the concept of mass tourism.

Thomas Cook, the pioneer of organised mass tourism had proclaimed, "God's earth in all its fullness and beauty is for the people." Travel from the earliest times has had a fascination for mankind. The urge to explore new places within one's own country or outside and seek a change of environment and experience has been there since ancient times. Rapid developments in the means of transport systems and communication have made the entire world practically one neighbourhood. Recent changes in information technology have given easy access to a large number of people the choice of a variety of destinations. Today millions of people seem to enjoy the prospect of moving from one continent to another in a matter of hours. Prosperity and leisure coupled with the quest for pleasure and recreation, are the principle motivating factors which sustain the development of mass movement of people. The force behind this phenomenon is tourism.

It is predicted that travel and tourism will be one of the world's highest growth sectors in the new century. UN World Tourism Organisation statistics indicate that the tourism industry will continue to grow from strength to strength. From 70 million international tourist movements in the year 1960 the number had increased to over 710 million in the year 2000. It is further estimated by UNWTO that international tourism arrivals worldwide would reach 1.5 billion by the year 2020.

The economic impacts the number of tourist movements globally has enormous. According to the latest report from World Travel and Tourism Council (WTTC), the sector accounts for 10.4% of global GDP and 313 million jobs or 9.9% of the total employment in the year 2017. The direct contribution of Travel and Tourism to GDP was USD 2,570.1 billion (3.2% of the total GDP in 2017) and is forecast to rise by 4.0% in 2018 and to rise by 3.8% p.a from 2018 to USD 3,890.0 billion (3.6% of total GDP) in 2028.

Although there have been temporary setbacks in the number of tourist movements due to increase in fuel costs and territorial crises, tourism has withstood the change of circumstances in national and international economies better than other sectors of the economy. Herman Kahn, one of the leading futurologist of the world, predicting a golden era for tourism has said, "I see a very bright future ahead for tourism and travel industry. There are clouds on the horizon, to be sure, but it will become a larger giant than it already is in the next decades."

Those responsible for managing the affairs of nations have almost universally recognised the economic advantages of tourism. Tourism is a painless procedure for transfer of real resources from industrially capital-surplus developed countries to low-income developing countries. It is a very important source for maximising scarce foreign exchange earnings, not only for developing countries but for many developed countries of the world too. For instance, there were more visitor arrivals in Spain in 2017 (81.8 million) than the actual population of the country (40 million). Countries in areas such as the Caribbean depend very heavily on tourist income, which often represents the major part of the Gross Domestic Product (GDP). In India in the year 2007, tourism ranks as the major foreign exchange earner for the country. Even developed nations like Canada (which derives over 10 per cent of its GDP from international visitors) rely heavily on the income from tourism. Tourism is also being recognised as a source of employment. It is a highly labour-intensive industry offering employment to both the semi-skilled and the unskilled. Being a service industry, it creates employment opportunities for the local population. It is a major source of income and employment for individuals living in places deficient in natural resources which cannot readily contribute to the economic prosperity of the area except through the medium of tourism. This aspect of provision of employment becomes more important in a developing country where the levels of unemployment and underemployment tend to be high. Besides, providing employment to a large number of people, tourism can be the instrument of regional policy aimed at achieving an equitable balance between major industrial areas and the rest of the country. Tourism enables the wealth earned in one part of the country to be transferred in part to another.

Tourism also makes a tremendous contribution to the improvement of social and political understanding. Travel fosters a better rapport between people with different lifestyles. Personal international contacts have always been an important way of spreading ideas about other cultures. Tourism is thus an important means of promoting cultural exchanges and international cooperation. The experiences gained through travel have a profound effect upon the life of the individual as well as upon society as a whole. Travel exercises a very healthy influence on international understanding and appreciation of other people's style of life. Tourism thus is a highly complex phenomenon. In addition to its economic significance it is also a significant human activity. As a mass phenomenon of an essentially social nature, tourism can no longer be viewed as a fringe activity. Both in the use it makes of time and space and its relationship with the production of goods and services, tourism has become one of the pivotal concerns of nations and of the international community.

Various academic disciplines are involved in the study of tourism phenomenon because of its complex nature. Some basic disciplines such as economics, psychology, and sociology and geography contribute a great deal. Certain newer disciplines of management and marketing have been introduced and play a significant role. In addition, techniques such as planning, statistics and market research are also involved and are used extensively by tourism enterprises. In order to explain the complex tourism phenomenon in its various manifestations, it is essential to have a systematic framework to explain it.

The book is designed to introduce the basic concepts of tourism. It serves as a comprehensive resource for the working manager, supervisor as also executive. The students pursuing both undergraduate and postgraduate college and university courses in tourism, the book serves as a valuable guide. The approach has been to provide a simple and comprehensive outline of various dimensions of tourism such as historical, psychological, social and cultural, economic, environmental and international.

Part II of the book examines the tourism services and tools available to assist industry professionals and students in understanding tourism activity. The chapters focus on various services for the traveller—planning and development, research and measurement, marketing and tourism policy.

Appendices make a book more valuable. I have believed all along that these add interest and provide good support to the subject matter. Later on in the book, a comprehensive glossary of tourism and travel terms, a list of tourism trade journals and periodicals, and publications of international organisations have been provided. A bibliography has been prepared to serve as a guide to the reader who wishes to study a particular subject more extensively. A list of international tourism organisations as also institutions imparting training in various courses in the field of tourism has also been appended.

The approach throughout has been to provide a simple and comprehensive outline of as many subjects as possible. The reader who wishes to make a detailed study of any subject will obviously have to do more reading. There is no one book available covering the wide range of subjects on tourism. It is the author's earnest hope that the fourth edition of this book will provide valuable material to both students as well as professionals and others engaged in the business of tourism.

Ex-Deputy Director General — A. K. Bhatia
Ministry of Tourism, Government of India
New Delhi
June, 2019

Contents

Part II

Abbreviations

ABTA	:	Association of British Travel Agents
AH & MA	:	American Hotel & Motel Association
AI	:	Air India
AIEST	:	International Association of Scientific Experts in Tourism
AAI	:	Airport Authority of India
APEX	:	Advance Purchase Excursion
AMTRAK	:	American Travel by Track
AP	:	American Plan
ASI	:	Archaeological Survey of India
ASTA	:	American Society of Travel Agents
ATC	:	Air Traffic Control
BIT	:	Bulk Inclusive Tour
BOP	:	Balance of Payments
BTA	:	British Tourist Authority
CLIA	:	Cruise Lines International Association
CRS	:	Computer Reservation Systems
DGCA	:	Directorate General of Civil Aviation
DIT	:	Domestic Independent Tour
DOT	:	Department of Tourism
E C A F E	:	Economic Commission for Asia and Far East
E C S O C	:	Economic and Social Council of the United Nations
E N I T	:	Ente Nazionale Italiano per il Turismo
E P	:	European plan
E S C A P	:	Economic and Social Commission for Asia and the Pacific
E T C	:	European Travel Commission
E T C	:	Euro-Traveller's Cheque
E T C I	:	Euro-Traveller's Cheque International
E C	:	European Community
F H R A I	:	Federation of Hotel and Restaurant Association of India
F I T	:	Foreign Individual Tour
F T T	:	Foreign Travel Tax
G I T	:	Group Inclusive Tour
G S A	:	General Sales Agent

G D S	:	Global Distribution Systems
I A	:	Indian Airlines
I A A I	:	International Airport Authority of India
I A P C O	:	International Association of Professional Congress Organisations
I A T A	:	International Air Transport Authority
I C A O	:	International Civil Aviation Organisation
I C C A	:	International Congress and Convention Association
I D A	:	International Development Association
I F T O	:	International Federation of Tour Operators
I H A	:	International Hotel Association
I L O	:	International Labour Organisation
I H R A	:	International Hotel & Restaurant Association
I A P A	:	International Airline Passenger Association
I F T O	:	International Federation of Tour Operators
I T	:	Information Technology
I S T O	:	International Social Tourism Organisation
I T A	:	International Touring Alliance
I T	:	Inclusive Tour
I T C	:	Inclusive Tour Charter
I T D C	:	India Tourism Development Corporation
I U O T O	:	International Union of Official Tourist Organisation
I U O T P O	:	International Union of Tourist Propaganda Organisation
I Y H F	:	International Youth Hostel Federation
I A T O	:	Indian Association of Tour Operators
I O T O	:	Indian Ocean Tourism Organisation
I C P B	:	India Convention Promotion Bureau
I T B	:	International Tourismus Borse
M A P	:	Modified American Plan
N C A E R	:	National Council of Applied Economic Research
N D C	:	National Development Council
N T B	:	National Tourism Board
N T O	:	National Tourism Organisation
O E C D	:	Organisation for Economic Cooperation and Development
O E E C	:	Organisation for European Economic Cooperation
P A T A	:	Pacific Asia Travel Association
P R	:	Public Relations
R T A C	:	Regional Tourist Advisory Committee
R T O	:	Regional Tourist Office
R T B	:	Regional Tourist Boards
S A R T C	:	South Asia Regional Tourist Council
S A T W	:	Society of American Travel Writers
S S T	:	Supersonic Transport

S T D C	:	State Tourism Development Corporation
S A A R C	:	South Asia Association for Regional Co-operation
T A	:	Travel Agent
T A A I	:	Travel Agents Association of India
T B R E	:	Tourist Baggage Re-Export
T G V	:	Train Grande Vitesse
S T C	:	Switzerland Tourism Council
T I M	:	Travel Information Manual
T I M	:	Tourism Income Multiplier
U F T A A	:	Universal Federation of Travel Agents Association
U S T O A	:	United States Tour Operators Association
U N	:	United Nations
U N CT A D	:	United Nations Conference on Trade and Development
U N E S C O	:	United Nations Educational, Scientific and Cultural Organisations
U S T T A	:	US Travel and Tourism Administration
U N D P	:	United Nations Development Programme
U N E P	:	United Nations Environment Programme
U N W T O	:	United Nations World Tourism Organisations
V F R	:	Visiting Friends and Relations
W A T A	:	World Association of Travel Agents
W H O	:	World Health Organisation
W T T C	:	World Travel & Tourism Council
W T M	:	World Travel Mart
Y H A I	:	Youth Hostel Association of India

List of Tables

PART I

apter

istorical Dimensions

The first instances of long-distance travel in the broader Mediterranean world occurred in what are today Egypt and Iraq. In Egypt the Nile served as a conduit for trade and transportation, while in the Near East, river travel on the Tigris and Euphrates was supplemented by long distance travel over land in wagon-like vehicles pulled by oxen. Later, the chariot developed, which was originally reserved for royalty, although it later became integrated into warfare. In the Near East, large but not particularly sophisticated systems of roads evolved; later these would be connected and developed by the Persians.

The primary motivation for the development of travel and infrastructure to support it in both Egypt and the Near East was conquest and subsequent rule, a trend that continued in Greece and Rome. There is evidence, however, of travel motivated by tourism in Egypt, with visitors and scribes coming to view and record the pyramids and other religious monuments.

Maritime and River Travel

The earliest maritime travel occurred on the Nile and other rivers in the Near East. Due to the lack of roads in ancient Greece, the most efficient way of shipping large amounts of goods, such as olive oil, was over the sea. Greek ships were built in varying sizes, with the largest accommodating as much as 500 tons of goods. Despite reliance on favourable weather, relatively little effort went into short sea voyages beyond the packing and management of the ship, although there was the danger of pirates and kidnapping for ransom.

For Romans, the seas were more or less clear of pirates due to the Roman military, although the fear of shipwreck by storm was greater, and often referenced in poetry and song. Passage by ship was considerably more pleasant than passage by land, but was not available throughout the year due to changes in tides and other weather conditions.

Land Travel

The earliest notable road system in the ancient Mediterranean world was the Royal Road. The most extensive incarnation of the system was unified and organised under Darius I, ruler of the Achaemenid Empire in the 5th century BCE. It was built from connecting and upgrading older systems, and was used to enable rapid communication and transportation throughout the empire, as well as the collection of taxes. Generally, other contemporary roads were not paved or well maintained, making land travel both on foot and horseback arduous and time-consuming.

Greece

Greece roads were poorly developed due to the fragmentation of Greek society at the state level, and due to the extreme cost of constructing roads in Greece's mountainous terrain. At least in Athens, when built, roads were funded through special taxes on wealthy. Some roads were difficult to traverse even on foot, and most could not be traversed with the heavy wagons built to haul goods. Notable exceptions were the roads between major cities and nearby sanctuaries and holy sites, which were built to endure all weather. However, no portion of the Greek highway system included state-sponsored way stations or milestones, as found later in Rome.

There was danger of violence on Greek roads. For the same reasons that roads in Greece were poorly and rarely constructed, there was essentially no oversight by official forces, and as such travellers were prone to being accosted by highwaymen. As such, having a large entourage was useful for protection, and the transportation of valuables was risky.

Rome

Roman roads were extensive, largely to facilitate the transportation of the military. They suffered from lack of maintenance, at least during the Roman Republic due to the fact that more visible projects (new city-centric construction, such as aqueducts, and arena games) took precedence. The roads were built with few resources, and had to be built to function in a variety of geographical and seasonal conditions. As Roman roads radiated away from towns, they became less elaborate, and were sometimes paved with gravel, or markers were used to illustrate the proper path. This lack of attention to detail is contrasted with the uniform stone highways that generally existed near major urban centres, typically built by soldiers overseen by army engineers. Romans tended to build their roads without curves as often as possible. The danger of violence was much less pronounced on Roman roads, due to the strong central military that did not attend the limited Greek highway network.

Due to the difficulty and stress of travel by land, few civilians chose to conduct long-distance travel or trade over Rome's roads. Instead, tax collectors, couriers, soldiers and other government officials would have been the primary users of the highway network.

Map Making and Itineraria

Without ready access to maps, both Greeks and Romans relied on *itineraria* to conduct sea travel, and the Romans used the documents for land travel as well. These documents were lists of cities or ports and the distances between them. Itineraria may have sometimes included crude illustrations, never to scale, to orient travellers as they moved through Roman or Greek territory.

Greek Maps

Greek maps were often either localised, intended to demonstrate the shapes of specific cities, or to represent abstract concepts. Divisions between continents and nations were often determined by bodies of water. Greek maps further separated the world into habitable and inhospitable zones. Later Greek scientists determined that the Earth was round, although there was some debate as to the veracity of this claim. During the conquests by Alexander the Great, Hellenistic knowledge of the world was expanded, resulting in an improved map of the world by Eratosthenes.

Roman Maps

Like the Greeks, the Romans did not possess the materials or technology to produce useful maps. Several examples of what may have been Roman maps have been introduced through archaeology, although both their validity as maps and even their authenticity have been debated. Romans used *itineraria* in warfare, to guide government postal workers, and for civilian travel. Those that contained illustrations to underscore the text would not have been to scale, and would have born more similarity to transit maps than contemporary to-scale maps. Although not used for travel, there is evidence of maps created after surveys by the Roman government, in a process known as centuriation in which the land was reduced to grids for cultivation.

History reveals the harsh realities of travel in ancient times and civilizations. The search for basic necessities of life—water, food, shelter and safety—kept early hunters constantly on the move from one settlement to another. This often meant dangerous and difficult travel for individuals, families or the entire communities. In the absence of any organised roads, people travelled by foot or on animal backs over open fields, forests, and marshy lands often facing great dangers. Movement across the land was a virtual adventure that required caution and skill.

Travel in Prehistoric Times

Travel in the prehistoric times Paleolithic Age, (30,000 B.C. to 10,000 B.C.) suggests that all human activity, as also movements, revolved upon day-to-day survival. Gradually, when the regions were explored, fire was discovered and tools were made, people were able to settle down in shelters. This resulted in increased activity in travel. The ability to make and use tools and build shelters enabled prehistoric man to travel to new hunting grounds even in very extreme and inhospitable weather. Subsequently, during the Neolithic Age, which began about 10,000 B.C., primitive people settled in more permanent regions and formed themselves into some kind of agricultural communities. The element of travel in humans can thus be traced to the beginning of time.

During the Neolithic Age, several innovations in the field of transport changed the very nature of travel. In Egypt, sailing vessels were built around 4000 B.C. This resulted in conscious travel in order to explore and see the world. There are early references to this effect. The invention of wheel and money by the Sumerians (Babylonia) around 3500 B.C. marks the beginning of the modern era of travel. All the above factors and inventions greatly affected travel. The money invented by the Sumerians was used by them in their various business and travel dealings. Many traders could pay for transportation as well as accommodation either with money or by exchange of goods. Shulgi, the ruler of ancient Babylonia, claimed to have protected roads and built rest houses at various places for respectable wayfarers. The forerunners of modern-day accommodation, these rest houses were the ideal places of rest for the travellers of those days.

Travel for Trade

From the earliest times, travel has fascinated man. Much of travel in the beginning was largely unconscious and rather a simple affair. The cumbersome procedures that we witness in travel today were not to be found in olden days. No travel formalities existed. Travel in the distant past was not a thing of pleasure as is the case now. The traveller of the past was a merchant, a pilgrim, a scholar in search of ancient texts, or even a curious wayfarer looking forward to new and exciting experiences. Trade and commerce was, however, the strongest force in the ancient times; it made people travel to distant lands in order to seek fortunes. Gradually, opening of the new trade routes gave a big boost to travel. Travellers from distant lands started moving about in large numbers and visited many places for the purpose of commerce. With the opening of the trade routes, travel became easier and more regulated. At the marketplaces, travellers made contacts with each other resulting in increased flow of trade and commerce. Trade relations matured into cultural relations and better understanding of each other's way of life.

Early travel in the Orient, particularly in India and China, was also largely based on trade and commerce. Travel to the Orient, especially to India, was undertaken by travellers from all over the world. This was done for a variety of reasons—the most important among them being trade and commerce. India and China enjoyed the reputation of being countries of fabulous wealth. It is on record that long before the Christian era, travellers visited India in search of fortune. This trend continued and became more marked in course of time with Europeans heading towards the Indian shores for the sole purpose of trade and commerce. Not only did India attract a series of invaders starting with Alexander of Macedonia, but also great travellers like Vasco da Gama. Many foreigners, Arabs and Europeans alike came to India to establish trading posts. The great explorer, Christopher Columbus, set out to find a new route to India and in the process discovered the New World. India always held a great fascination for foreign travellers. Mark Twain described it as a fabulous world of "Splendour and rags, the one country under the sun with an imperishable interest, the one land that all men desire to see".

Medieval Travel and Tourism

When people today are asked about retirement plans, they very frequently say, "I hope to travel." Being a tourist, travelling around to interesting places, is considered fun and worthwhile, even if only really available to those with leisure time (one wonders if those whose jobs require a great deal of travel have the same attitude toward retirement).

Travel in the Middle Ages was a lot harder than it is now. With human power (walking) the chief form of transport, much of the population might spend most of their lives within a twenty-mile radius. Horses were for the well to do, and carts, made to transport goods, would have been very uncomfortable to ride in over any distance. Yet people did travel. The aristocracy especially travelled a lot. It was easier to move people than to move food, so large courts would frequently move from place to place, eating up the food at one palace before moving on to the next. Without modern communication, the only easy way to tell what was happening somewhere was to go there, so kings, dukes, counts, and landlords were constantly on the move, checking things out, passing judgments, hearing complaints, collecting revenue. And of course you had armies marching back and forth and young men travelling to tournaments.

Tourism as we know it did not exist in the Middle Ages. Travel really began in the nineteenth century, when well to do young men (rarely women) would undertake a Grand Tour. Young English gentlemen would travel around the Continent for months, even a few years, picking up culture and art, admiring the scenery, and visiting places of historical significance. The very word "tourism" comes from taking the Tour.

Modern tourism essentially began with the automobile, after World War I. It is much easier to go visit interesting places when one can hop in the car. In France, after the Armistice, people wanted to visit the battlefields where so many of their young men had died. The automobile made this possible, and Michelin especially (maker of car tires) started putting out helpful booklets to let people figure out where to go and what to see.

Learning About History

Modern tourism is a combination of "broadening one's mind" by being exposed to different scenes and ideas, of entertainment by seeing lovely and interesting places, and of education, by learning about history and other useful subjects. The museums where all this educational information was made available developed along with tourism. Something that looks like tourism certainly existed in the Middle Ages, but its purpose was very different from broadening one's mind or being entertained or educated. It was called pilgrimage.

One travelled places to improve one's soul, and the difficulties of the journey were supposed to help improve it, by shaking one out of lethargy or luxury. The best pilgrimage goal was always Jerusalem, the scene of the Crucifixion, but most Europeans would choose more accessible places to go.

Rome was always a place for pilgrims, full of the bones of early martyrs, the graves of Saints Peter and Paul, and of course the papacy. Many other spots became pilgrimage centres, from Vézelay in Burgundy to Santiago in northern Spain (and a pilgrimage route ran between these two). Pilgrims were always interested in lovely architecture, important relics, and holy men (hermits could be visited as part of the pilgrim experience), but they do not seem to have paid as much attention to scenery.

Travel During the Middle Ages

During the Middle Ages how did people travel. Just what were there conveyances, how did they travel what did they see and visit, was it safe and where did they stay? How did the people of the middle ages travel if at all?

During the middle ages, pilgrimages were undertaken for a variety of purposes. Some individuals travelled to religious sites for the forgiveness of their sins, others to receive a "divine" cure for their health problems. While religion was the primary purpose for pilgrimage travel, adventure, learning and merriment were also on the trip venue and agenda.

Several shines or churches shaped a common itinerary. The most popular sites included Santiago de Compostela in Spain , the famous churches of Paris France, the seat of the Roman Catholic Church in Rome, and the Holy Land - especially of course Jerusalem. Since the pilgrim was in search of forgiveness or indulgence (years of forgiveness), proof had to obtain. This was often provided in the form of a pendant or pin - in essence a kind of "holy souvenir".

Travel was by foot or horseback; when possible pilgrims travelled by boat or horse-drawn coach or coaches. The mass pilgrimages required communities nearby the shrines or along popular routes to provide accommodations for these spiritual or "medical tourism", travellers and wayfarers. Some inns catered only to particular nationalities and clienteles; others varied by location and in terms of resources of the travellers and the traveller's groups and groupings. Very popular sites had an array of inns and hostels to accommodate weary travellers in search of salvation or specialised medical care for those in desperation of medical and health care - not available in their local areas and locales. In addition earthly pleasures and curiosities were provided by the "service and hospitality"industries.

Lastly people travelled in groups to guard against robbers and muggers on the roads, and as for and in addition for comfort and merriment. It can be said that although all types of people made pilgrimages, that this specific journey and most trips of this time period - that is the "Middle Ages" were by the far the most pleasant for those of means. Its amazing that even comparing travel currently in 2017 to the Middle Ages themselves that at least in travel , travelling and in the travel , tourism and hospitality industries the more things change - the more they stay the same.

Travel and Commerce a Strong Force

History thus reveals that trade and commerce remained a strong force for many travellers to undertake long journeys to distant lands. This was followed by an urge to explore new lands and to seek new knowledge in ancient and distant lands. There are many references to great explorers who spent many formidable years of their lives in search of knowledge. Even if we go back a few hundred years to the third century A.D., since the first exploration of Alexander the Great, or only about 700 years since Marco Polo and their amazing explorations crossing many lands, we get fascinating accounts of these great persons. These great explorers can perhaps be credited with the distinction of being the pioneers who subsequently paved the way for modern travel. When Alexander the Great reached India, he found well-maintained roads lined with shady trees. Along one royal highway, 1,920 kilometres long and about 19 metres wide, people travelled in chariots, palanquins, bullock carts, on horses, camels and elephants.

Young Marco Polo left Venice in the year 1271 with his father and uncle. They travelled through Persia and Afghanistan to the "roof of the world", the then unknown Pamir Plateau. After crossing the wind swept Gobi Desert, he reached Kublai Khan's palace and remained in China for over twenty years. On his way back home, he stopped in Sumatra, Java, India, and Ceylon. The first medieval traveller to reach the Orient was probably Benjamin of Tudela, a Jewish scholar who left Saragossa in A.D. 1160. He wrote a detailed account of his thirteen-year journey through Europe, Persia and India, giving information on the Jewish communities, and the geography of the various places he visited.

Yet another famous traveller who recorded interesting accounts of his travel experiences was Ibn Batuta. Ibn Batuta wrote a detailed diary of his travel experiences. He was born at Tangier (Morocco) in A.D. 1304. In A.D. 1325, he left his home, and passing through various countries in Africa and West Asia, crossed the Indus (also Sindhu) in A.D. 1333. The travels took him as far as Indonesia and China. Out of a total of more than 17,000 miles, he covered over 14,000 miles through India, Maldives and Ceylon.

There are also accounts of some European travellers who visited India during the period described above. The Franciscan friar, John of Monte Corrino, visited India on his way to and back from China during the last decade of the thirteenth century. Mention may also be made here of the famous Portuguese chronicle—the commentaries of the Great Alfonso D'Albuquerque. Later on in the sixteenth and seventeenth centuries many more European monks, travellers, and adventurers visited India and many other places in search of knowledge.

The expeditions of these great travellers rewarded them with new ideas and also with fabulously rich treasures from rich and highly advanced civilizations of Asia and other parts of the world. The actual number of individuals who participated in various explorations as travellers in search of knowledge, however, represented only a small proportion of the total population. Travel was considered difficult and not a thing of pleasure. Transport and communication systems of today were non-existent. Land migrations were done by foot and on horseback, elephant, camel and river craft in Europe, Asia and Africa, and the very limited exploration by rafts and primitive vessels moved by tides, oar and sail.

Early Pleasure Travel

The Romans probably can be considered the first pleasure travellers. They travelled for a variety of reasons and enjoyed attractions associated with natural beauty, arts, music and the Colosseum games. Travel for pleasure, religion and sports was recognised as an important pastime of well-to-do Romans. The Roman citizen had the resources and time—the two most powerful elements for travel. The Romans had easy and safe access to Greece, Egypt, Asia Minor and many parts of present-day Europe and Africa. All these regions provided excellent opportunities for pleasure travel and trade.

The fabled Silk Route was the creation of this period. Stretching across more than 12,000 kilometres from Mediterranean Sea to the Pacific Ocean, it was the world's main trade artery linking the great civilizations of China, India, Persia, Mesopotamia, Egypt, Greece and Rome. Along the fabled highway, cities and towns grew prosperous from the exchange of exotic, luxury goods. Their rulers built spectacular palaces, mosques, temples, caravanserais and other structures.

Travel received a great stimulus from the good communication system and security of the Roman Empire. There existed a fine network of roads and new roads were built increasingly wherever the Romans went. Travel literature was published extensively giving routes, names of major roads, distances between places and time required in travelling to them. The Romans were able to travel over a hundred miles in a day using relays of horses. They journeyed primarily to see famous temples in the Mediterranean areas, particularly the monuments and the famous Pyramids of Egypt. The Romans also travelled during holiday occasions, especially during the Olympic Games.

Spas and Seaside Resorts

Spas and seaside resorts, which developed during this period, may be associated with pleasure travel. Medicinal baths and seaside resorts, which were later named spas, were very popular with the Romans. The inland Spa had its origin in a belief in the efficacy of its mineral waters for medicinal purposes, either by drinking the water or by immersing in it. The patients using the spas would require certain diversions, and gradually, the spa resorts added facilities for pleasure and entertainment to their medical facilities. The visitors now not only enjoyed the medicinal baths but also various forms of entertainments. Theatrical productions, athletic competitions, festivals and other forms of entertainment and amusements were often provided at the sites where spas were located. The spas had become extremely popular with travellers.

Subsequent development of spas after their original use for recreational purposes by the Romans played a big role in the development of pleasure travel in many countries in Europe. Development of various seaside resorts is also linked with it. In the later half of the eighteenth century, people started realising the possible curative effects of sea water. Sea bathing also became very popular and many believed that bathing in sea water was more beneficial than inland spas. The seaside resorts began to appear as an alternative to the original inland spa. By the year 1865, there were major seaside resorts in Britain, France and few more countries of Central Europe. This development was a result of demand for vacation travel. However, the use of these resorts was still confined to those with considerable means. Nevertheless, both the spas and the seaside resorts paved the way for the modern pleasure travel all over the world where millions of people visited various seaside resorts each year.

The fall of the Roman Empire between A.D. 400 and A.D. 500 had a great impact on the development of travel in old Roman territories, across Europe and parts of Asia Minor for a number of centuries. It was a great setback particularly for pleasure travel in Europe. During the Dark Ages only the adventurous and brave would venture to travel. No one would, however, associate travel with pleasure. Also with the fall of the Roman Empire came a sharp decline in trade and commerce. In the absence of a prosperous community with the incentive to travel for pleasure, travelling ceased to exist for its own sake. The luxury of vacation travel almost disappeared, various facilities and resources required for the common people to travel were no longer available.

In the centuries that followed, to about A.D. 1100, the service, safety and comforts of travel almost disappeared and the people were no longer motivated to travel. The new rulers of the old Roman lands did not give any importance to the development of leisure activities for the masses.

Travel for Religious Purposes

Travel for religious purposes assumed a significant importance. The practice of travelling for religious reasons, going on a pilgrimage for instance, became a well-established custom in many parts of the world. By the end of the Middle Ages a large number of pilgrims were travelling to the main shrines in Europe, and travel again assumed an interesting character. However, it was still dominated by religious motivations. Very little actual pleasure travel was undertaken. The adoption and spread of Christianity subsequently led to numerous pilgrims making their way to the Holy Land. So deep and strong was the hold of faith that the ritual of pilgrimage flourished over the centuries. Religion was a great unifying force. Pilgrimages strengthened religious bonds. It provided the impetus for a 'stay-at-home' agrarian society to break out of its narrow geographical confines. It also exposed people to new manners and customs, different kinds of food and modes of dress. It encouraged exchange of ideas and also fostered trade. It served as a powerful means of forging unity and understanding between people from widely different regions. The powerful influences of a crusading religion that slowly penetrated a foreign land, such as Christianity in Europe and later in America, and Buddhism, Islam, and Hinduism in Asia took place to permit an assimilation and perpetuation of very distinctive languages, literature, music, art, architecture, philosophy and forms of government. Religion thus played and continues to play a crucial part in travel.

The travel for pilgrimages was largely undertaken by foot or horseback. However, some rich pilgrims travelled by boat or horse- drawn coach. There were no paved roads and travel was rather dangerous. Great threat to the pilgrims came from bandits and robbers, who used to waylay pilgrims and loot their belongings. In order to avoid such mishaps, groups of pilgrims usually hired the services of a brave and experienced guide who was familiar with dangerous tracts and the ways to avoid them. Generally pilgrims travelled by daylight and rested at night.

The forerunners of modern-day hotels, the roadside inns along popular routes provided accommodation for the spiritual travellers. Inns were the ideal place for night halts. Accommodation in these places was either provided free of cost or at a very nominal price. Some inns only catered to particular nationality. By about the fourteenth century, pilgrimage was a mass phenomenon as a very large number of people were participating in pilgrimages. Subsequently, the religious nature of travel gave way to education, learning and sightseeing. People began to appreciate the importance of education, arts science and culture. This period was called the Renaissance.

Pilgrimage Tourism

The word tourism derives from the verb tour meaning "travel." Travellers, whether alone or in a group, date back to ancient times—the sign, perhaps, of an innate need in man. In ancient Greece, for example, people would travel to attend the Olympic Games or to worship the gods in particularly important temples. In pre-Christian times, the oracle at Delphi played an especially important role in ancient Greece. The panhellenic religious feasts held at Olympia every four years and at Delphi led to the two sites becoming famous outside Greece. The oracle at Delphi, in particular, exercised a strong attraction, drawing a large number of pilgrims.

Latin literature in its turn often mentions the otia, the periods of free time that the upper classes devoted to activities other than work. The Middle Ages are marked by journeys and pilgrimages to holy places. This is the period in which religious tourism became popular with its interdependent means of transport, accommodation for pilgrims, and stops along the route at which peddlers would sell relics. The most common destinations of the period were Santiago de Compostela, Czestochowa, and Rome.

In the Middle Ages, pilgrimages were a collective phenomenon that was an integral part of the Christian world. Pilgrims were considered to be extremely spiritual and were held in high regard by society. Pilgrims were the initiated who sought to free themselves from the structures surrounding them and to ascend to a new level of existence. To go on a pilgrimage meant leaving behind the worldly aspects of life so as to concentrate on the purity of one's faith. When they returned home, pilgrims were greeted with admiration and were aware of having taken a further step toward spirituality.

In Medieval times, the pilgrimage represented elements of a very precise nature: the movement of the journey, the religious motivation, and the destination, which had to be a place that was considered holy. In general, pilgrimages arose from the search for salvation and, sometimes, the need to be physically healed. Medieval travellers undertook their journeys for a purpose—to increase their spirituality—and in this sense pilgrims in the Middle Ages were clearly different from those who travelled to satisfy their curiosity.

In the seventeenth century, those travelling for the purposes of tourism emphasised the search for truth, but the real change in the nature of tourism came about in the following century. With the reduction in working hours, more leisure time became available, and cultural tourism, with the accent on art and poetry, became popular. The major change dates to 1828, the year in which George Stephenson invented the steam locomotive. This was also the period of the Grand tour of Europe of the English aristocracy and the no less famous Journey to Italy of the German nobles, intellectuals, and artists who were treading in the footsteps of Goethe. This was soon followed by visits to spa towns.

As time passed, tourism came to mean the opportunities available to the increasing mass of individuals who felt attracted by these offers of excursions for pleasure. The growing demand led to the birth of travel agencies; the first was founded in Leicester in 1841 by Thomas Cook. He went on to become famous because, in 1866, he organised the first tour of the United States and, in 1872, the first round-the-world tour.

At the beginning of this century, tourism was turning into a business, although it slackened in the first half of the century, owing to the two world wars. After these difficulties, tourism came to signify the personal transfer from one place to another of income for the purposes of consumerism as the result of economic well-being and technological progress.

Tourism has led to the creation of new habits and different behaviour and life models as well as a different conception of time. It has generated a movement of culture that encourages travellers to see and understand social, cultural, and environmental differences.

Today, the old pilgrimage sites have begun again to attract masses of pilgrims, the difference now being that the pilgrims also come across tourists on holiday. The tourist industry and the media are offering pilgrimages as consumerism. Given that tourists share the same attitudes as pilgrims—in other words, the search for authenticity at different levels of depth and involvement—it could be said that pilgrims are partly tourists and that tourists are partly pilgrims. Thus they complement one another; the promotion of religious tourism today, seen as both devotional and cultural, is proof of the existence of this common search. The rediscovery of pilgrimages also shows that religious values, doctrines, and institutions have lost nothing of their status in, and their influence over, everyday behaviour . This means that the modern individual is seeking transcendental values to overcome the fragments, the discontinuity, of modern society and that he or she is the "pilgrim tourist" of modern times.

Religious Tourism

Religious tourism also commonly referred to as faith tourism, is a form of tourism, whereby people of faith travel individually or in groups for pilgrimage, missionary, or leisure (fellowship) purposes. Religious tourism has a big future in India. India is richly endowed with ancient temples and religious festivals. Religions originating in India, be it Hinduism, Sikhism, Jainism or Buddhism, have a vibrant culture and spiritual philosophy. Together, they present a viable, alternative way of life as compared to the materialism and confrontation prevalent in the West. The religions of Indian origin are also proving to be an attraction to many persons of non-Indian origin because these religions advocate a pacifist and inclusive approach to life. This is evident from the posts that can be read on then numerous blog sites devoted to religion. Also there can be no better way to introduce these aspirants to Indian religions than to entice them to come to India and undertake and experience religious tourism themselves.

Although no definitive study has been completed on worldwide religious tourism, some segments of the industry have been measured:

- According to the World Tourism Organisation, an estimated 300 to 330 million pilgrims visit the world's key religious sites every year.
- According to the U.S. Office of Travel and Tourism Industries, Americans travelling overseas for "religious or pilgrimage" purposes has increased from 491,000 travellers in 2002 to 633,000 travellers in 2005 (30% increase).
- The Christian Camp and Conference Association states that more than eight million people are involved in CCCA member camps and conferences, including more than 120,000 churches.
- Religious attractions including Sight & Sound Theatre attracts 800,000 visitors a year while the Holy Land Experience and Focus on the Family Welcome Centre each receiving about 250,000 guests annually.

Kumbh Mela

Kumbh Mela held in India twice a year is the world's largest gathering of humans. The number of pilgrims attending the mela is between 120 million to 150 million, equivalent to the combined population of Spain and Germany. In addition to devotees from all parts of India, visitors from over 100 countries attend the Mela.

The current Mela being held in Allahabad (Prayagraj) in north India (January 15-March 4, 2019), received 22 million devotees on the opening day. The Mela is spread over 32 square kilometers having over 1000 CCTVs, 40 firefighting centres, 15 fire outposts and 40 watch towers.

There are over 300 km of roads in the Mela area, 84 parking places where over five lakh (five hundred thousand) vehicles can be parked. There are over 200 water ATMs, 1,22,000 toilets, 20,000 dustbins with liner bags. A new air terminal at Allahabad (Prayagraj) civil Airport has been built. Luxury bed and breakfast units have also been constructed.

The Grand Tour and the Renaissance

The Renaissance marked the next important stage in the history of travel. The reappearance of tourism in Europe followed the Italian Renaissance and the development of a full-scale urban systems and network of roads. By the end of the fifteenth century Italy itself became the object of attention. At this time Italy was Europe's economic and cultural leader. It was, however, totally disunited politically. Wars were being fought on Italian soil. These wars played an important part in the dissemination of the Renaissance and the subsequent development of the 'Grand Tour'. Although in decline materially, Italy was still the intellectual capital of Europe. For the aristocracy and intelligentsia of north-west Europe, it represented both the classical heritage and all the latest ideas and inventions. A growing number of young noblemen were being sent abroad to complete their education in France and Italy.

The development of the Grand Tour followed a shift in the focus of culture, and of economic and political power. The wealthy and educated, of states whose position of dominance in the world was comparatively new, visited countries that had passed their peak of prestige but were still venerated for historical and cultural reasons. Thus Romans visited Greece and the eastern Mediterranean, the English, from the sixteenth century onwards, visited Italy. The Grand Tourist respected the learning, antiquities and social refinements of the Old World. The eighteenth century is conventionally considered the golden age of the Grand Tour, especially the thirty years between 1763 and 1793. With the new wealth of the English bourgeoisie the number of tourists had multiplied. The Grand Tour was no longer an aristocratic preserve. It had been invaded by the bourgeoisie. During this period a great many poets, authors and intellectuals visited Italy and other countries nearby with a view to broaden their knowledge and learn new arts and crafts. The Grand Tourist paved the way for the popular tourism of the nineteenth and twentieth centuries.

The Introduction of Annual Holiday

The introduction of annual holiday in Europe was another important landmark which encouraged many people to undertake travel in large numbers during the eighteenth century. The eighteenth century became the great age of travel. The annual holiday was the forerunner to the paid holiday which later was responsible for an extraordinary growth of tourism. The term holiday derives from "holy days" associated with religious observances. In the present day, it is used generally in a secular sense, meaning a respite from the routine of daily workday life and a time for leisure, recreation and amusement. A feature of ancient Rome, public holidays were among the most enjoyable of events. And the most enjoyable public holiday was the Saturnalia – the feast of Saturn – celebrated in December, when all classes indulged in feasting and frolic. Also, in Europe, certain days commemorating religious festivals and saints' days became holidays on which there was cessation from work. In 1552, an act was passed in England during the reign of Edward VI "for the keeping of holidays and fasting days". This act still continues to be in the statute-book. Subsequently, public and semi-official offices in England frequently closed on certain saints' days. There were, however, no general public holidays until the time of the Industrial Revolution. The concept of modern annual paid holiday is very largely an outcome of the Industrial Revolution.

The Middle Ages by and large did not constitute a favourable period for the pursuit and development of tourism. The process of the development of imagination, however, was continued by the innumerable events, for the most part connected with wars. Discoveries and expeditions, pilgrimages, wandering scholars and mercenary soldiers were the principal sources for information about the outside world. Nobles, accompanied by their retinues, visited the pivotal centres of religious and secular power. The education of young noblemen at foreign princely courts became a fashion which spread still further with these noblemen's educational travel, which naturally included the element of pleasure as well.

The travels of friends and the trips of students during those days to the different university towns enriched the popular imagination. The beginning of the eighteenth century saw the setting in of the practice of going to watering-places, which owed its renewal to a more liberal conception of life after the Roman bathing cult had fallen into oblivion with the fall of the Roman Empire. The increase in population and the resultant divisions of the social classes increased the interest of people in the activities and doings of others. Thus it was quite natural that the rising bourgeoisie took over the living habits of the nobility. The advent of Enlightenment in the eighteenth century and with it the introduction of a new attitude towards Nature gave rise to romanticism and fancifulness. These in their turn influenced and transformed the attitude towards the distant and the strange. Hitherto, in popular understanding, "foreign" had always been associated with danger and suffering. It was this emotional content of the term "foreign" which now underwent a complete transformation. The scientists who had initiated a new awareness were followed by poets and painters who widened further the orbit of the world of imagination and thus aroused desires, wishes and needs. The growth of communications, printing technique and multifarious dramatic events concerning mankind in the nineteenth and twentieth centuries enlarged the definition and conception of the world and increased man's desire to see it. The distant and the strange evinced a seductive quality. Social development made it possible for ever-larger classes to corroborate their conceptions and ideas with actual experiences.

Grand Tour

The term "**Grand Tour**" refers to the 17th and 18th century custom of a traditional trip of Europe undertaken by upper-class young European men of sufficient means and rank (typically accompanied by a chaperon, such as a family member) when they had come of age (about 21 years old). Young women of equally sufficient means ("debutantes"), or those of either gender of a more humble origin who could find a sponsor, could also partake. The custom—which flourished from about 1660 until the advent of large-scale rail transport in the 1840s and was associated with a standard itinerary—served as an educational right of passage. Though the Grand Tour was primarily associated with the British nobility and wealthy landed gentry, similar trips were made by wealthy young men of other Protestant Northern European nations, and, from the second half of the 18th century, by some South and North Americans. By the mid 18th century, the Grand Tour had become a regular feature of aristocratic education in Central Europe, as well, although it was restricted to the higher nobility. The tradition declined as enthusiasm for neo-classical culture waned, and with the advent of accessible rail and steamship travel—an era in which Thomas Cook made the "Cook's Tour" of early mass tourism a byword.

Three hundred years ago, wealthy young Englishmen began taking a post-Oxbridge trek through France and Italy in search of art, culture and the roots of Western civilization. With nearly unlimited funds, aristocratic connections and months (or years) to roam, they commissioned paintings, perfected their language skills and mingled with the upper crust of the Continent.

The primary value of the Grand Tour, it was believed, lay in its exposure to the cultural legacy of classical antiquity and the Renaissance, and to the aristocratic and fashionably polite society of the European continent. In addition, it provided the only opportunity to view specific works of art, and possibly the only chance to hear certain music. A Grand Tour could last anywhere from several months to several years. It was commonly undertaken in the company of a knowledgeable guide or tutor. The Grand Tour had more than superficial cultural importance. The legacy of the Grand Tour lives on to the modern day and is still evident in works of travel and literature. From its aristocratic origins and the permutations of sentimental and romantic travel to the age of tourism and globalisation, the Grand Tour still influences the destinations tourists choose and shapes the ideas of culture and sophistication that surround the act of travel.

Essence of Grand Tour

In essence, the Grand Tour was neither a scholarly pilgrimage nor a religious one, though a pleasurable stay in Venice and a residence in Rome were essential. Since the 17th century, a tour to such places was also considered essential for budding artists to understand proper painting and sculpture techniques, though the trappings of the Grand Tour—valets and coachmen, perhaps a cook, certainly a "bear-leader" or scholarly guide—were beyond their reach. The advent of popular guides, such as the book An Account of Some of the Statues, Bas-Reliefs, Drawings, and Pictures in Italy published in 1722 by Jonathan Richardson and its son Jonathan Richardson the Younger, did much to popularise such trips, and following the artists themselves, the elite considered travel to such centres as necessary rites of passage. For gentlemen, some works of art were essential to demonstrate the breadth and polish they had received from their tour. In Rome, antiquaries like Thomas Jenkins were also dealers and were able to sell and advise on the purchase of marbles; their price would rise if it were known that the Tourists were interested. Coins and medals, which formed more portable souvenirs and a respected gentleman's guide to ancient history were also popular.

Travel in the Industrial Age

The concept of modern tourism came into being in the second half of the nineteenth century hand in hand with the development of the industrialised societies of Western Europe and North America. Development of industrialised societies of Western Europe and North America can therefore be considered as responsible for growth of modern tourism. Though an accurate analysis of the history of tourism can be traced no further back than half a century, the scattered figures published from 1855 onwards, together with official statements, observations by various travel writers, and travel guides and other literature on sale at the time, point to the direct relationship between the birth of these societies and the expansion of tourist movements.

Development of industrialised societies was a direct result of Industrial Revolution in the West. The Industrial Revolution brought in its wake tremendous changes in society. As has been mentioned earlier, travel before the Industrial Revolution was mainly a matter of seeking knowledge, engaging in commerce and trade and undertaking pilgrimage. There is a little evidence of the extent and volume of private travel in the medieval period. During the Roman Empire, only the rich and leisured class indulged in pleasure travel.

Development of Health Resorts

The Industrial Revolution was responsible for the change in the economic and social systems. It threw up great factory towns, big and small. The working class was in the beginning burdened by long working hours and poor working and living conditions. For a large number of people there was little relief from routine of putting in long hours of work in difficult conditions in the factory set-up of those days. Sudden concentration of population in towns and cities created unhealthy social conditions. As the industrial momentum gathered and the cities and their populations increased at an enormous rate, the need for escape became even more acute. The prosperous and well-to-do proceeded to various resorts. Industrialisation also brought in an increase of material wealth and certain improvements in transport and communications during the second half of the nineteenth and early twentieth century. The factors, like increasing need to find relief from workday routine; the city dweller's yearning for physical adventure, comforts and pleasure; and development of resorts and spas for health and relaxation produced a fertile ground for the development of pleasure traffic on a big scale. Many resorts owe their present-day popularity to their original discovery by wealthy minorities during the Roman Empire. The nineteenth century saw the development of large-scale pleasure zones at some considerable distance from the large cities and metropolitan centres of Central Europe. The French Riviera with Nice, Cannes and Monte Carlo were some of these pleasure zones.

By the end of the century the Riviera was unmistakably the most popular pleasure zone. Its development became possible only when escape to the south had become a major feature of tourism in Europe. Many 'health' resorts were developed to cater to the increasing needs of wealthy people. Until the 1920s it remained a winter-resort area. The summer heat was considered not only intolerable in itself but a danger to health. As late as the 1920s, Cannes was trying to compete itself with the English health resorts with a view to attract the rich and respectable English clientele. In the late nineteenth century, the Italian Riviera also began to be popular with the English and French. By the early twentieth century, rich Americans started to appear in considerable numbers on the Riviera scene. The appearance of Americans on the Riviera was something of a new development as they were latecomers on the European tourist scene. One of the reasons could be the distance involved. Only the rich Americans could visit Europe at that time. It was, however, only after the First World War that Americans were to emerge as pioneers of a new tourism.

Rail Transport in Great Britain

The history of rail transport in Great Britain to 1830 covers the period up to the opening of the Liverpool and Manchester Railway, the world's first intercity passenger railway operated solely by steam locomotives. The earliest form of railways, horse-drawn wagonways, originated in Germany in the 16th century. Soon wagonways were also build in Britain. However, the first use of steam locomotives was in Britain. The invention of wrought iron rails, together with pioneering steam locomotive meant that Britain had the first modern railways in the world.

Early Rails

A wagonway was used by German miners at Caldbeck, Cumbria, England, perhaps from the 1560s. A wagonway was built at Prescot, near Liverpool, sometime around 1600, possibly as early as 1594. Owned by Philip Layton, the line carried coal from a pit near Prescot Hall to a terminus about half a mile away. Another wagonway was Sir Francis Willoughby's Wollaton Wagonway in Nottinghamshire built between 1603 and 1604 to carry coal.

As early as 1671 railed roads were in use in Durham to ease the conveyance of coal; the first of these was the Tanfield Wagon Way. Many of these *tramroads* or *wagon ways* were built in the 17th and 18th centuries. They used simply straight and parallel rails of timber on which carts with simple flanged iron wheels were drawn by horses, enabling several wagons to be moved simultaneously.

These primitive rails were superseded in 1767, when ironmaster Richard Reynolds probably for the first time replaced wooden rails with cast iron rails and in 1793 when the then superintendent of the Cromford Canal, Benjamin Outram, constructed a tramway with 'L'-shaped flanged cast-iron *plate rails* from the quarry at Crich: it was a little over a mile in length descending some 300 feet (91 m) and had a gauge of 3 ft 6 in (1,067 mm). Wagons fitted with simple flangeless wheels were kept on the track by vertical ledges, or plates. Cast-iron rails were a significant improvement over wooden rails as they could support a greater weight and the friction between wheel and rail was lower, allowing longer trains to be moved by horses. Outram's rails were superseded by William Jessop's cast iron *edge rails* where flanged wheels ran on the top edge of simple bar-shaped rails without the guiding ledges of Outram's flanged plate rails. The rails had been first employed in 1789 at Nanpantan at the Loughborough Charnwood Forest Canal.

Early Public Railways

The earliest railways were built and paid for by the owners of the mines they served. As railway technology developed, longer lines became possible, connecting mines with more distant transshipment points and promising lower costs. These longer lines often required public subscription to build and crossed over land not owned by the mine owners. As a result, they needed an Act of Parliament to build, to enforce the sale of wayleave by landowners. The Acts also protected investors from unrealistic, or downright fraudulent, schemes.

The first line to obtain such an act, in 1758, was a private coal-owner's wagonway, the Middleton Railway in Leeds. The first for public use, and on cast iron rails, was the Lake Lock Rail Road formed in 1796 and opened in 1798. Another early public railway, the Surrey Iron Railway obtained an Act of Parliament on 21 May 1801 to build a tramroad between Wandsworth and Croydon in what is now south London; the engineer was William Jessop. Although it survived only until 1845 and was for freight traffic only, it prefaced many others in different parts of the country. Meanwhile, the first passenger-carrying public railway was the Oystermouth Railway, authorised in 1807. All three of these railways were initially worked by horses; the Surrey Iron Railway remained horse-drawn throughout its life.

Introduction of Steam Locomotives

The liverpool and manchester railway (L&MR) was the world's first intercity passenger railway in which all the trains were timetabled and operated by steam locomotives. The Liverpool and Manchester Railway Company was founded on 24 May 1823. The 35-mile (56 km) line was a remarkable engineering achievement for its time. The line opened on 15 September 1830 with termini at Liverpool Road, Manchester (now part of the Museum of Science and Industry in Manchester) and Edge Hill, Liverpool.

Introduction of Railways

The introduction of railways in the nineteenth century was yet another crucial landmark in travel history. Passengers were first carried by rail in 1830 in England. The newly completed railway track between Liverpool and Manchester in England featured special provisions for carrying passengers in addition to freight. However, the birth of organised rail travel came in the year 1841. A baptist preacher of Derbyshire was on his way to a temperance meeting in Leicester when he struck upon the idea of engaging a special train to carry the friends of temperance society from Leicester to Loughborough and back to attend a quarterly delegate meeting. The man behind this was Thomas Cook. He broached his idea to his friends. A few weeks later 570 passengers made the journey by the Midland Countries Railway at a specially reduced fare. This venture was followed by various excursions to beauty spots. 3,000 schoolchildren were taken on a trip from Leicester to Derby in the year 1843. From 1848 to 1863 Cook conducted circular tours of Scotland, with 5,000 tourists a season.

The success of the Liverpool and Manchester railway encouraged many other countries in Europe to open railway lines. Railway tracks were laid in France, Austria and in Switzerland. Across the Atlantic the tracks were laid in America. This revolution in transport technology produced an immediate expansion in European tourism. In the year 1881, the railways carried over 600 million passengers over lines operated by one hundred odd companies. The railways were now keen to stimulate travel and to improve the system. There was also now an element of competition and the various railway companies tried to make travel as comfortable as possible. In the early 1870s, first-class railway travel was introduced by an American, G.M. Pullman, who developed the Pullman coaches with their luxury furnishing and dining facilities. Long-distance travel could now be undertaken in comfort and with pleasure. The Pullman cars manufactured in America were imported by some railway companies in England and other countries in Europe. The cars, which were very comfortable for long journeys, were first introduced in America. The longer distances in America necessitated assurance of greater comfort for passengers. By the year 1872 the Pullman Company had 700 cars working over 30,000 miles of railway under contract with over 150 different companies. The introduction of railways thus vastly increased the opportunities for escape from the rigours of city life as a result of urbanisation. The railways can be considered as one of the most powerful motives for mass travel in nineteenth as well as early twentieth centuries. The railways carried and continue to carry millions of passengers from all over the world, mostly from large urban centres.

Sea Transport

Like the railways, shipping also made significant contribution to travel during the nineteenth century. While railways were responsible for inland travel especially in Europe, the steamship crossed the boundaries and made strides in intercontinental travel. Shipping technology made a number of innovations in the nineteenth century. In America, a number of sailing ships were built which were considered to be superior to those built in England or elsewhere. The English felt a great need for improved communications across the Atlantic with America for the purpose of trade and commerce and passenger transportation. As a result of this, there were great strides in the development of deep-sea shipping. The history of the Cunard Steamship Company in England demonstrates important features in the growth of North Atlantic Shipping.

A subsidy in the form of the award of mail contract represented a recurring theme in the development of passenger transportation. With the passage of time, toward the last quarter of the nineteenth century, emigrant traffic became an important factor in North Atlantic travel. America was considered at that time the New World full of opportunities and fortunes for people in Europe. A great number of people from the Continent started going to America in search of fortune. Great Britain and Germany, along with other countries, became the principal generators of emigrants to the New World. Many travelled as tourists to see this new land. The opening of the Suez Canal in 1869 brought about the possibility of a much shortened route between the West and East and in turn stimulated the introduction of better steamship carriage to the Far East.

The use of chartered ships for cruising and operation of cruises on a limited scale dates from the mid-nineteenth century. One of the earliest cruises perhaps was that described by Mark Twain in his first book, *The Innocents Abroad*, published in 1869.

Cruising, however, did not play a significant part in the world of shipping until the beginning of the twentieth century. The period just before the First World War can be considered the heyday of passenger- liner service. It was an era of large and comfortable fast ships operated by relatively small number of companies in various countries.

The Glamour of the Deep-Sea Travel

The glamour of the deep-sea travel was, however, reserved for the wealthy Europeans and Americans. In the luxury liners, a big space reserved for the not too wealthy was used by the emigrant traffic. In fact, the biggest volume of transatlantic passenger trade was the emigrant traffic. In the first half of the twentieth century, the descendants of those migrants must have formed a large part of the transatlantic tourist movement. Transport by water makes a significant contribution to the development of travel on land and by air. Scheduled liner transport, formerly used for intercontinental travel, has presently almost vanished. The expansion of international tourism has, however, led to an increasing use of ferry boats by tourists on short-sea crossing. Tourist sea transport on the whole does not seem to have a promising future. Long-distance sea travel may continue to contract, although there will always be a limited demand for sea cruising, since this leisurely and attractive mode of travel has great appeal. In the recent past one of the most important developments in sea traffic has, in fact, been that of holiday sea cruises, especially in the Mediterranean and Caribbean and also in South-East Asia.

By the turn of the twentieth century all the main characteristics of modern tourism were evident in its embryonic form. Changes in mental attitudes towards pleasure seeking, the recognised value of travel for education, an increase in material wealth and improvements in transport, social prestige, the growing need to find relief from working routine—all these factors produced a fertile ground for the development of excursion traffic on a large scale.

Up to the first quarter of the twentieth century, tourism was essentially a luxury commodity within the reach of only a privileged few having both plenty of free time and considerable purchasing power. Admittedly, such tourism had a charm all its own, associated as it was with elegant luxurious hotels, such long-distance trains as the Orient Express and the blue-riband transatlantic liners like the *Queen Mary*. Although all the main characteristics of modern tourism were evident by this time, only the privileged few managed to indulge in this luxury. It is also true that certain associations, which recruited members from among the embryonic middle and working classes, organised excursions, holiday camps, family rest and holiday homes, etc., but only very few people benefited from such activities at that time.

Paid Holidays and Growth of Tourism

It was in the last quarter of the nineteenth century that increasing attention was paid to the desirability of holidays with pay or at least of cheap holidays for working-class people. During this period a few factories gave paid holidays to their workers in some countries in the West. The introduction of annual paid holiday is very largely of English origin and this had important repercussions on development of mass tourism. The annual paid holiday was established during the inter-War years as a reality for a considerable part of the working population. By the year 1939, in UK, some eleven million people were covered by the Holidays with Pay Act (1938). Introduction of paid holiday had led to greater mobility of the population, created new industries, resulted in the creation and growth of many towns of distinctive function and broadened the horizons of millions of people. In fact, the introduction of paid holidays can truly be associated with development of modern mass tourism.

In the year 1936, modern tourism really got under way when, at the instigation of its trade union representatives, the International Labour Organisation (ILO) adopted the first convention that was to support serious movements to promote paid holidays and, in turn tourism. That convention on paid holidays was an innovation well ahead of time, when only fourteen countries, mostly European, had enacted general legislation on paid holidays. Soon afterwards tourism experienced an extraordinary growth. Paid holidays are now established all over the world, and in most countries a minimum duration of one to three weeks is specified either by law or by collective agreements, between the employer and the workers.

Today the right to paid holidays has universal recognition. The trend is to grant longer holiday periods. The employers have realised that the paid holidays have not affected industrial production. The legal minimum in many countries at present is three weeks. Some countries have even gone beyond this and granted four weeks of paid holiday. Today it is recognised that in Western Europe the fifth week, even from the standpoint of output, may also be regarded as a productive investment. Sweden has recently enacted legislation introducing this additional week of paid holidays. Worldwide, more than 800 million wage-earners are entitled to paid holidays. Out of this number, roughly half are in Europe, little less than 30 per cent in the Americas, and the rest in Asia and the Pacific. Presently the main potential for tourism markets is made up of wage-earners and their families. As a result of economic and social changes due to further industrialisation the world over and the rationalization of the tertiary sector, the number of wage-earners in the world is bound to grow at a much faster rate than before. This in turn will give wage-earners increasingly longer holidays. The concept of paid holidays, which originated with the advent of industrialisation in the West, has given modern tourism a tremendous boost.

The First World War was responsible for a temporary halt to tourist movements. There was considerable decline in tourist travel not only within Europe but also all over the world. However, soon after the War, tourist travel quickly reached prewar levels, and within three or four years, greatly exceeded them. The War also brought about many changes which were destined to influence the volume of tourism. The War was, for example, responsible for breaking down international barriers, and resulting in the fostering of an ideal, optimistic, peaceful internationalism – just the climate in which tourism was most likely to flourish. The Second World War marked a watershed. Before it, in the twenties and thirties, organised tourism was chiefly a matter of trains, boats or coaches. In the post-l945 era, such travel was made increasingly by aeroplane, thus allowing the pleasure periphery to expand into new mass destinations like Spain, Greece, Bermuda, Cuba, Hawaii, etc. Each decade has seen a massive increase in the importance of aircraft in this process until today, when we are on the verge of truly global tourism.

Rise in Incomes of Working Class

Rise in the standard of living of the working and the middle classes in America and in certain European countries was yet another factor responsible for growth in tourism. Soon after the War the tourists began to appear in countries where tourism had been practically unknown a few years earlier. The early traveller had advanced from the scholar and the pilgrim of the past to the pleasure seeker of today. The major tourist countries enjoyed an unprecedented boom in the late twenties. In the year 1929 there were nearly one and a half million visitors to Switzerland, over one million visitors to Italy and about two million to Austria. Great Britain also received a considerable number of visitors.

A Decree "Tourism for All" in 2003

In 2003, the decree "Tourism for All" replaced the Royal Decree of 1980. It was a response to the changing societal context and gives new interpretation to social tourism. "Tourism for All" refers to a non-commercial form of tourism and recreation, with the focus on objectives that differ from merely economic activities. On the one hand, a choice was made for a target group -focused approach to support the manner in which specific target groups experience holidays.

On the other hand, "Tourism for All" implies a new structure for supporting the organisations that focus on these target groups.

Often, persons living in poverty do not have access to the commercial holiday circuit. Work done by the Holiday Participation Centre is fully focused on this target group.

Making holidays possible for the disabled also implies providing the requisite supporting initiatives. The initiatives for this target group principally concern the quality of the accommodation infrastructure. To advertise their services to the target group, a accessibility label is awarded.

Children and young people constitute a fully - fledged target group within "Tourism for All". The goal of the decree is to provide sufficient capacity, diversity and basis quality within the youth tourism sector.

In addition, many families and senior citizens still fall by the wayside when it comes to experiencing holidays away from home. The existing social vacation centres continue to play a very important role in support of this target group.

History of the Struggle for Paid Leave

With the spread of factory work after the industrial revolution, people in Britain ceased to enjoy the seasonal breaks from work that farming offered. Most workers had the Sunday off, but apart from that the only other time off was during the religious holidays of Christmas and Good Friday. In 1871, the Bank Holiday Act gave workers a few paid holidays each year - four new public holidays were introduced in England and Wales, and 3 new ones in Scotland.

In the 19th century and early decades of the 20th century, additional paid leave was only granted to senior managers and supervisors in UK factories. At the end of the 19th century most people had no paid holidays except bank holidays. The Trade Union Congress first began to campaign for a paid holiday for workers in 1911.

In the 1930s, paid vacation time became a very important issue for workers. Trade unions raised this issue through campaigns and lobbied the government of the day for a two week paid holiday. In 1936, the International Labour Organisation (ILO) adopted the Holidays with Pay Convention (no.52), which called for an annual holiday with pay of at least six working days after one year of continuous service. This was not ratified by the United Kingdom.

Following pressure from trade unions on behalf of their members, in the latter half of the 1930s, European workers were typically granted an average of one to two weeks of paid vacation. Following a general strike, the French government signed the Matignon Accords in 1936, which mandated 12 days (2 weeks) of paid leave for workers each year. In the UK, the Holidays with Pay Act 1938 gave those workers whose minimum rates of wages were fixed by trade boards, the right to one weeks' holiday per year. This was the first law on paid leave in this country, but it fell short of the two weeks demanded by the trade unions and did not cover all workers.

The idea of paid leave and the importance of leisure was reiterated in 1948 by the United Nations' Universal Declaration of Human Rights, which states, 'Everyone has the right to rest and leisure, including reasonable limitation of working hours and periodic holidays with pay' (Article 24). In 1970, the ILO convention recommended a minimum of three weeks' annual paid leave (No. 132).

By the 1970s, there was growing international recognition of the need for a statutory paid annual leave. Many countries in Western Europe passed new legislation concerning minimum paid vacations of two to three weeks. Providing statutory rights to four weeks' paid annual leave for workers was the subject of much debate in the European Union through the 1980s.

The EU Working Time Directive stipulating four weeks' annual leave was agreed on 23 November 1993, with the United Kingdom abstaining from the vote. The UK government did not implement a general statutory right to paid annual leave but continued to leave it to individual and collective bargaining in the workplace. However, on 1st October 1998, the Labour government in the UK implemented the EU Working Time Regulations granting workers 4 week's annual leave.

The Law on Paid Leave in the UK (2013)

The statutory minimum annual leave for full-time employees in the UK is 20 days and 8 national holidays (28 days in all). Self employed workers are not entitled to annual paid leave. Workers who are in the armed forces, the police or the civil protection services don't have the right to statutory holiday.

apter

Development o odern Transport stems

Development of road and air transport, especially the former, is the major factor which was largely responsible for and continues to be so for the great spurt in modern tourism. Transport is the necessary precondition of travel. For the greater part of contemporary tourism, transport means airlines and the private cars. As a broad generalization it can be said that holidaymakers travelling away from home to a foreign country spend the major portion of their total holiday money on transport and travel. Travel costs as much as about 40 per cent of the total holiday expenditure. This fact has been brought about by a number of studies. Tourist traffic, as we know it today, could not have developed without relatively inexpensive and efficient modes of transportation.

Road Transport

Up to the beginning of the twentieth century, people travelled almost exclusively by rail and steamship. With the invention of the new transport medium, travel by a private car and coach received its first great impetus in the ten years which preceded World War I. The entire shape of tourist industry was therefore transformed by the invention of this new transport medium. The growth of the private car may be identified as a major cause of the decline of the railways. In both USA and the United Kingdom, passenger rail traffic almost halved in the first ten years or so after the First World War. The motor car gradually came to be the alternative means of transport for both short-and medium-range journeys. Subsequently, with the growth of a fine network of fast and superfast national and international highway systems, long journeys were also performed by motor car and motor coach.

The motor car has revolutionised holiday habits. Although the first motor car had come into operation by the end of the nineteenth century, up to the time of the First World War their numbers were small. After the Second World War their numbers jumped manifold. It became increasingly important in the pursuit of leisure and tourism. The actual number of holidaymakers travelling by road increased tremendously as more and more people took holidays away from home. The provision of good motor roads and road services were important factors in the development of both domestic and international tourism. With the tremendous increase in road traffic, improved roads and dual carriageways were introduced after 1930. In 1930s the Germans pioneered the development of motorways with their autobahns. Improvements in road transport facilities stimulated travel in many European countries such as France, Spain and Germany. Mention may also be made of the great progress made in the United States in building highways, expressways and superhighways. In many other countries of the world newer and faster roads were built which made movement of traffic by road faster and comfortable.

Development of Motor Transport

Mobility can perhaps be considered as one of the major causes of the development of the motor transport. The motor car had provided the actual mobility so that people are no longer anchored to a particular holiday centre as they tended to be when they mostly travelled by train. Speed is yet another important factor which economises on time and therefore makes it possible for people with limited amount of time to travel to distant places. People with even one week of holiday considered it sufficient to travel. The gradual spread of the network of roads opened up many new areas and made many places hitherto not very accessible, easy to get to. The railways, on the other hand, tended rather to concentrate and restrict movement to particular channels.

Road transport made striking advances in subsequent years. Soon after 1950, when the difficulties and restrictions of the immediate post-War years had begun to straighten themselves out, there were rapid developments in transport; whereas the car ownership multiplied, the motor coach appeared in increasing numbers and the coach tour became popular. Greater use of motor car and coach is being made at present for the purpose of tourism. A great majority of people travel by the above modes in Europe. Increasing use of this mode of transport is being made in USA and Canada as also in other major tourist countries. The construction of motorways in many countries has made speedy travel over long distances by car and the coach easy and have made many remote places more accessible. The development of 'motorail', the carrying of cars and coaches over extended distances by train, is making it possible for holidaymakers to use their motor cars in holiday areas. Though economic conditions in the recent years, as a result of increasing fuel costs and the energy crisis, have not favoured travel by private motor car, road transport remains the mode most used by international visitors. The world economic crisis, which brought about cut backs in the use of transport facilities, did not however seriously impair the growth of road transport. In many countries of Europe increasing emphasis is being given to the construction of new roads. Several countries are continuing to build motorways and highways.

There are large-scale highway programmes in the pipeline at present in different regions of the world. When completed, these will cater to the ever-increasing demands of the tourists. Mention may be made of the following highway programmes:

Trans-African Highway Network

The Trans-African Highway network comprises transcontinental road projects in Africa being developed by the United Nations Economic Commission for Africa (UNECA), the African Development Bank (ADB), and the African Union in conjunction with regional international communities. They aim to promote trade and alleviate poverty in Africa through highway infrastructure development and the management of road-based trade corridors. The total length of the nine highways in the network is 56,683 km (35,221 mi).

In some documents the highways are referred to as "Trans-African Corridors" or "Road Corridors" rather than highways. The name Trans-African Highway and its variants are not in wide common usage outside of planning and development circles, and as of 2014 one does not see them signposted as such or labelled on maps, except in Kenya and Uganda where the Mombasa-Nairobi-Kampala-Fort Portal section (or the Kampala-Kigali feeder road) of Trans-African Highway 8 is sometimes referred to as the "Trans-Africa Highway".

Countries Served

The network as planned reaches all the continental African nations except Burundi, Eritrea, Somalia, Equatorial Guinea (Rio Muni), Lesotho, Malawi, Rwanda, South Sudan, and Swaziland. Of these, Rwanda, Malawi, Lesotho and Swaziland have paved highways connecting to the network, and the network reaches almost to the border of the others.

Trans–West African Coastal Highway

The Trans-West African Coastal Highway is a transnational highway project to link 12 West African coastal nations, from Mauritania in the north-west of the region to Nigeria in the east, with feeder roads already existing to two landlocked countries, Maliand Burkina Faso.

The eastern end of the highway terminates at Lagos, Nigeria. Some organisations such as the Economic Community of West African States (ECOWAS) consider its western end to be Nouakchott, Mauritania, and others such as the United Nations Economic Commission for Africa consider it to be Dakar, Senegal, giving rise to these alternative names for the road:

- Nouakchott-Lagos Highway
- Lagos-Nouakchott Highway
- Dakar-Lagos Highway
- Lagos-Dakar Highway
- Trans-African Highway 7 in the Trans-African Highway network.

Trans-European North – South Motorway (TEM) Project

- The oldest regional transport infrastructure project in Europe
- Initiated by Poland and Hungary who asked the United Nations assistance in preparing, designing and constructing motorways
- Opening the Project Central Office in Warsaw, Poland in 1977
- At the beginning 10 countries participated in the TEM Project : Austria, Bulgaria, Czechoslovakia, Greece, Hungary, Italy, Poland, Romania, Turkey and Yugoslavia
- Its network total length was 10,400km

Further Milestones

- Political and economic changes in Europe lead to decision to expand the system by adding east - west connections in 1991
- Since 1992 independent and self - sustaining funding of the Project activities by participating countries only
- 14 TEM member countries in 2006: Armenia, Bosnia and Herzegovina, Bulgaria, Croatia, Czech Republic, Georgia, Hungary, Italy, Lithuania, Poland, Romania, Slovakia, Slovenia and Turkey.
- Associated member: Austria
- Observers: Serbia, Sweden and Ukraine

Pan-American Highway

The **Pan-American Highway** is a network of roads stretching across the American continents and measuring about 30,000 kilometres (19,000 mi) in total length. Except for a rainforest break of approximately 160 km (100 mi), called the Darién Gap, the roads link almost all of the Pacific coastal countries of the Americas in a connected highway system. According to Guinness World Records, the Pan-American Highway is the world's longest motorable road. However, because of the Darién Gap, it is not possible to cross between South America and Central America with conventional highway vehicles. Without an all-terrain vehicle, it is necessary to circumnavigate this terrestrial stretch by sea.

The Pan-American Highway passes through many diverse climates and ecological types, from dense jungles, to arid deserts, to barren tundra, some of which are passable only during the dry season, and in many regions driving is occasionally hazardous. The Pan-American Highway system is physically mostly complete and extends in de facto terms from Prudhoe Bay, Alaska, in North America to the lower reaches of South America. Several southern highway termini are claimed to exist, including the cities of Puerto Montt and Quellón in Chileand Ushuaia in Argentina. West and north of the Darién Gap, it is also known as the Inter-American Highway through Central America and Mexico where it splits into several spurs leading to the Mexico-US border.

Countries Served

The Northern Pan-American Highway travels through 9 countries:

- Canada (unofficial)
- United States (interstate highway system official)
- Mexico
- Guatemala
- El Salvador
- Honduras
- Nicaragua
- Costa Rica
- Panama

The Southern Pan-American Highway travels through 8 countries:

- Colombia
- Ecuador
- Peru
- Chile
- Argentina

Important spurs also lead into 4 countries:

- Bolivia
- Brazil
- Paraguay
- Uruguay

Northern Section

Alaska and Canada

The Alaska Highway through Alaska, Yukon and British Columbia is commonly considered a de facto northerly extension of the Pan-American Highway, as well as the Dalton Highway in Alaska. In Canada, no particular road has been officially designated as the Pan-American Highway. The National Highway System, which includes but is not limited to the Trans-Canada Highway, is the country's only official interprovincial highway system. However, there are several Canadian routes that are a natural extension of several key American highways that reach the Canada-US border. British Columbia Highway 97 and Highway 2 to Alberta both pick up where the southern end of the Alaska highway leaves off. Highway 97 becomes U.S. Route 97 at the Canada-US border. British Columbia Highway 99 provides an alternate route from Highway 97 just north of Cache Creek that runs through Whistler and Vancouver before ending at the Canada-US border at the north end of Interstate 5 in Washington State, the beginning of the official Pan-American route south of British Columbia. Meanwhile, Alberta Highway 2 runs south and east to Alberta Highway 3 leading into Lethbridge, then south on Alberta Highway 4 to the Canada-US border where it becomes Interstate 15 in Montana, the first official stretch of the Pan-American Highway south of the Alberta route.

Asian Highway Network

The **Asian Highway Network** (**AH**), also known as the **Great Asian Highway**, is a cooperative project among countries in Asia and Europe and the United Nations Economic and Social Commission for Asia and the Pacific (ESCAP), to improve the highwaysystems in Asia. It is one of the three pillars of the Asian Land Transport Infrastructure Development (ALTID) project, endorsed by the ESCAP commission at its 48th session in 1992, comprising Asian Highway, Trans-Asian Railway (TAR) and facilitation of land transport projects.

Agreements have been signed by 32 countries to allow the highway to cross the continent and also reach to Europe. Some of the countries taking part in the highway project are India (Look-East connectivity projects), Sri Lanka, Pakistan, China, Iran, Japan, South Korea and Bangladesh. Most of the funding comes from the larger, more advanced Asian nations like Japan, India, Taiwan, South Korea and China as well as international agencies such as the Asian Development Bank.

The project aims to make maximum use of the continent's existing highways to avoid the construction of newer ones, except in cases where missing routes necessitate their construction. *Project Monitor*, an Asian infrastructure news website, has commented that "early beneficiaries of the Asian Highway project are the planners within the national land transport department of the participating countries [since] it assists them in planning the most cost-effective and efficient routes to promote domestic and international trade. Non-coastal areas, which are often negligible, are the other beneficiaries.

However, in the mid-2000s some transportation experts were sceptical about the viability of the project given the economic and political climate in both South and Southeast Asia.

The Asian Highway Network is going to take over 2 projects, one is the AH 45 and the other is the new AH 45A. AH 45A is the new highway all over Asia from Tonghua to Sana'a.

Routes

Route AH1 is proposed to extend from Tokyo to the border with Bulgaria west of Istanbul and Edirne, passing through both Koreas, China and other countries in Southeast, Central and South Asia. The corridor is expected to improve trade links between East Asian countries, India and Russia. To complete the route, existing roads will be upgraded and new roads constructed to link the network. US$25 billion has been spent or committed as of 2007, with additional US$18 billion needed for upgrades and improvements to 26,000 km of highway.

First Car Crossing

What is believed to be the first car crossing of the full extent (East to West) of the new Asian Highway was achieved by Britons Richard Meredith and Phil Colley in 2007 driving an Aston Martin.

Following the AH1 and the AH5 from Tokyo (the Highway grid's furthest point East) to Istanbul (furthest West), they drove a total of 12089 km (7512 miles) before joining the European motorway network for another 3259 km (2025 miles) to London.

Including ferry trips and customs clearance delays, the journey took 49 days and crossed 18 countries.

The completed route was verified by Aston Martin and the UN's Asian Commission (UNESCAP) in Bangkok, whose director of transport and tourism confirmed "I can warrant that, to my best knowledge, this was the first car to undertake this journey".

Eurowatch in London provided independent corroboration by tracking the car's location from satellite position reports and plotting the vehicle's location throughout the journey.

Air Transport Industry

The earliest projectiles in the history of mankind that travel through the air have been known to be stones and spears. These made way for the boomerang in Australia, the hot air lantern, and kites. If we look into the history of air transport, we will come across early legends of human flight such as the story of Icarus, Jamshid in Persian myth, and may more. The flying automaton of Archytas of Tarentum later, the winged flights of Abbas Ibn Firnas and the hot-air Passarola of Bartolomeu Lourenço de Gusmão in the air transport history is to some extent more credible claims of short-distance human flights. The main purpose of this article is to trace the origin of air transport. Read on.

The modern age in the history of air transportation began with the hot air balloon designed by the Montgolfier brothers in 1783, which was the first untethered human lighter-than-air flight. But the flights were limited as the balloon could only travel downwind. In 1784, a steerable balloon by Jean-Pierre Blanchard was the first human-powered dirigible. He crossed the English Channel in one in 1785. However, the concept of the modern airplane, as a fixed-wing flying machine with separate systems for lift, propulsion, and control was only set forth in 1799 by Sir George Cayley, as per the history of air transport. The first assisted take-off flight was in December 17, 1903 by the Wright Brothers, who are known to be the first to fly in a powered and controlled aircraft.

Following the new standards in the air transport history, there were extensive adoption of ailerons versus wing warping made aircraft which were much easier to control. At the start of World War I, only a decade later, heavier-than-air powered aircraft were used for investigation, artillery spotting, and even attacking against ground positions.

The history of air transportation reflects hoe following this, as designs grew larger and more reliable; the aircraft began to carry people and cargo. There were giant rigid airships transporting passengers and cargo over large distances. The German Zeppelin company became the best known manufacturers of these type of aircrafts in the air transport history. The most triumphant Zeppelin was the Graf Zeppelin, which flew over one million miles.

However with the advancement in the airplane design, the dominance of the Zeppelins in this period of history of air transport was soon to end. During the 1920s and 1930s there was huge progress in the field of aviation. The first airliner that was commercial carrying passengers exclusively was the Douglas DC-3. This began the modern era of passenger airline service ever since the origin of air transport. With the World War II, one also saw many towns and cities building airports. There were numerous qualified pilots available too. The first jet aircraft and the first liquid-fueled rockets brought many improvements to air transport.

After World War II, a boom was seen in general air transport, both private and commercial. Many inexpensive war-surplus transport and training aircraft became available and thousands of pilots were released from military service. Manufacturers like Cessna, Piper, and Beechcraft swelled their production to supply light aircraft for the new middle-class market. As the history of air transportation reveals, the first widely-used passenger jet was the Boeing 707 which was also the most economical.

Ever since the 1960s, the composite airframes have become lighter and quieter. The engines have become more competent. But the most significant lasting improvements have taken place in instrumentation and control, as we study the air transport history. The influx of solid-state electronics, the Global Positioning System, satellite communications have radically changed the cockpits of airliners. Small and powerful computers and LED displays help the pilots in navigating and viewing the terrain much more accurately, even at night or in low visibility.

In 2004, SpaceShipOne became the first privately funded aircraft to make a spaceflight. This has opened the likelihood of an aviation market competent of leaving the Earth's atmosphere.

History of Aviation

The **history of aviation** extends for more than two thousand years, from the earliest forms of aviation such as kites and attempts at tower jumping to supersonic and hypersonic flight by powered, heavier-than-air jets.

Kite flying in China dates back to several hundred years BC and slowly spread around the world. It is thought to be the earliest example of man-made flight.

Leonardo da Vinci's 15th-century dream of flight found expression in several rational but unscientific designs, though he did not attempt to construct any of them.

The discovery of hydrogen gas in the 18th century led to the invention of the hydrogen balloon, at almost exactly the same time that the Montgolfier brothers rediscovered the hot-air balloon and began manned flights. Various theories in mechanics by physicists during the same period of time, notably fluid dynamics and Newton's laws of motion, led to the foundation of modern aerodynamics, most notably by Sir George Cayley.

Balloons, both free-flying and tethered, began to be used for military purposes from the end of the 18th century, with the French government establishing Balloon Companies during the Revolution.

The term aviation, noun of action from stem of Latin avis "bird" with suffix -ation meaning action or progress, was coined in 1863 by French pioneer Guillaume Joseph Gabriel de La Landelle (1812–1886) in "Aviation ou Navigation aérienne sans ballons".

Experiments with gliders provided the groundwork for heavier-than-air craft, and by the early-20th century, advances in engine technology and aerodynamics made controlled, powered flight possible for the first time. The modern aeroplane with its characteristic tail was established by 1909 and from then on the history of the aeroplane became tied to the development of more and more powerful engines.

The first great ships of the air were the rigid dirigible balloons pioneered by Ferdinand von Zeppelin, which soon became synonymous with airships and dominated long-distance flight until the 1930s, when large flying boats became popular. After World War II, the flying boats were in their turn replaced by land planes, and the new and immensely powerful jet engine revolutionised both air travel and military aviation.

In the latter part of the 20th century the advent of digital electronics produced great advances in flight instrumentation and "fly-by-wire" systems. The 21st century saw the large-scale use of pilotless drones for military, civilian and leisure use. With digital controls, inherently unstable aircraft such as flying wings became possible.

Air Transport

The role of air transport in the development of international tourism is becoming increasingly important. Air transport has certainly been a key factor in the growth of international tourism especially in respect of long-distance and intercontinental travel. Although commercial travel took place before the Second World War, air transport for the masses has essentially been a post-War phenomenon. The main period of growth was during the 1960s when overseas holiday became a symptomatic benefit of a society experiencing rising living standards.

In Europe, the years immediately after World War I witnessed the attempts to create commercial airlines. The war itself had a direct bearing on the development of air transport in a similar way as had with motor transport. Certain commercial civil air services were inaugurated and developed in this period. Besides Europe, air transport, however, was developed in many other countries including in India during this period. Although international air travel was born at the end of World War I and slowly grew between the two wars, it was only at the end of World War II that it made a tremendous breakthrough. It emerged into a practical mode of transport over long distances only in the late forties when the aircraft industry in America applied the technical and manufacturing resources it had developed during the war. This period saw the development of large pressurised civil aircraft like the Douglas Corporation's DC-6s and the Lockheed Constellations followed by the DC-7s and the super-constellations operating at twice the speed and flying attitudes of their predecessor war planes.

The removal of wartime restrictions on international travel and the tremendous increase in speed, safety and comfort provided by the new aircraft released the long pent-up wanderlust of the people, the world over. In the year 1952 the two-class travel was introduced which was made possible by the larger capacity of the new aircraft. The larger capacity of the new aircraft resulted in lowering air fares. The steady fall in the real cost of flying has been chiefly productive in traffic across the Atlantic and within the USA, stimulated by the introduction of tourist fares in the year 1952. This period also saw the first post-War attempt to build a "package holiday" around air transport, the model for most of today's global tourism. The growing willingness of tourists to take to air travel during this period was responsible for the annual flood of North Americans across the Atlantic to Europe. This trend continues even today. Within Europe, there has been the spectacular growth of the Mediterranean resorts.

Advent of the Jet Technology

The advent of jet travel in 1958 was the most dramatic event which introduced an entirely new dimension of speed, comfort and efficiency to air transport and brought mass travel to its present level. As a result of the introduction of jets, air travel from 1960 grew tremendously. The most decisive development during this period was, however, the development inclusive tours in which travellers are carried on charter flights at rates substantially below those of normal scheduled services. It only slowed down after 1973 because of the worldwide oil crises which resulted in widespread recession and galloping inflation. In spite of this, the volume of world air travel today is several times more than what it was in 1960s.

Despite rising fuel costs and inflation, the industry was able to control successfully the fare levels; as a result of the economies of scale provided by the very big aircraft. The improved fuel efficiency of later models of jet engines and the ingenuity and marketing expertise of the airlines, travel agencies and tour operators are other factors. The latter is illustrated by the North Atlantic route—the golden route of tourist traffic—which saw the successive introduction of excursion fares in 1948, coach fares in 1952, family fares in 1955, economy class fares in 1958, affinity group fares in 1963, group inclusive tour fares in 1967, youth fares in 1972 and apex fares in 1975. As a result of these innovations in air travel, fares per seat mile declined in real terms, between 1963 and 1975.

Great advances have been made in air travel in the recent years, more particularly for overseas holidaymaking. Tourism in turn has had a significant impact on the aircraft industry and on the carriers. Factors like comfort, speed, and safety influence the tourists' choice of mode of transport. New wide-bodied jets such as Boeing 747, the McDonnell Douglas DC-10, the Airbus A300 and Lockheed TriStar L-1011 are all part of response to the requirements of the ever-growing travel market. The technical brilliance of supersonic aircraft like the Concorde and Tupolev Tu-144 are remarkable landmarks in aviation history.

Long Range Air Travel

The industry has a bright future in spite of the rising fuel costs and inflation engulfing the entire world. As far as long-range international travel in future is concerned, the large majority of the aircraft used will continue to be of the current wide-bodied generation. In order to achieve further economy in running the aircraft to offset the increase in aviation fuel costs, the subsequent decades of the present century may make further advances in the form of still larger aircraft such as the double-deck 600-seater derivative of the Boeing 747 and Airbus. The skytrain concept, which is the latest introduction in the aviation world, has brought about a considerable reduction in Atlantic fares. Conceived by Fred Laker, the skytrain type of fares introduced some years ago on the Atlantic route considerably reduced air fares resulting in big increase in tourist traffic. The application of the concept to long-distance international travel is likely to stimulate the growth of tourist traffic in the coming years. With a view to meet the competition of the skytrain fare, the stand-by and budget fares were also introduced by the schedule airlines on the Atlantic route. The future of the air transport is bright. Airlines will continue to play a vital role in the growth of international tourism for a long time to come.

Transport thus is the single key factor which has largely been responsible for the spurt in tourism, especially modern tourism. Tourist traffic, as we know it today, could not have developed without the development of various modes of transport from time to time. Early travel in the nineteenth century was dominated by the railway and the steamship. Up to the beginning of the twentieth century tourists travelled almost exclusively by rail, internally and by steamship, overseas. World War I witnessed the development of motor and air transport, and in the years which preceded the War, private car and coach travel made much progress. However, the years between the two world wars mainly witnessed the significant development of the private motor car and also of the bus and coach travel. Post-World War II period saw the great development of civil aviation. It was the aeroplane—the most glamorous of all modes of transport—which came into its own in the—fifties and gave international tourism a real shot in the arm. International tourism as, we know it today, has been largely shaped by air travel.

Advent of High-Speed Trains

A recent and interesting development in the field of transportation is the advent of high-speed trains. The energy crisis since 1974, which resulted in widespread recession and galloping inflation, had adversely affected travel by air and the private motor car. It was becoming increasingly expensive to travel by air and by the private car and coach. The fuel consumption per passenger kilometre is two to four times more in automobiles and ten times more in aeroplanes as compared to trains. This factor of increase in oil prices was responsible for the remarkable achievement in recent years in the growth of faster and cheaper rail transport. Besides the cost factor, the railways also have an advantage over the airlines in that the terminal stations are often located in the heart of the cities and the train timings are generally more convenient. To add to this, the growing congestion on highways and airports has given a further impetus to the trend. All the above factors coupled with advanced technology and increasing needs for mobility are leading to a renaissance of the rail transport. The railways, which were pioneers in the growth and development of early mass travel and were relegated to a secondary place with the introduction of motor and air transport, are once again assuming an important role. In almost all the European countries, the United States, the countries of Asia and elsewhere, revolutionary ideas for achieving higher speeds and comfort are being conceived and put into practice.

Intercity Rail System

The trend, however, was discernible before the world was affected by the energy crisis. It was in Europe when the designs for faster and comfortable trains were first formulated. In the year 1960 British Railways electrified its London-Manchester line, which was a very busy line, to achieve the speed of 160 kilometres per hour. The new high-speed trains on this line reduced their running time by full one hour from the former three-hour-forty-minute trip. Passenger traffic almost doubled in five years. In former West Germany, a new inter-city system introduced in 1971 provided rapid train service at two-hour intervals between every major city in the country and brought over 30 per cent more passengers in the first twelve months. Passengers were provided with extra conveniences like telephones, secretarial services, latest stock quotations and *à la carte* dining-car service round the clock. Similarly, in France, the 160-kilometres-per-hour turbine-train service, which began in 1970 between Paris and Caen in northern France, cut travel time by almost one-fifth. Passenger loads went up by 25 per cent in the first year. High-speed train services elsewhere in Europe connect Paris and Lyons in France, Rome and Milan in Italy and Moscow and Leningrad in Russia.

In the United States of America, the combination of rail cruise and railbus offered by Amtrak (American Travel by Track) resulted in 1974 in a rise of 11.2 per cent over 1973 in the number of passenger kilometres performed. Long-distance trains running on the Amtrak system between New York and San Francisco have been lately modernised. Amtrak is adding new double-decked Pullman coaches gradually on the system with a view to encourage more rail travel. High-speed train services now connect the highly populated Washington–Baltimore–Philadelphia–New York–Boston corridor in the United States.

In Asia, it was Japan which took the epoch-making decision, to use the latest technology and convert the rail line between Tokyo and Osaka, covering a distance of 515 kilometres into a high-speed track. This ambitious project was completed in the year 1964. The super-fast train known as Hikari Express (is popularly known as Bullet Train) travels on the new Tokaido line at a crashing speed of 210 kilometres per hour cutting the journey time to less than three hours against six and a half hours taken earlier. Encouraged by the success of its bold venture, it went further and built the new Sanyo line, 565 kilometres in length on which trains travel even faster at a maximum speed of 260 kilometres per hour. Elsewhere in Asia, new and faster rail tracks are being introduced. The number of passengers carried by rail have been increasing in Malaysia, Philippines and Thailand.

Indian Railway Network

In India, railways have made great strides in technology, resulting in increased speed, comfort and carrying capacity. Efforts were initiated as early as in 1964 to increase the speed of some trains to 120 kilometres per hour. The tests enabled the railway authorities to introduce the first high-speed train, Rajdhani Express, between New Delhi and Calcutta (Kolkata). It was originally meant to run at a cruising speed of 120 kilometres per hour to cover a distance of 1,441 kilometres in 17 hours and 30 minutes. A fully air-conditioned comfortable train now runs at 130 kilometres per hour reducing the running time to 16 hours and 20 minutes. The special coaches for the train have been manufactured in India. In 1972, another such train was introduced between New Delhi and Bombay (Mumbai) at a speed of 120 kilometres per hour to cover a distance of 1,384 kilometres in 16 hours and 50 minutes. Trials have already been successfully conducted over small sections on both these routes to run the trains at 160 kilometres per hour. Taking advantage of improvements in track for the Rajdhani Express trains, a number of other important trains on trunk routes were designed as super-fast trains and the speeds were increased up to 120 kilometres per hour. A number of new high-speed trains have been introduced linking large metropolitan cities with important tourist centres.

Super Fast Trains

More and more railway systems in different parts of the world are experimenting with newer concepts. Research is going on to run the trains at even faster speeds. Today a train traveller between Paris and Lyon in France is able to cover the 460-kilometre distance in less than two hours. The passengers will then ride at 350 kilometres per hour in turbine-powered train that, despite its 5,000 horsepower engines, will be smoother and more silent than an aeroplane. In September 1981 a new high-speed train owned by the state-run SNCF Railroad Company shattered the 26-year-old world record for rail speed by clocking 380 kph (236 mph). The record-breaking time was achieved near the central French city of Tonnerre during a test run of the French-manufactured TGV (Trains à Grande Vitesse; literally, of great speed) train. It broke the previous record of 331 kph (205 mph) that was set in 1975. The TGV train began its commercial operation in September 1981 between Paris and Lyon in France. It has a speed of 260 kph (161 mph) and covers a distance of 560 kilometres (287 miles) between Paris and Lyon in one hour and forty-five minutes. In the comfortable sound-proofed cars, the only noises were the quiet hiss of air-conditioning, the strains of Chopin and the popping of champagne corks.

Some experts today even visualize potential speeds of 500 kilometres per hour on rails. The day is not very far off when trains will cruise at such high speeds. The new technology aims at dispensing the conventional rails. It aims at providing an air cushion to replace the conventional run on the rails. The projected aero-trains will not only be fast but also relatively sleek looking, noise and pollution free and, above all, will cause no wear and tear on the track because they never touch it. In France and Japan many such trains are already operating.

High-Speed Rail

High-Speed rail is a type of rail transport that operates significantly faster than traditional rail traffic, using an integrated system of specialized rolling stock and dedicated tracks. While there is no single standard that applies worldwide, new lines in excess of 250 kilometres per hour (160 mph) and existing lines in excess of 200 kilometres per hour (120 mph) are widely considered to be high-speed, with some extending the definition to include lower speeds in areas for which these speeds still represent significant improvements. The first such system began operations in Japan in 1964 and was widely known as the bullet train. High-speed trains normally operate on standard gauge tracks of continuously welded rail on grade-separated right-of-way that incorporates a large turning radius in its design.

Many countries have developed high-speed rail to connect major cities, including Austria, Belgium, China, Finland, France, Germany, Ireland, Italy, Japan, Morocco, the Netherlands, Poland, Portugal, Russia, Saudi Arabia, South Korea, Spain, Sweden, Taiwan, Turkey, the United Kingdom, the United States, and Uzbekistan. Only in Europe does HSR cross international borders. China has 22,000 kilometres (14,000 mi) of HSR as of end December 2016, accounting for two-thirds of the world's total.

History

Railways were the first form of rapid land transportation and had an effective monopoly on long distance passenger traffic until the development of the motor car and airliners in the early-mid 20th century. Speed had always been an important factor for railroads and they constantly tried to achieve higher speeds and decrease journey times. Rail transportation in the late 19th Century was not much slower than non-high-speed trains today and many railroads regularly operated relatively fast *express* trains which averaged speeds of around 100 km/h (62 mph).

Early German High-Speed Network

On 15 May 1933, the Deutsche Reichsbahn-Gesellschaft company introduced the diesel-powered "Fliegender Hamburger" in regular service between Hamburg and

Berlin (286 km or 178 mi), thereby achieving a new top speed for a regular service, with a top speed of 160 km/h (99 mph). This train was a streamlined multi-powered unit, albeit diesel, and used Jakobs bogies.

Following the success of the Hamburg line, the steam-powered Henschel-Wegmann Train was developed and introduced in June 1936 for service from Berlin to Dresden, with a regular top speed of 160 km/h (99 mph). Incidentally no train service since the cancellation of this express train in 1939 has travelled between the two cities in a faster time as of 2018.

Further development allowed the usage of these "Fliegenden Züge" (flying trains) on a rail network across Germany. The "Diesel-Schnelltriebwagen-Netz" had been in the planning since 1934 but it never reached its envisaged size.

All high-speed service stopped in August 1939 shortly before the outbreak of World War II.

First Narrow-Gauge Japanese High-Speed Service

In 1957, the engineers at the private Odakyu Electric Railway in Greater Tokyo Area launched the Odakyu 3000 series SE EMU. This EMU set a world record for narrow gauge trains at 145 km/h (90 mph), giving the Odakyu engineers confidence they could safely and reliably build even faster trains at standard gauge.[20] The original Japanese railways generally used narrow gauge, but the increased stability offered by widening the rails to standard gauge would make very high-speed rail much simpler, and thus standard gauge was adopted for high-speed service. With the sole exceptions of Russia, Finland and Uzbekistan (where even wider gauge is used) all high speed rail lines in the world are still standard gauge, even in countries where the preferred gauge for legacy lines is different.

Bullet Train (Shinkansen)

The Shinkansen, meaning new trunkline, but colloquially known in English as the bullet train, is a network of high-speed railway lines in Japan. Initially, it was built to connect distant Japanese regions with Tokyo, the capital, in order to aid economic growth and development. Beyond long-distance travel, some sections around the largest metropolitan areas are used as a commuter rail network. It is operated by five Japan Railways Group companies.

Starting with the Tōkaidō Shinkansen (515.4 km, 320.3 mi) in 1964, the network has expanded to currently consist of 2,764.6 km (1,717.8 mi) of lines with maximum speeds of 240–320 km/h (150–200 mph), 283.5 km (176.2 mi) of Mini-Shinkansen lines with a maximum speed of 130 km/h (80 mph), and 10.3 km (6.4 mi) of spur lines with Shinkansen services. The network presently links most major cities on the islands of Honshu and Kyushu, and Hakodate on northern island of Hokkaido, with an extension to Sapporo under construction and scheduled to commence in March 2031. The maximum operating speed is 320 km/h (200 mph) (on a 387.5 km section of the Tōhoku Shinkansen). Test runs have reached 443 km/h (275 mph) for conventional rail in 1996, and up to a world record 603 km/h (375 mph) for SCMaglev trains in April 2015.

The original Tōkaidō Shinkansen, connecting Tokyo, Nagoya and Osaka, Japan's three largest cities, is one of the world's busiest high-speed rail lines. In the one-year period preceding March 2017, it carried 159 million passengers, and since its opening more than five decades ago, it has transported more than 5.6 billion total passengers The service on the line operates much larger trains and at higher frequency than most other high speed lines in the world. At peak times, the line carries up to thirteen trains per hour in each direction with sixteen cars each (1,323-seat capacity and occasionally additional standing passengers) with a minimum headway of three minutes between trains.

Japan's Shinkansen network had the highest annual passenger ridership (a maximum of 353 million in 2007) of any high-speed rail network until 2011, when the Chinese high-speed railway network surpassed it at 370 million passengers annually, reaching over 1.7 billion annual passengers in 2017, though the total cumulative passengers, at over 10 billion, is still larger. While the Shinkansen network has been expanding, Japan's declining population is expected to cause ridership to decline over time. The recent expansion in tourism has boosted ridership marginally.

Mumbai–Ahmedabad High-Speed Rail Corridor

The Mumbai-Ahmedabad high-speed rail corridor is an under-construction high-speed rail line connecting the cities of Ahmedabad, Gujarat, and India's economic hub Mumbai, Maharashtra. It will be India's first high-speed rail line.

Construction of the corridor was began by August 2018 by acquiring land for Sabarmati terminus, and the first high speed train is scheduled to leave for its first run on 15 August 2022. The corridor will use Japan Railways Shinkansen E5 Series Electric multiple unit for it's rolling stock

Background

The Mumbai-Ahmedabad corridor, along with 5 other high-speed rail corridors, was introduced for a feasibility study in the 2009-2010 Rail Budget. A 650 km long high-speed rail corridor was proposed to run from Pune railway station to Ahmedabad railway station via Mumbai. The point at which this route would touch Mumbai was to be decided when the feasibility report was prepared. The pre-feasibility study for the Ahmedabad-Mumbai-Pune corridor was completed by a consortium of RITES, Italferr and Systra.[4] The top speed expected for the corridor was up to 350 km/h. The proposed stations included Lonavala on Mumbai-Pune section and Surat, Bharuch and Vadodara on Mumbai-Ahmedabad section. It was proposed to have 32 services between Mumbai and Ahmedabad. Railway officials also proposed extending the corridor up to Bangalore.

A Memorandum of Understanding (MoU) was signed in New Delhi on 14 February 2013 between the Ministry of Railways and the Société Nationale des Chemins de Fer Français(SNCF), the French national railways, for technical cooperation in the field of railways. The parties agreed to carry out jointly an "operations and development" feasibility project on the Mumbai-Ahmedabad high-speed rail corridor. The project was funded by the SNCF with support from the French Ministry of Finance. In March 2013, the Railway Board decided to drop the Mumbai-Pune section and operate the high-speed rail service only between Mumbai and Ahmedabad. The Board took the decision due to financial constraints, as the ghat section between Pune and Mumbai would escalate the budget for the project. According to V.A. Malegaonkar, Chief

Public Relations Officer (PRO), Western Railway, "It's basically a Western Railway project and very little portion of Maharashtra was being covered under it. Hence, the Maharashtra government was showing little interest in the project and was also reluctant to bear a financial burden. That is the reason why the Railway Board has decided against including the Pune-Mumbai portion in the high-speed corridor."

India and Japan signed a MOU to undertake a joint feasibility study of the Mumbai-Ahmedabad route in New Delhi in September 2013. This was in pursuance of the Joint Statement between then Prime Minister of India Manmohan Singh and the Prime Minister of Japan Shinzō Abe on 29 May 2013, which provided that the two sides would co-finance a joint feasibility study of the route. The objective of the joint study was to prepare a feasibility report of the system with a speed of 300–350 km/h. The cost of the study (¥500 million) was borne equally by India and Japan. The study was scheduled to be completed within 18 months from its commencement, i.e. it would complete by July 2015. The study carried out traffic forecasting, alignment surveys and undertook a comparative Study of high-speed railway technology and systems.

Japanese International Cooperation Agency (JICA) and the SNCF carried out studies on the project. JICA researched the technology, alignment and traffic-related aspects, while SNCF worked on business projections. The feasibility study included an alignment survey concerning aspects such as land acquisition, environmental challenges and building of tunnels and bridges. It also suggested a financial model based on fare and non-fare box revenue.

Route of the Train

The line will have 12 stations. Proposed stations are Mumbai, Thane, Virar, Boisar, Vapi, Bilimora, Surat, Bharuch, Vadodara, Anand and Ahmedabad, Sabarmati. High speed rail stations will be constructed either above or next to existing railway stations to provide transfer with the Indian Railways network. The Director of the Railway Bureau of Japan's Ministry of Land, Infrastructure, Transportation and Tourism stated that "this makes construction extremely difficult".

Mumbai Terminal

The Indian Railways proposed constructing the proposed terminus at BKC as a three-storey underground station. However, the Maharashtra state government planned to construct the International Financial Services Centre (IFSC) at BKC on the same plot. JICA's report had cited the BKC plot as the most suitable location to build the Mumbai terminus. In February 2016, the Railways and the state government came to an agreement to construct both projects at the BKC. However, in April 2016, the state government refused to permit construction of the underground station at BKC, citing the lack of availability of land in the area for an underground station after the completion of the proposed IFSC and its multi-level underground car park. The state government also stated that IFSC would begin generating revenue for the government shortly, while the rail corridor was only expected to be completed by 2023. It instead suggested relocating the proposed BKC terminus to either Matunga or Kanjurmarg. The issue was resolved in January 2017, when the Maharashtra Government and the MMRDA agreed to provide 5.4 hectares of land in BKC to construct a terminus.

apter

T e mer ence o odern ass Tourism

Emergence of Leisure Travel

Leisure travel was associated with the Industrial Revolution in the United Kingdom – the first European country to promote leisure time to the increasing industrial population. Initially, this applied to the owners of the machinery of production, the economic oligarchy, factory owners and traders. These comprised the new middle class. Cox & Kings was the first official travel company to be formed in 1758.

The British origin of this new industry is reflected in many place names. In Nice, France, one of the first and best-established holiday resorts on the French Riviera, the long esplanade along the seafront is known to this day as the Promenade des Anglais; in many other historic resorts in continental Europe, old, well-established palace hotels have names like the Hotel Bristol, Hotel Carlton, or Hotel Majestic - reflecting the dominance of English customers

A pioneer of the travel agency business, Thomas Cook's idea to offer excursions came to him while waiting for the stagecoach on the London Road at Kibworth. With the opening of the extended Midland Counties Railway, he arranged to take a group of 540 temperance campaigners from Leicester Campbell Street station to a rally in Loughborough, eleven miles (18 km) away. On 5 July 1841, Thomas Cook arranged for the rail company to charge one shilling per person; this included rail tickets and food for the journey. Cook was paid a share of the fares charged to the passengers, as the railway tickets, being legal contracts between company and passenger, could not have been issued at his own price. This was the first privately chartered excursion train to be advertised to the general public; Cook himself acknowledged that there had been previous, unadvertised, private excursion trains.

During the following three summers Cook planned and conducted outings for temperance societies and Sunday school children. In 1844 the Midland Counties Railway Company agreed to make a permanent arrangement with Cook, provided he found the passengers. This success led Cook to start his own business running rail excursions for pleasure, taking a percentage of the railway fares.

In 1855, Cook planned his first excursion abroad, when he took a group from Leicester to Calais to coincide with the Paris Exhibition. The following year he started his "grand circular tours" of Europe. During the 1860s he took parties to Switzerland, Italy, Egypt and the United States. Cook established "inclusive independent travel", whereby the traveller went independently but his agency charged for travel, food and accommodation for a fixed period over any chosen route. Such was his success that the Scottish railway companies withdrew their support between 1862 and 1863 to try the excursion business for themselves.

The first fifty years of the twentieth century made tourism a major worldwide industry. The emergence of the middle class in Europe along with the technological, political and social events of the day gave a great thrust to tourism. A large number of people were travelling both for leisure and business purposes. This period saw the mass movement of people annually from their home location to another country for temporary stay for a few days or a week. This mass movement of tourists was, however, predominant between Europe and America as the conditions of travel between the two continents were perfect. A fairly good infrastructure was already in existence. The necessary elements for travel like time, money and motivation were present. In addition to international movements, there was also growth in domestic tourism. The invention of the motor car in Europe and USA, along with the technological advancements in rail transport and the construction of networks of highways, gave a boost to domestic tourism.

Although the annual migration of people began rather more than a century ago, the present-day exodus especially in relation to international tourists is essentially a post World War II phenomenon. The period between the two world wars can also be associated with the great movement of people for the purposes of tourism as a result of development of the various modes of transport, especially the motor car and the aeroplane. The encouraging trend, however, received a setback as the Second World War intervened.

Tourism is sensitive to global economic and political conditions. It can occur on a large scale where the great majority of people enjoy some prosperity and security. Tourism and holidaymaking, on global as well as national scale, is a manifestation of prosperity and peace. As a great number of people in many countries have higher living standards, they can afford to set aside a proportion of their incomes for holidays and recreation.

Air travel blossomed during the post World War II period resulting in rapid development of tourism. As the world began to settle down after years of readjustments immediately after the War in 1945, there had been a rapid increase in both domestic and international tourism. The United Nations reported that in the ten-year period between 1955 and 1965, the number of tourist arrivals in some sixty-five countries increased three times, from around 51 million to over 157 million. This, however, was only a beginning.

Table 3.1

The Main Tourist Generators, 1961

Country	*Total world arrivals generated (millions)*	*World arrivals generated per 1000 population*
USA	21.7	112
UK	7.5	138
France	10.0	204
Germany	21 .6	318
Canada	6.7	340
Belgium	3.8	387
Luxembourg	NA	NA
Netherlands	4.1	332
Italy	3.1	61
Switzerland	2.2	369
Sweden	1.4	185
Denmark	1.4	287
Austria	2.1	287
Total	85.6	181

Source: International Union of Official Travel Organisations (IUOTO)

In the 1960s, USA, Germany, UK, France, Canada, Belgium, Luxembourg, Netherlands, Italy, Switzerland, Sweden, Denmark and Austria represented the twelve main tourist- generating countries. These twelve countries accounted for some three quarters of all international tourist arrivals in the world. The first two—USA and Germany—accounted for more than one-third of the world tourist arrivals. The reasons for this are very clear. These were the countries which enjoyed prosperity and higher standards of living, the two main factors conducive to growth of tourism. The development in the means of speedy transport and communication was also witnessed in these countries more significantly. This rapid increase in tourism in the above countries was therefore the outcome of factors such as prosperity and higher standards of living that lead to increased leisure, improved education and, above all, the rapid strides they made in speedy transport and communication.

The trend in the growth of international tourism continues since the mid-1960s. The growth continues to be determined by the higher living standards in the developed countries. The widespread introduction of holidays with pay to a large majority of people is yet another important factor responsible for growth of tourist traffic. Tables 3.1-3.7 and Figures 3.1-3.3 show the international tourist arrivals and the annual percentage of growth in recent years.

In 2005, there were 808 million international tourist arrivals in the world (see Table 2.2). This was a huge increase from 1965. During 2000-2005, which was a period of intensive economic development in most industrialized countries, international tourism grew at an average rate of over 7 per cent annually. During this period, most of the developing countries were also able to benefit from the growing trend in the developed countries to consume tourist products. As mentioned elsewhere, tourism and its development are closely related to the consumers' purchasing power and, in turn, to any domestic or international economic fluctuations.

In recent years, the world economy was affected by the increased cost of Aviation Turbine Fuel (ATF) as also by the incident of 9/11 which occurred at the end of 2001. As a result, there was a decline in tourist arrivals globally with special reference to the United States of America. In subsequent years the problems like SAARS and TSUNAMI were also responsible for reduction in tourist arrivals. Tourism, like all other sectors of production and consumption, suffered the economic consequences of these crises. Table 2.2 clearly shows this. The total international tourist arrivals in 2003 dropped by 1.7% over 2002 and 0.3% in 2001 over 2000.

Table 3.2

International Tourist Arrivals, 2000–2005

Region	*2000*	*2001*	*2002*	*2003*	*2004*	*2005*
WORLD						
Arrivals	685.5	683.8	702.8	690.9	766.0	808.0
% Annual change	6.9	-0.3	2.8	-1.7	10.9	5.6
AFRICA						
Arrivals	28.6	29.2	29.9	30.8	33.4	36.8
% Annual change	4.9	2.3	2.2	3.1	8.4	10.0
AMERICAS						
Arrivals	128.2	122.2	116.6	113.0	125.9	133.6
% Annual change	5.1	-4.7	-4.5	-3.1	11.4	6.1
ASIA & THE PACIFIC						
Arrivals	114.9	120.5	131.1	119.3	145.4	156.7
% Annual change	12.3	4.9	8.8	-9.0	21.9	7.8
EUROPE						
Arrivals	389.6	387.8	397.3	399.0	424.5	441.6
% Annual change	5.8	-0.5	2.4	0.4	6.4	4.0
MIDDLE EAST						
Arrivals	24.3	24.0	27.9	28.8	36.3	39.7
% Annual change	13.0	-1.0	16.1	3.4	26.0	9.5
INDIA						
Arrivals	2.6	2.5	2.4	2.7	3.5	3.9
% Annual change	6.7	-4.2	-6.0	14.3	26.8	13.2
SHARE OF INDIA	0.39	0.37	0.34	0.39	0.45	0.49

Source: World Tourism Organisation

In the year 2004–2005, as a result of concerted efforts made by the governments of industrialized and developing countries to keep the economy moving faster, there was accelerated growth in the economic development in the main generating countries. As a consequence, there was likewise a resumption of international travel. The total international tourist arrivals in the year 2005 amounted to 808 million. The total number of international tourist arrivals in the year 2007 was estimated at between 850 and 876 million, which is a considerable rise over previous years.

According to the most recent estimates produced by the Secretariat General of UN World Tourism Organisation, international tourist arrivals in 2010 are estimated to be a total of over 900 million, an increase of manifolds from 1975.

Europe and North America continue to be the principle generating as well as receiving areas for international tourism, accounting for 70 per cent and 20 per cent respectively, of the international tourist arrivals. The statistics show continuous trend of increase in international tourist arrivals in these areas since the year 1965. It may be stressed here that intra-regional tourism—tourism between countries of the same region—has an appreciable influence on the distribution of world arrivals. Thus, while domestic tourist movements tend to increase more and more, holidaymakers and tourists tend at the same time to travel farther from their usual place of residence, first in their own region and afterwards beyond it. Of the total international tourist movements within Europe and North America, over 74 per cent are intra-regional. For Africa, it may be estimated that nearly 40 per cent of the tourist flows are intra-regional. In Americas, the United States and Canada alone account for nearly 50 per cent of all international tourist traffic in the region, where intra-regional international tourist movements are therefore predominant. In South Asia, intra-regional tourist movements may be estimated at between 20 and 30 per cent of the total tourist traffic in the region. In Europe, intra-regional tourism accounts for over 73 per cent of international tourist movements.

Table 3.3 shows the top 15 tourist destinations in 2005. However, a glance at the figures would indicate that most of the destinations are the same which were prominent in the year 1961. There is nevertheless a significant change in the number of arrivals in each of the destination. For instance, in 1961, France had generated 10.0 million tourists. This has been increased to almost 72 million in the year 1999. The big surprise, however, is China which received 27 million tourists in 1999.

Table 3.3

Top 15 Tourist Destinations in 2003-2005

Rank	*Country*	*International tourist arrivals (000)*		
		2003	*2004*	*2005*
1	France	75048	75121	76001
2	Spain	50854	52430	55577
3	United States	41218	46085	49402
4	Italy	39604	37071	36513
5	China	32970	41761	46809
6	Hungary	31412	33934	10048
7	UK	24715	27755	29970
8	Russian Fed	20443	19892	19892
9	Austria	19078	19373	19952
10	Mexico	18665	20618	21915
11	Germany	18399	20137	21500
12	Canada	17534	19095	18612
13	Greece	13969	13969	13969
14	Poland	13720	14290	15200
15	Turkey	13341	16826	20273

The values shown in Table 3.4 and Figures 3.1 and 3.2 are based upon preliminary data estimated for the full year supplied to the UN World Tourism Organisation (WTO) secretariat by the tourism authorities of the countries and territories concerned. Most countries and territories do not have the figures available for the whole year. However, experiences from the earlier years have shown that projections tend to be somewhat conservative. This implies that total figures might increase slightly when final figures are computed.

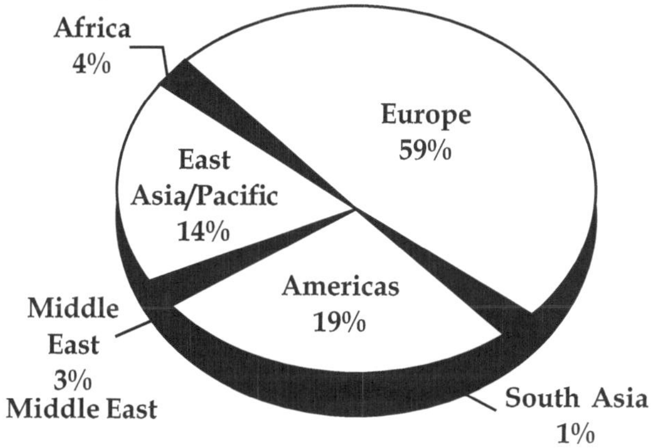

Fig. 2.1: International Tourist Arrivals:
Share of World Total (Estimates)

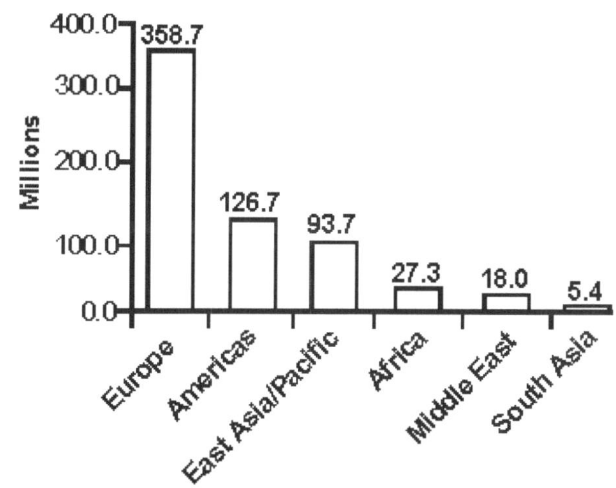

Fig. 3.2: International Tourist Arrivals, 1999 (Estimates).
(Source: World Tourism Organisation)

The most significant expansion of tourism has taken place primarily in the advanced industrialized countries, where tourism has become a part of lifestyle and consumption pattern of most people. Europe and Americas together account for almost 78 per cent of the total international tourist arrivals (see Table 3.6). The remaining 22 per cent is shared between East Asia/Pacific, Africa, Middle East and South Asia. South Asia's share is just one per cent of the total.

Table 3.4

International Tourist Arrivals and Receipts Worldwide 1970–1993

Years	*Arrivals (thousand)*	*Change*	*Receipts (US million)*	*Change*
1970	165,787	–	17,900	–
1975	222,290	34.08	40,702	127.38
1980	287,771	29.46	103,356	153.93
1985	329,634	14.55	116,149	12.38
1986	340,800	3.39	140,556	21.01
1987	366,743	7.61	172,334	22.61
1988	402,123	9.65	198,839	15.38
1989	431,327	7.26	213,153	7.20
1990	457,954	6.17	257,810	20.95
1991	456,502	-0.32	260,535	1.06
1992	481,672	5.51	296,375	13.76
1993	500,142	3.83	324,080	9.35

Source: World Tourism Organisation (WTO)

Table 3.5

International Tourist Arrivals and Receipts Worldwide and by Region 1985–1993

Regions	*Series*	*1985*	*Share World Total Percentage*	*1993*	*Share World Total Percentage*	*Average annual growth rate 1985-93*
World	A(1)	329,634	100.00	500,142	100.00	6.1
	R(2)	116,149	100.00	324,080	100.00	15.8
Africa	A(1)	9,706	2.95	17,875	3.57	9.1
	R(2)	2,601	2.24	6,364	1.96	13.6
Americas	A(1)	66,495	20.17	106,525	21.30	7.0
	R(2)	33,315	28.68	95,545	29.48	16.2
East Asia/	A(1)	30,389	9.22	68,548	13.71	12.3
Pacific	R(2)	12,849	11.06	52,587	16.23	22.3
Europe	A(1)	214,264	65.00	296,535	59.29	4.7
	R(2)	61,181	52.67	162,573	50.17	15.0
Middle	A(1)	6,240	1.89	7,200	1.44	2.1
East	R(2)	4,032	3.47	4,996	1.54	3.1
South	A(1)	2,540	0.77	3,459	0.69	4.3
Asia	R(2)	1,667	1.44	2,015	0.62	2.7

Source: World Tourism Organisation (WTO)
Notes: Figures on receipts exclude international transport
A(1) = Arrivals (thousand)
R(2) = Receipts (US$ million)

Table 3.6

World's Top Tourist Destinations based on International Tourist Arrivals

Rank 1992	*Country*	*Tourist arrivals (thousands) 1992*	*1985*	*Rank 1985*	*Average annual growth rate percentage 1985/92*	*Percentage Share of arrivals worldwide 1992*	*1985*
1	France	59,590	36,748	1	7.15	12.37	11.15
2	USA	44,647	25,417	3	8.38	9.27	7.71
3	Spain	39,638	27,477	2	5.37	8.23	8.34
4	Italy	26,113	25,047	4	0.60	5.42	7.60
5	Hungary	20,188	9,724	11	11.00	4.19	2.95
6	Austria	19,098	15,168	5	3.35	3.96	4.60
7	UK	18,535	14,449	6	3.62	3.85	4.38
8	Mexico	17,271	11,907	9	5.46	3.59	3.61
9	China	16,512	7,133	12	12.74	3.43	2.16
10	Germany	15,147	12,686	8	2.57	3.14	3.85
11	Canada	14,741	13,171	7	1.62	3.06	4.00
12	Switzerland	12,800	11,900	10	1.05	2.66	3.61
13	Greece	9,331	6,574	13	5.13	1.94	1.99
14	Portugal	8,921	4,989	14	8.66	1.85	1.51
15	Czechoslov+	8,000	4,869	15	7.35	1.66	1.48
16	Hong Kong	6,986	3,370	17	10.98	1.45	1.02
17	Turkey	6,549	2,230	20	16.64	1.36	0.68
18	Romania	6,280	4,772	16	4.00	1.30	1.45
19	Netherlands	6,049	3,329	18	8.91	1.26	1.01
20	Malaysia	6,016	2,933	19	10.81	1.25	0.89
World Total		481,672	329,634		5.57	100.00	100.00

Table 3.7

World Top 10 Tourism Destinations During 2002

(Figures In Thousands)

Sr No.	*Country*	*Arrival*
01.	France	76722
02.	Spain	51748
03.	United States	41892
04.	Italy	39799
05.	China	36803
06.	United Kingdom	23942
07.	Canada	20032
08.	Mexico	19668
09.	Germany	17969
10.	Hong Kong (China)	16566

It may be stated that France continued to hold the number one position even in the year 2007. The tourist arrivals in France far exceed the total population of the country. Followed by France, Spain holds the second position in terms of global tourist arrivals. In fact, the number of tourist arrivals in Spain also exceeds the total population of the country. China continues to surprise the world as far as the international tourist arrivals and the growth rate is concerned. In fact, China has the fastest growth rate not only in Asia but globally as well.

Mass Tourism

Academics have defined mass tourism as travel by groups on pre-scheduled tours, usually under the organisation of tourism professionals.This form of tourism developed during the second half of the 19th century in the United Kingdom and was pioneered by Thomas Cook. Cook took advantage of Europe's rapidly expanding railway network and established a company that offered affordable day trip excursions to the masses, in addition to longer holidays to Continental Europe, India, Asia and the Western Hemisphere which attracted wealthier customers. By the 1890s over 20,000 tourists per year used Thomas Cook & Son.

The relationship between tourism companies, transportation operators and hotels is a central feature of mass tourism. Cook was able to offer prices that were below the publicly advertised price because his company purchased large numbers of tickets from railroads.One contemporary form of mass tourism, package tourism, still incorporates the partnership between these three groups.

Travel developed during the early 20th century and was facilitated by the development of the automobiles and later by airplanes. Improvements in transport allowed many people to travel quickly to places of leisure interest, so that more people could begin to enjoy the benefits of leisure time.

In Continental Europe, early seaside resorts included: Heiligendamm, founded in 1793 at the Baltic Sea, being the first seaside resort; Ostend, popularised by the people of Brussels; Boulogne-sur-Mer and Deauville for the Parisians; Taormina in Sicily. In the United States, the first seaside resorts in the European style were at Atlantic City, New Jersey and Long Island, New York.

By the mid-20th century the Mediterranean Coast became the principal mass tourism destination. The 1960s and 1970s saw mass tourism play a major role in the Spanish economic miracle.

Table 3.8

Most Visited Destinations by International Tourist Arrivals

In 2017, there were 1.323 billion international tourist arrivals worldwide, with a growth of 6.8% as compared to 2016. The top 10 international tourism destinations in 2017 were (2017 numbers are preliminary.

Rank	Destination	International tourist arrivals (2017)[1]	International tourist arrivals (2016)[1]	Change (2016 to 2017) (%)	Change (2015 to 2016) (%)
1	France	86.9 million	82.7 million	5.1	2.1
2	Spain	81.8 million	75.6 million	8.6	10.5
3	United States	-	75.6 million	-	2.1
4	China	60.7 million	59.3 million	2.5	4.2
5	Italy	58.3 million	52.4 million	11.2	3.2
6	Mexico	39.3 million	35.1 million	12.0	9.3
7	United Kingdom	37.7 million	35.8 million	5.1	4.0
8	Turkey	37.6 million	30.3 million	24.1	23.3
9	Germany	37.5 million	35.6 million	5.2	1.8
10	Thailand	35.4 million	32.6 million	8.6	8.9

UNWTO

Africa

In 2016, there were over 57.8 million international tourist arrivals to Africa, an increase of 7.8% from 2015. Preliminary numbers for 2017 indicate a similar increase.[1] In 2016, the top ten African destinations were:

Rank	Destination	International tourist arrivals (2016)[1]	International tourist arrivals (2015)[2]	Change (2015 to 2016) (%)	Change (2014 to 2015) (%)
1	Morocco	10.3 million	10.2 million	1.5	1.0
2	South Africa	10.0 million	8.9 million	12.8	6.8
3	Tunisia	5.7 million	5.4 million	6.8	25.2
4	Egypt	5.3 million	9.1 million	42.5	5.1
5	Zimbabwe	2.2 million	2.0 million	5.4	9.4
6	Algeria	2.0 million	1.7 million	19.2	25.7
7	Nigeria	1.9 million	1.3 million	50.5	-
8	Mozambique	1.6 million	1.6 million	5.6	6.6
9	Ivory Coast	1.6 million	1.4 million	9.9	205.9
10	Namibia	1.5 million	1.4 million	5.8	5.1
Note: Egypt is classified under "Middle East" in the UNWTO.					

UNWTO

Americas

In 2017, there were 208.7 million international tourist arrivals to the Americas, an increase of 4.0%.[1] In 2017, the top ten destinations were (2017 numbers are preliminary, US and Cuba numbers not yet available):

Rank	Destination	International tourist arrivals (2017)[1]	International tourist arrivals (2016)[1]	Change (2016 to 2017) (%)	Change (2015 to 2016) (%)
1	United States	-	75.6 million	-	2.1
2	Mexico	39.3 million	35.1 million	12.0	9.3
3	Canada	20.8 million	20.0 million	4.1	11.1
4	Argentina	6.7 million	6.6 million	1.0	15.7
5	Brazil	6.6 million	6.5 million	0.6	3.8
6	Chile	6.5 million	5.6 million	14.3	26.0
7	Dominican Republic	6.2 million	6.0 million	3.8	6.4
8	Cuba	-	4.0 million	-	13.4
9	Peru	4.0 million	3.7 million	7.7	8.4
10	Colombia	4.0 million	3.3 million	21.4	11.4

UNWTO

Asia-Pacific

In 2017, there were over 323 million international tourist arrivals to Asia-Pacific, an increase of 5.6% over 2016.[1] In 2017, the top ten destinations were (2017 numbers are preliminary):

Rank	Destination	International tourist arrivals (2017)[1]	International tourist arrivals (2016)[1]	Change (2016 to 2017) (%)	Change (2015 to 2016) (%)
1	China	60.7 million	59.3 million	2.5	4.2
2	Thailand	35.4 million	32.6 million	8.6	8.9
3	Japan	28.7 million	24.0 million	19.4	21.8
4	Hong Kong	27.9 million	26.6 million	5.0	0.5
5	Malaysia	26.0 million	26.8 million	3.0	4.0
6	Macau	17.3 million	15.7 million	9.9	9.8
7	India	15.5 million	14.6 million	6.7	9.7
8	Singapore	13.9 million	12.9 million	7.7	7.2
9	South Korea	13.3 million	17.2 million	22.7	30.3
10	Indonesia	12.9 million	11.0 million	16.9	11.1

UNWTO

Europe

In 2017, there were over 670 million international tourist arrivals to Europe, an increase of 8.3% over 2016.[1] In 2017, the top ten destinations were (2017 numbers are preliminary):

Rank	Destination	International tourist arrivals (2017)[1]	International tourist arrivals (2016)[1]	Change (2016 to 2017) (%)	Change (2015 to 2016) (%)
1	France	86.9 million	82.7 million	5.1	2.1
2	Spain	81.8 million	75.6 million	8.6	10.5
3	Italy	58.3 million	52.4 million	11.2	3.2
4	United Kingdom	37.7 million	35.8 million	5.1	4.0
5	Turkey	37.6 million	30.3 million	24.1	23.3
6	Germany	37.5 million	35.6 million	5.2	1.8
7	Austria	29.5 million	28.1 million	4.8	5.2
8	Greece	27.2 million	24.8 million	9.7	5.1
9	Russia	24.4 million	24.6 million	0.7	8.5
10	Poland	18.4 million	17.5 million	5.4	4.4

UNWTO

Middle East

In 2016, there were 55,6 million international tourist arrivals to the Middle East (excluding Turkey, Iran and Israel), a decrease of 4.4% over 2015. Preliminary numbers for 2017 indicate an increase of 4.6%.[1] In 2016, the top ten destinations were:

Rank	**Destination**	**International tourist arrivals (2016)[1]**	**International tourist arrivals (2015)[2]**	**Change (2015 to 2016) (%)**	**Change (2014 to 2015) (%)**
1	Turkey	30.3 million	39.5 million	23.3	5.3
2	Saudi Arabia	18.0 million	18.0 million	0.3	1.5
3	United Arab Emirates	14.9 million	14.2 million	4.7	7.6
4	Egypt	5.3 million	9.1 million	42.5	5.1
5	Iran	4.9 million	5.2 million	5.6	5.4
6	Jordan	3.6 million	3.8 million	5.2	5.7
7	Qatar	2.9 million	2.9 million	0.1	3.7
8	Israel	2.9 million	2.8 million	3.6	4.4
9	Oman	2.3 million	1.9 million	20.1	17.8
10	Lebanon	1.7 million	1.5 million	11.2	12.1
Note: Iran is classified as part of "South Asia" in the UNWTO.[3] Turkey and Israel are classified as part of "Southern/Medit. Europe" in the UNWTO.					

UNWTO

Table 3.9

International Tourism Receipts

International tourism receipts grew to US$1,340 billion in 2017, corresponding to an increase in real terms of 4.9% from 2016.[1] The World Tourism Organisation reports the following destinations as the top ten tourism earners for the year 2017, with the United States by far the top earner.

Rank	Region	International tourism receipts (US$ billion) (2017)[1]	International tourism receipts (US$ billion) (2016)[1]	Change (2016 to 2017) (%)
1	United States	210.7	206.9	1.9%
2	Spain	68.0	60.5	10.1%
3	France	60.7	54.5	9.0%
4	Thailand	57.5	48.8	13.1%
5	United Kingdom	51.2	47.9	12.1%
6	Italy	44.2	40.2	7.7%
7	Australia	41.7	37.0	9.3%
8	Germany	39.8	37.5	4.2%
9	Macau	35.6	30.4	17.6%
10	Japan	34.1	30.7	14.4%

UNWTO

Africa

Rank	**Region**	**International tourism receipts (US$ million) (2017)[1]**
1	South Africa	8,818
2	Egypt	7,775
3	Morocco	7,417
4	Nigeria	2,549
5	Tanzania	2,339
6	Mauritius	1,748
7	Tunisia	1,299
8	Sudan	1,029
9	Kenya	926
10	Uganda	918

UNWTO

Americas

Rank	Region	International tourism receipts (US$ million) (2017)[1]
1	United States	210,747
2		21,333
3	Canada	20,328
4	Dominican Republic	7,178
5	Brazil	5,809
6	Argentina	5,060
7	Colombia	4,821
8	Panama	4,452
9	Puerto Rico	4,090
10	Costa Rica	3,876

UNWTO

Asia-Pacific

Rank	Region	International tourism receipts (US$ million) (2017)[1]
1	Thailand	57,477
2	Australia	41,732
3	Macau	35,575
4	Japan	34,054
5	Hong Kong	33,304
6	China	32,617
7	India	27,365
8	Singapore	19,707
9	Malaysia	18,323
10	South Korea	13,427

UNWTO

Europe

Rank	Region	International tourism receipts (US$ million) (2017)[1]
1	Spain	67,964
2	France	60,681
3	United Kingdom	51,211
4	Italy	44,233
5	Germany	39,823
6	Turkey	22,478
7	Austria	20,400
8	Switzerland	17,003
9	Greece	16,528
10	Netherlands	15,867

UNWTO

Middle East

Rank	Region	International tourism receipts (US$ million) (2017)[1]
1	Turkey	22,478
2	United Arab Emirates	21,048
3	Saudi Arabia	12,056
4	Lebanon	7,611
5	Egypt	7,775
6	Israel	6,821
7	Qatar	5,971
8	Jordan	4,639
9	Iran	3,713*
10	Iraq	2,423*
Note: Numbers for Iran and Iraq are for 2016.		

UNWTO

Table 3.10

International Tourism Expenditures

The World Tourism Organisation reports the following source countries as the top ten spenders on international tourism for the year 2017, with China by far being the top spender:

Rank	Country	International tourism expenditure (2017)[1]	International tourism expenditure (2016)[4]	Change (2016 to 2017) (%) [1]
1	China	$257.7 billion	$250.1 billion	4.7
2	United States	$135.0 billion	$123.6 billion	9.3
3	Germany	$89.1 billion	$79.8 billion	9.4
4	United Kingdom	$71.4 billion	$64.8 billion	2.4
5	France	$41.4 billion	$40.3 billion	0.8
6	Australia	$34.2 billion	$30.8 billion	7.7
7	Canada	$31.8 billion	$28.7 billion	8.5
8	Russia	$31.1 billion	$24.0 billion	29.7
9	South Korea	$30.6 billion	$27.2 billion	12.3
10	Italy	$27.7 billion	$25.0 billion	8.9

UNWTO

Causes of Rapid Growth

The basic causes of this rapid growth of demand for tourism in the highly developed industrialized countries in the course of the recent decades are economic, social and technological in nature. Rising per capita incomes leading to higher purchasing power and an increase in discretionary incomes have made tourism accessible to a large majority of people. Today in advanced countries, a large majority of people can afford an annual holiday. In fact, many can even afford to take a 'second holiday' of longer or shorter duration. In the case of more affluent members of the society, establishment of what may be called 'recreation homes'—seaside flatlets, country cottages, caravans, cruising boats, etc., have become a fashion and a status symbol. Secondly, more and diverse types of holiday and recreation are becoming popular. For example, in addition to comparatively recent developments such as holiday camps, caravans and coach tours, there are even newer fashions such as yachting, trail riding, safari and archaeological holidays. Increased mobility as a result of use of motor car for travel is another important economic factor which is responsible for growth in tourism in Europe and North America. Ownership of private motor cars in these areas grew tremendously resulting in more travel, including travel for the purpose of tourism.

Social Causes

The social causes of the rapid growth of tourism are linked with new attitudes towards travel and leisure. Traditionally considered a luxury, both are now held to be a normal, virtually indispensable part of the lifestyle and consumption pattern of all but the lowest income groups of the population. The entire concept of pleasure travel has changed quite drastically. Foreign travel in the prewar days was reserved to the more affluent and well-to-do who enjoyed travel for its own sake and who were content to enjoy scenery and works of arts and theatres in foreign places. This concept has now changed with change in attitudes towards travel. The present day tourist has a different kind of background and his ideas about travel are very different. He comes from a wider social mileu and his tastes and desires are much more varied. His leisure time is much more restricted and, accordingly, he desires to pack into it as much as possible. 'Democratization' of leisure pursuits is yet another factor of growth in tourist traffic. Winter sports, for example, were an activity almost exclusively confined to wealthier members of the society until recently. Some of the other exclusive pursuits such as riding, boating, yachting, surf-riding, shooting, etc., are now available to even a low-budget tourist who is interested in these. A large number of people are now going abroad to participate in more exciting and exotic activities like mountaineering, waterskiing, trekking, underwater swimming and the like.

Technological Causes

The impact of modern transport technology, especially in the field of aviation, has brought about a completely new meaning to tourism. Travel to even remote destinations has now become a reality. During the last twenty years there has been a remarkable increase in the number of long-distance journeys undertaken by tourists. The technological developments in transport have made it possible for millions of people to travel to faraway places, places which only a few generations ago were regarded as being almost entirely inaccessible. Today holidaymakers can be transported a thousand miles or more in a matter of few hours. The gradual evolution of the originally homogeneous air-travel market into two separate and distinct segments—charters and schedule air travel—has greatly increased the demand. The recent introduction of wide bodied Aircrafts like Airbus A-380 with a carrying capacity of 800 passengers has revolutionized global international tourism. This Aircraft was introduced in the year 2007 and many international Airlines have already placed an order for purchase of the Aircraft.

Newer Marketing Style

The newer marketing style of organising a 'package tour' is a major contributing factor to the growth of tourism. By preparing organised holiday trips complete with all arrangements like transport, accommodation, sightseeing tours, etc., and selling these on a large scale to the public, the average price per tour has been significantly reduced. This price is much below the price of the trip arranged individually. Opening up of new travel destinations, particularly in developing countries, creation of new facilities to receive larger flow of tourists, and increasing tourism promotion efforts by tourist-service enterprises and by official tourist organisations have increased the tourist flows. The participation of a large number of people in tourism activities, as seen in highly developed industrialized countries, is essentially a manifestation of prosperity. As a great number of people in these countries enjoy higher living standards, they can afford to set aside a proportion of incomes for holidays.

International tourism has now become one of the leading items of international trade and exceeds many other commodities including wheat, automobiles and machine tools. Tourism's importance was exemplified in the sponsorship by the

United Nations of the Conference on International Travel and Tourism held in Rome in August–September, 1963. At this conference, which was attended by over 500 persons from some 84 countries, world attention was focussed on international travel and tourism "as economic and social force of major proportions in the world." Many countries realised the benefits of tourism.

The most significant advantage which tourism has for many countries, more especially the developing countries, is the lure of foreign exchange. Most developing countries suffer from a more or less acute shortage of foreign currency. As a result, they have difficulties in obtaining the goods and services necessary for development. For a significant number of developing countries, international tourism has become a major and, in many instances, the largest source of foreign exchange earnings. This has resulted in increased attention of these countries in the development of tourism. Presently in the developing world, over one hundred countries are getting increasingly interested in tourism. Some of these countries are calling upon international consulting firms to prepare their tourism development plans, asking the World Bank group to grant loans to finance tourism projects and also putting in requests to United Nations Development Programme to finance technical assistance projects for tourism. Almost all developing countries set aside substantial financial allocations every year for the development and promotion of tourism. The dynamic efforts made by certain countries, especially the developing countries, both to build and strengthen the basic infrastructure and accommodation and to promote their products, have led to an intensification of tourist flows to those countries. Even the countries of Eastern Europe, that were only a few years ago virtually closed societies, have thrown open their doors to a large number of visitors in a bid to win a fair share of foreign exchange. The lure of foreign exchange has made China open its door to a large number of visitors. Though China was always a closed society, the country is now receiving a large number of foreign tourists from many countries of the world. Hoping to enlarge currency reserves with a large slice of tourist trade, the authorities have made travel in China more liberal and at the same time comfortable by building several new hotels, modernising airports and providing new accommodation at different tourist sites.

Reasons for Growth / Increase in Tourism

- Better/Quicker Air Travel- Making Previously Remote areas accessible.
- More Paid Holidays- People tend to take many small holidays rather than one big one.
- Increase in amount of Disposable income- People can afford to spend more.
- Awareness of attractions- People are becoming more aware of travel from travel shows and advertising.
- 2 working parents
- Smaller families
- Longer life expectancy
- Cheaper/ Easier Travel
- Internet booking/advertising
- More unusual tourist destinations and attractions/destinations
- Newer Marketing Techniques
- Influence of the Internet
- E-Bookings

apter

Ps c olo ical Dimensions

Psychology and Tourism

Psychology is the study of an individual's mentality which focuses on behaviour and mental processes to provide a comprehension and understanding of human behaviour . Psychology attempts to understand the motivation, personality, attitudes and environment of an individual. In tourism, psychology is used to understand the motivations driving people to become tourists. Psychology also studies the needs relating to tourism at a destination for an individual because they are changing with their age, life circle and past tourist experiences. The studies try also to predict tourist behaviour by exploring the personalities of tourists and by seeing how tourists interact with the environment around them.

Motivation Theory

To understand why people travel is the main point, psychology study the travellers motivation. Indeed, understanding why people travel can minimise leakages and allow a bigger tourists' satisfaction. According to Parrinello (1993) the motivation in tourism is one of the most important thing. Indeed, without motivation to travel, there would be no tourism. Psychology schools study many sectors like behaviourism, cognitive, humanistic and psychoanalytic (Holden, 2005). No psychological theory is established for the moment because of the absence of universal agreement upon conceptualisation of the tourist motivation construct. Psychology is not a physical thing we can not touch it, it is why it is difficult to agree; everyone has their own opinion. The study of the motivation with a psychological approach started in the beginning of the twentieth century and there are different approaches upon the subject. In one side, the 'rationalists', they believed that pain avoidance and pleasure seeking directed human behaviour, it is also known as the concept of 'hedonism'. In the other side, there are the 'rationalists', to them the concept of motivation seems unnecessary because they believe that it is the own actions of people who push them to travel (Holden, 2005).

According to Atkinson et al. (1983, cited in Holden, 2005) psychologists based the motivation upon the instinct theory. It is when the instincts of an individual controls their behaviour. What exactly is an 'instinct?' It depends on each person, the definition is too vague (Holden, 2005). Another theory that was applied is the 'drive-reduction' theory, it was popular during the 1920s. Defined by Atkinson et al. (1983, cited in Holden, 2005), this theory is based upon essential needs including: food, shelter and sex, and these needs influence the motivation. After 1950, psychologists included the concept of externals factors upon human behaviour . All individual decisions are based not only on the instinct but also on external stimuli (Holden, 2005). There are a lot of theories that need to be confirmed, but as stated before, psychology in tourism is reasonably new, and very subjective, and at the moment people have very different opinions.

The Application of Motivational Theories to Tourism Studies

In reality, there are two categories of tourist motivations can be observed (Holden, 2005). The first one is people influenced by '**extrinsic**' motivations. This type of motivation comes from outside yourself, from, for example, winning trophies, medals - as a reward. The second one is people influenced by '**intrinsic**' motivations, this is when you do something only for yourself, without any external aspects influencing you. For example, going for a run because it makes you feel better, not because it will benefit anything or anyone else.

Travel Career

Travel career is another theory which is considerable and describes that people are working while experiencing tourism as well as in their workplace. It argues that a tourism career is significantly desired and also follows a specific aim. Even though taking part in tourism is usually out of choice, one's travel career has a tendency to be mostly due to the intrinsic pushes instead of extrinsic ones. The main concept of the theory argues that the factors which make people tourists differ in different stages of life related to the age and also previous experiences as tourists (Pearce, 1998 cited in Holden, 2005).

The results of examining the theory puts the five types of needs in the case of tourism; 'relaxation' is the first group of the 'leisure ladder' where the tourist is just looking for his basic needs in a place that makes the feeling of being free of all the responsibilities and escapism. People in the 'stimulation' group are often interested in fun, unusual and unordinary activities, open to try new things and are concerned with controlling their arousal levels. The members of the 'relationship' group are keen on interacting with others and joint activities and try to make good shared memories. The 'self-esteem and development' group includes people who are working and concentrated on their skills and talents, seeking to improve and be productive respected. 'Fulfilment', which is the last stage of the ladder, belongs to the people who are more focused on living in peace and joy and spirituality (Holden, 2005). This theory brought a vision which clears that the several factors influencing the motivation in tourism change according to the age and different stages of life and this makes planner makers to concentrate to evaluate the tourism needs (Holden, 2005).

Personality

Personality is another effective factor in behaviour and is the most popular topic related to psychology. There is no exact and complete definition for it (Holden, 2005). It can be defined as the reaction of the individual in difficulties and his particular merits which changes him to be firm on his approach to repeat the environmental boosts and catalysts (Decrop, 1999 cited in Holden, 2005). However, there is no exact agreement as to what personality is, but the theories are still beneficial for anticipating the behaviour (Ross, 1998 cited in Holden, 2005). The personality theory as a means of predicting has been examined by the psychographic research which lets the researcher feel exactly what tourist feels and get the reasons for choosing different destinations (Plog, 1994 cited in Holden, 2005). It illustrates that the characteristics such as social class, age, and gender which are called socio-demographic characteristics are becoming less useful in the case of forecasting and anticipating leisure and tourism behaviour in postmodern societies (Holden, 2005). Since the type of trips or activities which belonged just to the population who had the power are involving more people from different groups and classes of society (Holden, 2005). The method categorises typologies of tourists ranging from the term 'psychocentrics' to 'allocentrics.' It shows that 'psychocentrics' are mostly self-inhibited, anxious and not interested in adventure, while 'allocentrics' tend to be more confident and keen on variety and adventure and new destinations have often been discovered by this type since they are keen on interaction by sharing their experiences they make the destination well-known and afterwards becomes the host of the 'near-allocentric' group which are higher in quantity compared to 'allocentrics' and their attention and attraction pushes the developed facilities appear in the destinations. The spreading of the popularity of the destination attracts the 'mid-centric' group and the whole process results in development into the mature stage (Holden, 2005). High rates in population belong to the 'mid-centric' group who usually carry dominant characteristics (Plog, 1973 cited in Holden, 2005). It shows that the different types choose different destinations which are suitable for their personalities. There has been also an established connection between the typology of the tourists and the way that destinations develop and change during which the 'allocentrics' in the path of their adventure would come to check the destination that they have discovered once but this time they find it too far from the nature that it was once (Holden, 2005). At this time the destination is being overused that it reached its maximum potential. Following the process the destinations changes to a suitable place for psychocentric (Plog, 1973 cited in Holden, 2005).

Attitudes

Holden (2005) states that attitudes from the tourist in a destination can influence the types of activities they may choose to participate in. "Attitude refers to the knowledge and positive or negative feelings about an object or activity. The objects or acts towards which we have attitudes may be tangible or intangible, living or non-living" (Dibb et al. 1994: 115, cited in Holden, 2005).

Attitudes can be divided into three components:

- the cognitive which concerns perceptions or beliefs,
- the affective which involves feelings or emotions generated by an object,
- the behavioural (or conative response) which is linked to behaviour intention (based on cognitive and affective responses).

According to Holden (2005), attitudes suggest a cognitive dimension for the information process. Tourist perception is described by Decrop (1999, cited in Holden, 2005) as a process which translates tourist information from an 'external world' to an 'internal' (or mental) one.

Attitudes are permanent sets of evaluations that affect how people see and interpret what is around them. Attitudes make them more predictable in their responses and acts, but it can change or be changed because attitudes are based upon a cognitive component so people can assimilate new information and this can influence the affective and behavioural parts of the attitudes. This is used in tourism marketing: the informations are presented in a way that makes people re-think about the unfavourable cognitions or beliefs about a destination. This is also used for tourist behaviour (negative impacts) and for minority groups in society (racism and homophobia) (Holden, 2005)

Environmental Psychology

Environmental psychology is studying more comprehensively and deeper the perceived and experienced foreign environments by the tourists at a destination. According to Ittleson et al. (1976, cited in Holden, 2005), five modes of interaction can be experienced by tourists in the environment:

- **external:** little attachment to the surroundings, nature and environment seen as separated from tourists;
- **setting for action:** the environment is seen useful because tourists can have activities depending on it;
- **social system:** tourists see environment as a way to strengthen the relationships with their family and friends;
- **emotional territory:** places that tourists have already seen and remind them some emotions; and
- **self:** environment is a part of the person's personality. He/she spends all his/ her free time visiting the place.

In addition, some of these modes of interaction can be experienced at the same time. Holden (2005) insists on the fact that it is how someone sees an environment that determines how this person will interact with it. The more tourist sees the environment as "self", the more he/she will take care of and protect it.

The Visitor Experience

The visitor experience is a factor in which relates to the attitudes and environmental psychology. Psychological theories are applied in order to augment the visitor's experience. Factors used in order to achieve this may include providing the visitor with a service which may make their time at the destination easier, and implement environmental interpretation of what they see (Holden, 2005).

Cognitive maps are a representation of how humans and animals find their way around, mentally .This is because they help you to determine and remember the most unique or distinct features or monuments in a foreign area and this is called the 'anchor point' theory (Holden, 2005).

Holden (2005) states that there has been a lack of research conducted on cognitive mapping, but potential research in this area could help to understand how a person mentally absorbs something that is new or previously unknown to them. Understanding how the human mind works would be extremely useful in this case because it can help to determine what could be done to benefit the visitor and also the destination.

Moscardo (1999) noticed that a large amount of people who use maps tend not to follow compass points or directions, and therefore it has been found that maps that present big landmarks and features may be found more useful and easy to follow than a traditional map due to the way people subconsciously think (cited in Holden. 2005). This is an example of the 'anchor point' theory.

Another observation by Moscardo (1999) found that another factor that could help to intensify the visitor's experience is understanding the environment. This can be done through communication (Ross, 1998 cited in Holden, 2005). 'Mindfulness' is an important part of this as it relates to how we pay attention to our surroundings, and often if when you are open to gaining a better understanding of the environment itself.

Mindfulness could be encouraged by:

- unfamiliar settings;
- changed and varying situations;
- preference and authority; and
- relevance to the individual

Mindfulness is an important factor of the discipline of psychology as it determines how the visitor sees the destination (Moscardo, 1999 cited in Holden, 2005).

If you were to find a reason as to why your neighbour or friend is taking a holiday, that neighbour or friend could probably give you a long list of good reasons. These reasons however would be influenced by his personality type, education, values he attaches to a holiday and so on. Among the several reasons he may include rest and relaxation, seeing different places than his own, meeting his family members or enjoying sun, surf and sea. Therefore, it becomes important to differentiate between various stated reasons and motivations for travel. The various reasons stated by tourists to travel may not all be motivations. Many of these may be of the destination facilities and amenities which are available at the destination. Although important, these reasons are not motivations. Motivation can be defined as a force within an individual which compels him/her to do something to fulfil a psychological or a biological desire.

Tourism as Behaviour

In attempting to account both for consistency of and change in behaviour, psychologists have found it useful to use certain concepts. We have been able to understand behaviour by determining (a) the motives, drives, or concerns which are being satisfied by the action, and (b) the attitudes and information that the person uses to decide what response he should make in a given situation. A motive can be defined as a person's basic predisposition to reach for or to strive toward a general class of goals. Motivated striving may be based upon biological needs and desires acquired through an extended period of past experience. Attitude, on the other hand, is a more circumscribed concept. It can generally be conceived of as an inner factor predisposing one to react positively or negatively towards particular objects, acts, or institutions. As person's disposition or attitude towards an object is likely to depend upon (a) the basic motive with which the object is associated and (b) the degree to which the object is received as instrumental for satisfying or blocking these motives.

The question of motivation is basically the question of "why". Why does Mr. X go to a temple? Why does his brother go out on strike and parade in the picket-line four hours a day? Why does his aunt rigorously observe all the cultural taboos? Why has his cousin complained against him to his employers? The answers to these questions are usually given in terms of individual motivations: because Mr. X seeks social approval, because his brother seeks more benefits from his employer, because his aunt seeks status and security, because his cousin seeks to express his rebellion against the family of Mr. X.

In any account of the behaviours of people we start our description with reference to some kind of active driving force: "the individual seeks", "the individual wants", "the individual fears", and so on. In addition, we specify an object or condition towards which that force is directed: "he seeks wealth", "he wants peace", "he fears something". The study of the relationships between these two variables, the driving force and the object or condition towards which that driving force is directed, is the study of the dynamics of behaviour or motivation. The basic principles or dynamics accounting for the behaviour of going to a temple, joining a particular association, choosing a mate, etc., are the same no matter how simple or how complex the activity.

Predicting Individual Behaviour

Such principles, if they are to be helpful in making accurate predictions of individual behaviour and in increasing our understanding of social phenomenon, must answer questions such as: What induces these driving forces of wanting, seeking fearing in the individuals? What determines, for different individuals the specific nature of the objects or conditions towards which these driving forces are directed? How does it happen that in achieving his goal the individual sometimes carries out this integrated series of acts? What happens when the individual, no matter how strong the driving force, fails to achieve his goal? Knowing the answers to such questions, certain other important questions arise. Does everyone have the same wants, needs, and fears? Can an individual's wants, needs and fears be changed? Can one goal be substituted for another goal to satisfy the same wants? How can conflicting demands be resolved? The answers to these involve basic principles of perception, thinking and learning, as well as of motivation.

The question of motivation is the question of "why". Why do some people travel and others not? Why in a particular country do more people engage in tourism than in another? Or for that matter why one member in a family undertakes travel and others do not? The answers to all these questions have been given in the preceding paragraphs. Various studies of tourism psychology and motivation show that individuals normally travel for more than one reason, and for many, perhaps the majority, tourism is the outcome of a combination of motivations.

Early Influences

Prior to the emergence of mass tourism, particularly since the First World War, the growth of tourism was the result of certain sets of influences which were observed more particularly in the Western world. As a result of the Industrial Revolution in the nineteenth century, there emerged a large and prosperous group in the Western society. The group subsequently became richer since there was a general increase in the material wealth as industrialisation grew and trade and commerce developed. This increase in industrial activity in turn gave rise to new settlements and towns and cities were built to accommodate the increasing number of workforce which was engaged in industries, trade and commerce. Population came to be increasingly concentrated in towns and cities. The introduction of the railway system first in England and then elsewhere in other parts of Europe and America resulted in provision of cheap and quick means of inland travel. The steamship met the need for international travel. A number of steamship companies both in Europe and America came up resulting in increase in international travel. To cater to the needs of tourists, many big hotels and other accommodation facilities were built. Travel came to be organised with the emergence of travel organisers, tourist literature and certain other travel services.

The three major developments—increase in the wealth of the industrial society, development of the means of transport and the organisation of travel—were first witnessed in England and America. However, their influence soon spread across into other countries in Europe and elsewhere. The basic motives to engage in tourism, which had been apparent even much before the middle of the nineteenth century, can be said to be curiosity, seeking material gains by engaging in trade and commerce and education and health. To this another motive—recreation—can be added, which certainly is a result of industrialisation. As no scientific studies were made in that period to determine the motive for travel, it can be safely said that there could have been many more motives besides the basic motives of curiosity, trade and commerce, education and health and recreation. Motivation also includes secondary needs such as success, prestige, achievement, recognition and socialization.

Travel Motivations

Travel motivators are those factors that create a person's desire to travel. They are the internal psychological influences affecting individual choices. Motivations for travel incorporate a broad range of human experiences and behaviours. A brief list of travel motivations might include rest and relaxation, recreation, excitement, social interactions with friends and relations, status, adventure, physical challenges, status and escape from routine work and stress. With the advent of mass tourism, especially after the Second World War, various studies have been made to find out the reasons as to why people wish to travel and become tourists.

McIntosh has stated that basic travel motivators may be grouped into the following four categories.

(i) ***Physical motivators,*** which are related to physical relaxation and rest, sporting activities and specific medical treatment. All are connected with the individual's bodily health and well being.

(ii) ***Cultural motivators,*** which are connected with the individual's desire to travel in order to learn about other countries and their people and their cultural heritage expressed in art, music, literature, folklore, etc.

(iii) ***Interpersonal motivators,*** which are related to a desire to visit relatives, friends, or to escape from one's family, workmates or neighbours, or to meet new people and forge new friendships, or simply to escape from the routine of everyday life.

(iv) ***Status and prestige motivators,*** which are identified with the needs of personal esteem and personal development. These are related to travel for business or professional interests, for the purpose of education and the pursuit of hobbies.

The above-mentioned categories of motivators can be broken down and elaborated to give us more reasons as to why an increasing number of people engage in tourism. These include :

(i) ***Pleasure*:** Getting away from all that routine of everyday life is perhaps the most important motive of all in recent times. The individual's desire and need for pure pleasure is very strong indeed. An individual likes to have fun, excitement and good time whenever possible. The significance of the pleasure factor is widely utilized by travel agents and tour operators who are astute psychologists when it comes to selling the tours. Various brochures and folders particularly emphasise the pleasure aspects of the holidays and travel.

(ii) ***Relaxation, rest and recreation*:** Industrialisation and urbanization has created great pressures on modern living. The stress and strain of modern city life has made it still more necessary than ever before for people to get away from all this and relax in an atmosphere which is more peaceful and healthy. Relaxation is very essential to keep the body and mind healthy. There may be various forms of relaxation and rest. To some it is secured by a change in the environment. Others seek sunshine and excitement at seaside or other resorts. Some seek relaxation in seeing new places, meeting strangers and seeking new experiences. Whatever form the holiday takes, relaxation is always sought in a certain measure by the holidaymaker.

(iii) ***Health* :** The benefits to be gained from fresh air and sunshine have long been recognised. The development of spas during the Roman Empire was the result of people's desire to seek good health. The subsequent establishment of many sanatoria is Switzerland was the result of awareness on the part of the people of the various benefits of good health. These sanatoria laid the foundations for future resort developments. Many travel to spas and clinics for curative baths and medical treatment. In some countries like Italy, Austria and Germany, great importance is given to spa treatment. In Russia along the Black Sea coast and in the foothills of the Caucasus Mountains, there are many world-famous sanatoria where millions of Russians and international tourists throng every year.

(iv) ***Participation in sports***: There has been an increasing participation in a wide variety of sporting activities such as mountaineering, walking, skiing, sailing, fishing, sunbathing, trekking, boating, surf-riding, etc. More and more people these days are taking holidays involving physical activities. In recent years there has been a big increase in sporting holidays. The visitors go to places primarily to indulge in a sporting activity to which all their energies are directed.

(v) ***Curiosity and culture*** : An increasing number of people are visiting different lands, especially places having important historical or cultural associations with the ancient past or places holding special art festivals, music festivals, theatre and other cultural events of importance. Curiosity has been one of the major reasons for tourism. There has always been curiosity in man about foreign lands, people and places. In the present- day world technological developments in the area of mass media have made it possible for people to read, see and hear about different places. The increasing interest shown by many in architecture, art, music, literature, folklore, dance, paintings and sports, of other people's culture or in archaeological and historical remains and monuments is but another aspect of man's curiosity to seek more knowledge. This curiosity has been stimulated by more education. International events like the Olympic Games, Asian Games, national celebrations, exhibitions, special festivals, etc., attract thousands of tourists.

(vi) ***Ethnic and family***: This includes visiting one's relatives and friends, meeting new people and seeking new friendships. A large number of people travel for interpersonal reasons. There is considerable travel by people wanting to visit friends and relatives. A large number of Americans visit European countries in order to see their families or because they feel they are visiting their homeland. Every year thousands of people visit India for ethnic reasons. Many friendships have been made as a result of holiday acquaintances.

(vii) ***Spiritual and Religious***: Travel for spiritual reasons has been taking place since a long time. Visiting religious places has been one of the earliest motivators of travel. A large number of people have been making pilgrimages to sacred religious places or holy places. This practice is widespread in many parts of the world. In the Christian world, for instance, a visit to Jerusalem or the Vatican is considered auspicious. In the Arab–Muslim world, a pilgrimage to Mecca is considered a great act of faith. In India there are many pilgrimage centres and holy places belonging to all the major religions of the world. A large number of pilgrims from all over the world come to India every year.

(viii) ***Status and prestige*:** This concerns the ego needs and personal development. Many people undertake travel with a view to talk about it to their relatives and friends. They like to impress them by relating their experiences in the various places visited. They also travel because they think it is fashionable to do so and, perhaps, show that they can afford to do it. Foreign tour is a magic word and people like to mention it to their friends and other acquaintances.

(ix) ***Professional or business*:** Attending conventions and conferences related to the profession, industry or commerce or to some organisation to which the individual belongs has become very popular. Convention travel has made great strides in recent times. In order to attract more tourists many countries have established grand convention complexes where all kinds of modern facilities are provided for business meetings and seminars. Hotels also provide facilities for conventions as a large number of people travel for business and professional reasons. Conventions and conferences associated with education, commerce, industry, politics and various professions are increasingly being held in various parts of the world. Although some people travel strictly for business purposes, the majority link business travel with pleasure.

Motivations can also be classified as (i) **destination related** and (ii) **non-destination related.**

Destination-related travel motivators are those that allow a tourist to select any area/attraction where he/she would like to go. Tourists are not restricted to a specific destination or an area within a destination. A cost comparison can always be made before making a decision. On the other hand, non-destination related factors are not directly related to a destination. The determining factor in this travel is the cause rather than the destination itself. This would include travel for business, education, visiting friends and relations (VFR travel), health and pilgrimage.

In his summary to the history of tourism, Professor Krapf cites a series of motivations which he considers as the determining impulses of tourism in the past and present. As the first motivating factor, Krapf mentions the exploration of the close and distant neighbourhood. If we proceed from the fact that foreign lands and people were originally looked upon as dangerous and even hostile, it is obvious that considerable personal courage was required to visit or confront them. Only a strong man with initiative could dare to forsake the security of the family or the clan and travel to nearby or distant places.

The second motivation advanced by Krapf is divine service. Originally, this also implied an exceptional social position, for it was a prerogative reserved for priests to visit places considered as abodes of the deities, and it was only gradually that the worldly high-ranking persons were able to approach them.

The same held true for the third motivation, which is participation in events of religious or secular authority. Such participation was again reserved for the selected few, i.e., those of higher social positions.

The utilisation of natural medical cures or journeys to watering-places, as the fourth motivating factor, is again characterized by being restricted to particular social classes, at first the nobility and later the well-to-do bourgeoisie. Here the restrictions followed from the fact of long distances and the related high costs of travel and sojourn.

The final motive force mentioned by Krapf is the enjoyment of nature which must, however, be regarded as of relatively late validity at a time when man began to take a pleasure in nature and did not look upon it as something self-evident to be taken for granted or even to some extent dangerous. It was the intellectual call for a "return to Nature" which first exercised the spell and made trips into what was now considered as "magnificent Nature" a favourite social practice. But here again the high costs resulted in this practice being restricted to the well off, that is the higher social classes.

Some of the motivations cited in respect of modern tourism can be enumerated as follows:

(i) The exploration of the close and distant neighbourhood has become travel aimed at knowing other countries, regions or people, and also travel for studies and cultural ends.

(ii) Divine service as a travel-motivating force subsists in journeys to sacred religious places and in pilgrimages.

(iii) Participation in events of religious or secular authority manifests itself today in the form of travel to political meetings and ceremonies.

(iv) The utilisation of natural medical cures comprises in the widest sense all travel undertaken with the object of rest and relaxation, medical care or treatment of diseases.

(v) Travel for the enjoyment of the beauties of the landscape has undergone modifications both in the conception of what is beautiful and in the expression of sentiment.

(vi) A further motive of tourism is constituted by sports travel. This includes travel for the sake of travelling, the joy felt in motion. In fact, this is only one sports activity projected on the travel screen in addition to the numerous other motive forces connected with sports for which landscape and nature provide the setting for the best possible practice and exercise of sports.

Various reasons as to why people wish to become tourists have been considered. In considering the reasons we are thus dealing with the motivations. After examining the motivations, two broad distinguishable groups of travellers emerge. The first group consists of those who have to visit a particular place and includes businessmen and those who may be described as common-interest travellers, such as those visiting relatives and friends. The decision to travel, when and where to go, how much to spend, etc., is to a great extent outside the control of this group of travellers. They are also less influenced by the price or distance factor. Particularly business travel is relatively price-inelastic and is not susceptible to price inducements. The second group consists of tourists in the pure sense who have a freedom of choice. This group decides for themselves whether they should apply a part of their leisure time to participate in tourism. They also decide for themselves where and when to go. The demand for travel for this group as compared to the demand for the former group is highly price-elastic, that is susceptible to price inducements.

The reason for travel in the case of businessmen and others in the first group are self-evident. Each may, indeed, be marginally influenced by those considerations which affect the second group, the pleasure travellers. This may be reflected in the frequency of visits or the consideration of alternatives as, for example, in the choice of venues for conventions and conferences. However, no particular problem is faced in identifying the motivations. In pleasure or holiday travel, on the other hand, the reasons are varied and not always clearly evident or easily identifiable. It may be stated that the prime motivation to engage in tourism is to be elsewhere and to escape, however temporarily from the routine of everyday life. From this basic motivation, two principal and distinct motivations may be stipulated as dominant.

These have been described by Professor Gray as:

(i) wanderlust

(ii) sunlust

Wanderlust describes the desire to exchange the known for the unknown or familiar with the unfamiliar, to leave things familiar and to go and see different places, people and cultures or architecture of the past in places famous for their historical monuments and also past associations. This also involves seeing current fashions. *Sunlust,* on the other hand, generates a type of travel which depends on the existence elsewhere of better amenities and facilities for a specific purpose than are available in the home country of the traveller. It is commonly associated with such activities as sports and search for sunshine. Wanderlust calls for facilities geared to short-stay visitors and for means of movement at the destinations. Sunlust, on the other hand, requires facilities for a longer stay and for recreation.

apter

conomic Dimensions

The World Tourism Conference held at Manila, Philippines in October, 1980 considered the nature of tourism phenomenon in all its aspects and the role tourism is to play in a dynamic and vastly changing world. Convened by the World Tourism Organisation (WTO), the conference also considered the responsibility of various countries for the development and enhancement of tourism as more than a purely economic activity of nations and peoples.

The significance of tourism to developing countries came up for detailed discussion during the conference. The participants in the World Tourism Conference attached particular importance to its effects on the developing countries. The conference from the beginning pronounced itself on this subject. It stated its conviction that "the world tourism can contribute to the establishment of a new international economic order that will help to eliminate the widening economic gap between developed and developing countries and ensure the steady acceleration of economic and social development and progress, in particular of the developing countries". The Manila Declaration on world tourism considered almost all the aspects of the tourism phenomenon. Besides the economic aspects, social, cultural, spiritual aspects also were considered. The conference was also convinced that world tourism can be a vital force for world peace and can provide the moral and intellectual basis for international understanding and interdependence.

The Manila Declaration States:

(i) Tourism is considered an activity essential to the life of nations because of its direct effects on the social, cultural educational and economic sectors of national societies and their international relations. Its development is linked to the social and economic development of nations and can only be possible if man has access to creative rest and enjoys the freedom to travel within the framework of free time and leisure whose profoundly human character it underlines. Its very existence and development depend entirely on the existence of a state of lasting peace, to which tourism itself is required to contribute.

(ii) On the threshold of the twenty-first century and in view of the problems facing mankind, it seems timely and necessary to analyse the phenomenon of tourism, in relation fundamentally to the dimensions it has assumed since the granting to workers of the right to annual paid holidays, which moved tourism from a restricted elitist activity to a wider activity integrated into social and economic life.

(iii) As a result of people's aspirations to tourism, the initiatives taken by States regarding legislation and institutions, the permanent activities of voluntary bodies representing the various strata of the population and the technical contribution made by specialized professionals, modern tourism has come to play an important role within the range of human activities. States have recognized this fact and the great majority of them have entrusted the World Tourism Organisation with the task of ensuring the harmonious and sustained development of tourism, in cooperation, in appropriate cases, with the specialized agencies of the United Nations and the other international organisations concerned.

(iv) The right to use of leisure, and in particular the right to access to holiday and to freedom of travel and tourism, a natural consequence of the right to work, is recognized as an aspect of the fulfilment of the human needs by the Universal Declaration of Human Rights as well as by the legislation of many States. It entails for society the duty of providing for its citizens the best practical, effective and non-discriminatory access to this type of activity. Such an effort must be in harmony with the priorities, institutions and traditions of each individual country.

(v) There are many constraints on the development of tourism. Nations and groups of nations should determine and study these constraints, and adopt measures aimed at attenuating their negative influence.

(vi) The share of tourism in national economies and in international trade makes it a significant factor in world development. Its consistent major role in national economic activity, in international transactions and in securing balance of payments equilibrium makes it one of the main activities of the world economy.

(vii) Within each country, domestic tourism contributes to an improved balance of the national economy through a redistribution of the national income. Domestic tourism also heightens the awareness of common interest and contributes to the development of activities favourable to the general economy of the country. Thus, the development of tourism from abroad should be accompanied by a similar effort to expand domestic tourism.

(viii) The economic returns of tourism, however real and significant they may be, do not and cannot constitute the only criterion for the decision by States to encourage this activity. The right to holidays, the opportunity for the citizen to get to know his own environment, a deeper awareness of his national identity and of the solidarity that links him to his compatriots and the sense of belonging to a culture and to a people are all major reasons for stimulating the individual's participation in domestic and international tourism through access to holidays and travel.

(ix) The importance that millions of our contemporaries attach to tourism in the use of their free time and in their concept of the quality of life makes it a need that governments should take into account and support tourism.

(x) Social tourism is an objective which society must pursue in the interest of those citizens who are least privileged in the exercise of their rights to rest.

(xi) Through its effects on the physical and mental health of individuals practising it, tourism is a factor that favours social stability, improves the working capacity of communities and promotes individual as well as collective well-being.

(xii) Through the wide range of services needed to satisfy its requirements, tourism creates new activities of considerable importance which are a source of new employment. In this respect, tourism constitutes a positive element for social development in all the countries where it is practised irrespective of their level of development.

(xiii) With respect to international relations and the search for peace based on justice and respect of individual and national aspirations, tourism stands out as a positive and ever-present factor in promoting mutual knowledge and understanding and as a basis for reaching a greater level of respect and confidence among all the peoples of the world.

(xiv) Modern tourism results from the adoption of a social policy which led to the workers' gaining annual paid holidays and represents the recognition of a fundamental right of the human being to rest and leisure. It has become a factor contributing to social stability, mutual understanding among individuals and peoples and individual betterment. In addition to its well-known economic aspects, it has acquired a cultural and moral dimension which must be fostered and protected against the harmful distortions which can be brought about by economic factors. Public authorities and the travel trade should accordingly participate in development of tourism by formulating guidelines aimed at encouraging appropriate investments.

(xv) Youth tourism requires the most active attention since young people have less income than others for travelling or taking holidays. A positive policy should provide youth with the utmost encouragement and facilities. The same attention should be provided for the elderly and handicapped.

(xvi) In the universal efforts to establish a new international economic order, tourism can under appropriate conditions, play a positive role in furthering equilibrium, cooperation, mutual understanding and solidarity among all countries.

(xvii) Nations should promote improved conditions of employment for workers engaged in tourism and confirm and protect their right to establish professional trade unions and collective bargaining.

(xviii) Tourism resources available in various countries consist of space, facilities and values at the same time. These are resources whose use cannot be left uncontrolled without running the risk of their deterioration, or even their destruction. The satisfaction of tourism requirements must not be prejudicial to the social and economic interests of the population in tourist areas, to the environment or, above all to natural resources, which are the fundamental attractions of tourism, and historical and cultural sites. All tourism resources are part of the heritage of mankind. National communities and the entire international community must take the necessary steps to ensure their preservation. The conservation of historical, cultural and religious sites represents at all times, and notably in time of conflict, one of the fundamental responsibilities of States.

(xix) International cooperation in the field of tourism is an endeavour in which the characteristics of peoples and basic interests of individual States must be respected. In this field, the central and decisive role of the World Tourism Organisation as a concept-utilizing and harmonizing body is obvious.

(xx) Bilateral and multilateral technical and financial cooperation cannot be looked upon as an act of assistance since it constitutes the pooling of the means necessary for the utilization of resources for the benefit of all parties.

(xxi) In the practice of tourism, spiritual elements must take precedence over technical and material elements. The spiritual elements are essentially as follows:

(a) the total fulfilment of the human being;
(b) a constantly increasing contribution to education;
(c) equality of destiny of nations;
(d) the liberation of man in a spirit of respect for his identity and dignity;
(e) the affirmation of the originality of cultures and respect for the moral heritage of peoples.

(xxii) Preparation for tourism should be integrated with the training of the citizen for his civic responsibilities. In this respect, governments should mobilize the means of education and information at their disposal and should facilitate the work of individuals and bodies involved in this endeavour. Preparation for tourism, for holidays and for travel could usefully form part of the process of youth education and training. For these reasons, the integration of tourism into youth education constitutes a basic element favourable to the permanent strengthening of peace.

(xxiii) Any long-term analysis of mankind's social, cultural and economic development should take due account of national and international tourist and recreational activities. These activities now form an integral part of the life of modern national and international societies. Bearing in mind the acknowledged values of tourism which are inseparable from it, the authorities will have to give more increased attention to the development of national and international tourists and recreational activities, based on an ever-wider participation of peoples in holidays and travel, as well as the movement of persons for numerous other purposes, with a view to ensuring the orderly growth of tourism in a manner consistent with the other basic needs of society.

(xxiv) The States and other participants in the Conference, together with the World Tourism Organisation, are strongly urged to take into account the guidelines, viewpoints and recommendations emanating from the Conference so that they can contribute, on the basis of their experience and in the context of their day-to-day activities, to the practical implementation of the objectives set with a view to broadening the process of development of world tourism and breathing new life into it.

(xxv) The Conference urges the World Tourism Organisation to take all necessary measures, through its own internal machinery and, where appropriate, in cooperation with other international, inter-government and non-governmental bodies, so as to permit the global implementation of the principles, concepts and guidelines contained in this final document.

The Manila Declaration on world tourism considered almost all aspects of tourism phenomenon, which included economic, social, cultural, spiritual and environmental aspects. The economic and social impacts of tourism for the countries promoting and developing tourism, however, found a special mention in the declaration. The economic returns of tourism, according to the declaration, were real and significant in terms of employment generation, balance of payments, and improved balance of the national economy through a redistribution of the national income.

Understanding of tourism impacts is very important as this would provide clear insight into the way it should be developed and promoted. Tourism impacts come in different shapes and forms. These are often discussed in terms of economy, physical environment of destination, area, social structure and environmentally sustainable development.

Economic aspects broadly concern issues of employment generation, regional development of underdeveloped areas, balance of payments and foreign exchange.

Social Structure relates to issues of culture, traditions, interpersonal relationships and lifestyles of both visitors and host communities.

Physical Environment issues concern landscape, ecological conservation and land use in both built-up and natural areas.

Economic Impacts

Most countries develop tourism because of its economic impact. The main reasons for encouraging tourism development have been the income and employment generation benefits created by visitor expenditure in the host areas. The income and employment impacts can be spread over to several areas/regions of a country in the following manner:

- Most directly in areas with a buoyant level of tourism.
- Labour-intensive accommodation units such as hotels spread over in a large number of attractions.
- Ground-handling arrangements of several types.
- In underdeveloped areas where there are few other jobs available.

- Income from interest payments on loans advanced to various sectors with special reference to purchase of high-value equipment like aircraft.
- Income from taxation on tourism activities such as value-added tax on hotels.
- Direct taxation on tourism to raise additional public income (tax imposed on accommodation or departure tax at airports).

The status of tourism as a major economic activity is recognised as an expenditure by international visitors (visitor exports) amounting to about 600 billion US dollars in the year 1999. The total number of international visitors involved in the year 1999 were estimated to be about 700 million.

According to a report by the World Travel and Tourism Council (WTTC) travel and tourism is "expected to generate about 3.5 trillion US dollars of GDP and almost 200 million jobs across the world economy in 1999; approximately one third of this comes from the industry itself and the remainder from its very strong catalytic flow-through effect in other sectors such as retail and construction. World travel and tourism GDP is forecast to increase in real terms at 3.0 per cent per annum in the decade 2010. In the same period employment in travel and tourism is expected to grow at 2.6 per cent per annum."

WTTC Highlights

The World Travel and Tourism Council has summarised the world highlights concerning travel and tourism industry as follows:

- The travel and tourism economy will account for 11.7 per cent of world GDP in 1999.
- Travel and tourism has emerged strongly from the Asia Crisis with leisure tourism expected to grow by 4.7 per cent in 1999 and business travel by 4.4 per cent.
- Spending by international visitors will amount to 8 per cent of world exports in 1999 with further impact by export of travel and tourism-related goods.
- Travel and tourism-related GDP is forecast to increase at 3 per cent per annum in real terms.
- Over 8 per cent of all jobs worldwide will depend upon travel and tourism.
- Travel and tourism will support the creation of over 5.5 million jobs per year over the next decade.

Travel and tourism can be considered the world's largest industry and the largest creator of employment across the economy. Looking back, much work on tourism impacts or significance focussed mainly on the economic benefits only. There was hardly mention of any social or environmental impacts or cost-benefit recognition. The emphasis towards economic benefits during earlier periods of tourism development was, however, not surprising considering the fact that most countries considered tourism as potential economic development activity. The massive economic gains derived from tourism, however, are seldom exclusive of social or environmental change. The environmental changes as a result of mass movement of tourists to host areas (destinations) leave behind profound social and environmental impacts. The manner in which these impacts are managed by the governments as also by private and public sectors in the host areas could determine the positive or negative results.

Tourism has been recognised by almost all the countries as a major force. The question, however, arises as to whether tourism is an industry. Should this be judged primarily or even mainly through its economic impact? Do the tourists themselves think of travel as a primary economic activity? Are not the social and environmental issues of tourism as crucial as economic? Does tourism not help in the development of international understanding? Many attempts to evaluate tourism benefits fail because they limit their coverage only to economic issues. Proper understanding of tourism impacts can only be appreciated on a broad base which could include not only economic aspect but also socio-cultural and environmental aspects.

Economic Significance

Tourism has major economic significance for a country. The receipts from international tourism can provide a valuable source of earnings for both developed as well as developing countries. Visitor spending generates income for both public and private sectors, besides effecting wages and employment opportunities. Although tourism is sensitive to the level of economic activity in the tourist-generating countries, it provides more fixed earnings than primary products. The income from tourism has tended to increase at a higher rate than merchandise export in a number of countries, especially in countries having a low industrial base. There is now an almost assured channel of financial flows from the developed countries to the developing countries raising the latter's export earnings and rate of economic growth. According to the World Tourism Organisation (WTO), among the world's top 40 tourism earners in 1995 about 18 were developing countries including India. Regarding the number of visitor arrivals, in some countries there were more visitor arrivals than the population. France with a population of 57 million received 70 million visitors in 1998; similarly, Spain with a population of 37 million received 47 million visitors during the same year.

Several island countries in such areas as the Caribbean depend very heavily on tourist income resulting from visitor arrivals, which often represents the major part of the GDP. Even developed countries like Canada, which derived over 13 per cent of its GDP from international visitors in 1995, rely heavily on income from tourism. Tourism thus forms a very important source of income, especially foreign exchange for several countries. Although the quantum contributed in foreign currency per visitor varies from one destination to another, the importance of receipts from tourism in the balance-of-payment accounts and of tourist activities in the national revenue has become considerable for a number of countries.

Major Economic Benefits

The major economic benefit in promoting the tourism industry has therefore tended to be the earning of foreign exchange. Income from foreign tourism in the form of foreign exchange earnings adds to the national income and, as an invisible export, may offset a loss on the visible trading account and be of critical importance in the overall financial reckoning. This is more true in case of developing countries. For many developing countries, particularly the small countries, which are mainly dependent upon primary products such as a few basic cash crops, tourism often offers a more reliable form of income. In the case of some European countries, notably Spain, Portugal, Austria and Greece, the invisible earnings from tourism are of major significance and have a very strong positive effect on the balance of payments. Tourism is thus a very useful means of earning the much-needed foreign currency. It is almost without a rival as an earning source for many developed as well as developing countries. These earnings assume a great significance in the balance-of-payment calculations.

Balance of Payments

The balance of payments shows the relationship between a country's total payments to all other countries and its total receipts from them. In other words, it may be defined as a statement of income and expenditure on international account. Payments and receipts on international account are of three kinds: (i) the visible balance of trade (relating to the import and export of goods); (ii) invisible items (relating to the services such as shipping and insurance); and (iii) capital transfers. The receipts from foreign tourism form an 'invisible export', similar to other 'invisibles' which come from transportation and shipping, banking and insurance, income on investments, etc. Because most countries from time to time have serious problems with the balance of their international payments, much attention comes to be focussed on tourism because of its potentially important contribution to, and also effect upon, the balance of payments.

The receipts from international tourism, however, are not always net. Sometimes expenditures are involved which must be set against them. Net foreign exchange receipts from tourism are reduced principally by the import cost of goods and services used by visitors, foreign exchange costs of capital investment in tourist amenities and promotion and publicity expenditure abroad. Peters has said: "Certain imports associated with tourist expenditures must be deducted. . . . the importation of material and equipment for constructing hotels and other amenities, and necessary supplies to run them; foreign currency costs of imports for consumption by international tourists; remittances of interests and profits on overseas investment in tourism enterprises, mainly hotel construction; foreign currency costs of conducting a tourism-development programme, including marketing expenditure overseas."

Reliance on imports to meet tourist's needs does not, however, deny developing countries the opportunity of earning foreign exchange in supplying such goods and services. Imports are, to a large extent, as essential to the operation of the tourist sector as to that of other sectors. The important question is whether the value added domestically on an export good or service is maximized. Maximization of import substitution without due regard to the effect on overall tourism receipts (i.e., demand) may be counter-productive. Secondly, differences in the pattern and level of reliance on imported goods and services, capital equipment and manpower are very wide depending upon the level of development of a country. In some cases, this reliance is simply due to a lack of resources that will be transformed into items to be sold to the industry. In others, the industry has not yet drawn on such supply potential, for which it may be an important stimulus. There is a general need for a careful programme of import substitution.

The Economic Contribution of Travel & Tourism

The economic contribution of travel & tourism travel and tourism is an important economic activity in most countries around the world. As well as its direct economic impact, the industry has significant indirect and induced impacts. The UN Statistics Division-approved Tourism Satellite Accounting methodology (TSA:RMF 2008) quantifies only the direct contribution of Travel & Tourism. But WTTC recognises that Travel & Tourism's total contribution is much greater, and aims to capture its indirect and induced impacts through its annual research.

Direct Contribution

The direct contribution of Travel & Tourism to GDP reflects the 'internal' spending on Travel & Tourism (total spending within a particular spending by government on Travel & Tourism services directly linked to visitors, such as cultural (eg. Museums) or recreational (eg. National Parks). The direct contribution of Travel & Tourism to GDP is calculated to be consistent with the output, as expressed in National Accounting, tourists. The direct contribution of Travel & Tourism to GDP is calculated from total internal spending by 'netting out' the purchases made by the different tourism sectors. This measure is consistent with the definition of Tourism GDP, specified in the 2008 Tourism Satellite The total contribution of Travel & Tourism includes its 'wider impacts' (i.e. the indirect and induced impacts) on the economy. The 'indirect' contribution includes the GDP and jobs supported by: Travel &Tourism investment spending - an important aspect of both current and future activity that includes investment activity such as the purchase of new aircraft and construction of new hotels; Government 'collective' spending, which helps Travel & Tourism activity in many different ways as it is made on behalf of the Domestic purchases of goods and services by the sectors dealing directly with tourists - including, for example, purchases of food and cleaning services by hotels, of fuel and catering services by airlines, and IT services by travel agents.

The 'induced' contribution measures the GDP and jobs supported by the spending of those who are directly or indirectly employed by the Travel & Tourism industry

Travel & Tourism's Contribution to GDP

The direct contribution of Travel & Tourism to GDP in 2017 was USD2,570.1bn (3.2% of GDP). This is forecast to rise by 4.0% to USD2,674.2bn in 2018. This primarily reflects the economic activity generated by industries such as hotels, travel agents, airlines and other passenger transportation The direct contribution of Travel & Tourism to GDP is expected to grow by 3.8% pa to USD3,890.0bn (3.6% of GDP) by 2028.

The total contribution of Travel & Tourism to GDP (including wider effects from investment, the supply chain and induced income impacts,

It is forecast to rise by 3.8% pa to USD12,450.1bn by 2028 (11.7% of GDP)

Travel & Tourism's Contribution to Employment

Travel & Tourism generated 118,454,000 jobs directly in 2017 (3.8% of total employment) and this is forecast to grow by 2.4% in 2018 to 121,356,000 commuter services). It also includes, for example, the activities of the restaurant and leisure industries directly supported by tourists. By 2028, Travel & Tourism will account for 150,139,000 jobs directly, an increase of 2.2% pa over the next ten years.

The total contribution of Travel & Tourism to employment (including wider effects from investment, the supply chain and induced income was 313,221,000 jobs in 2017 (9.9% of total employment). This is forecast to rise by 3.0% in 2018 to 322,666,000 jobs (10.1% of total employment).

By 2028, Travel & Tourism is forecast to support 413,556,000 jobs (11.6% of total employment), an increase of 2.5% pa over the period.

Visitor Exports and Investment

Visitor Exports

Money spent by foreign visitors to a country (or visitor exports) is a key component of the direct contribution of Travel & Tourism. In 2017, the world generated USD1,494.2bn in visitor exports. In 2018, this is expected to grow by 3.9%, and the world is expected to attract 1,395,660,000 international tourist arrivals. By 2028, international tourist arrivals are forecast to total 2,094,210,000, generating expenditure of USD2,311.4bn, an increase of 4.1% pa.

Investment

Travel & Tourism is expected to have attracted capital investment of USD882.4bn in 2017. This is expected to rise by 4.8% in 2018, and rise by 4.3% pa over the next ten years to USD1,408.3bn in 2028. Travel & Tourism's share of total national investment will rise from 4.5% in 2018 to 5.1% in 2028.

Table 5.1

The Economic Contribution of Travel and Tourism: Real 2017 Prices

WORLD (USDbn, real 2017 prices)	**2012**	**2013**	**2014**	**2015**	**2016**	**2017**	**2018E**	**2028F**
1. Visitor exports	1221.4	1289.0	1355.5	1396.7	1432.6	1494.2	1552.6	2311.4
Domestic expenditure 2. (includes government individual spending)	3258.3	3367.1	3488.2	3617.1	3789.2	3970.5	4132.4	6051.5
3. Internal tourism consumption (= 1 + 2)	4479.7	4656.1	4843.7	5013.8	5221.8	5464.8	5684.9	8362.8
4. Purchases by tourism providers, including imported goods (supply chain)	-2,392.9	-2,487.0	-2,585.2	-2,651.5	-2,765.6	-2,894.6	-3,010.7	-4,472.8
5. **Direct contribution of Travel & TourismtoGDP** (= 3 + 4)	2,086.8	2,169.1	2,258.5	2,362.3	2,456.2	2,570.1	2,674.2	3,890.0
Other final impacts (indirect & induced) 6. Domestic supply chain	2,070.1	2,161.8	2,253.2	2,321.7	2,429.3	2,526.9	2,629.6	3,897.2
7. Capital investment	705.6	724.4	760.6	804.8	848.6	882.4	924.5	1,408.3
8. Government collective spending	393.9	401.2	408.8	421.5	434.0	444.4	456.8	603.4
9. Imported goods from indirect spending	301.3	314.8	326.6	359.3	381.7	418.7	438.9	593.8
10. Induced	1,201.2	1,246.6	1,290.1	1,337.2	1,386.9	1,429.8	1,480.6	2,057.4
11. **Total contribution of Travel&TourismtoGDP** **(= 5 + 6 + 7 + 8 + 9 + 10)**	6,758.8	7,017.8	7,297.8	7,606.7	7,936.7	8,272.3	8,604.5	12,450.1
Employment impacts ('000) 12. Direct contribution of Travel & Tourism to employment	108,131	109,640	111,658	114,014	116,095	118,454	121,356	150,139
13. **Total contribution of Travel &Tourism to employment**	276,819	283,329	290,135	298,802	306,003	313,221	322,666	413,556
Other indicators 14. Expenditure on outbound travel	1,050.4	1,123.9	1,235.7	1,287.8	1,332.8	1,391.7	1,447.7	2,037.3

Tourism Income Multiplier (TIM)

Multipliers are a means of estimating how much extra income is produced in an economy as a result of initial spending or injection of cash. Every time the money changes hands it provides 'new' income and the continuing series of conversions of money spent by the tourists form what the economists term the multiplier effect. The more often the conversion occurs, the greater its beneficial effect on the economy of the recipient country.

Earnings from tourism occupy an important place in the national income of a country. Without taking into account receipts from domestic tourism, international tourism receipts alone contribute a great deal. The flow of money generated by tourist spendings multiplies as it passes through various sections of the economy. In addition to an important source of income, tourism provides a number of other economic benefits, which vary in importance from one country to another and also depending upon the nature and scale of tourism. Tourist facilities such as hotels, restaurants, museums, clubs, sports complexes, public transport, national parks are used also by domestic tourists and visitors, businessmen and residents; yet a significant portion of the costs may be borne by international tourists. Tourists also contribute to tax revenue both directly through sales taxes and indirectly through property, profits and income taxes. Tourism provides employment, brings infrastructural improvements and may help regional development. Each of these economic aspects can be dealt with separately, but they are all closely related and are considered together. Let us first look at the income aspect of tourism.

Multiplier Mechanism

Tourism as a source of income is not easy to measure, at least with any degree of accuracy. This is because of the multiplier effect. The flow of money generated by tourist spending multiplies as it passes through various sections of the economy through the operation of the multiplier effect. The multiplier is an income concept. The multiplier theory emerges from the work of Kahn and Keynes. It can be systematically explained as follows: from an initial impulse, such as investment or expenditure, there springs one or more primary effects such as income, savings, etc. These primary effects, in their turn, and in the course of a second period, produce secondary effects of the same type as the first. The process is repeated several times in a given lapse of time. The multiplier makes it possible to calculate the sum of the various primary, secondary and tertiary effects of the same type, and hence the relation between the total effects of the same nature and the primary effect. This relation is represented by the multiplier, which is then applied to the primary effect in order to arrive at the total effect.

The multiplier mechanism has also been applied to tourism and in particular to tourist expenditure. The nature of the tourism multiplier and its effect may be described as follows: "The money paid by a tourist in, say, paying his hotel bill will be used by the hotel management to provide for the costs which it had incurred in meeting the demands of the visitor, e.g., such goods and services as food, drink, furnishing, laundering, electricity and entertainment. The recipients, in turn, use the money they have thus received to meet their financial commitments and so on". In other words, tourist expenditure not only supports the tourist industry directly but helps indirectly to support many other industries which supply goods and services to the tourist industry. In this way money spent by tourists may be said to be used several times and to spread into various sectors of the economy. In sum, the money paid by the tourist, after a long series of transfers over a given period of time, passes through all sectors of the national economy, stimulating each in turn throughout the process.

Leakages

However, this transfer of money is not absolute as there are 'leakages' which occur. Such leakages may occur as a result of, say, importing foreign goods, paying interest on foreign investments, etc. Any leakage of these kinds will reduce the stream of expenditure which, in consequence, will limit and reduce the multiplier effect. Income generated by foreign tourist expenditure in countries possessing more advanced economies, which generally are more self-sufficient and less in need of foreign imports, will tend to have higher multipliers than countries which are less self-sufficient and need to support their tourist industries by substantial imports. If the developing countries are to gain maximum economic benefits from tourism, they should control very strictly those imported items of tourist consumption and to keep foreign investment expenditure to a reasonable level. The benefits, otherwise, accruing from tourism would be reduced or even cancelled by the leakages. The other leakages include:

(i) remittance of incomes outside the host area, for example, by foreign workers;
(ii) indirect and direct taxation where the tax proceeds are not respent in the host area; and
(iii) savings out of income received by the workers in the host area.

The most important leakage would appear to arise from expenditures on importation of agricultural products like food and drink. In a primary macroeconomic approach to the prospects opened up by tourism establishment in a developing country, it is regarded as advantageous that a good portion of tourist consumption should consist of food products. It is estimated that the major part of these products can be found in those countries whose economic structure is largely agricultural in character. In this sense, tourist consumption, derived from international flow, can offer an assured outlet to a production which is already active within the country, without raising problems connected with export of such products in the international markets. Home-grown products could thus be substituted for imported foodstuffs and a significant saving effected.

Such savings would help to increase the tourism multiplier, which, in turn, would help the host country to derive maximum economic benefits from its tourist industry. This aspect of the question is all the more important in that the multiplier effect maintains its efficiency as long as no importation takes place. It follows that if the national economy is to derive the maximum benefit from the impact of international and national tourism, there is an elementary obligation to find all those products needed for tourist consumption. The dynamics of agricultural production in recent years appear to confirm the ability of developing countries to produce the major part of their agricultural products required for tourist consumption without resorting to massive imports. The tourist economy of any country, if it is to remain healthy, must rely upon local agricultural production and this elementary condition seems today to be on the way to realization in the majority of developing countries.

In an economy with a high proportion of leakages such as high tax rate or high import levels, tourism income multiplier (TIM) tends to be low and tourism will not stimulate the local economy much. On the other hand, with a low proportion of leakages, tourism income multiplier tends to be high resulting in the high contribution of tourism to the local economy. In general, the value of tourism income multiplier has been found to range between about one and two and a half.

Infrastructure

Expansion and modernisation of infrastructure is perhaps the single most important challenge to travel and tourism in reaching its potential for wealth and employment generation. Many regions in the world are not in a position to reap the benefits of tourism simply because of the lack of infrastructure. In fact, if we look at the countries and the regions within the countries, the ones having adequate infrastructure are the greatest beneficiaries. The world's top 40 tourist generating and receiving countries all have excellent infrastructure.

Income from tourism is an important source for expansion and modernisation of infrastructure in a country. The benefits from infrastructure investments, justified primarily for tourism—airports, hotels, roads, water supply, information systems and other public utilities—may be shared by the other sectors of economy. In addition to development of new infrastructure, the improvements and upgradation in the existing infrastructure which are undertaken in order to attract visitors is also of crucial importance. These improvements would also confer benefits upon the resident population by providing them with amenities which, hitherto, they had not enjoyed. Furthermore, the provision of infrastructure may provide the basis or serve as an encouragement for greater economic diversification. A variety of secondary industries may be promoted which may not serve the needs of tourism. Thus, indirectly, tourist expenditure may be responsible for stimulating other economic activities.

One of the characteristics of underdevelopment is that of deficiencies in the basic infrastructures, which lie at the root of a series of serious problems related to the development of tourism. Construction of primary infrastructures represents the foundation of any future economic growth even though they are not directly productive. The tourist industry illustrates the elementary need for basic infrastructures. It has today the important benefit of being able to profit from the existing infrastructures and thus to make a decisive contribution to the growth of the national economy. The traffic arising from international and national tourism, moreover, represents a reward for the capital invested and can contribute to the financial efforts required for maintenance. The satisfactory degree of development achieved in this specific sector permits major tourist progress, while giving further proof of the complementary character of tourism in relation to other economic sectors. Creation of basic infrastructures for tourist usage will also be of service to the other sectors of the economy like industry and agriculture. The outcome of this is better equilibrium of general economic growth.

Regional Development

Another important domestic effect relates to the regional aspects of tourist expenditure. Such expenditure is of special significance in marginal areas, which are relatively isolated, economically underdeveloped, and have unemployment problems. The United Nations Conference on International Travel and Tourism held in Rome in 1963 noted that tourism was important not as a source of foreign exchange, but also as a factor in the location of industry and in the development of less-developed regions. It further stated that in some cases the development of tourism may be the only means of promoting the economic advancement of less-developed areas lacking in other resources.

The underdeveloped regions of the country can greatly benefit from tourism development. Many of the economically backward regions contain areas of high scenic beauty and of cultural attractions. These areas, if developed for use by tourists, can bring a lot of prosperity to the local people. Tourism development in these regions may become a significant factor in redressing regional imbalances in employment and income. Tourist expenditure at a particular tourist area greatly helps the development of the areas around it. Many countries, both developed as well as developing, have realised this aspect of tourism development and are creating and developing tourist facilities in underdeveloped regions with a view to bringing prosperity there.

Khajuraho in Madhya Pradesh, which is now an internationally famous tourist attraction, is an example of one such region. A remote and unknown village about forty years ago, Khajuraho is now on the world tourist map attracting thousands of tourists both domestic as well as international. Today, Indian Airlines flies a jet plane between New Delhi and Khajuraho, and seats are not easy to come by. Thousands of tourists visit the place by air, rail and road-transport every month to see the architectural beauty of temples and erotic sculptures built by the Chandela kings, who held sway in North India from the ninth to thirteenth centuries. Out of the 80 odd temples built in Khajuraho, only 22 temples remain today; yet they are among the most glorious embodiments of Indian temple architecture, wreathed in seemingly living sculpture. Together they represent the finest expression of the art of medieval India.

Development of Heritage Areas

The area around Khajuraho now pulsates with life. The place has provided employment to hundreds of local people in hotels and shops. There is already a thriving clay model industry devoted to making replicas of the famous temple sculptures. A number of shops dealing with items of presentation, handlooms and handicrafts have created jobs for many. As a result of this, local people are recipients of additional income which has resulted in their increased prosperity. The subsequent development of areas around Khajuraho will provide additional employment opportunities resulting in general prosperity of the people.

But for the development of tourism in the area, Khajuraho would have remained a remote unknown village.

Many such areas of tourist interest where industrial development is out of question because of distance from markets, lack of raw materials and transportation facilities, scarcity of power, water, etc., can greatly benefit if developed properly. There is no dearth of areas which could, after they are developed for tourism, become great assets to the region in particular and to the country as a whole. The French government has created a series of new resorts particularly to bring prosperity to the areas which traditionally have been underdeveloped. The Italian government is likewise attempting to develop tourism in southern Italy in order to redress the economic imbalances which have long existed between the north and the south. Tourism is to be regarded not as an area of peripheral investment but as one of primary investment whose benefits will help in creating employment opportunities and in the regeneration of backward regions.

Employment

Tourism creates employment. As mentioned earlier, the World Travel and Tourism Council had estimated that in the year 1999 travel and tourism was expected to generate almost 200 million jobs across the world economy, both direct and indirect. Approximately one-third of these jobs were to be directly from the industry itself and the remainder from its very strong catalytic flow-through effect in other sectors such as retail and construction. WTTC further expected that over 8 per cent of all jobs worldwide will depend on travel and tourism in 1999 and that the industry will support the creation of over 5.5 million jobs per year over the next decade. Looking forward, WTTC states that in the decade 2010, employment in travel and tourism is expected to grow at 2.6 per cent per annum. WTTC has further projected that by the year 2017 Travel and Tourism would generate 313 million jobs across the world.

The majority of jobs associated with travel and tourism tend to come in the form of direct-service jobs in tourist-related facilities and attractions at the destination and in tourist-generating areas. However, the bulk of the jobs are in tourist destinations. These jobs are available primarily in accommodation sector (e.g., hotels), with travel intermediaries (travel agents, tour operators) supplying services, restaurants, shops selling discretionary goods and travel enterprises. In addition, employment opportunities are also available in other sectors of the economy which service and supply the main tourism sector, such as manufacturing and transport services, banking, agriculture and fisheries. Many of the jobs are created in areas where few alternative employment opportunities are available.

Labour Intensive Service Industry

The tourist industry is a highly labour-intensive service industry and hence is a valuable source of employment. It employs large number of people and provides a wide range of jobs which extend from the unskilled to the highly specialised. In addition to those involved in management, there are a large number of specialist personnel required to work as accountants, housekeepers, waiters, cooks and entertainers, who in turn need large number of semi-skilled workers such as porters, chambermaids, kitchen staff, gardeners, etc. In addition, it should be emphasised that tourism is also responsible for creating employment outside the industry in its more narrowly defined sense and, in this respect, those who supply goods and services to those directly involved in tourism equally are beneficiaries from tourism. Such indirect employment includes, for example, those involved in the furnishing and equipment industries, souvenir industries and farming and food supply.

The construction industry is another very big source of employment. The basic infrastructure—roads, airports, water supply and other public utilities and also construction of hotels and other accommodation units—create jobs for thousands of workers, both unskilled and skilled. This important sector represents appreciable source of employment of manpower. In many of the developing countries, where a high rate of unemployment often exists, the promotion of tourism can be a great encouragement to economic development and, especially, employment. When discussing about employment, it is necessary to consider the seasonal nature of the tourism industry. In areas where general diversification alternatives are scarce, a combination of heavy dependence on tourism and highly marked seasonality calls for measures to develop off-season traffic.

Employment Multiplier

Like income multiplier, employment multiplier does the same for employment. Employment multiplier can be expressed in one of the following two ways:

(a) As a ratio of the combination of direct employment. At the destination, the jobs are directly created in the industry there.

(b) As a ratio of secondary employment generated per additional unit of tourist expenditure to direct employment. The workers and their families require their own goods and services giving rise to further indirectly created employment in shops, schools, health-care institutions, etc. The value of the employment multiplier is similar to that of tourism income multiplier (TIM), assuming that jobs with average wage rates are created.

Cultural Resources

It may appear strange to discuss cultural tourism in this era of mass tourism. As an example of this conception of tourism, a statement by J. Fourastie may be quoted here: "It is necessary for us to learn to look, to behold, to meditate, to question actions virtually unknown if we are to judge by the bands of tourists who are content with a brief glance which will allow them to affix the mention 'seen' to the greatest number of countries or monuments. We can then hear them say 'I have done Italy, Greece, Mexico'—as if it were sufficient to pass through a place to know it. A man who has seen ten cathedrals once has not seen a single one, a man who has seen the same cathedral ten times may perhaps have seen something."

Nevertheless, the first appearance of tourism in the world had a cultural motivation, and tourism has always stood as a unique vehicle for the cultural propagation that is necessary to a deeper understanding of peoples. Tourism, with its basic element of movement, stands for the possibility of communication between differing civilizations and it has served in this sense since its first emergence. Tourism has always been an essential medium for broadening the limits of human knowledge. From the very early times, a mainspring of the urge to travel has been that based on the cultural interest. Even today we can witness large masses of people travelling to foreign countries to become acquainted with the usages and customs, to visit the museums and to admire works of art. As Medlik says: "When the tourist comes in contact with the place he visits and its population, a social exchange takes place. His social background affects the social structure and mode of life of his destination; he is in turn affected by it and sometimes carries back home with him new habits and ways of life." Every type of civilization, from the most sophisticated and advanced to the most primitive, is a source of attraction and curiosity for mankind.

Tourism remains basically a cultural phenomenon. One way of hastening the beneficial effects resulting from tourism is to bring the cultural heritage into the economic circuit, thus justifying the investments made at the cost of the national community for its preservation. Taking a strictly economic view of the cultural heritage of a nation may not be altogether justified, considering that the preservation of its culture is one of the basic responsibilities of any community. But considering the financial obstacles especially for the developing countries, this may appear to be a rational approach. Hence mass tourism can contribute unique benefits to the exploiting of the cultural heritage of a nation and can serve indirectly to improve the individual cultural levels of both citizens and foreigners, while at the same time developing into national wealth. The circle thus closes: cultural and tourist economy, instead of standing in opposition, derive reciprocal advantage from one another.

An Italian illustrated review, the *Milan Tempo*, sometime back published a full-page advertising display featuring a middle-aged lady of unmistakably foreign origin, wearing a flowered hat, sunglasses and gloves and laden with an assortment of parcels. The caption in the advertising display reads: "A foreign tourist stands admiringly before a work of art. She came to Italy for this purpose. She bought six pairs of shoes in Milan, nine tablecloths in Florence and seven dresses in Rome. Our artistic heritage is an inexhaustible source of culture and wealth. Let us protect it!" There is an affirmation in the above publicity slogan as to how cultural resources are brought into the economic circuit of the country.

Cultural Heritage

Cultural resources have another specific characteristic which can act as a positive element in the developing countries. Those developing countries that possess an ancient civilization or an original culture can benefit greatly from tourism as many people would like to experience the exotic. There will be a great urge on the part of the tourist to visit and become acquainted with the ancient civilization. The greater part, if not the totality, of the developing countries possesses clearly determined and original characteristics capable of attracting flows of tourists from industrialized countries who are in quest of novel human knowledge. The main justification for cultural tourism is, in fact, not solely the cultural heritage alone. It also means the prospect of contact with other civilizations, their original and varied customs and traditions with their distinct characteristics. The entire process creates a powerful lever on motivation towards travel. A factor favourable to the developing countries is the unequalled and characteristic novelty of the different civilizations, ancient or recent, so revealed, which can only add a further and decisive motivation for undertaking the journey.

A two-way exchange is thus achieved between the industrialized and the developing countries. This two-way exchange is expressed in the following terms by Boyer: "We can say that the tourist process provides or should provide for exchanges between economic values (from the countries which send out tourists) and cultural values (from the countries that receive tourists)." It may be added that Boyer is clearly referring to the industrialized countries as generators of tourists, and to the developing countries as receivers of tourists. The characteristic benefit resulting from cultural tourism for the national economies and the balance of payments of the developing countries are quite significant.

International Understanding

Tourism can be a vehicle for international understanding by way of bringing diverse people face to face. Tourism has played a major role in improving international understanding. It has been a contributor to international goodwill and as a prime means of developing social and cultural understanding among all peoples of the world. The interaction of a large number of people with the local population of the country visited results in making friends and goes a long way in increasing friendships. Tourism can greatly enrich and promote friendship and goodwill. People belonging to different countries, practising different lifestyles and speaking different languages come together to make friends. There is a mingling of cultures which has positive effects. Tourism helps to break down prejudices, barriers and suspicions that exist between nations. The best way of getting to know another country is to go there, and when vast numbers travel, the narrow, rigid boundaries that keep people in compartments naturally tend to shrink and a positive move towards better international understanding begins to operate.

Tourism thus is not only an economic activity of importance inasmuch as it earns a country the foreign exchange. It is an important medium of social and cultural development and also of promoting lasting goodwill and friendship among the nations of the world. It also helps in the regional development of the country and acts as a means of social education and better understanding among the peoples in different regions of the country. In the long run, the most important contribution of tourism is developing understanding among varied cultures and lifestyles.

apter

easurement o Tourism

Tourism has become not only a major force in world trade but also a vital factor in a country's economic, cultural and social development. However, the development of statistical concepts and frameworks for tourism have not kept pace with this changing environment. A stronger statistical base is essential for a deeper understanding by governments, private and public industries, academics and the public, of tourism's contribution to the social, cultural and economic development of all countries in the world.

The faster rate of expansion of international tourism is a result of increasing leisure, higher standards of living, technological advances in transport and communication, emergence of the new patterns in world tourist flows as a result of psychological, sociological and economic factors related to purchasing power and efforts by various countries put into the marketing of tourist products. The swift pace at which tourism has grown over the past decades, especially the decades following the Second World War, clearly indicates the importance of this sector of activity not only from the economic standpoint, but above all, as an essential need of people everywhere. The economic advantages of tourism are, however, enormous and this fact is realised all over the world. Various countries are spending huge amounts of money to develop infrastructure and other facilities with a view to attract more tourists and thereby get their share from this sector. It is a fact that developed countries in Europe and North America are the ones which are the main receiving areas for international tourism and are therefore the principal receivers of the economic advantage. However, because of the constant growth of tourism throughout the world at present, the developing countries are also getting a larger share of the international tourist markets. The main economic advantages to these countries are in terms of foreign currency earnings.

The Statistical Measurement

Tourism today has little in common with the tours that characterized the beginning of the century and were limited to a privileged few who had the means to afford it. Subsequently, the labour legislations enacted in many countries freed vast sectors of population from the constraints imposed by exclusively productive activities and afforded them both leisure time and greater purchasing power. This produced tourism on the scale we know today, amounting to about 650 millions of international tourist movements a year. The statistical measurement of this phenomenon is very essential.

Tourism can only be grasped in all its complexity, and its multiple relations with other economic and social sectors properly understood, if there is a statistical tool able to measure its development according to the determinant factors and at the same time permit a country comparison of such development. This is possible only by the use of statistics. Statistics can be defined as that branch of science which deals with the frequency of occurrence of different kinds of things or with the frequency of occurrence of different attributes. It is a method specially adapted to the elucidation of quantitative data affected by a multiplicity of causes. The objective of statistics is not merely the description of an existing situation, but also the study of procedures of scientific inference and proof.

Tourism is a fast growing economic activity in many countries around the word, and plays an important role in the economic and technological development of nations. Tourism serves to stimulate the development of basic infrastructure, contributes to the growth of domestic industries, attracts foreign investment, and facilitates the transfer of technology and information.

Despite its obvious importance, however, tourism still needs to be defined precisely and measured consistently. Even among tourism experts, consensus has not been reached on what tourism is and how it should be measured. For example, the World Travel and Tourism Council (WTTC) reported in its 1995 report that tourism contributed 13% (or $63.79 billion US dollars) to Canadian Gross Domestic Product (GDP) in 1988 and 14.7% (or $1.8 millions) of its total employment]. But, a study of the Statistics Canada reported that tourism accounted for 3% (or $13.4 billion Canadian dollars) of Canadian GDP and 5% (467,000 persons/year) of its total employment in 1988. These huge differences highlight the necessity of a common conceptual framework for tourism statistics.

A conceptual framework for tourism statistics should give a definition of what tourism is, draw a boundary of where tourism begins and ends, and provide ways to measure different dimensions of tourism based on the definition and within the boundary. Such a framework is crucial to the usefulness and the credibility of tourism statistics. Without it, meaningful comparative analyses of tourism would be impossible and tourism statistics may fail to facilitate the understanding of the importance of tourism in an economy and its relationship with various industries. The World Tourism Organisation's "A Satellite Account For Tourism" and OECD Tourism Committee's "Manual On Tourism Economic Accounts" represent two important progresses in this area. Yet, a consistent conceptual framework for tourism statistics remains to be consummated, particularly about how tourism should be measured.

The tourism is a multi dimensional phenomenon with a demand and a supply side. But the supply side cannot be defined as an industry. Hence aggregate measures of tourism should be built from the demand side. The initial tourism demand as the measure of tourism size and tourism driven GDP as the measure of tourism contribution. While our size measure is free of double counting and comparable to GDP, contribution measure traces tourism from demand to supply and captures the impacts of not only tourism final demand but also of business travel. It is shown that in the presence of international trade, the size of tourism so defined may differ significantly from its contribution to GDP. However, they are on a consistent basis. The method developed here provides consistent estimates for both measures.

Difficulties in Measuring Tourism

No matter how we measure tourism, the two most important issues we have to deal with are conceptual comparability and definitional consistency. Since people frequently ask how big tourism is compared to the whole economy, a size measure of tourism without comparability and consistency is obviously of limited credibility and use. With GDP as the most widely used size measure of an economy, it is a natural desire to measure tourism in a way that is conceptually comparable to GDP.

Tourism is primarily a consumption activity. Therefore, the total expenditure on tourism as a measure of tourism size seems to be a natural choice. However, the existence of business tourism causes the following problem.

Double counting. GDP as the total final demand includes tourism final demand but not business tourism demand, which is part of the intermediate demand. Therefore, the combination of tourism final demand and business tourism demand is not comparable to GDP. Fundamentally, this non-comparability is caused by two sources of double counting inherent in the total tourism expenditure in comparison to GDP. First, part of business tourism is used as input to produce tourism final demand and hence its value is already embodied in and counted as part of the value of tourism final demand. Second, the production (or supply) of business tourism uses business tourism as inputs. For example, in the business of providing hotel services the hotel industry uses hotel services as part of the inputs to its production. The value of business tourism used as inputs to the production of business tourism is double counted in the output of business tourism.

However, business tourism expenditures can not be completely excluded from the measure of the size of tourism, because it is mostly driven by non-tourism final demand and forms an additional net value of tourism. If business tourism expenditures are excluded, the measure of the size of tourism in an economy would be incomplete. The challenge is therefore to find a measure which takes into account both final demand tourism expenditure and business tourism expenditure, and at the same time maintains the comparability with GDP, namely, avoids double counting. The demand approach currently proposed or practiced does not face up to this challenge.

Defining and measuring tourism supply side as an industry has its own difficulties. Within both International Standard Industrial Classification (ISIC) and System of National Accounts (SNA)], industries are classified according to what they produce and how they produce rather than for whom they produce. Defining one industry according to whom it serves while defining all the others according to what and how they produce is conceptually inconsistent. It also creates the following problems.

Incomparability

For many industries in the economy directly supplying to tourists, tourists are only a portion of their customers. To avoid misestimating the size of tourism, those industries have to be splitted into a tourism part and a nontourism part and then regrouped to form the tourism industry. But a tourism industry so defined overlaps with other industries defined in the System of National Accounts. Unless all tourism related industries in the central framework are redefined accordingly, it will be impossible to make meaningful comparisons between the tourism industry and other industries.

Inter-Industry Relationship

Intuitively, a "tourism industry" should have inputs from many tourism related industries. Since the tourism part of an industry which directly provides goods and services to tourists is counted as part of the "toursim industry", the "tourism industry" by definition (and to avoid double counting) would not need any input from those industries anymore. For example, inputs from the food industry and the transportation industry to the "tourism industry" would be zero, because, by definition, they are a part of the output of the "industry" rather than of its inputs.

Hard to Implement

To estimate the output of the "tourism industry", it was proposed that a survey be conducted to find out what proportion of industries' outputs is for tourism. Although this is conceptually straightforward, it is also obviously impractical since many industries supporting tourism have no interest or no easy way to find out what portion of their outputs are used to support tourism.

Domestic Tourism

Domestic Tourism is concerned with travelling within the country. It does not need a pass¬port and visa or conversion of one currency into another. Domestic tourism has greater scope in countries of large dimensions such as India as compared to smaller countries. From a geographical viewpoint, domestic tourism may range from local excursion, regional trips to national level travels.

On the basis of purpose of tour or the motives of tourists, tourism is of three types, viz., (a) common interest tourism, (b) holiday tourism and (c) business tourism. In case of common interest tourism, the purpose of visiting and the visited persons in common.

Visiting friends and relatives in this type puts very low pressure on the provision of tourist facilities at the destination. Holiday tourism is the most popular type. A fine weather favourable for sightseeing, touring, recreation and going round different cultural sites are sought after by incoming tourists of this category.

Business tourists travel to boost their business, attend trade fairs and conferences pertaining to commerce or professions. They combine business with recreation using same facilities as provided for holiday tourists.

Data Sources in Travel and Tourism

Big data is merely the most popular and widely used term to explain data availability and exponential growth in the changing modern world. It is a comprehensive term for data-sets that are big or complicated. Large data has challenges regarding search, capture, storage, visualization, analysis and information privacy, and they require innovations to expose the hidden values from expansive data-sets that are complex, diverse and massive in scale.

Large data has evolved to bring new opportunities for modern living. These vast repositories of data sources can provide managers, researchers, and policymakers with the data-driven proof required to make decisions. On the premise of numbers and analysis other than guesswork, anecdotes, intuition or previous experience, may help you to more confident decision-making, accurate analytics and greater operational efficiencies, and risk and cost reductions.

Large Data Tourism

The industry of tourism thrives on information. Large data can deliver up-to-date and immensely informed inferences regarding behaviour and human activity that enhances the tourism industry. Tourists leave various digital traces behind when using mobile technologies on the web. Through every tourist, enormous amounts of data are present about everything that is relevant to different stages of travel – before, between and after a voyage. Due to the vast amounts of data availability in the cloud, analytics has become a need to make sense of the information present in the data. If you are a new customer planning for a trip, you probably acquire more sources from the internet when you are buying tickets, researching attractions or reserving accommodations. Members of the tourism industry are slowly turning to large data to find new ways for improving opportunities, decision-making and overall performance, for example, an interconnection of scattered information can be made possible through large data.

Merchants and agencies involved in tourism can find various methods to use a diversity of data resources to interact with potential guests at each stage of a tour and use these large data sources to timely and better understand the increasing visitor statistics. They can also re-market to aim customers who have chosen a particular destination on an agency travel website.

Benefits of Large Data Tourism

Previous studies on tourism have been based mostly on expert's views and surveys, which possibly mean that they have retrieved samples from the population as a whole and the real data of the tourists are not available. Large data tourism using particular methods have benefits over traditional methodologies, which are discussed below.

New Information Flows

Tourism large data is typical information produced by travellers themselves. It improves the thought process of tourism businesses by analysing the customers demand for various services and products.

Reliability

Large data is not based on surveys but users' real actions. In other words, these actions - not stated queries or intentions – have been examined. Collecting all the data sources together, large data enhances the sample base on which conventional groundwork tends to be established by several orders of magnitude. We all are living in a period of unprecedented flux in customer beliefs, company business models and consumer response created by technologies that are simultaneously disrupting established institutions and producing new ones. In any case, tourism large data indicate noteworthy changes in the relationship between clients and businesses. We can utilize large data to support experiences and provide superior predictive analytics to enhance customer decisions and expectations.

Survey Sampling

In statistics, survey sampling describes the process of selecting a sample of elements from a target population to conduct a survey. The term "survey" may refer to many different types or techniques of observation. In survey sampling it most often involves a questionnaire used to measure the characteristics and/or attitudes of people. Different ways of contacting members of a sample once they have been selected is the subject of survey data collection. The purpose of sampling is to reduce the cost and/or the amount of work that it would take to survey the entire target population. A survey that measures the entire target population is called a census.

Survey samples can be broadly divided into two types:

(i) Probability samples

(ii) Non-probability samples

Probability-based samples implement a sampling plan with specified probabilities (perhaps adapted probabilities specified by an adaptive procedure). Probability-based sampling allows design-based inference about the target population. The inferences are based on a known objective probability distribution that was specified in the study protocol. Inferences from probability-based surveys may still suffer from many types of bias. Surveys that are not based on probability sampling have greater difficulty measuring their bias or sampling error. Surveys based on non-probability samples often fail to represent the people in the target population.

In academic and government survey research, probability sampling is a standard procedure.

Selecting samples using generally accepted statistical methods (e.g., probabilistic methods that can provide estimates of sampling error). Any use of non-probability sampling methods (e.g., cut-off or model-based samples) must be justified statistically and be able to measure estimation error.

Besides, random sampling and design-based inference are supplemented by other statistical methods, such as model-assisted sampling and model-based sampling.

For example, many surveys have substantial amounts of non-response. Even though the units are initially chosen with known probabilities, the non-response mechanisms are unknown. For surveys with substantial non-response, statisticians have proposed statistical models, with which data sets are analysed.

Probability Sampling

In a probability sample (also called "scientific" or "random" sample) each member of the target population has a known and non-zero probability of inclusion in the sample. A survey based on a probability sample can in theory produce statistical measurements of the target population.

A probability-based survey sample is created by constructing a list of the target population, called the sampling frame, a randomised process for selecting units from the sample frame, called a selection procedure, and a method of contacting selected units to enable them complete the survey, called a data collection method or mode. For some target populations this process may be easy, for example, sampling the employees of a company by using payroll list. However, in large, disorganised populations simply constructing a suitable sample frame is often a complex and expensive task.

Common methods of conducting a probability sample of the household population are:

(i) Area Probability Sampling
(ii) Random Digit Dial telephone sampling
(iii) Address-Based Sampling.

Within probability sampling, there are specialized techniques such as stratified sampling and cluster sampling that improve the precision or efficiency of the sampling process without altering the fundamental principles of probability sampling.

Stratification is the process of dividing members of the population into homogeneous subgroups before sampling. The strata should be mutually exclusive: every element in the population must be assigned to only one stratum. The strata should also be collectively exhaustive: no population element can be excluded. Methods such as simple random sampling or systematic sampling can be applied within each stratum. This often improves the representativeness of the sample by reducing sampling error.

Bias in Probability Sampling

Bias in surveys is undesirable, but often unavoidable. The major types of bias that may occur in the sampling process are:

- **Non-response bias:** When individuals or households selected in the survey sample cannot or will not complete the survey there is the potential for bias to result from this non-response. Non-response bias occurs when the observed value deviates from the population parameter due to differences between respondents and non respondents
- **Response bias:** This is not the opposite of non-response bias, but instead relates to a possible tendency of respondents to give inaccurate or untruthful answers for various reasons.
- **Selection bias:** Selection bias occurs when some units have a differing probability of selection that is unaccounted for by the researcher. For example, some households have multiple phone numbers making them more likely to be selected in a telephone survey than households with only one phone number. This selection bias would be corrected by applying a survey weight equal to [1/(# of phone numbers)] to each household.
- **Self-selection bias:** A type of bias in which individuals voluntarily select themselves into a group, thereby potentially biasing the response of that group.
- **Participation bias:** Bias that arises due to the characteristics of those who choose to participate in a survey or poll.

- **Coverage bias:** Coverage bias can occur when population members do not appear in the sample frame (undercoverage). Coverage bias occurs when the observed value deviates from the population parameter due to differences between covered and non-covered units. Telephone surveys suffer from a well known source of coverage bias because they cannot include households without telephones.

Non-Probability Sampling

Many surveys are not based on probability samples, but rather on finding a suitable collection of respondents to complete the survey. Some common examples of non-probability sampling are:

- **Judgement Samples:** A researcher decides which population members to include in the sample based on his or her judgement. The researcher may provide some alternative justification for the representativeness of the sample. The underlying assumption is that the investigator will select units that are characteristic of the population. This method can be subjected to researcher's biases and perception.
- **Snowball Samples:** Often used when a target population is rare. Members of the target population recruit other members of the population for the survey.
- **Quota Samples:** The sample is designed to include a designated number of people with certain specified characteristics. For example, 100 coffee drinkers. This type of sampling is common in non-probability market research surveys.
- **Convenience Samples:** The sample is composed of whatever persons can be most easily accessed to fill out the survey.
- **In non-probability samples** the relationship between the target population and the survey sample is immeasurable and potential bias is not known. Sophisticated users of non-probability survey samples tend to view the survey as an experimental condition, rather than a tool for population measurement, and examine the results for internally consistent relationships.

Systematic Measurement of Tourism

The systematic measurement of tourism began not very long ago. The need was felt as the volume of tourist traffic began to reach significant proportions in the early years of the twentieth century. As the tourist movements grew tremendously, particularly in the last eight decades following the First World War, their measurements became very significant for various purposes. The frequency of occurrence of tourist movement in various countries engaged the attention of the statisticians and the social scientists in Europe, Switzerland, Italy, Austria and France which emerged clearly as tourist countries early in the century. Before the commencement of the World War I, Switzerland was a very popular destination for the rich and leisured class and was known to have received half a million foreign visitors annually. In the year 1929, foreign visitors to Austria were estimated at about two million, to Switzerland about one and a half million and to Italy about a million and a quarter. In Europe such statistics of tourism as did exist up to the First World War were mainly derived from government controls and enumeration records for health, safety and taxation and, in particular, for police and migration purposes. No distinction was made between tourists and other travellers. These statistics provided only some indication of the volume and value of tourist traffic.

Some other principal sources of quantitative data about tourism were the records of individual passenger transport and accommodation operators, the former giving numbers of travellers carried on particular routes and the latter giving numbers of travellers staying in hotels and similar accommodation establishments. These sources continue to be still utilised for quantitative data about tourism by many countries. In the absence of clear-cut definition of the term 'tourist', these sources rarely distinguished in any way between actual tourists and other travellers and also between different groups of tourists. These were thus of limited value in the assessment of the volume and the value of tourism. Tourism had not yet received recognition as an economic phenomenon and therefore not much efforts were made to systematically and scientifically measure it.

The post-World War I period witnessed a large-scale movement of tourists and tourism received recognition as a great economic phenomenon in the decade that followed. In the 1920s and early 1930s tourism came to be examined against the background of economic problems of most European countries. World War II, however, temporarily stopped the tourist movements. Most of the European countries suffered tremendous economic losses as a result of the War. In the years immediately following the War, European economies were dominated by reconstruction and recovery, by balance-of-payment problems, and, in particular by the dollar gap. Tourism in these countries was seen as an important factor to the solution of various economic problems, especially the problems of the balance of payments.

Importance of Tourist Statistics

It was however in the 1960s—the United Nations Development Decade—that much attention was focussed on the developing countries, their problems and solutions. Various development plans were prepared by the experts in which tourism played a significant and a dominant role. The need arose for primary data on tourism to measure the tourist flows to particular destinations and of the tourist expenditure to provide a basis for planning the future development. Statistics thus became an essential tool of measurement of the tourist phenomenon. The emphasis, however, was on international tourism. Most of the statistics which were collected and analysed concerned the international tourist. During this period domestic tourism also gathered momentum. The governments realizing the importance of tourism gave a thought to its development. It was felt that both international and domestic tourism can contribute towards regional development within a country. Hence, in recent years, many countries have felt the need for the collection of tourist statistics of domestic tourist movements and expenditure and for the statistics related to particular destinations within a country.

Market research in recent years has brought about the need for quantified data in addition to the basic statistics about the movement and expenditure. A prospective tourist's choice of a particular destination or destinations is from a certain priority and related to his wants which could be physiological, psychological and/or sociological. These wants could be related to factors like recognition, a new learning experience, response from others, relaxation, etc. Marketing, decision-making and formulation of promotion strategies involve specialized knowledge and information of the buyer's likes and dislikes, preferences, etc. Therefore, it becomes necessary for a country to know about the potential tourist, his interests and needs and the level of the satisfaction for each of the interests. The characteristics of tourists and details of their behaviour are thus necessary for the purposes of marketing of the tourist product. Hence the need for obtaining quantified data became necessary.

The measurement of tourism phenomenon therefore is very vital. The importance of statistical measurement in tourism may be summarised as follows:

(i) For evaluating the magnitude and significance of tourism to a particular tourist destination. The destination could be a country, a region or a district within a region. The data collected can be utilized to quantify the role and contribution of tourism to a country's economy.

(ii) For planning and development of physical facilities and for infrastructural requirements. It is not merely that statistics are useful to know the numbers of tourist arrivals for a series of consequent years to show whether tourist trade in any particular country is growing, stagnant or declining. It is important to know the other attributes like the mode of arrival, the kind of accommodation used, the amenities desired by the traveller, the length of stay, the amount that he spends, the purchases he makes, etc. All this information is necessary for tourism planning.

(iii) For marketing and promotion, it is essential to know the profile of tourists, both actual and potential. It is only after ascertaining the physiological, psychological and sociological wants of the visitors that an effective marketing campaign can be launched.

(iv) To know about the changes in tourist fashions. Regular returns of statistics help the countries to find out the flow of tourist traffic to various destinations. The flow will indicate whether a tourist patronises a beach holiday, winter resort, a historical place or any other place.

Definition of the Term 'Tourist'

When we talk about measurement we must know as to what is to be measured. It is the 'tourist' who is the principal character in the phenomenon called tourism. Without his being around, the tourism phenomenon is meaningless. And when we talk about measurement, we mean measuring a 'tourist'. In other words, the tourist becomes the unit of measurement. The next question which comes up is, who is a tourist? How should a tourist be defined for the purposes of tourist statistics and for measuring the tourism phenomenon?

The origin of the word 'tourist' dates back to A.D. 1292. It has come from the word 'tour', a derivation of the Latin word *tornus,* meaning a tool for describing a circle or a turner's wheel. In the first half of the seventeenth century, the term was used for travelling from place to place, a journey, an excursion, a circuitous journey touching the principal parts of a country or region.

The *19th-Century Dictionary* defines 'tourist' as a "person who travels for pleasure of travelling, out of curiosity, and because he has nothing better to do". The term 'tourist', the *Oxford English Dictionary* tells us, was used as early as the year 1800. According to the *Dictionnaire Universal*, the 'tourist' is a person who makes a journey for the sake of curiosity, for the fun of travelling; or just to tell others that he has travelled.

The term 'tourist' in the sense of a pleasure tour is, however, of recent origin. In the words of Jose Ignacio De Arrillaga, "tourism in its first period was considered as a sport or rather as a synthesis of automobiles, touring, cycling, camping, excursions and yachting. In the early nineteenth century, the term 'tourist' assumed a meaning of 'one who makes a tour or tours, especially one who does this for recreation or who travels for pleasure, object of interest, scenery or the like'."

Definition by League of Nation and the UN

All the above definitions of the term 'tourist' are of general nature and therefore could not serve the purpose of measurement. It was, however, the League of Nations which did a pioneering work in defining the term for the purposes of statistical measurements. Realising the importance of collecting tourist statistics and of securing international compatibility, the Committee of Statistical Experts of the League of Nations in the year 1937 established the definition of the term 'tourist'. The League of Nations, with the concurrence of member countries, defined the term 'foreign tourist' as "any person visiting a country, other than that in which he usually resides, for a period of at least 24 hours."

The following persons were to be considered tourists within this definition:

(i) Persons travelling for pleasure, for domestic reasons, for health, etc.

(ii) Persons travelling to meetings, or in a representative capacity of any kind (scientific, administrative diplomatic, religious, athletic, etc.).

(iii) Persons travelling for business purposes.

(iv) Persons arriving in the course of a sea cruise, even when they stay for less than 24 hours. (The latter should be reckoned as a separate group, disregarding if necessary their usual place of residence.)

The following categories were not to be regarded as tourists:

(i) Persons arriving, with or without a contract of work, to take up an occupation or engage in any business activity in the country.

(ii) Persons coming to establish a residence in the country.

(iii) Students and young persons in boarding establishments or schools.

(iv) Residents in a frontier zone and persons domiciled in one country and working in an adjoining country.

(v) Travellers passing through a country without stopping, even if the journey takes more than 24 hours.

The above definition was confirmed by the United Nations in the year 1945 and it was stated that the 'tourist' was a person who stayed in a foreign country for more than 24 hours and less than six months for any non-immigrant purpose. The definition was adopted by many countries for the compilation of travel statistics.

European Travel Commission

The European Travel Commission (ETC), the Organisation for European Economic Cooperation (OEEC), and the International Union of Official Travel Organisations (IUOTO) were the agencies through which the first regular reporting was developed on the basis of the definition established by the Committee of Statistical Experts of the League of Nations. The European Travel Commission is a non-governmental body chiefly concerned with the promotion of American travel to Europe. The members of this commission are the national tourist organisations of some countries of Western Europe. The IUOTO (later the World Tourism Organisation), representing national tourist organisations on international basis, established the Study Commission on International Travel Statistics, and in 1947 began the publication of its *Digest of Tourist Statistics*. The document was a collection of national statistics of tourist arrivals and travel payments of some countries. In the year 1950 a permanent IUOTO Research Commission was established to study and recommend improvements in statistical methods. In December 1960 the Organisation for Economic Cooperation and Development (OECD) was set up under a convention signed in Paris. It took over the work in tourism of its predecessor, the Organisation for European Economic Cooperation. Up to the year 1963, the Tourism Committee of OECD recommended to its member countries the adoption of the definition of the term 'foreign tourist' established by the Committee of Statistical Experts of the League of Nations in 1937. Both the OECD and the IUOTO brought out many publications in the subsequent years concerning tourist statistics.

United Nations Rome Conference

In 1963, the United Nations Conference on International Travel and Tourism held in Rome considered a definition and recommended that it be studied by the United Nations Statistical Commission. A revised definition was prepared and adopted. The conference considered an overall definition of the term 'visitor' for statistical purposes and defines him as "any person visiting a country other than that in which he has his usual place of residence, for any reason other than following an occupation remunerated from within the country visited."

This definition covered:

(i) Tourists, i.e., temporary visitors staying at least twenty-four hours in the country visited and the purpose of whose journey can be classified either as (a) leisure (recreation, holiday, health, study, religion, and sport) or (b) business, family, mission, meeting.

(ii) Excursionists, i.e., temporary visitors staying less than twenty-four hours in the country visited (including travellers on cruises).

The above definition excludes travellers who, in the legal sense, do not enter the country (e.g., air travellers who do not leave an airport's transit area).

The Expert Statistical Group on International Travel Statistics convened by the United Nations Statistical Commission recommended in 1967 that countries use the definition of 'visitor' proposed by the United Nations Conference on International Travel and Tourism in Rome in 1963. The group considered that it would be desirable to distinguish within the definition of visitor a separate class of visitors, who might be described as 'day visitors' or 'excursionists' defined as consisting of visitors on day excursions and other border-crossers for purposes other than employment, cruise passengers, and visitors in transit who do not stay overnight in accommodation provided within the country. The special characteristic of this category of visitors, distinguishing it from the main class of visitor, is that there is no overnight stay. In 1968 the United Nations Statistical Commission approved the Rome definition. These definitions are gradually receiving general acceptance. According to the studies published by World Tourism Organisation, nearly 80 per cent of the countries use these definitions in the collection of international travel statistics.

The definition of 'foreign tourist' adopted by the Government of India's tourist department as per the recommendation of the United Nations Conference on International Travel and Tourism, Rome, 1963 is as follows:

"A foreign tourist is a person visiting India on a foreign passport, staying at least twenty-four hours in India and the purpose of whose journey can be classified under one of the following headings:

(i) Leisure (recreation, holiday, health, study, religion and sport);

(ii) Business, family, mission, meeting."

The following categories are not regarded as foreign tourists in India:

(i) Persons arriving, with or without a contract, to take up an occupation or engage in activities remunerated from within the country;

(ii) Persons coming to establish residence in the country;

(iii) 'Same-day visitors', i.e., temporary visitors staying less than twenty-four hours in the country (including travellers on cruises).

The following categories of travellers are not included in the data on foreign tourism:

(a) Nationals of Nepal entering India through land routes along Indo-Nepal border;

(b) All foreigners entering India from Bhutan by land; and

(c) Children aged less than three years.

Distinction Between Domestic and Foreign Tourism

A distinction is drawn between domestic or internal and foreign or international tourism. In domestic tourism, people travel outside their normal domicile to certain other areas within the country as compared to travelling outside the boundaries of a country in international tourism. The basic difference between domestic and international tourism is that of jurisdiction of travel. The tourist activity of residents of a country within their own country, which does not cross the boundaries of the country, is thus described as internal or domestic tourism. Since the travel takes place within the limits of the boundaries of a country, the various travel formalities which are necessary in international tourism are not to be observed. The travel becomes an easy affair. The barriers of currency exchange, language, passport, visa, health documents, etc., are not to be faced by a domestic tourist. A tourist's own language serves as a medium of communication. The currency which they use in their everyday transactions continues to be the medium of exchange.

Presently there exists no generally accepted definition of the term 'domestic tourist'. The domestic tourist is generally regarded as a person travelling for a purpose other than exercising a gainful activity or settling at the place visited. The XXIII General Assembly of IUOTO held in Caracas, Venezuela in October 1973 recommended that a study should be carried out at the international level with a view to arriving at a standardized definition of domestic tourism. The following definition was put forward by IUOTO in 1974–75:

"For statistical purposes, the term 'domestic tourist' designates any person who travels within the country where he resides to a place other than his usual place of residence for at least twenty-four hours or one night, for a purpose other than exercising a gainful activity and which may be classified under one of the following headings:

(i) leisure (recreation, holiday, health, study, religion and sport);

(ii) business, family, mission, meeting."

The above definition, however, was not adopted as an official definition but merely as a basis for discussion.

Three elements are common to the definitions normally in use. These elements are: (i) place of residence; (ii) geographical setting of travel; and (iii) duration of travel. With regard to place of residence most countries regard domestic tourism as travel by country's residents, within that country. The geographical setting is the national territory. Duration of travel is an important element in a number of definitions. The unit most often mentioned is the night spent at an accommodation establishment. By analogy with the accepted definition of 'international tourist', the domestic tourist is one who spends not less than twenty-four hours or makes an overnight stay away from his usual residence. Two further elements are common to most definitions of domestic tourism. These are (i) distance travelled and (ii) travel motivation.

With regard to distance travelled, some countries specify a minimum distance in their definitions. This may vary between 25 and 100 miles (between 40 and 160 kilometres approximately). The concept of travel motivation is considered important by most countries. The domestic tourist is generally considered as a person travelling for a purpose other than exercising a gainful activity at the place visited. Sometimes, domestic tourism is considered as including holiday or leisure travel only.

General Problems of Measurement

McEven has said that almost all international tourists have three actions in common:

(i) they cross international frontiers,

(ii) they exchange their own currency for foreign currency, and

(iii) they spend time outside their own country

This implies using some form of accommodation. It is possible to use these actions as methods for measuring international tourism, i.e., by enumerating arrivals at frontiers, by recording currency transactions and by recording number of nights in various types of accommodation units by the foreign visitors. None of these methods is, however, foolproof. Each method has its limitations in respect of recording and enumerating foreign visitors. Counting foreign visitor arrivals is the most usual and most widely adopted method.

Risk of Double Counting

The tourist statistics is basically concerned with arrivals and departures and more particularly with the former. In arriving at these figures, it is, as indicated above, concerned with events rather than individuals, and as far as these are concerned, half a dozen visits by the same person is counted as six separate events or six tourist arrivals. There are certain difficulties in the matter of counting. The main difficulty is perhaps the risk of double counting. Absolute figures of tourists visiting almost every country tend to be inflated because of double counting. For example, an Italian tourist on his way to holiday in Spain may travel by car for two days through France and on his return journey to Italy will also travel two days through France, hence his journey, i.e., his arrival in France is recorded twice. Another problem of statistical measurement in tourism arises from the difficulty of differentiating between tourists and other travellers and between them and the resident and working populations. In their movements and in their stay at various places at destinations it becomes difficult at times to distinguish between them and the residents and the working populations. Also regarding the use of transport to destinations, tourists may use public transport or use their own private transport. They normally enter various destinations without stopping and often without registering their arrival. They do so increasingly even when crossing many national frontiers. At the destination the tourists use a variety of accommodation ranging from hotels, pension apartments and guesthouses to friends' and relatives' homes. They eat in the same catering establishments and buy items for use and other services from the same sources from which these are bought by those who are not tourists.

It may, however, be stated that the various general problems of statistical measurements in tourism discussed above are to be encountered in countries having common borders. It is in these countries that distinction becomes difficult. A number of countries in Europe, Middle East, South America and South-East Asia encounter such problems of measurements.

Types of Tourist Statistics

The tourist statistics is basically concerned with the figures of arrivals and departures, and more particularly the former. In addition to statistics of arrivals and departures, the statistics of tourist spendings during their stay at a destination have an important implication for the country's economy and on its balance of payments. Yet another type of tourist statistics is concerned with the information on the tourist himself. This information, which is very crucial for the purposes of tourism marketing and development, deals with various aspects of tourist behaviour and his characteristics. The main categories of the tourist statistics are:

(i) volume
(ii) expenditure and
(iii) characteristics

Volume Statistics

The basic volume statistics consist of the number of tourists to a particular destination over a given period. The unit of period could be a month, six months or a year. Most of the countries, however, consider a year as the unit of the period. While counting, it is normally the number of arrivals or visits and not the number of tourists. This is because it is impracticable to allow for those who visit the same destination more than once in the same period. It is the events rather than individuals with which the basic statistics of volume are concerned. As already stated, half a dozen visits by the same person is counted as six separate events or six tourist arrivals. Thus 650 million tourist arrivals in the world in the year 1999 denote 650 million visits made by a somewhat smaller number of individual visitors. Length of stay is another main volume statistic. This is measured in terms of days or nights spent by a tourist at the destination and is normally expressed as the average length of stay. Thus the average length of stay of overseas tourists to India in the year 1998 was 28.6 days. This could be further subdivided in respect of nationals of different countries and regions. Thus the average duration of stay of nationals of South-East Asia in India in the year 1998 was 41.5 days compared to 28.0 days in case of nationals from Western Europe.

Statistics of numbers provide a general indication of the volume of tourist traffic to particular destinations. The statistics of length of stay, on the other hand, provide a general indication of the nature of the traffic, in particular of the extent of transit and terminal visitors and of their demand for overnight accommodation.

Data Sources for Travel and Tourism

The need for identifying the various data sources in the field of tourism has assumed a greater importance in the recent past. The data sources are very crucial as these help the practitioners of the tourism field to properly know at a glance the trends in tourism patterns, the markets and their requirements as also for planning and promotion. Over the past few decades there has been a multiplicity of these sources. The sources of information available today on travel and tourism have mushroomed and continue to grow with the growth in tourism activity all over the world.

Not only have the sources of information multiplied in volume, these have multiplied in range also. The wide range of data incorporate information of accommodation units, travel agencies and tour operations, transportations, recreation, research studies, books, periodical, journals, tourist statistics, regional tourism developments, employment, marketing trends and projections, etc. In fact, there is hardly a single tourism activity on which information is not available.

Together with the volume and range of information available on travel and tourism, the sources of information have also multiplied. There are a wide range of sources from where the information is made available. These include both private and government sources, travel agencies and tour operators, airlines companies, travel trade journals, reports and research studies. International organisations dealing with tourism and allied areas are yet another important source of supply of information. National tourist organisations of various countries contribute a great deal of material.

Trade and professional associations are yet another source. Bibliographies, yearbooks, handbooks are other important sources of information.

The range, volume and the sources of information on travel and tourism are, however, not available at one place. There is a great need for development of a comprehensive list of volume, range and sources of information available on tourism so that it can be gainfully utilized by all concerned. Travel executives, officials in government and private sectors, international organisations, academicians as also the students of the subject require the above information and there is, therefore, an urgent need for providing the same to them. Such information can be used in not only analysing but also solving problems related to the travel industry.

Tables 6.1–6.4 show the data required and their availability for obtaining a proper perspective of the tourism sector, for meeting the needs of development planning, for evolving marketing strategies, and for facilitating investment decisions, respectively.

Table 6.1

Data Required for Obtaining a Proper Perspective of Tourism Sector

	Data Required		*Availability*
1.	Number of tourist arrivals	(a)	Data on foreign tourist arrivals are available on a regular basis from disembarkation cards
		(b)	Data on domestic tourist traffic are not available from some of the regions and the data received from most others are unreliable
2.	Tourist nights		Data on foreign tourists available on a regular basis
3.	Outbound	(a)	Total figures of citizens going abroad is available traffic from airports
		(b)	Details of purpose of visit, destination, country, etc., are not available
4.	Foreign exchange earnings from tourism		Available on a regular basis
5.	Contribution to GDP		Derived from national income estimates
6.	Employment generation		Derived from national income estimates and employment records
7.	Multiplier effect		Calculated on the basis of input-output tables
8.	Regional impact		Not available
9.	Social impact		No specific studies available
10.	Ecological and environmental impact		No specific studies available

Table 6.2

Data Required to Meet the Needs of Development Planning

Data Required	*Availability*
1. Demand	
(a) Place-wise tourist visits and tourist	Periodical foreign tourist surveys provide details in respect of major centres. Partial information is available from the regional governments through monthly return-nights submitted by them.
(b) Occupancy statistics of hotels	Response is good in the case of approved hotels. There is no system in the case of unapproved hotels.
2. Supply	
(a) Hotel rooms	Details of approved hotels and rooms are available place-wise. Similar details in respect of unapproved and supplementary accommodation are not available in general.
(b) Restaurants	No details available
(c) Shopping	No details available
(d) Entertainment facilities	No details available
(e) Tourist activities	No details available
(f) International air seat capacity to a country	There is no regular flow of data on the subject from civil aviation authorities.

Table 6.3

Data Required For Evolving Marketing Strategies

Data Required	*Availability*
1. Global trends	Available from WTO regularly
2. Country profiles	
(a) Outbound traffic	Not available regularly
(b) Preferred destinations	Available from WTO for certain nationalities
(c) Economic situation	GDP figures are available from WTO
(d) Political situation	Normally reported by the overseas tourist offices

(e) Legislations, regulations and advisories	Overseas tourist offices usually report them
(f) Market segments	Not much information available
3. Profile of tourists	
(a) Age	In the case of tourists who visit the country details of (a) and (c) are available from disembarkation cards.
(b) Sex	Details of (a) to (c) are also available from
(c) Occupation	periodical foreign tourist surveys.
(d) Place of residence	No such details are available in the case of (a) to (b) except through PATA
(e) Purpose of travel	Co-operative Market Research Studies and certain studies undertaken by the respective countries.
(f) Travel habits	
(g) Travel planning	
(h) Choice of destination factor	
(i) Motivations	
(j) Perceptions	
(k) Media affinity	
(l) Reading habits	
4. Reactions of tourists to facilities	Available from periodical foreign tourist surveys
5. Activities of competing destinations	Not much being documented
6. Feedback/ evaluation	
(a) Awareness created	Tourist offices abroad maintain certain basic information
(b) Response received	
(c) Departure rates	

Table 6.4

Data Required to Facilitate Investment Decisions

Data Required	*Availability*
1. Locational details	
(a) Availability of land, water electricity, etc.	Being compiled
(b) Transport facilities	Being compiled

2. Incentives available	Being compiled
3. Profitability of existing units	Not available
4. Occupancy rates	Not available for most of the centres due to non-reporting of data
5. Taxation policies	Information is available in bits and pieces

The importance of statistical data on travel and tourism today is well recognised by all the concerned authorities responsible for policy planning and marketing and promotion of tourism. No organisation can effort to neglect this vital source of information on which depends the accurate assessment of the sector and its role in the economic development of a country.

Planning a Survey

Social research is becoming increasingly an important activity. It is extremely important for the agency which wants to undertake any research to understand the basic research procedures. The knowledge about the basic rudiments of careful and systematic inquiry is very essential for undertaking any research.

There are a number of steps or closely related activities involved in research. All these steps follow a prescribed sequence. However, all the steps need not follow a rigid sequence but may overlap as well. The steps in research are also very much interdependent. One step determines the nature of another. Every step of the research process is so wide that separate chapters can be written on them. However, only a brief account of the steps is given.

(i) Formulation of the Problem

Formulation of the problem is one of the very important steps in research. We have to put a great deal of thought into the formulation of our questions if we hope to get anything out of an effort to answer them. In order to solve the problem, it has first to be carefully formulated. The more carefully the problem is formulated the more satisfactory is the solution we obtain. Before formulating a problem we have to first determine what a 'problem' is. The problem must be clearly defined as it should give guidance in the construction of research design. By allowing design considerations to influence problem definition, the researcher tends to limit his choice to those problems about which objective data can be readily obtained. Hence, we find that formulation of the problem is a very essential step of research.

(ii) Specifying Objectives of the Survey

The objectives of the survey must be clearly spelt out. This is very important and helps in achieving and measuring the results. Both general as well as specific objectives of the survey must be clearly defined. The objectives make it clear as to why we are conducting the research and what we are trying to get out of it. Where do we look for the objectives and how do we go about formulating them? In general, there are three sources to take into account before formulating objectives. These are (a) the research consumer, (b) the researcher and (c) those who will be affected by use of the research results. All pertinent objectives are the most important in order to know how to evaluate any potential solution to the problem. The objectives, however, should be simple and clear. They should be framed in a simple language.

(iii) Selecting a Survey Area and Survey Population

The particular area where the survey is to be undertaken must be carefully chosen. Great care should be taken before choosing an area. Many important factors such as importance, feasibility, personnel available for study, its use to community, organisation, etc., must be taken into consideration. Regarding study population, it should be carefully selected. Obtaining information on results by observing or by questioning the entire group of people potentially affected would be an extremely difficult task. Therefore, a sample of population is to be selected. By observing or questioning only a fraction (sample of the group) the desired information can be obtained more economically, more quickly and accurately. But samples, whether random or stratified, should be selected properly without introduction of personal bias or other biases as to its size and representativeness.

(iv) Deciding the Nature and Scope of Survey

Yet another essential step of research is the decision regarding the nature and scope of the survey. The decision about the type of survey will also depend upon its purpose. There are different types of studies. Broadly, the surveys can be classified by (a) purpose and (b) approach used. Surveys of foreign tourism may be divided into several types according to purpose and scope and according to where and when interviews take place. The survey may not, however, be classified according to some precise or rigid system. What is important is that they should be well designed and carefully done, whatever type they may be. It is also important that specific nature of the survey should be determined early, particularly when time and resources are limited.

(v) Selecting Methods and Techniques

Great care is to be taken in the selection of methods and techniques of data collection. The findings of the survey will greatly depend on how scientifically methods have been selected. The methods by which data are to be collected or obtained must be devised after the problem has been formulated. Techniques are to be devised for collection of information. There are various methods of data collection, namely, interviewing, observation, questionnaires, projective techniques, examination of records, etc. All these methods have advantages and limitations. Selection of a particular type of method will also depend upon the type of survey for which data is to be collected.

(vi) Selection or Designing Survey Instrument

Selection of appropriate instrument for data collection is a fundamental step in a research project. This carries heavy implications for the entire study. Instrument must therefore be selected very carefully. Once it is decided as to which instrument will be used in the survey, the question of its designing or construction comes. While constructing the instruments care should be taken to see that it is simple, and not loaded and confusing. The questions should be so framed that the respondent may not have any difficulty in answering them. It should produce useful information. The questions should be clear and straightforward and easy to comprehend.

(vii) Pretesting and Revising Instruments

After the data-collection instruments have been framed, they must be pretested before they are used in the final study. Questions, which at first may seem simple and straightforward, may prove difficult to comprehend during trials . They may prove to be ambiguous or simply not productive of useful information. In addition, the categories may be inappropriate. To avoid all this it is essential to pretest the instruments and subsequently revise it for the final use. Pretesting the instrument's will ensure that they will collect the right type of information.

(viii) Data Collection

Data denote all the relevant materials, past and present, which serve as basis for study and analysis. The data must be carefully collected. Adequate care should be taken to see that they are collected honestly and consistently. They should be unbiased and free from errors. They should be checked for completeness, comprehensibility and reliability. Such checking will prevent difficulty at later stages when the data are arranged. Care should also be taken to ensure that the timing of data collection is convenient to the respondent.

(ix) Analysis of Data

The collection of data, however, is only one important step in research. The data are to be analysed for meaningful interpretation. The amount of data collected may be huge and extremely varied. This has to be systematically arranged. The process of analysis includes: editing, classification and coding (placing each item in the appropriate category) and tabulating (counting the number of items in each category) and statistical computations. In order to save time at the later stages, it is necessary that the analysis be planned in detail before actual work on it is started. A simple basic outline of analysis should be prepared in advance.

(x) Interpretation of Data

The data analysed are to be meaningfully interpreted. The interpretation of findings is interrelated with the analysis. Both are involved in the writing of survey report. Interpretation takes the results of analysis, makes inferences pertinent to the research questions studied, and draws conclusions about these questions. Interpretation of data should be done very carefully. Results of the survey greatly depend on this. Care should be taken to ensure that a major portion of the data analysed should be interpreted. It is advisable that a plan should be prepared beforehand as to the manner in which the data are to be interpreted.

(xi) Writing of the Report

Writing the report is the final step of research. The process of research becomes incomplete until the report has been written and distributed. The report should be written in a simple and meaningful language so that different consumers may not have difficulty in grasping its findings. It should also be brief and precise. At the end, a summary containing the essential points should be given. The final report can be utilized in different ways. It can be useful for the guidance of the agency sponsoring the research in dealing with some practical problem. It may be useful for a wider audience with similar problem. Finally it may be of use to administrators in formulating policies.

Sample Surveys

Sample surveys of foreign tourism can be divided into several types according to scope and purpose and also according to where and when interviews take place. The more comprehensive survey endeavours to include all or most visitors to a country and obtain volume and expenditure data as well as qualitative data about the tourists themselves and about various aspects of their trip. This survey is carried out at points of arrival and departure or en route. In order to be representative of the total traffic, interviews must be carried out at all major points of arrival and departure of foreign tourists throughout the year. When, on the other hand, it is desired to obtain more detailed information about one part of the traffic, sample surveys may be used to cover that particular part only. For example, interviews of industrialists or motorists, which are carried out only with the visitors on business or those arriving and departing by car, may be restricted to certain times of the year.

Sample surveys may cover separately visitors of particular nationality or countries of origin. In this case, interviews may be conducted at points of arrival and departure, but sometimes there are advantages in the survey being undertaken in the country of origin rather than the country visited. The biggest advantage in this is that interviews can be conducted in the visitor's own language. Since only a small proportion of the total population in a particular country have visited the country studied as a destination, it is necessary to locate them in the first instance. This can be done, for example, by including questions in an omnibus survey in the country of origin, from which names and addresses of past visitors provide the contacts for interviews. The sample survey method is independent of the administrative process and has the advantage of making contact with the tourists from whom all kinds of information relevant to the industry may be elicited.

Statistical measurement of tourism is very important as it helps the tourism organisation in a variety of ways. Tourist statistics are required for planning as well as for marketing and promotional purposes. Different countries have developed statistics of international tourism and also of domestic tourism to meet their need for measurement of the volume and value of tourism. These countries use methods which have been earlier derived from immigration and exchange-control systems. In recent years, however, increasing efforts have been made to produce on the one hand more specific statistics and on the other to achieve a greater measure of comparability between statistics produced by individual countries. It is not possible to obtain adequate information by way of indirect methods derived from administrative systems as the volume of international travel has grown tremendously. Direct methods based on sample surveys of tourists are increasingly used, in addition to and in place of indirect methods in order to obtain adequate information.

apter

r anisation o Tourism

An organisation is an entity comprising multiple people, such as an institution or an association, that has a particular purpose. The word is derived from the Greek word organon, which means "organ".

Types

There are a variety of legal types of organisations, including corporations, governments, non-governmental organisations, political organisations, international organisations, armed forces, charities, not-for-profit corporations, partnerships, cooperatives, and educational institutions.

A hybrid organisation is a body that operates in both the public sector and the private sector simultaneously, fulfilling public duties and developing commercial market activities.

A voluntary association is an organisation consisting of volunteers. Such organisations may be able to operate without legal formalities, depending on jurisdiction, including informal clubs.

Organisations may also operate secretly or illegally in the case of secret societies, criminal organisations and resistance movements.

Structures

The study of organisations includes a focus on optimising organisational structure. According to management science, most human organisations fall roughly into four types:

- Committees or juries
- Ecologies
- Matrix organisations
- Pyramids or hierarchies

Formal Organisations

An organisation that is established as a means for achieving defined objectives has been referred to as a formal organisation. Its design specifies how goals are subdivided and reflected in subdivisions of the organisation. Divisions, departments, sections, positions, jobs, and tasks make up this work structure. Thus, the formal organisation is expected to behave impersonally in regard to relationships with clients or with its members. According to Weber's definition, entry and subsequent advancement is by merit or seniority. Each employee receives a salary and enjoys a degree of tenure that safeguards him from the arbitrary influence of superiors or of powerful clients. The higher his position in the hierarchy, the greater his presumed expertise in adjudicating problems that may arise in the course of the work carried out at lower levels of the organisation. It is this bureaucratic structure that forms the basis for the appointment of heads or chiefs of administrative subdivisions in the organisation and endows them with the authority attached to their position.

Informal Organisations

In contrast to the appointed head or chief of an administrative unit, a leader emerges within the context of the informal organisation that underlies the formal structure. The informal organisation expresses the personal objectives and goals of the individual membership. Their objectives and goals may or may not coincide with those of the formal organisation. The informal organisation represents an extension of the social structures that generally characterise human life - the spontaneous emergence of groups and organisations as ends in themselves.

In prehistoric times, man was preoccupied with his personal security, maintenance, protection, and survival. Now man spends a major portion of his waking hours working for organisations. His need to identify with a community that provides security, protection, maintenance, and a feeling of belonging continues unchanged from prehistoric times. This need is met by the informal organisation and its emergent, or unofficial, leaders.

Leaders emerge from within the structure of the informal organisation. Their personal qualities, the demands of the situation, or a combination of these and other factors attract followers who accept their leadership within one or several overlay structures. Instead of the authority of position held by an appointed head or chief, the emergent leader wields influence or power. Influence is the ability of a person to gain cooperation from others by means of persuasion or control over rewards. Power is a stronger form of influence because it reflects a person's ability to enforce action through the control of a means of punishment.

Factors Influencing Organisation Structure

The organisation function is the immediate logical function after planning. To achieve the objectives set in the plan, somebody should work and should do the right work. The organising function makes the people to work. The function "involves managers in decisions which result in a system of specialised coordinated jobs." In an organisation structure so many aspects are involved. Human and non-human elements will be working. Organisational structure is an integrated whole. Job of each worker is specified, control measures are adopted for performing those jobs effectively. An organisational chart depicts tangibly the reporting relationships and channels of communication. Work flow and accountability are also shown. What factors actually determine the organisation structure? It is grouping activity of men, machine and material for attaining a specific objective. Hence the following factors determine the organisation structure.

1. Size of the unit.
    (a) Capital employed.
    (b) Development of Science, and Technology.
    (c) Men employed.
    (d) Nature of activity.
2. Job design.
3. Grouping of activities.
4. Span of control.
5. Delegation of authority.

1. Size of the Unit.

Size indicates the scale of operation. Normally there are three scales of operation, viz., small, medium and large. Size is an important factor governing cost, efficiency and profitability of a business enterprise. Before any business or non-business enterprise is started, the organisers will have to decide the most profitable and viable size of the unit. Optimum or the best size is a dynamic concept and it changes with the development of science and technology. Therefore, technology is one factor which determines the size and the organisation structure. To introduce new technology, in business enterprise, the activity has to be expanded and hence the structure changes.

The size of the organisation is also determined by the capital employed in the unit. There may be heavy capital outlay but it may be less labour intensive. In such cases the size will be small as authority relation will be less. However, capital outlay is one factor which determines the size of the organisation.

Another important factor which determines the size of the organisation is "men employed." If more men are employed there will be more level of management and more authority relationships. If men employed are less, the size of the organisation will be less and less levels of management and authority relationships.

The nature of business unit also determines the size and organisation structure. If it is capital goods industry with huge capital outlay, the organisation structure will be complex in nature. Consumer goods industries will have more authority relationships in marketing division and less in production and finance line. Thus the nature of activity also determines the organisation structure.

2. Job Design.

The bricks that develop an organisation structure are jobs. What are the jobs to be done in an organisation has to be decided by the top brass. Job design is the first managerial decision of the organisation structure. Jobs in a task have to be specified as one person cannot perform a task. It is a team work. Job in each task is to be specified and assigned. What an individual has to do to contribute to the overall tasks and objectives has to be decided. Therefore the fundamental factor, which determines the organisation structure is "Job designing" and "numbering" them. These numbers decide the size of the organisation.

3. Grouping of Activities.

The designed jobs have to be formed into groups according to the nature of activity. Grouping of activities are essential to achieve coordination. Each group is termed as "DEPARTMENT." Departmentation is another factor which determines the organisation structure. Thus in each business organisation we observe departments like Marketing Department, Production Department, Finance Department etc which discharge their functions. In each department we find authority relationships like Finance

Manager, Assistant Finance Section Officer, Finance Supervisor etc., each assigned with specific job and responsibility to perform. There will be accountability to higher ups also. Like this in every business or non-business activity, there will be grouping of similar jobs in the form of departments which are responsible to perform to specific task. There will be sub-departments in each basic department like Production Department in which we find (i) Purchase Department (ii) Stores Department (iii) Technical Design Department etc. These sub-departments constitute Production Department. All the functional departments put together forms an organisation. Grouping of the designed jobs according to their nature and activity is another factor which determines the organisation structure.

4. Span of Control.

Another factor that determines the organisation structure is the number of persons to be managed by each manager. This is called "Span of management." Depending upon the nature of organisation some departments will be big in size and some will be small. Therefore, each manager should be assigned with manageable tasks and personnel. If the tasks are many in a department, there should be splitting the tasks into number of divisions and lower levels are to be created. All this takes place depending upon resources and personnel available. However, the span of management, i.e., the number of persons to be managed by each manager, has to be decided and that becomes one of the major factors to decide the size of organisation structure. The number varies from manager to manager and the number determines the span. Manageable span found out by experience is six, i.e., one manager can manage six, persons effectively.

5. Delegation of Authority.

Authority relationship also decides the organisation structure. If the span is more, there will be more authority levels and top management has to delegate authority to each level. Authority, means "the right to make decisions without having to obtain approval from a higher up." In an organisation structure, if the span and levels of management are more, the delegation of authority will be more and there will be decentralisation of authority for smooth functioning of tasks. If the span is narrow, less levels and more centralisation of authority. Thus delegation of authority decides the organisation structure.

The specialised job designs will have narrow spans, homogenous departments, little control, little authority and small structure will be designed. Job designs with less or no specialisation will have heterogeneous departments, more spans of management, more delegation of authority and forms a complex organisation structure. Although these are the factors which decide the organisation structure, research and experience have shown that performance, attitudes, satisfaction and other factors also influence the structure.

Need for an Organisation

For any industry to develop, an organisation is a must as it plays a vital role in its planning, development and growth. Organisation consists of individuals whose primary role is the achievement of the objectives for which it has been set up. Administration as a general field may be divided into two constituent areas: (i) administrative organisation, which deals with the internal structure and arrangement of the personnel of the agency, and (ii) administrative management, which is concerned with the direction of the personnel, fiscal control and other techniques related to operation. The aim of the organisation is 'to arrange people into working groups, associating those with similar functions or purposes in order to move efficiently to obtain a desired result from their combined action. In other words, organisation means combination of a group of individuals whose main purpose is to achieve through group action the objectives for which it has been set up. It is the framework within which an industry works. It relates to the structure of the industry, and is concerned with the issues involved in, and the approaches to it. This could be any industry including the tourism industry.

The basic determinants of success in the field of tourism can be threefold: (i) attractions, e.g., climate, scenery, historical and cultural features; (ii) accessibility, i.e., distance of destination, their location and transport facilities; (iii) amenities, e.g., accommodation, catering and entertainment facilities. An appropriate mix of all the above three components is necessary for the success of tourism, and it is the task of the organisation to achieve this success. The organisation of tourism may be divided into two parts. First, there are sectors of tourism, i.e., the various providers of tourist services—the hotel and catering services, the transport services and the entertainment services; second, there are the levels of tourist organisation—national, regional and local. The organisation of tourism can therefore be horizontal as well as vertical. It also varies widely from country to country as there are a number of considerations which influence the nature of organisational set-up.

Today almost all the countries have a tourist organisation. Rapidly growing awareness of the economic, financial and social advantages of tourism development, together with the recognition that such advantages can best be achieved through systematic efforts to expand tourism, has led many states especially after the Second World War to extend and enlarge their direct interest in tourism. To manage tourism on scientific lines, many nations have set up organisations to deal specifically with the subject of tourism. However, the pattern and nature of these organisations differ widely from one country to another.

Factors Influencing Type of Tourist Organisation

The type of a tourist organisation in a particular country is influenced by a number of factors in that country:

(i) The political, economic and social system

(ii) The importance of Tourism to national economy

(iii) The stage of Tourism Development

(i) The political, economic and social system in a country will have an important bearing upon its tourist organisation. In countries where there is a centralised government, this is likely to be reflected in the tourist organisation, as is the case, for example, in Spain and the Russian Federation. In these countries the tourism industry is centralized and dominated by the government. By contrast, in countries such as Switzerland, Austria, Germany, Great Britain, with a federal state organisation, the tourist industry is decentralised with a minimum of governmental interference. In these countries, the tourist organisations consist of one or more cooperative bodies at the national level and there is also a high degree of devolution to individual states or regions in various matters concerning tourism.

(ii) The importance of tourism to a national economy is another factor which influences the character of an organisation. In countries where tourism is very important in relation to other industries, or conversely, where tourism is well developed and of substantial economic importance, the tourism organisation is likely to be well developed and the government actively concerned with tourism. This type of organisation is functioning in large number of countries. In Italy, it is a dual Ministry of Tourism and Entertainment, which is concerned with tourism as also with historical monuments, theatres and other forms of entertainment. Similarly, in Spain the dual ministry controls the press, radio and television along with tourism, while in France, the dual ministry controls tourism and entertainment.

(iii) The stage of tourism development is yet another important factor likely to have a considerable influence on the organisation. For instance, in countries where tourism is not yet fully developed or is just beginning to develop (as is the case in many developing countries including India), better results can be achieved if the industry is centralised and under direct government control. In such countries direct government intervention would seem to be not only desirable but indispensable. Also as these countries would require huge sums of money for the development of infrastructure, these would come from the state as the private enterprise may not be in a position to invest because of lack of resources at their disposal. On the other hand, in countries with highly developed tourist industries, it is common to find flexible, decentralized tourist organisations, which have evolved over many years as is the case in Austria, Germany and Switzerland. Switzerland has a long history of tourism and as such there is a highly developed tourism organisation which is decentralized and also reflects the federal character of the state. The organisation of tourism, therefore, is complex and involves many forms and is influenced by a variety of factors. A study of tourism organisation should logically begin with the official tourist organisation called the National Tourist Organisation followed by other semi-official or private organisations which together serve the objectives of tourism.

Recommendations of UN Conference

The United Nations Conference on International Travel and Tourism held in Rome in 1963 considered the role of organisations in the development of tourism. The resolutions and recommendations of the conference are contained in the third part of the documents, which deals with tourism development. In a general resolution on the organisation of tourism, it states that the conference.

(i) considers it incumbent on governments to stimulate and coordinate national tourist activities;

(ii) is convinced that this task can in the main be carried out through the medium of national tourist organisations;

(iii) recommends that national tourist organisations should be granted the authority and resources necessary to enable them to take effective action, as desired by governments, for the development and promotion of national and international tourism.

The conference was unanimously of the opinion that national tourist organisations having governmental or semi-governmental support were an essential foundation for building up a prosperous tourist industry. Various forms of a national tourist organisation were considered during the conference. In some countries the organisation was in effect a government department directly responsible to a minister; in others it was a section of a government department. In many countries the tourist organisation was a separate government agency. The conference noted that the degree of direct government control over such agencies varied a great deal from one country to another. In yet other countries the organisation, though wholly or mainly financed by the government, could properly be described as non-governmental. Some non-governmental tourist organisations also received financial contributions from various sectors of the travel industry.

The conference was of the opinion that it was necessary, especially in developing countries, that the government should leave the organisation responsible for tourism—whether a governmental or semi-governmental organisation or a government agency—complete autonomy in the exercise of its functions. The conference considered it desirable that, in the case of national tourist organisations which did not include representatives of the principal administrative and private (producer and consumer) activities related to tourism, those activities should be represented by an advisory body with, if possible, spokesmen for organised labour in its membership. The conference also agreed that government should make adequate funds available to enable the national tourist organisations to carry out their work effectively. In view of the fact that tourism was an important social, economic and cultural factor, and recognising that, in the interest of their peoples, governments should assume their responsibilities in the field of tourism, the conference considered that such responsibilities should be delegated so far as possible to national tourist organisations.

The conference was of the opinion that the activities of the national tourist organisations should not be restricted to promotional questions alone, but should also cover the establishment, improvement and development of tourist equipment through either direct or coordinate or consultative action, as might be appropriate in each specific case. In developing countries, private enterprise was often unwilling or unable to invest in hotels and other enterprises connected with tourism because it lacked resources. In such cases, the conference felt, the state should lend assistance. The conference also believed that in order to be able to carry out their proper functions, national tourist organisations should be endowed by the government with the necessary authority and resources.

The conference expressed the opinion that where no national tourist organisation existed, the government cognizant of its social responsibilities should take the initiative in setting up such an organisation, which would aim at the development of both domestic and international tourism. That should be done in consultation with the private sector of the industry and where that sector was not sufficiently developed, the government should take action to stimulate its development.

The conference recommended that national tourist organisations should be awarded wider competence, increased responsibility and larger resources, so that they could promote the development of domestic tourism and thus assist in the development of international tourism. It recognized that in certain cases international tourism can encourage the rise and development of domestic tourism.

In every country governments are concerned about the tourism industry. There are several reasons for this. The important and obvious reasons are related to the economic impacts of tourism, e.g., employment generation, balance of payments and the contribution of tourism to the country's gross domestic product (GDP). Tourism also has social, cultural and environmental impacts which may be positive or negative. Governments are generally concerned in maximising the benefits and minimising the costs.

Governments are also responsible for framing the overall tourism policy. Policy is a guideline for the future or a course of action to meet defined goals and objectives. Tourism policy refers to guidelines and decisions designed to assist in meeting tourism goals and objectives. National, regional, state or local governments formulate tourism policies concerning their respective regions. At the national level, governments have an important role in influencing tourism. They can influence tourism both on demand and supply sides. Tourism is influenced on demand side to maximise net income and minimise costs. This can be achieved by

(i) removing the requirements of visas to stimulate demand;
(ii) promoting and marketing by way of funding tourist organisations which advertise at home and abroad;
(iii) exchanging controls on outbound tourists;
(iv) exchanging requirements on inbound tourists;
(v) levying entry/departure taxes;
(vi) providing subsidies to tourists; and
(vii) taking any action affecting disposable income/free time.

On the supply side the governments can influence tourism with a view to protecting the consumer and obtaining quick economic benefits. This can be achieved by

(i) providing infrastructure like roads, airports, wayside facilities, etc.;
(ii) improving level of public services like water, sewage treatment, medical facilities etc.;

(iii) manpower development including education and training;
(iv) providing range of investment incentives by way of granting loans, subsidies, grants, tax holidays, etc.;
(v) planning permissions zoning building regulations;
(vi) Legislation regarding protection of resources like national parks etc.; and
(vii) framing rules regarding flow of foreign investment.

National Tourist Organisation

The National Tourist Organisation (NTO) is the body responsible for the formulation and implementation of national tourist policy. It is the proper agency and instrument for the execution of the national government's responsibilities for the control, direction and promotion of tourism. All countries which are engaged in tourism have a national tourist organisation which plays a leading role in both the formulation and the implementation of the government's tourism programme. This organisation is also responsible for coordinating the different activities of all the bodies interested in tourism development. The national tourist organisation may be a full-fledged ministry, a directorate general, a department, corporation or a board.

There is, however, no set formula as to what constitutes the most satisfactory constitutional arrangement for the national tourism body. Tourism ranks as a full ministry in some countries with a minister enjoying a cabinet rank. Another arrangement in many countries is for tourism to share a minister with information or with arts, sports and culture. Yet other possibilities include attaching the tourism office to the presidency of the council, putting it in the charge of an official of the rank of a deputy secretary with an occasional voice in the council of ministers. In others, it has semi-autonomous status of a corporation and functions not as an organ of the government but rather as a professional body outside it. It will be apparent that the arrangement and the constitution for the national tourist organisation vary widely. It depends on factors like political structure of the country, the level of economic development, of potential value of tourism to the economy, the level of tourism development and also availability of capital for tourism development including infrastructural developments.

Functions of the National Tourist Organisation

The National Tourist Organisation is primarily concerned with control, direction and promotion of tourism. The object and functions of the NTO are therefore to ensure that the maximum possible value from international tourism accrues to the country for its economic and social benefit. The functions of the NTO, however, will vary quite widely in relation both to (i) the degree of the direct intervention that the government desires to exercise and (ii) the level of development of tourist industry in the country concerned.

At the Estoril Seminar in 1966 in England, it was agreed that the NTO would normally undertake the following functions.

(i) Research,
(ii) Information and promotion within the country,

(iii) Regularisation of standards of lodging and restaurants,
(iv) Control of activities of private travel agencies,
(v) Publicity overseas,
(vi) Technical and juridical problems,
(vii) International relations,
(viii) Development of selected areas, and
(ix) Overall tourism policy and promotion.

Research is a basic function of a national tourist organisation. A concomitant of institutional promotion is research into the tourism potential of the principal markets and investigation into the marketability of the country's tourist product. This is an important direct responsibility of NTO.

Information and promotion within the country helps not only the actual international tourist but also the domestic tourist. The information offices located at important tourist centres serve as a facility to the tourists. These are a major aid to tourists both overseas as well as local. These centres provide accurate and up-to-date information to tourists visiting various places. In most countries, NTO has its own branch offices in strategic places throughout the country. These offices are responsible for information and reception services for visitors and liaison with the local tourist interests. It is also the responsibility of the NTO to encourage and promote tourism consciousness among the government agencies and the public so that they will realise the benefits that a country can derive from tourism.

Regularisation of standards of lodging and restaurants is very essential for tourist satisfaction. Since the growth of tourism depends directly on consumer satisfaction, the NTO, in its role of administrator, manager and promoter of the tourist product, acts as the government watchdog to ensure the maintenance of appropriate standards of quality and service of lodging establishments. This supervisory role has been enlarged and strengthened because of the complex problems arising from the growth of tourism and the expanding needs for safeguarding the interests of tourists. The degree of tourism development, and of the travel sectors' maturity, naturally determine the extent to which the travel industries are self-regulating and the scope of NTO's supervisory role.

Control of activities of private travel agencies is another important supervisory role of the NTO. More and more tourists are utilizing the services of private travel agencies. It is essential that the tourists should get good and efficient service and protection. NTO should be responsible for the maintenance of appropriate standards of quality and service of the travel agents. Travel agents should be regarded as having professional status and this could best be brought about by introducing appropriate legislation.

Publicity overseas is a major function of the NTO. One of the most important activities of any national tourist office is promotion of the country as a destination for tourists. Among other activities, promotion includes advertising, publicity of all kinds, public relations, the provision of information and the distribution of printed sales material. Planned publicity and promotion on behalf of the country are among the basic functions common to all NTOs. Normally no other government agency exercises this function. The NTOs cooperate with other governmental departments and the travel trade in promoting tourism for their country.

Technical and juridical problems are those which are related with the administration of law. This is very crucial as on it will depend the quality of various services provided by various sectors. NTOs have to be very cautious while administering law. Technical problems on the other hand are concerned with the development and maintenance of various services. Continuous detailed assessment has to be made of the extent to which the infrastructure, superstructure and organisation plans are likely to meet future tourism demand. It is imperative that the NTO should take part directly in each of these stages. The optimum development of tourism in any country implies a close knowledge of the attractions of the country; acquaintance with the motivations and the needs of the market; the processing and presentation of the country's attractions in the manner most favourable and acceptable to the market; action of the market to create effective demand; and the provision of adequate facilities, amenities and services to ensure the maximum satisfaction of tourists. All these areas are of technical nature and the NTOs have to take proper care for their efficient maintenance.

International relations are also a very essential part of tourism. International contacts resulting from tourism have always been among the most important ways of spreading ideas about other cultures. Tourism can be a vehicle for international understanding by way of bringing diverse people face to face. It has been cited as a major contributor to international goodwill and as a prime means of developing social and cultural understanding among all people of the world. The interaction of a large number of people with the local population of a country visited results in making friends. It is the responsibility of the NTO to deal with aspects of tourism development that have a bearing on relations with foreign countries. It maintains offices and representatives abroad for the promotion of tourism traffic to the country, and has close relations with foreign tour operators, travel agents and carriers. It cooperates with NTOs of neighbouring countries in mounting joint regional travel promotion programmes. Governments also empower NTOs to represent the country's tourism interests in international organisations and, wherever necessary, to join with other government agencies in negotiations for the conclusion of agreements in the field of tourism with foreign governments.

Development of selected areas to attract tourists is necessary. In every country there are hundreds of areas of tourist potential. However, due to various constraints it is not possible to develop all these areas. It is important to identify and select certain areas which have the maximum potential for tourism development. A detailed scientific survey of these areas will help in avoiding wasteful expenditure. To the extent permitted by its economic resources, the NTOs should encourage development of selected resorts. Existing possibilities of attracting tourists—mountaineering, winter sports, beaches, national parks, game sanctuaries, national monuments, sites and shrines, pilgrim centres, folk traditions and customs, festivals and sporting events—should be developed and protected. In a developing country the NTO should consider obtaining a preliminary survey in order to assess clearly what positive tourist attractions the country already had, what potential tourist attractions existed, and how they could most effectively be developed within the limits of the resources available.

Overall tourism policy and promotion is very essential as it helps in the optimum utilization of resources. In calculating returns from investments in tourism, the national tourist policy cannot restrict itself to limited considerations of immediate financial and economic profitability. It has to consider the beneficial effects of tourism on general national development where considerations of non-economic character may be equally or even more important, than purely economic returns, viz., cultural considerations, social considerations, political considerations, etc.

The NTOs should take all these factors into consideration while formulating overall tourism policy and promotion. They should not consider tourism from its balance-of-payments aspect alone, but should take into account the contribution which tourism makes to international trade by developing the national economy and enhancing social values.

WORK OF NTO

The National Tourist Organisation is likely to be concerned with four broad areas:

(i) administration
(ii) production
(iii) marketing
(iv) financing.

The administration will be concerned with the personnel of the organisation, with the part to be played by tourist in the overall national developmental plan; with effective liaison with concerned government departments like finance, home, planning, health, transport, communications, education, culture, public works, labour etc.; regional cooperation and legal matters and advisory services, etc.

The production part will be concerned with all those elements and activities which make up the tourism product. Production will include the inventory and assessment of the country's natural attractions and the development and protection of these assets; the listing, assessing and forecasting the country's tourism plant, the requirements in infrastructure where tourist development is planned, the drawing up of plans for regional or area development, the establishment of close relations with the hotel, catering and transport sectors of tourism, the recruitment and training of personnel for the tourist industry, etc.

The marketing area will be concerned with research into the principal and potential tourist markets, their size, socio-economic characteristics, preferences of tourists for food and accommodation, spending power and the like, with sales promotion, public relations, advertising, maintenance of overseas offices, etc.; and collaboration with other countries in the same region.

Finally, **the *financial*** work will involve investment in and financing of tourism in the country. It will, for example, provide financial assistance for approved tourist projects, approve loans or grants for hotels, seek and encourage private investment in various tourism projects and, where these are not enough, seek funds from international agencies such as World Bank, or International Bank for Reconstruction and Development. The role of foreign participation in tourism development is important in many of the developing countries which have not the necessary capital available for investment.

Another important area of the work of a national tourist organisation is its role as the spokesperson for private tourism industries, to communicate their needs to the government and to strive for the most satisfactory solutions. The NTO has to ensure that the expectations and operations of the private tourist operators are consistent with the aims and objectives of the national tourist programme and policy. With the recognition of tourism as an industry through the formation of large integrated travel enterprises and the development of package travel, NTOs are experiencing the need to foster the integration of their country's tourist industries (travel agencies, tour operators, hotels) so as to enable them to become more efficient and effective partners in promoting tourism in the country.

Whatever the tasks that the national tourism body is called upon to do, what is most important is that it should have the full powers necessary to carry them out. The NTO can carry out its task most effectively and satisfactorily only when it has broad powers and adequate resources. The governments should make adequate funds available to enable the national tourist organisations to carry out their work effectively. The NTO must, above all, have authority. It must be able to present effectively and forcefully the case for tourism among the claims of other sectors competing for government support and finance. Lastly, it is essential that the tourist organisation maintains a close and harmonious liaison with all other interests that may be involved in tourism development. To sum up, the national tourist organisation has to mobilize all potential national forces and resources available for stimulating the growth and development of tourism.

Tourist Organisation in India

Tourism as a separate organisation was set up rather late in India. Prior to the formation of a separate organisation, tourism was a part of the Ministry of Transport. The government, had, however, started devoting considerable time and attention to the development of tourist traffic immediately after independence. By that time it was recognised that tourist traffic was an important source of earning foreign exchange as well as promoting international understanding.

The first step towards the development of the tourist industry in India was initiated in the year 1945 when the Sargent Committee was appointed. This committee, set up by the then Government of India under the chairmanship of Sir John Sargent, the then educational adviser to the government, submitted its report in the year 1946. The main recommendation of the committee was that a separate tourist organisation should be set up at the Centre with regional offices in metropolitan cities of Bombay (now Mumbai), Delhi, Calcutta (Kolkata) and Madras (Chennai). The committee also recommended setting up of tourist publicity cells in Indian embassies and consulates all over the world. As a follow-up, an adhoc tourist traffic committee was appointed in 1948. This committee was entrusted with the job of suggesting ways and means of promoting tourist traffic to India.

Ad Hoc Tourist Traffic Committee

It was in 1948 that the independent Government of India took the first step towards promotion of tourism in India. The Ministry of Transport constituted an ad hoc tourist traffic committee consisting of representatives of the concerned ministries and of tourist, transport and hotel industries. One of the major recommendations of the Sargent

Committee appointed in 1945 was that the work of development of tourist traffic in India should be undertaken on a "methodical basis by a separate organisation". As a result of this recommendation, a separate tourist traffic branch was set up in the Ministry of Transport in 1949 with the main objective of development of tourist traffic in India. The subsequent years witnessed an expansion of the branch and its activities in various directions. In 1955–56, its headquarters establishment was increased from one branch to four branches, each having wide- ranging duties. The four sections looking after various subjects were (i) tourist traffic section (ii) tourist administration section (iii) tourist publicity section and (iv) distribution section.

The *tourist traffic section* was to look after a larger number of travel trade subjects which included development of both internal and external tourist traffic, legislative matters, five-year plans, travel agencies, hotels and rest houses, facilitation, tourist statistics and monthly reports. It also dealt with international conferences on tourism and conferences relating to United Nations and its agencies, coordination with railways, establishment of tourist bureaus in States and development of tourist centres and the training of guides. The *tourist administration section* was to deal with administration work relating to tourist offices both in India and abroad, budget, delegation of financial powers to tourist offices, opening of new tourist offices in India and abroad and periodical inspection of tourist offices. The *tourist publicity section* was to deal with publication of tourist literature such as pamphlets, guidebooks and posters, issue of advertisements and participation in exhibitions and fairs. The *distribution section* was to deal with the distribution of tourist publicity literature in India and abroad.

Within a short period of time there was manifold increase in the activities of the Tourist Traffic Branch. The four branches as they developed during the years 1955–56 performed a variety of duties covering almost all the important segments of tourism. These branches were functioning under one deputy secretary and two under secretaries. At this stage there was a proposal for the creation of a directorate general of tourism. One reason advanced in favour of this proposal was that the policy making and executive functions were combined in the existing staff of the tourist division of the secretariat and that these should be separated. However, this proposal did not find favour as it was felt that the subject of tourism had not yet developed to an extent as would justify an immediate separation of these two functions.

Information Offices in India

Another important step during this period was the opening of a chain of tourist offices both in India and abroad. Steps were taken to establish regional offices at important ports of entry. Tourist offices were opened in Delhi, Bombay (now Mumbai), Calcutta (Kolkata) and Madras (Chennai). This was followed by the establishment of a chain of information offices all over the country. By the year 1955, nine such offices were opened. The staff in the regional offices in India consisted of one regional officer, one assistant regional officer, one receptionist and two clerks. The staff in information offices consisted of one information officer and one clerk. Regional tourist officers and the information officers had to perform wide-ranging duties. The duties of the former included liaison with State governments, the local tourist agencies, the railway authorities, airlines, shipping agencies and hotels with regard to travel trade of the region. Other duties were as follows: (i) making suggestions for improvement of tourist traffic facilities in the region, (ii) assisting Ministry of Transport in the preparation and distribution of publicity material, (iii) selling tourist literature supplied by the Ministry of Transport and State governments and the Publications Division, (iv) issue of permits and cards to foreign tourists holding tourist visas, issue of tourist introduction cards, distribution of embarkation and disembarkation cards to the airlines, travel agents and security control for observance of frontier formalities, (v) attending to the complaints of tourists and travel trade regarding lack of amenities and bringing the same to the notice of the Ministry of Transport and the local authorities.

The duties of the information officers included (i) surveying tourist resources in the region and maintaining an up-to-date record of available facilities, (ii) organising tourist promotional activities, (iii) attending to all enquiries regarding tourist amenities and tourist attractions which may be made at the Tourist Information Office whether personally or by correspondence, (iv) receiving parties of tourists at aerodromes and railway stations and rendering assistance to them, and (v) keeping close liaison with the travel trade and local authorities.

The details of the functions of the tourist offices are as follows:

(i) Attending to personal and postal enquiries of Indian and foreign tourists.

(ii) Collecting and compiling of detailed up-to-date information for dissemination to tourists.

(iii) Preparation of handouts containing information on places of tourist interest for distribution among tourists.

(iv) Assistance in expeditious clearance of travel formalities of tourists arriving by air and sea.

(v) Issue of liquor permits, tourist introduction cards, railway concession forms, etc.

(vi) Making various arrangements for departmental guests consisting of travel agents, writers and film makers including booking of accommodation, airline seats, arrangements for sightseeing, transport, entertainment, etc.

(vii) Rendering non-financial assistance to important tourist groups, individual tourists, travel writers, journalists, etc., who are on tour of India.

(viii) Publicity and tourist promotion by contributing articles to press and travel magazines, organising film shows, talks on radio, lectures, club meetings, etc.

(ix) Taking up problems of various sections of the travel trade in order to ensure that tourists face no difficulty whatsoever. This involves liaison with various Central and State government departments.

(x) Enquiries into the complaints of tourists against shopkeepers, taxi drivers, etc., and getting them refund wherever necessary.

(xi) Liaison with archaeological department, State government tourist departments and other local bodies for the maintenance and improvement of tourist facilities.

(xii) Arranging regular film shows at airports for a large number of tourists.

(xiii) Distribution of tourist literature to travel agencies, hotel counters, airlines, etc., as also publicising tourist centres through display of posters at focal points.

(xiv) Allotting guides on rotation basis for tourists and travel agencies, supervision of the quality of services rendered by guides, and conducting periodical training courses for guides.

(xv) Inspection of hotels from time to time, screening shops, shikar agencies, travel agencies and car operators for approval, and generally supervising the services of all branches of the travel trade.

(xvi) Organising special programmes for tourist cruise ships such as cultural shows, fashion shows, etc., and arranging sightseeing tours for tourists from these ships.

(xvii) Arranging meet-the-people programmes and Indian home visits for foreign tourists.

(xviii) Assisting foreign journalists, TV and radio publicists, film producers, etc., in getting facilities so that the country gets maximum publicity abroad through such media.

(xx) Maintaining a statistical section for compiling tourist statistics.

(xxi) Promotion of sightseeing tours and inducing tour operators/agents to start new tours where necessary.

(xxii) Supervision of the working of tourist bungalows/youth hostels, etc., put up by the Department of Tourism.

(xxiii) Participation in meetings and conferences related to tourism promotion like Pacific Asia Travel Association (PATA), World Tourism Organisation (WTO), etc.

In short, the functions of the tourist offices in India include supply of up-to-date information on places of tourist interests after tourists had arrived in India, keeping in touch with all the segments of travel trade, assisting the tourists in clearance of various travel formalities, distribution and display of tourist literature and periodic inspection of various facilities available for tourists. Tourist offices were also to ensure that the various amenities are developed and maintained in each region. In addition to attending to foreign tourists, the tourist offices were also to cater to the needs of domestic tourists.

Tourism Offices in India

The Ministry of Tourism has five Regional offices located at Kolkata (East), Mumbai (West), Delhi (North), Chennai (South) and Guwahati (North East), which are headed by an officer of the level of Deputy Director General designated as Regional Director. Each Regional Officer (called RD Office) has sub regional officers in their jurisdiction, totalling 15 in number. Details of these Regional & Sub Regional Officers are as under.

- Andaman & Nicobar (Port Blair)
- Arunachal Pradesh (Naharlagun)

- Assam (Guwahati)
- Bihar (Patna)
- Delhi (Delhi)
- Goa (Panaji)
- Karnataka (Bangalore/ Bengaluru)
- Kerala (Kochi)
- Madhya Pradesh (Indore)
- Maharashtra (Aurangabad)
- Maharashtra (Mumbai)
- Manipur (Imphal)
- Meghalaya (Shillong)
- Odisha (Bhubaneswar)
- Rajasthan (Jaipur)
- Tamil Nadu (Chennai)
- Telangana (Hyderabad)
- Uttar Pradesh (Agra)
- Uttar Pradesh (Varanasi)
- West Bengal (Kolkata)

Tourist Offices Overseas

The Central government decided to open a chain of tourist offices overseas with a view to attracting foreign tourists to India. The first step in this direction was the establishment of Government of India Tourist Office in New York in the United States of America in December 1952. The reason for opening an office in the United States was that as an affluent country its people had enough money and leisure to afford a holiday in India. Nearer home, special staff was also provided in the offices of the High Commissioners for India in Sri Lanka and Australia for tourist promotion work in these countries. To arouse interest among Europeans to visit India, a chain of offices were also opened in the continent. The first office in Europe was opened in London in July 1955. Two more offices were opened, one in Paris in February 1956 and the other in Frankfurt in September of the same year. In order to promote tourist traffic from Australia and New Zealand, a tourist office was opened in Melbourne in September 1956. Also in 1956 an office was opened in Colombo on the occasion of the 2,500th anniversary of Gautama Buddha. The office in Colombo was responsible for helping and promoting a large Buddhist traffic from Sri Lanka.

Functions of Overseas Offices

The functions performed by the tourist offices abroad were more or less similar to those performed by the regional offices in India, with the difference that while the regional offices in India mainly assisted the foreign tourists who had arrived in India, the tourist offices abroad furnished preliminary information to tourists intending to visit India. Their duties included publicity and public relations, sales promotion and reporting to the Department of Tourism about the trends in the tourist travel abroad.

The details of the functions of the tourist offices abroad are as follows:

(i) To establish and maintain continuous contacts with travel agents, airlines, shipping companies, professional clubs and international tourist promotion societies.

(ii) To establish and maintain continuous contact with heads of national tourist offices of the other governments, tour promoters, travel writers, film and TV producers, etc.

(iii) Tourist publicity and promotion by way of sponsoring articles in press, by television and radio programmes, by advertisement campaign and through participation in exhibitions, etc.

(iv) To supply up-to-date information about tourist facilities in India through various channels to the potential visitors.

(v) To supply information to Central government's Department of Tourism about current trends in tourism in the area of their respective jurisdiction.

(vi) To organize film shows of tourist documentaries and other films of tourist interests for various groups.

(vii) To organize and supervise the advertisement programmes geared towards promotion of tourist traffic to India.

(viii) To attend to various personal and postal enquiries made by potential tourists and to assist in preparation of itineraries.

(ix) To prepare a monthly newsletter giving all the information of tourist interest.

(x) To distribute tourist literature to travel agents, wholesalers and other agencies responsible for promoting tourist traffic and maintaining a mailing list for distribution of publicity material.

(xi) To participate in social functions, conferences and meetings with a view to acquainting the potential visitor about India and its tourist attractions.

In short, the functions of tourist offices abroad include acquainting the potential visitor about the various tourist attractions and facilities available in India through publicity, public relations and sales promotion.

Criteria for Opening Overseas Offices

The most effective way of developing tourist traffic from abroad is to establish direct link with the countries concerned by opening tourist offices there. The tourist offices set up in other countries work for the promotion of tourism traffic to their home country. Although the main criteria for opening new offices abroad is the number of tourists coming from the country concerned, factors are also taken into consideration. The following are some of them:

(i) The potentiality of the tourist market in the area.

(ii) The spending capacity and the travel consciousness of the population of the country.

(iii) The need to develop a particular area from the foreign- exchange point of view, e.g., hard-currency areas.

(vi) The cultural and/or historic affinity between India and the country concerned.

(v) The importance of the place from the international tourism point of view. An office at such a place can persuade the transit tourists to include India in their itineraries.

Tourism Offices Overseas

- China (Beijing)
- France (Paris)
- Germany (Frankfurt)
- Japan (Tokyo)
- Singapore (Singapore)
- United Kingdom (London)
- United States (New York)
- United Arab Emirates (Dubai)

Setting up of Department of Tourism

It was on March 1st, 1958 that a separate tourism department was created in the Ministry of Transport to deal with all matters concerning tourism. Thus a long-felt need of such a department was at last met. The new department was put under the charge of the director general who had under him one deputy director general and four directors each in charge of administration, publicity, travel relations and planning and development.

By a presidential order dated 14 March, 1967, the Department of Aviation and Tourism, which was under the Ministry of Transport and Civil Aviation, was formed into a separate ministry designated as the Ministry of Tourism and Civil Aviation, with two constituent departments: (i) Department of Tourism and (ii) Department of Civil Aviation. The ministry was under the charge of a full-time minister. It was after nearly eighteen years that subject 'tourism' was accorded a separate entity and became independent of transport. With the formation of the new Ministry of Tourism and Civil Aviation, tourism got the importance due to it and thereby achieved all-round expansion in its activities.

The Department of Tourism now became an attached non-participating office of the Ministry of Tourism and Civil Aviation headed by the director general of tourism. The director general of tourism carried an ex-officio status of an additional secretary to the Government of India. Although an attached office, the department is both a policy-making and an executive organisation and corresponds directly with the other ministries and departments of the Central government and State governments.

Recently tourism has been accorded the status of a full-fledged ministry and is designated as Ministry of Tourism and Culture. It is headed by a minister who is assisted by a secretary and a director general. The Ministry of Tourism is both a policy-making and an executive organisation and corresponds directly with other ministries and departments of the Central and State governments.

The functions of the Ministry of Tourism are both promotional and organisational which are conducted by the following divisions:

(i) Planning and Programming;
(ii) Publicity and Conference;
(iii) Travel Trade and Hospitality;
(iv) Accommodation
(v) Supplementary Accommodation and Wildlife;
(vi) Market Research; and
(vii) Administration.

The activities of the ministry have since increased manifold and cover a wide range of subjects. The various activities fall under the following broad heads:

(i) Collection, compilation and dissemination of tourist information in India and abroad and attending to enquiries from international tourists, tour operators and travel industry such as airlines, steamship companies and hotels.
(ii) Cooperation with international travel and tourist organisations at government and non-government levels.
(iii) Development of tourist facilities of interest to international tourists.
(iv) Publicity at home and abroad with the object of creating an overall awareness of the importance of tourism.
(v) Simplification of frontier formalities in respect of international tourists.
(vi) Regulation of activities of the various segments of the travel trade such as hotels, youth hostels, travel agents, wildlife outfitters, guides, tourist car operators and shopkeepers catering to tourist needs.
(vii) Compilation of statistics and market research on international tourist traffic to India and their utilization for more effective tourist promotion.

The ministry has a chain of twenty-five tourist information offices established in important cities in India. Five of these offices (regional offices) are located at Mumbai, Delhi, Kolkata, Chennai and Guwahati (Assam) which are major ports of entry. The remaining sub-offices are functioning at focal points of tourist interest in Agra, Aurangabad, Kochi, Varanasi, Bangalore, Bhubaneswar, Hyderabad, Panaji, Patna, Port Blair, Indore and Kochi. With a view to attract tourists to the north-eastern region, offices have been opened Guwahati, Shillong, Imphal, Itanagar and Naharlagun (Arunachal Pradesh). The tourist offices in India furnish information to the tourists regarding travel and tourist attractions in India and also render assistance of non-financial nature. These offices help the department in exercising some measure of control over various segments of travel trade and try to ensure that the foreign tourists get various services at reasonable cost and are not inconvenienced in any way during their period of stay in India. All these offices work in close collaboration with State governments, travel agencies, excursion agencies, hoteliers, carriers, 'shikar' outfitters and tourist car operators.

For overseas promotion, the ministry has eight offices. The offices located at New York. Covering USA, Latin America and the Carribean islands. The regional director, with headquarters in New York, supervise the functioning of these offices. In Europe the offices are located at London, Paris, Frankfurt, Vienna and Milan.

These offices cover Continental Europe under the directions of a regional director stationed at Frankfurt. The tourist office in Tokyo covers Japan, Philippines, Hong Kong and Thailand. The office in Singapore, which is also under the guidance of Tokyo office, covers Singapore, Malaysia and Indonesia. The tourist office in Beijing covers China. West Asia is covered by the tourist office located in Dubai.

The overseas tourist offices form a direct link between the department and the travel trade in foreign countries. Their functions include handling of enquiries, dissemination of accurate information, advertising, publicity, public relation with press and travel trade and supply of up-to-date information to the department about current trends in tourism in the area of their jurisdiction.

From a small beginning in 1949, the tourist organisation as it stands now has passed through various facets. The recognition given to tourism as an industry paved the way for its standing as an independent discipline. In between 1949 and today there has been a tremendous amount of work which has helped in strengthening the organisation. The appointment of various expert committees, advisory commitments, councils and boards from time to time has helped the organisation grow tremendously.

Tourism Organisation in Italy

Italy, like India, is one of the oldest countries where civilization and culture have enjoyed a long history. Both Italy and India are endowed with ancient traditions, art, architecture, religion, philosophy, etc. Italy is a long, narrow peninsula and lies at the foot of the European continent. It is a beautiful country with numerous picturesque lakes, rivers and mountains. The northern mountains and lakes and the southern seas, forests of fir trees and Indian prickly pears, the fog of the lagoons, Gothic cathedrals and Greek temples, the rationality of the Renaissance have combined to make Italy a country where nature and culture blend superbly. The warm Mediterranean climate and the protection afforded by the Alps make Italy a land of sunshine where pine trees grow at the foot of snow-capped mountains and a deep blue sky spans equally over the cliffs of the Riviera, the soft hills of Tuscany and the historic monuments of Sicily. It is because of the magic spell of its scenic splendours and artistic grandeurs that Italy today is one of the most sought-after eldorados for tourists all over the world. It is truly a tourist paradise and the tourist trade in Italy has become an economic and social factor of enormous importance. The tourist arrival figures in Italy are simply startling. The foreign visitors to Italy have grown from two million in 1931 to over 36 million in 1999. The yearly increases are far beyond those registered in other European countries attracting foreign visitors.

The Italian authorities, considering tourism as an economic and social factor of enormous importance, have created special agencies and departments to manage and organize tourism in the country. These special agencies and departments operate under the overall supervision of the Ministry of Tourism and Entertainment. Earlier in the chapter it has been discussed that organisation of tourist industry in any country varies very widely and depends upon a number of considerations which influence the nature of organisational set-up. One of these factors is the importance of tourism in a national economy. This factor is likely to influence the character of the organisation. Where tourism is developed and is of substantial economic importance to a country, the organisation is also likely to be well developed and the government actively concerned. Tourism organisations in such countries may have a government department wholly or substantially concerned with tourism. In Italy it is the dual Ministry of Tourism and Entertainment, which is concerned in addition to tourism with historical monuments, theatres, and other forms of entertainment. The following paragraphs will discuss how tourism is organised in Italy.

At the top of the organisational pyramid lies the Ministry of Tourism and Entertainment (Ministero del Tourismo e dello Spettacolo). This is the central authority. It was created by the Legislative Act of July 1959 absorbing the former Commission for Tourism created in 1947. The Ministry of Tourism and Entertainment has two departments (general directorates): one for tourism and the other for entertainment. The Directorate General of Tourism has six main divisions (i) tourist organisation inside the country, (ii) reception and tourist resources, (iii) tourist aids, (iv) international relations and festivals, (v) professional training and tourist industries and (vi) legal and technical affairs.

In 1969, the country was divided into 20 regions. There was a shift to decentralization of the administration which involved the reorganisation of regional administration and the creation of regions. Fifteen new regions, besides the other five which existed for several years with special statutory provisions, came into existence. The ministry's functions before the formation of these states as a result of shift to decentralization were much wider in scope and covered a wide range of subjects. However, since 1971, with so many fields of competence in tourism transferred to the regions, a decree was enacted limiting the ministry's field competence mainly to the following:

(a) International relations,
(b) Creation and managing tourist offices at the frontiers;
(c) Tourist promotion abroad through the National Italian Tourist Organisation; and
(d) Guiding and coordinating regional administrative activities.

Planning of tourism within the framework of overall national development plans remains with the ministry through its consultative capacity to other ministries concerned. The implementation of those plans at a regional level is now entrusted to the regional boards [Ente Provincial del Tourismo (EPT)]. Such matters as tourism policy, the administration of loans, the grading of hotels and the general coordination of tourist services all come under the control of the Directorate General of Tourism, which is the tourist part of the Ministry.

Central Tourist Council

The Central Tourist Council (Consiglio Central del Turismo) is created within the Ministry of Tourism and Entertainment to exercise functions of advisory and research nature. The council is called together twice a year by the minister and may address itself to any question or questions relating to tourism in general and criteria of tourist publicity in particular. The council's recommendations become binding in certain cases, namely, measures necessary for creating cure, sojourn and tourist resorts and their revocation.

Presided over by the minister, the council is composed of 59 members, some of whom represent ministries such as tourism, the interior, foreign affairs, finance, public works, education, defence, civil aviation, transport, industry and commerce, agriculture and forests, health, etc. Besides there are the representatives from National Italian Tourist Organisation [Ente National Italiano per il Turismo (ENIT)], the national committee for the Olympics, automobile club, etc. Representatives of the employees in industries or enterprises concerned with tourism, workers in these enterprises and specialists in tourism are also represented in the council. The council is formed for a term of four years. It has a secretary who is usually a high official of the ministry. The Central Tourist Council was reorganised by a presidental decree of August 1964.

National Italian Tourist Organisation

The chief function of the National Italian Tourist Organisation [Ente National Italiano per il Turismo (ENIT)] is propaganda and promotion. This organisation is responsible at the national level for the Italian tourist promotion overseas. ENIT has 26 tourist overseas promotion offices. It has also correspondence offices abroad in collaboration with Alitalia Airlines. The main functions of this organisation can be summed up as promoting and developing the foreign tourist movement to Italy. In order to achieve this task the ENIT has to perform the following functions:

(i) carry out tourist promotion abroad through its overseas promotion offices;

(ii) create and administer overseas tourist offices;

(iii) collect and analyse statistical data pertaining to the international tourist movements;

(iv) carry out tourist marketing research and studies; and

(v) within its terms of reference, perform any other duties entrusted to it by the Ministry of Tourism and Entertainment.

ENIT is a public law body created in 1923 and reorganised by a presidential decree in August 1960. It has an autonomous legal status and is subject to the control of the Ministry of Tourism and Entertainment. The chief executive of this body is the president who is appointed by the Minister of Tourism and Entertainment. The president presides over the board of directors and the executive committee. In the case of his absence or inability to attend the board meetings, he is replaced by the senior most official among the three representatives of the Ministry of Tourism on the board. Following the president in the administrative structure of ENIT, the director general is the chief professional officer. Other senior officials are the inspector general, the chiefs of divisions and the directors of tourist offices abroad.

The ENIT supreme authority is invested in a council of administration which is nominated by a ministerial decree and comprises, in addition to the president, 28 members among whom 16 represent various ministries, regional boards of tourism, the autonomous bodies for cure, sojourn and tourism of whom four represent employers and four workers in the tourist enterprises. The executive committee comprises the president of ENIT and four board members to be nominated by the council. The committee adopts the necessary measures to implement the programmes of tourist activities laid down by the council of administration. ENIT has an independent operational budget which is financed by allocations put at its disposal by the ministry.

Regional Tourist Boards

The Regional Tourist Board (Ente Provinciale per il Turismo) is an intermediate level between the national and local levels. The boards were created first by the law decree of June 1935 and were reorganised by the presidential decree of August 1960. They have administrative autonomy and a public law status. The boards are situated in each regional capital and are subject to the ministry's supervision in carrying out their functions. The boards cover almost all activities in the region concerned with tourism. The following are the specific functions with which the regional tourist boards are concerned:

(i) to promote and develop the foreign tourist movement to the region;

(ii) to study tourist problems in the region and take necessary measures towards the growth of the regional tourist economy;

(iii) to take action aiming at exploitation of tourist attractions and resources;

(iv) to coordinate, within the region, all activities of a touristic nature and those activities exerted by various organisations concerned with tourism;

(v) to maintain relations with the regional, provincial and local authorities, with industry, chambers of commerce and other such organisations or associations having any tourist impact;

(vi) to collect and analyse tourist statistics;

(vii) to carry out inspection and classification of hotels and other types of accommodation and judge their rates; and

(ix) to carry out other duties which may be delegated to them by the minister of tourism and entertainment.

Each regional board is managed by a president, an administrative council and an executive committee. The president of the board is nominated by a ministerial decree for a term of four years. He is a political nominee and is the legal representative of the board. The president presides over the administrative council and the executive committee. The board is technically managed by a director who is usually a professional from a tourism field. The regional boards are financed through public funds by way of allocations by the ministry in its annual budget, and also partly through subsidies and contributions of organisations, associations and various bodies directly or indirectly interested in tourism. Close scrutiny of the functions of the boards will reveal that these are chiefly concerned with the development and growth of tourism in a region. The product development is the key function of the board in a particular region. A region often becomes a separate main destination within a country for a foreign tourist. As such, regions provide a basis for the formulation of tourist products which can be promoted in appropriate markets and which call for information services.

Autonomous Bodies for Cure, Sojourn and Tourism

The Autonomous Bodies for Cure, Sojourn and Tourism [Azienda Autonoma de Cura, Soggiorno e Turismo (ACST)] were instituted by the state in 1926 with the scope to promote tourism in their respective territorial zones under their competence. These were reorganised by the Presidential Decree of August 1960. These autonomous bodies, working on a local level, have the task of exerting all necessary efforts to expand the visitor traffic to the locality. They have administrative autonomy and public law status and are subject to the supervision of the Ministry of Tourism and Entertainment. The recognition of such a status is conferred on localities comprising the whole or part of the territory of one or more adjacent towns of the same province where the visitors' traffic constitutes an essential element of the economy of that locality. There are certain conditions specified pertaining to the minimum amount of sojourn tax required, availability of sufficient accommodation capacity, appropriate hygienic installations, satisfactory public services and sports equipments, etc. Each autonomous body for cure, sojourn and tourism has a president and a council of administration.

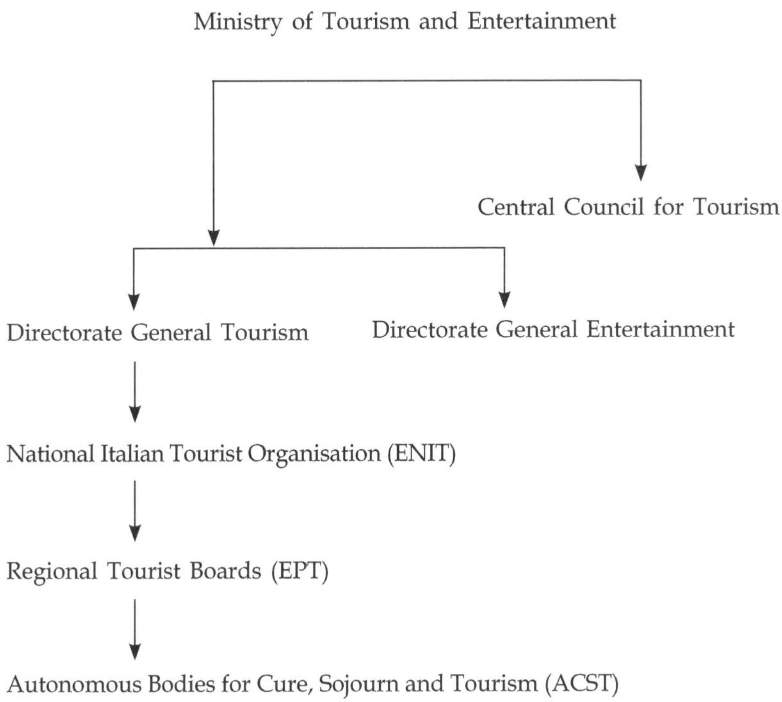

Fig 7.1 Organisation chart of the Ministry of Tourism and Entertainment (Italy)

Tourism in China

Tourism in China is a significant industry. The rate of tourism has greatly expanded over the last few decades since the beginning of reform and opening. The emergence of a newly rich middle class and an easing of restrictions on movement by the Chinese authorities are both fuelling this travel boom. China has become one of the world's most-watched and hottest inbound and outbound tourist markets. According to Xinhuanet, world is on the cusp of a sustained Chinese tourism boom.

As of 2015, China is the fourth most visited country in the world, after France, United States, and Spain, with 56.9 million international tourists per year.

In 2017, tourism contributed about CNY 8.77 trillion (USD 1.35 trillion), 11.04% of the GDP, and contributed direct and indirect employment of up to 28.25 million people. There were 139.48 million inbound trips and five billion domestic trips. Data from 2016 indicated that the majority of China's foreign tourists came (transferred) from Hong Kong, Macau, and Taiwan. Among the number of tourist arrivals who stayed for at least a night, 27.72 million came from Hong Kong, 4.81 million from Macau and 5.09 million from Taiwan. When adjusted to exclude transfers from Hong Kong, Macau and Taiwan, the number of tourist arrivals from foreign countries directly to China is 21.65 million.

China ranked second in the world for travel and tourism's contribution to GDP in 2014 ($943.1 billion), and first in the world for travel and tourism's contribution to employment (66,086,000 jobs in 2014). Tourism, based on direct, indirect, and induced impact, accounted for 9.3 percent of China's GDP in 2013.

Since 2012, tourists from have been the world's top spender in international tourism, leading global outbound travel. In 2016, the country accounted for 21% of the world's international tourism spending, or $261 billion. (Do note that the stats include journeys made to the special administrative regions of Hong Kong and Macau, as well as Taiwan; in 2017, these accounted for 69.5m of the so-called "overseas" journeys.) At the time, only 7% of Chinese had a passport, so the "potential for further growth is staggering", according to a UK news report.

History

Between 1949 and 1974, the People's Republic was closed to all but selected foreign visitors. In the late 1970s, when Deng Xiaopingdecided to promote tourism vigorously as a means of earning foreign exchange, China started to develop its tourist industry. Major hotel construction programs greatly increased the number of hotels and guest houses, more historic and scenic spots were renovated and opened to tourists, and professional guides and other service personnel were trained.

The expansion of domestic and international airline traffic and other tourist transportation facilities made travel more convenient. Over 250 cities and counties had been opened to foreign visitors by the mid-1980s. Travellers needed only valid visas or residence permits to visit 100 locations; the remaining locales required travel permits from public security departments. In 1985 approximately 1.4 million foreigners visited China, and nearly US$1.3 billion was earned from tourism.

Inbound

Sightseeing boats ply the river in Shanghai, providing just a tiny percent of the revenue from tourism China has become a major tourist destination following its reform and opening to the world in the late 1970s instigated by Deng Xiaoping. In 1978, China received about 230,000 international foreign tourists, mostly because of the severe limitations that the government placed on who was allowed to visit the country and who was not.

In 2016, overnight visitors increased 4.2% over the same period of 2015 to 59.27 million (of which over 60% came from Hong Kong, Macau and Taiwan). The corresponding income increased to USD 120 billion, an increase by 5.6% over the same period of 2015.

China National Tourism Administration

The China National Tourism Administration (CNTA; simplified Chinese, traditional Chinese: pinyin: GuójiāLuyóuJú) is a dissolved Chinese government authority responsible for the development of tourism in the country. The CNTA is subordinate to the State Council. Its headquarters are in Beijing, with regional branches in various provinces.

CNTA does not have the authority of a full department within the Chinese government to enforce regulations, but in other respects it acts as a ministry. Provincial CNTA offices in each Chinese province report to the central office in Beijing. CNTA has eighteen overseas offices called CNTO (China National Tourism Offices) that are charged with promoting tourism to China.[1] In Europe, there are CNTO offices in London and Paris.

CNTA is unique as a tourism office in that it is also responsible for controlling the outflow of tourists from China abroad.

The CNTA is dissolved on March 19, 2018; the duties are merged to the Ministry of Culture and Tourism.

Agency Structure

The agency is organised into the following areas.

- Office (Comprehensive Coordination Department)
- Department of Policy and Legal Affairs
- Department of Tourism Promotion and International Liaison
- Department of Planning
- Development and Finance
- Department of Quality Standardization and Administration
- Department of Affairs on Tourism of Hong Kong
- Macau & Taiwan, Department of Personnel
- Party Committee, Office of Retired Cadres

Directly Administered Agencies

- Service Center of CNTA
- Information Center of CNTA
- China Tourism Association, formerly known as the China National Tourism Institute
- China Tourism News Office
- China Travel and Tourism Press
- China Tourism Management Institute
- China Tourism Management Institute

Subordinate Associations

- China Association of Travel Services
- China Tourist Hotels Association
- China Tourism Automobile and Cruise Association and China Association of Tourism Journals

China National Tourism Administration

Chinese President Xi Jinping has pointed out that tourism is an important channel for communications and mutual learning between different countries and cultures, an effective means for developing the economy and increasing employment. In recent years, the world tourism industry has kept growing and become the largest and fastest-growing industry in the global economy. China National Tourism Administration (CNTA in short) is an institution in charge of China tourism directly affiliated to the State Council. It is one of those very important institutions in china that foreigners' issues get involved.

Responsibilities of CNTA

1. Coordinating the development of tourism, making development policies, planning and standards, drafting relevant laws and regulations and to supervise the implementation, as well as guiding the work of local tourism.
2. Establish and organize the implementation of the market development strategies of domestic tourism, inbound tourism and outbound tourism, organize the implementation of the publicity of the image of the National Tourism and other major promotional activities, as well as guide the work of overseas tourism offices.
3. Organize the survey, planning, development and protection of the tourism resources. Guide the planning and development of the key tourist areas, tourist destinations and tourist routes, and guide the leisure vocation industry. Monitor the operating of tourism economy and take charge of issuing tourism statistics and tourism industry information. Coordinate and guide holiday tourism and red tourism.
4. Standardize tourist market order, supervise the quality of service and maintain legal rights of tourists and operators. Normalize the operation and services of tourist enterprise and practitioners. Organize the drafting of standards on tourist regions, tourist services and tourist products, etc., and organize the implementation. Take charge of the overall coordination, supervision and management of tourist safety and emergency rescues. Guide the construction of the ideological infrastructure and the credibility system as well as operations of trade organisations.
5. Promote the international communication and cooperation of tourism and take charge of affairs relating to the cooperation with international tourism organisations. Make and organize the implement of policies of outbound tourism and border tourism. Examine and approve foreign travel agencies established

in China, examine the market access qualifications of foreign-invested travel agencies and travel agencies engaged in international tourism, examine and approve overseas (outbound) tourism and border tourism cases. Take charge of affairs on special tourism.

6. Establish policies on travel to Hong Kong, Macao & Taiwan with relevant departments and organize the implementation. Guide the promotion of tourist markets in Hong Kong, Macao & Taiwan. Take charge of the relevant issues on mainland residents travelling to Hong Kong, Macao and Taiwan, examine and approve Hong Kong, Macao and Taiwan's travel agency in mainland. Examine the market entry quantifications of travel agency investment of Hong Kong, Macao and Taiwan.
7. Formulate and organize implementation of the planning of educate tourism talent. Guide the tourism training work. Establish the eligibility criteria and rating standard of tourism practitioners with relevant authorities and supervise the implementation
8. Undertake other issues assigned by the State Council.

Structure of CNTA

Internal Institutions of CNTA:

Offices, Tourism Promotion and International Cooperation Department, Personnel Department, Supervision and Management Department, Party Membership Committee, Retired Cadres Office,

Organisations Directly Affiliated:

Authority Service Center, Information Center, China Tourism News, China Travel & Tourism Press, China Tourism Research Institute

Main Associations:

China Tourism Association, China Association of Travel Agents, China Tourist Hotel Association, China Tourism Automobile and Cruise Association, China Tourism Association Tourism Education Branch of the China Tourism Association, Hot Springs Branch of the China Tourism Association , Foreign Institutions of China Association Of Tourism Journals

China National Tourism Overseas Offices

Administration set up 18 overseas institutions in 15 countries and regions. These are:

- Tourism Office in Tokyo
- Tourism Office in Osaka,
- Tourism Office in Singapore,
- Tourism Office in Kathmandu,
- Tourism Office in Seoul,

- Tourism Office in New York,
- Tourism Office in Los Angeles,
- Tourism Office in Toronto,
- Tourism Office in London,
- Tourism Office in Paris,
- Tourism Office in Frankfurt,
- Tourism Office in Madrid,
- Tourism Office in Zurich,
- Tourism Office in Sydney,
- Tourism Office in Moscow.

Assistant Provided by CNTA

As tourism has become an important resource of economy growth and driving force for job creation, earning foreign exchange through export and promoting infrastructure construction. Chinese government especially the CNTA has attached great concern of travel service control, regulations and quality supervises. In recent years the quality service improvement of Chinese tourism industry has made a remarkable leap leading by the CNTA. Because we believe that the quality of tour guides and the services they provide is the key to the tourism industry perceive in China and abroad.

On 6th November 2017, CNTA had laid out new rules for tour guides ensuring the tourists in China could get a decent tour service. The new rules including punishments for tour guides who involved in misbehaviour clarified, forced shopping, charge extra money against a client's wishes, steering their clients to illegal or immoral activities, such as gambling, drugs or sex. Those who break the rules will have their licenses revoked and fined as well.

Apart from those new rules, over the past a few years, Chinese CNTA has spared no effort in a hygiene program called Toilet Revolution. Many important tourist cities in China have taken part in this toilet revolution and built thousands more modern and hygiene toilet in cities especially within tour site areas to serve the tourists better in a much more comfortable and more convenience condition.

To sum up, CNTA supervise the quality of service, maintain legal rights of tourists and operators, normalize the operation and services of tourist enterprise and practitioners. In addition taking complaints and dealing with related punishments are also the important services of CNTA for the tourists. In any rare occasion that you might need the detailed information listed below in contacting the CNTA Institute to Receive Complain of China Tourism: Tourism Quality Supervision Management Institute of National Tourism Administration.

The foregoing description of the tourism organisation in Italy shows the interest which the country takes in development and promotion of tourism. Although the ministry exercises a strong directing and controlling role, there appears to be a great degree of decentralisation in the organisation of Italian tourism. Not only local promotion, but also the whole of the tourist administration in individual regions, districts and towns is in the hands of local bodies with a substantial degree of autonomy, which are in turn represented at higher levels.

apter

ole o nternational Tourism r anisations

An organisation of a particular discipline having affiliation with an international body greatly helps in the promotion and development of a particular discipline. Global tourism development and promotion is influenced by various international agreements and mutually beneficial bilateral agreements. The various international and regional tourism organisations emerged with the objective of developing and promoting tourism. The role of these organisations in strengthening tourism by means of combined efforts is therefore of vital importance.

The world bodies or the international organisations provide a platform where ideas are exchanged and problems of mutual interest discussed. The subject specialists of various disciplines—be it arts, science or commerce—meet together on a common platform and discuss areas of mutual interest. This results in growth, development and promotion of the discipline. For any industry or discipline to develop, an organisation is an essential prerequisite as it plays a vital role in its proper planning, development and growth. An organisation consists of individuals whose primary role is the achievement of the objectives for which it has been set up. The aim of the organisation is to deploy staff into working groups, associating those with similar functions or purposes so as to move efficiently to obtain a desired result from their combined effort. In other words, organisation means combination of a group of individuals whose main purpose is to achieve through group action the objectives for which it has been set up.

The increasingly international character of modern tourism and the growing influence of international agencies in various fields are reflected in the growth and development of international cooperation and organisation in tourism. Organizers and the providers of various tourist services, whether in private or public sector, come together at various forums at the international level to discuss and share common problems and arrive at certain conclusions. The providers of tourist services sometimes meet as individuals or as individual firms, but more often when their national sectoral organisation is a member of a particular international body which has been set up for general or specific purposes.

There are numerous international organisations existing today. Some of these organisations are specifically concerned with development and promotion of tourism at the international level while others deal with the development and promotion of tourism in a particular region. There are other international organisations which do not concern themselves specifically with tourism but with fields indirectly connected with tourism like airlines, travel agents and the hoteliers.

Early History of Cooperative Endeavour

The history of cooperative endeavour in tourism can be traced back to the year 1908. Three countries—France, Spain and Portugal—felt the need of pooling their resources in the interest of promoting tourism and founded the Franc Hispano Portuguese Federation of Tourist Association. This might perhaps be considered as the first international tourist organisation. Although started in a modest way and limited to a small region in Europe, this association made a beginning in cooperative endeavour in the field of tourism and paved the way for future endeavours on a very large scale.

The need for international collaboration in the field of tourism found favour with many countries in the years following World War I. This need found its expression in setting up in 1924 of the International Union of Official Organisations for Tourist Propaganda. The first congress of the organisation was held at The Hague, the Netherlands, in 1925, and was attended by delegates from national tourist organisations of fourteen European countries. The aims of this congress were to exchange information on tourist publicity, to obtain international customs concessions for the export and import of tourist publicity material and to alleviate frontier formalities or other obstacles to free international tourist traffic. This organisation functioned with a considerable degree of success until the eve of the last World War. The International Union of Official Organisations for Tourist Propaganda was the forerunner of the International Union of Official Travel Organisations. In 1946, the representatives of various national tourist organisations met in London and the following year, in 1947, the International Union of Official Travel Organisations (IUOTO) was founded.

Although cooperative endeavour in the field of tourism began as early as in the year 1908 and the international organisation formed in the year 1924, the vital encouragement, however, came from the United Nations in 1963. The importance of the work of the international organisations in the field of tourism was recognised by the United Nations Conference on International Travel and Tourism held in Rome, in 1963. The conference recommended that the United Nations should consider the International Union of Official Travel Organisations (IUOTO) as its "main instrument for the promotion of tourism". The encouragement given by the United Nations to IUOTO paved the way for greater cooperation at international level in the field of tourism. India's first contact with the international tourism organisations was, however, established in the year 1950 when it joined the International Union of Official Travel Organisations.

International Union of Official Travel Organisations (IUOTO)

It was in 1925 that the international cooperation in tourism development had its beginning. The growth of international tourism in the twenties, and the consequent need for cooperation between national tourist bodies, led to the holding of an international conference in 1925 called by the National Tourist Office of Holland. Representatives of fourteen countries took part in the conference. Further conferences led to the setting up of the International Union of National Tourist Propaganda Organisations (IUNTPO) at The Hague. This body sought to promote facilitation and overcome the obstacles to free international tourist traffic; such obstacles having come about as a result of the First World War. IUNTPO, whose general aims were more streamlined than its title, established close contact with the economic committee of the then League of Nations.

With the advent of the Second World War, IUNTPO had to discontinue its activities. It was with the object of contributing to post-War reconstruction that one of its members, the Travel Association of Great Britain and Northern Ireland, decided in the spring of 1946 to call a world conference of national tourist organisations to discuss the restoration and reconstruction of travel facilitation destroyed by the War. The conference took place in London in October 1946 and the following year, in 1947, the International Union of Official Travel Organisations (IUOTO) was founded. The organisation represented over one hundred national tourist offices of various countries as full members and about eighty-eight national and international organisations, of both public and private sector, as associate members. It was at that time the only organisation whose activities related to every aspect of tourism throughout the world. One of its major tasks was the stimulation and coordination of tourism development. The category of full members was restricted to national tourist organisations or other organisations set up to promote the development of tourism established or recognised by the governments of the countries. The category of associate members was confined to international or national organisations, either commercial or non-commercial, representing tourist interest or interested in promotion of tourism.

The Aim of the IUOTO

The IUOTO was the only international organisation which grouped together the governmental or official tourist organisations of all parts of the world on the basis of one for each country and territory. The principal aim of the organisation was to stimulate and increase the free flow of persons in the interest of economic development and to strengthen social and cultural relations. This it tried to do by way of resolving the problems arising in the field of tourist movements and in the adoption of a common policy amongst the members for all questions dealing with international travel. The organisation tried in various ways to develop the tourist industry in the member countries, and particularly by promoting measures on a national as well as on an international level aimed at reducing travel barriers and stimulating the movement of travellers.

A technical and specialised organisation, IUOTO was granted consultative status by the United Nations. The supreme body of the IUOTO was the General Assembly which held its meeting once a year. It had various committees and commissions which were assigned different subjects. The executive committee consisted of full members, while the regional commissions covered specific areas. The technical commissions aimed at examining all problems on a universal scale. The Secretariat General, whose headquarters were located at Geneva in Switzerland, was responsible for ensuring liaison between the members.

Figure 7.1 shows the various IUOTO bodies responsible for drawing up and implementing its policy.

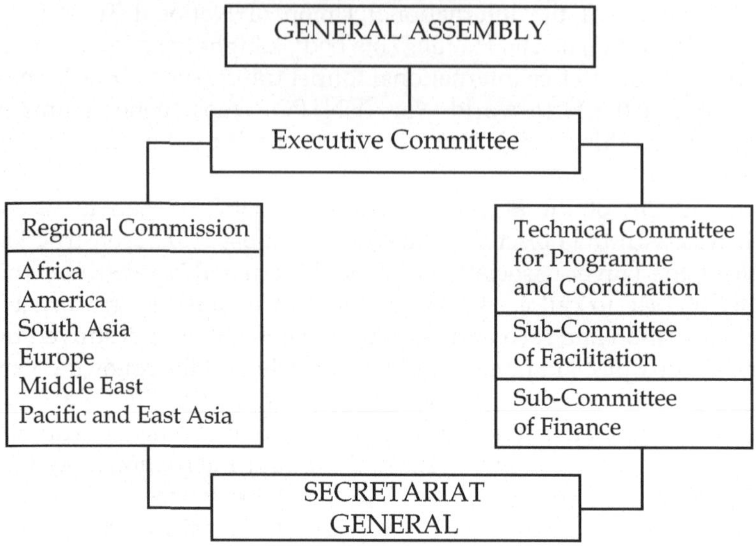

Fig 8.1 Organisation chart of IUOTO

The General Assembly

The General Assembly, which consisted of full and associate members, was a sovereign body of the IUOTO. It met once a year. It elected the president and the vice president of the IUOTO, the members of the executive committee and the auditors and decided upon the applications for new membership. Laying down general policy of the organisation and the actions to be carried out was another important function of the General Assembly.

The Executive Committee

The Executive Committee consisted of eighteen full members, representing the various geographical areas and, in an ex-officio capacity, the presidents of the regional and technical commissions. Presided over by the president of the IUOTO and assisted by the vice presidents, the Executive Committee was responsible to the General Assembly for the direction of the affairs of the IUOTO.

Regional Commissions

The following regional commissions were created by the IUOTO:

(a) The Regional Travel Commission for Europe included the countries of western and eastern Europe. The countries of western Europe were also grouped in the European Travel Commission which was an independent body responsible in particular for the collective publicity campaigns carried out in the United States of America.

(b) The African Travel Commission was responsible for tourism in African areas which had vast possibilities for growth.

(c) The Regional Travel Commission for the Pacific and East Asia had members who were also members of the Pacific Area Travel Association (PATA), which had accepted to act as the regional commission for the Pacific and the east Asian areas.
(d) The South Asian Travel Commission was responsible for developing modern travel facilities in a very extensive area which had become travel conscious.
(e) The Middle East Travel Commission was responsible for developing travel facilities in the area. It had also created sub-commissions of the Arab and non-Arab countries.
(f) The Regional Travel Commission for the Americas was created following the acceptance of the Inter-American Travel Congress to act as regional travel commission of the IUOTO for the American continent as a whole.

Technical Committees

IUOTO had the following technical committees:

(1) The Committee on the Elimination of Travel Barriers was concerned with the easing up of passport and visa requirements, frontier formalities including restrictions on the free circulation of publicity material, health regulations, taxes borne directly or indirectly by the tourists and tourist industry, currency controls and other matters which slow down travel.
(2) The Research Committee was charged with studying international travel statistics as well as carrying out other special studies with the assistance of the Advisory Committee.
(3) The Travel Plant Committee was responsible for studies on hotels as well as motels, hotel accommodation and classification, standardization of hotel guides, state aid to the hotel industry, the training of hotel personnel and additional means of accommodation.
(4) The Committee on Travel Development offered assistance to member countries in the field of travel, counselled national tourist offices on publicity activities, dealt with social tourism and youth and credit travel. The committee also dealt with travel films, which came to be regarded as one of the most important means of tourist publicity.
(5) The Transport Committee was responsible for examining the existing conditions in the field of rail, road, sea and air transportation and suggesting better facilities and improvements. It studied and recommended measures to improve the conditions and facilities available at airports, seaports and land frontier entry points.

The Secretariat General

The Secretariat General, which was located in Geneva, was the principal executive body for the decisions of the assembly and the executive committee as well as the presidency. It ensured the liaison between the members of the IUOTO, carried out the studies entrusted to it by the IUOTO members and was charged with the administration. It maintained contact with other international organisations. It produced various IUOTO publications and ensured the functioning of the Tourist Documentation Centre.

IUOTO had closer cooperation with the United Nations Economic and Social Council (ECOSOC), the Wold Health Organisation (WHO), the International Labour Organisation (ILO), the International Civil Aviation Organisation (ICAO) and the Inter-Governmental Maritime Consultative Organisation (IMCO). It also had permanent links with the regional commissions of the United Nations.

The Objectives of IUOTO

The organisation was set up with the following objectives:

(i) To promote the economic development of countries through tourism.

(ii) To enhance the social and cultural role of tourism in the life of nations.

(iii) To further the vital contribution of tourism to international trade.

(iv) To foster the steady expansion of international tourist flow.

(v) To supply its members with the results of the permanent tourist market research to enable them to keep abreast of development in this field.

(vi) To protect the interests of tourists and the tourist industry.

(vii) To gain recognition of the value of tourism as a means of promoting international understanding and world peace.

In order to achieve its objectives, the organisation undertook various activities like monitoring and identifying trends in world tourism, studies on travel demands, market trends, tourist motivation, surveys of environmental effects of travel expansion and formulation of recommendations for the protection of natural and cultural resources. Other activities included acting as clearing house for tourist information, keeping its members informed of tourism development and its economic and social aspects, publication of material, fostering research in the field of tourism, organising vocational training programmes and promoting the implementation of international agreements.

IUOTO's dynamic activities resulted in countless significant achievements. Some of the achievements were undertaken jointly with other organisations. These included preparation and participation in the United Nations on Customs Facilities and Tourism (1954), initiation, preparation and participation in the United Nations Conference on International Travel and Tourism in Rome (1963) and initiation and realization of International Tourist Year (1967). Besides establishing the Tourist Documentation Centre, the IUOTO has been responsible for organising various international travel research seminars and workshops. Another significant achievement of IUOTO has been the establishment of the International Centre for Advanced Tourism Studies at Turin, Italy and organisation of inter-departmental or specialized seminars on marketing, management, physical planning and promotion. It had also organised correspondence courses for the staff working in the field of tourism. Annual compilation and publication of official international travel statistics is yet another significant achievement of the IUOTO.

The IUOTO was the only non-governmental organisation whose activities covered every sector of tourism throughout the world. The organisation made a pioneering effort in the stimulation and coordination of tourism development at the international level. This pioneering task of the organisation is now being carried out by the World Tourism Organisation. The World Tourism Organisation came into existence as a result of the transformation of IUOTO on January 2, 1975. It was called upon to succeed IUOTO.

India joined the International Union of Official Travel Organisations in 1950.

World Tourism Organisation

History

The origin of UNWTO stems back to 1920 when the International Congress of Official Tourist Traffic Associations (ICOTT) was formed at The Hague. Some articles from early volumes of the Annals of Tourism Research,[4] claim that the UNWTO originated from the International Union of Official Tourist Publicity Organisations (IUOTPO), although the UNWTO states that the ICOTT became the International Union of Official Tourist Publicity Organisations first in 1934.

Following the end of the Second World War and with international travel numbers increasing, the IUOTPO restructured itself into the International Union of Official Travel Organisations (IUOTO). A technical, non-governmental organisation, the IUOTO was made up of a combination of national tourist organisations, industry and consumer groups. The goals and objectives of the IUOTO were to not only promote tourism in general but also to extract the best out of tourism as an international trade component and as an economic development strategy for developing nations.

Towards the end of the 1960s, the IUOTO realised the need for further transformation to enhance its role on an international level. The 20th IUOTO general assembly in Tokyo, 1967, declared the need for the creation of an intergovernmental body with the necessary abilities to function on an international level in cooperation with other international agencies, in particular the United Nations. Throughout the existence of the IUOTO, close ties had been established between the organisation and the United Nations (UN) and initial suggestions had the IUOTO becoming part of the UN. However, following the circulation of a draft convention, consensus held that any resultant intergovernmental organisation should be closely linked to the UN but preserve its "complete administrative and financial autonomy".

It was on the recommendations of the UN that the formation of the new intergovernmental tourism organisation was based. Resolution 2529 of the XXIVth UN general assembly stated:

In 1970, the IUOTO general assembly voted in favour of forming the World Tourism Organisation (WTO). Based on statutes of the IUOTO, and after ratification by the prescribed 51 states, the WTO came into operation on November 1, 1974.

The World Tourism Organisation (WTO), an inter-governmental technical body dealing with all aspects of tourism, began its legal existence on January 2, 1975. It was born of the International Union of Official Travel Organisations (IUOTO). The swift expansion of travel had created the need for a world body able to deal with tourism problems at the government level, and this led to the transformation of IUOTO into WTO. Like its predecessor, the WTO has a very emphatic technical character, essentially creative and dynamic, performing a well-defined service for its member states. The aims of the organisation, its raison d'êter, are defined with clarity in Article 3 of the statute which is divided into three sections:

(i) The fundamental aim of the organisation shall be the promotion and development of tourism with a view to contributing to economic development, international understanding, peace, prosperity, and universal respect for, and observance of, human rights and fundamental freedoms for all without distinction to either race, sex, language or religion. The organisation shall take all appropriate action to attain this objective.

(ii) In pursuing this aim, the organisation shall pay particular attention to the interests of the developing countries in the field of tourism.

(iii) In order to establish its central role in the field of tourism, the organisation shall establish and maintain effective collaboration with the appropriate organs of the United Nations and its specialized agencies. In this connection the organisation shall seek a cooperative relationship with and participation in the activities of the United Nations Development Programme (UNDP), as a participating and executing agency.

The World Tourism Organisation was originally conceived as an inter-governmental organisation in a UN General Assembly resolution (Number 2529) on December 5, 1969. This resolution called for establishment of WTO to play a "central and decisive role" in the field of tourism and to maintain effective collaboration with the appropriate organs of the United Nations and its specialized agencies.

At Torremolinos (Spain), in June 1977, the second General Assembly of WTO approved an agreement with the United Nations for cooperation and relationships. On December 20, 1977 the 32nd General Assembly of the UN approved this agreement which is now in force. In immediate implementation of this agreement, the UN General Assembly in December 1977 also approved a resolution sponsored by the Philippines with 24 co-sponsors, including India, requesting the WTO "to intensify its efforts to promote tourism, particularly in developing countries, through international cooperation and to report to the General Assembly at its 33rd session on action taken". The WTO became an executing agency of the UNDP in May 1976. A few months later, UNDP resident representatives throughout the world became WTO representatives for all matters concerning technical cooperation in the field of tourism. The WTO has already completed its first project in Jordan and is now processing many more requests from member states, including Asian members, for both national and regional assistance programmes and projects.

Membership of WTO

There are three categories of members:

(i) full members

(ii) associate members

(iii) affiliate members.

Full members are the sovereign states. Associate members are the territories or groups of territories not responsible for their external relations but whose membership is approved by the state assuming responsibility for their external relations. Affiliate members are international bodies, both inter-governmental and non-governmental, concerned with specialized interests in tourism, as well as commercial and non-commercial bodies and associations whose activities are related to the aims of WTO.

The activities of the organisation include: (i) clearing house for all available information on international and domestic tourism including statistical data, legislation and regulation and special events and its systematic collection, analysis and dissemination; (ii) making travel easier by reducing and simplifying frontier formalities and removing barriers to the free movement of tourists; (iii) organising and convening international conferences, seminars, round tables and technical meetings on all aspects of tourism; (iv) preparation of draft international agreements on tourism; and (v) examining vocational training programmes with a view to contributing to the establishment of suitable teaching programmes tailored to specific needs, especially in the developing countries. The permanent activities of WTO include the collection and updating of available information on training needs. Special activities include participation in technical cooperation projects for vocational training.

Functioning of WTO

There are three following organs through which WTO functions:

(i) ***General Assembly***: This is the supreme organ and sovereign body of WTO composed of delegates representing full members, associate members and representatives of affiliate members. It meets every two years and may consider any question and make recommendations on any matter within the competence of WTO. The General Assembly has created six regional commissions. The regions covered are Africa, the Americas, Europe, Middle East, the Pacific and East Asia and South Asia. The regional commissions ensure the implementation, within their respective regions, of the decisions and recommendations of the General Assembly and the Executive Council. They function and operate within the framework of the organisation. There are the regional secretariats which are an integral part of the WTO Secretariat and help the regional commissions in organising and covering their conferences and meetings.

(ii) ***Executive Council***: It consists of full members elected by the assembly at the ratio of one member for every five full members of WTO organisation with a view to achieving fair and equitable geographical distribution. The Executive Council, among other matters, takes all necessary measures in consultation with the Secretary General, for the implementation of the decisions and recommendations of the assembly, and reports thereon to the assembly. The Council meets at least twice a year.

(iii) ***The Secretariat***: The Secretariat consists of the Secretary General and such staff as the organisation may require. The Secretary General is responsible for carrying out the general policy and work programme of the organisation in accordance with the directions of the General Assembly and Executive Council. The Secretary General ensures the legal representation of the organisation.

By the decision of the first General Assembly of WTO in May 1975, the headquarters were set up in Madrid (Spain) in January 1976. The activities of the organisation cover all sectors of tourism on a worldwide basis. The WTO works in cooperation with all international organisations, the United Nations in particular, as well as with commercial and non-commercial bodies involved in tourism. The organisation is performing extremely useful service of concrete and creative character by facilitating the exchange of technical information; the making of specialized studies, the holding of special seminars adapted to world regional requirements and advanced vocational training courses. The essentially practical nature of its work programme, tailored as it is to regional requirements, takes full cognizance of the problems peculiar to countries and regions in all stages of development, such as investments, financial questions, physical planning and area development, economic analysis, marketing and market surveys—all this not only with a secretarial approach but with a comprehensive concern from the point of view of the state.

The creation of WTO coincided with the universal recognition of tourism as an important instrument of economic and social development and its consequent ascendancy to full government responsibility. An inter-governmental body of tourism officials, the WTO is empowered to act in the name of their governments and speak in terms of the impact of tourism on the balance of payments. The creation of WTO thus is not only a proof that the states are fully conscious of their own responsibilities in the field of tourism, but also of the establishment of tourism to its rightful ranking at international level.

Like its predecessor, the IUOTO, the WTO's activities cover all sectors of tourism on a worldwide basis. It provides an international forum where tourism officials, whether governmental or non-governmental, can discuss problems and exchange ideas. Representatives of the private sector also have access to its membership. WTO works in close cooperation with almost all international organisations, the United Nations' organisations in particular, as well as with commercial and non-commercial bodies involved in tourism.

India is a full member of the World Tourism Organisation.

Member States of WTO

As of July 2017, membership of the UNWTO included 156 states, six territories (Flemish Community (1997), Puerto Rico (2002), Aruba (1987), Hong Kong (1999), Macau (1981), Madeira (1995)), and two permanent observers (Holy See (1979), Palestine (1999)). Seventeen state members have withdrawn from the organisation for different periods in the past: Australia, Bahamas, Bahrain, Belgium, Canada, Costa Rica, El Salvador, Grenada, Honduras, Kuwait, Latvia, Malaysia, Myanmar, Panama, Philippines, Qatar, Thailand, United Kingdom and Puerto Rico (as an associate member).The Netherland Antilles was an associate member before its dissolution.

Non-members are: Antigua and Barbuda, Barbados, Belgium, Belize, Comoros, Denmark, Dominica, Estonia, Finland, Grenada, Guyana, Iceland, Ireland, Kiribati, Latvia, Liechtenstein, Luxembourg, Marshall Islands, Micronesia, Nauru, New Zealand, Palau, Saint Kitts and Nevis, Saint Lucia, Saint Vincent and the Grenadines, Samoa, Singapore, Solomon Islands, Somalia, South Sudan, Suriname, Sweden, Tonga, Tuvalu, United Kingdom, United States.

The United Arab Emirates (UAE) rejoined the organisation in May 2013, 26 years after having left UNWTO.

Additionally, for a United Nations specialized agency, UNWTO has over 500 affiliate members, representing the private sector, educational institutions, tourism associations and local tourism authorities, non-governmental entities with specialised interests in tourism, and commercial and non-commercial bodies and associations with activities related to the aims of UNWTO or falling within its competence.

Member States

List of the 158 Member States of the UNWTO and the year of admission in the Organisation.

Table 8.2

List of Member States of UNWTO

Country	Region	Admission	Previously	
1	Afghanistan	South Asia	1975	
2	Albania	Europe	1993	
3	Algeria	Africa	1976	
4	Andorra	Europe	1995	
5	Angola	Africa	1989	
6	Argentina	Americas	1975	
7	Armenia	Europe	1997	
8	Austria	Europe	1975	
9	Azerbaijan	Europe	2001	
10	Bahamas	Americas	2005	1975 → 1978
11	Bahrain	Middle East	2001	1977 → 1984
12	Bangladesh	South Asia	1975	
13	Barbados	Americas	2015	
14	Belarus	Europe	2005	
15	Benin	Africa	1975	
16	Bhutan	South Asia	2003	
17	Bolivia	Americas	1975	
18	Bosnia and Herzegovina	Europe	1993	
19	Botswana	Africa	1995	
20	Brazil	Americas	1975	
21	Brunei Darussalam	East Asia and the Pacific	2007	
22	Bulgaria	Europe	1976	
23	Burkina Faso	Africa	1975	
24	Burundi	Africa	1975	
25	Cabo Verde	Africa	2001	
26	Cambodia	East Asia and the Pacific	1975	
27	Cameroon	Africa	1975	
28	Central African Republic	Africa	1995	
29	Chad	Africa	1985	
30	Chile	Americas	1975	

31	China	East Asia and the Pacific	1983	
32	Colombia	Americas	1975	
33	Congo	Africa	1979	
34	Costa Rica	Americas	1995	1975 → 1988
35	Côte d'Ivoire	Africa	1975	
36	Croatia	Europe	1993	
37	Cuba	Americas	1975	
38	Cyprus	Europe	1975	
39	Czech Republic	Europe	1993	
40	Democratic People's Republic of Korea	East Asia and the Pacific	1987	
41	Democratic Republic of the Congo	Africa	1979	
42	Djibouti	Africa	1997	
43	Dominican Republic	Americas	1975	
44	Ecuador	Americas	1975	
45	Egypt	Middle East	1975	
46	El Salvador	Americas	1993	1975 → 1981
47	Equatorial Guinea	Africa	1995	
48	Eritrea	Africa	1995	
49	Eswatini (the Kingdom of)	Africa	1999	
50	Ethiopia	Africa	1975	
51	Federal Republic of Somalia	Africa	2017	
52	Fiji	East Asia and the Pacific	1997	
53	France	Europe	1975	
54	Gabon	Africa	1975	
55	Gambia	Africa	1975	
56	Georgia	Europe	1993	
57	Germany	Europe	1976	
58	Ghana	Africa	1975	
59	Greece	Europe	1975	
60	Guatemala	Americas	1993	
61	Guinea	Africa	1985	
62	Guinea-Bissau	Africa	1991	
63	Haiti	Americas	1975	
64	Honduras	Americas	2001	1975 → 1989
65	Hungary	Europe	1975	
66	India	South Asia	1975	
67	Indonesia	East Asia and the Pacific	1975	
68	Iran, Islamic Republic of	South Asia	1975	
69	Iraq	Middle East	1975	
70	Israel	Europe	1975	

71	Italy	Europe	1978	
72	Jamaica	Americas	1975	
73	Japan	East Asia and the Pacific	1978	
74	Jordan	Middle East	1975	
75	Kazakhstan	Europe	1993	
76	Kenya	Africa	1975	
77	Kuwait	Middle East	2003	1975 → 1998
78	Kyrgyzstan	Europe	1993	
79	Lao People's Democratic Republic	East Asia and the Pacific	1975	
80	Lebanon	Middle East	1975	
81	Lesotho	Africa	1981	
82	Liberia	Africa	2011	
83	Libya	Middle East	1977	
84	Lithuania	Europe	2003	
85	Madagascar	Africa	1975	
86	Malawi	Africa	1975	
87	Malaysia	East Asia and the Pacific	1991	1975 → 1987
88	Maldives	South Asia	1981	
89	Mali	Africa	1975	
90	Malta	Europe	1978	
91	Mauritania	Africa	1976	
92	Mauritius	Africa	1975	
93	Mexico	Americas	1975	
94	Monaco	Europe	2001	
95	Mongolia	East Asia and the Pacific	1990	
96	Montenegro	Europe	2007	
97	Morocco	Africa	1975	
98	Mozambique	Africa	1995	
99	Myanmar	East Asia and the Pacific	2012	1995 → 1999
100	Namibia	Africa	1997	
101	Nepal	South Asia	1975	
102	Netherlands	Europe	1976	
103	Nicaragua	Americas	1991	
104	Niger	Africa	1979	
105	Nigeria	Africa	1975	
106	Oman	Middle East	2004	
107	Pakistan	South Asia	1975	
108	Panama	Americas	1996	1975 → 1993
109	Papua New Guinea	East Asia and the Pacific	2005	
110	Paraguay	Americas	1992	
111	Peru	Americas	1975	

112	Philippines	East Asia and the Pacific	1991	1975 → 1989
113	Poland	Europe	1976	
114	Portugal	Europe	1976	
115	Qatar	Middle East	2002	1977 → 1986
116	Republic of Korea	East Asia and the Pacific	1975	
117	Republic of Moldova	Europe	2002	
118	Romania	Europe	1975	
119	Russian Federation	Europe	1975	
120	Rwanda	Africa	1975	
121	Samoa	East Asia and the Pacific	2015	
122	San Marino	Europe	1975	
123	Sao Tome and Principe	Africa	1985	
124	Saudi Arabia	Middle East	2002	
125	Senegal	Africa	1975	
126	Serbia	Europe	2001	
127	Seychelles	Africa	1991	
128	Sierra Leone	Africa	1975	
129	Slovakia	Europe	1993	
130	Slovenia	Europe	1993	
131	South Africa	Africa	1994	
132	Spain	Europe	1975	
133	Sri Lanka	South Asia	1975	
134	Sudan	Africa	1975	
135	Switzerland	Europe	1976	
136	Syrian Arab Republic	Middle East	1975	
137	Tajikistan	Europe	2007	
138	Thailand	East Asia and the Pacific	1996	1975 → 1990
139	The former Yugoslav Republic of Macedonia	Europe	1995	
140	Timor-Leste	East Asia and the Pacific	2005	
141	Togo	Africa	1975	
142	Trinidad and Tobago	Americas	2013	1975 → 1977
143	Tunisia	Africa	1975	
144	Turkey	Europe	1975	
145	Turkmenistan	Europe	1993	
146	Uganda	Africa	1975	
147	Ukraine	Europe	1997	
148	Union of the Comoros	Africa	2017	
149	United Arab Emirates	Middle East	2013	1975 → 1987
150	United Republic of Tanzania	Africa	1975	
151	Uruguay	Americas	1977	
152	Uzbekistan	Europe	1993	

153	Vanuatu	East Asia and the Pacific	2009	
154	Venezuela	Americas	1975	
155	Vietnam	East Asia and the Pacific	1981	
156	Yemen	Middle East	1977	
157	Zambia	Africa	1975	
158	Zimbabwe	Africa	1981	

Associate Members

Member States

- Member States
- Associate Members
- Observers

Regions

- Africa
- Americas
- East Asia & the Pacific
- Europe
- Middle East
- South Asia

Table 8.3

Associate Members

Associate Member				
	Country	**Region**	**Admission**	**Previously**
1	Aruba	Americas	1987	
2	Flanders	Europe	1997	
3	Hong Kong, China	East Asia and the Pacific	1999	
4	Macao, China	East Asia and the Pacific	1981	
5	Madeira, Portugal	Europe	1995	
6	Puerto Rico	Americas	2002	1985 → 199

UNWTO Affiliate Members

The **Affiliate Members** are companies (public or private), organisations, destinations, NGOs, educational institutions or bodies whose activities are related to tourism and which contribute to the **UNWTO** their knowledge and expertise to promote the development of tourism that's responsible, sustainable and accessible for everyone.

The Affiliate Member organisations are:

- **Advanced**: They are at the vanguard of innovation, developing new technologies, carrying out research and training the tourism professionals of the future.
- **Diverse**: The variety of organisations that are affiliated to **UNWTO** brings great value and enriches the exchange of ideas and knowledge.

For example, the members belong to airlines, travel agencies, destination promotion agencies, hotel groups, universities, business schools, trade unions, IT companies, specialized training centres and businesses involved in services, environmental research and sustainability.

- **International**: Being located across five continents means that the **Affiliate Members** can keep up to date with specialist national, regional and local knowledge. It also allows them to form partnerships with similar organisations in other parts of the world.

UNWTO Affiliate Members - Facts and Figures

- Have **Affiliate Members** with bases in **more than 80 countries**.
- **Over one million + people - employed** among the **Affiliate Members** and their partners.
- Highly internationalized: **70% operate in more than one country**.
- **1 in 5 Members operates in all world** regions.
- **More than 100 universities**, research centres and training schools dedicated to investigating, generating and sharing their research.

WTO's General Programme of Work

The World Tourism Organisation (WTO) is the only worldwide organisation focusing upon all aspects of tourism. It is a leading inter-governmental organisation in tourism. It provides a vital forum for governments and the industry to meet and address issues of common interest and concern. The WTO's general programme of work covers six broad areas:

(i) ***Cooperation for Development*:** Advice and assistance to governments on a wide range of tourism issues including master plans and feasibility studies, investment needs and technology transfer to marketing and promotion.

(ii) ***Education and Training*:** A strategic framework for the organisation of tourism education and training including courses on educating educators, short term and distance- learning courses and a growing network of WTO education and training centres.

(iii) ***Statistics and Market Research*:** WTO functions as the foremost centre for the collection, analysis and dissemination of tourism data from over 180 countries and territories. It continuously monitors and analyses trends around the world. A comprehensive series of publications is produced for members and the industry.

(iv) ***Environment and Planning***: WTO is working for sustainable tourism development and the translation of environmental concerns into practical measures. It participates in forums and summits concerning global issues on environment.

(v) ***Communication and Documentation:*** WTO's communication and documentation work relates to publication and distribution of several books, monographs, technical papers, and news and information bulletins such as *Yearbook of Tourism Statistics, Compendium of Tourism Statistics, Forecasts of Tourism Trends, World Directory of Tourism Education, National and Regional Planning and Sustainable Tourism Guides,* etc. The communication and documentation section of WTO also works as press contact point for the organisation.

(vi) ***Quality of Tourism Services***: Liberalization, health and safety reflect the broad and interconnected range of issues related to improving the quality of tourism services. WTO is working towards the removal of barriers to tourism and is encouraging the liberalization of trade and tourism services. Additional activities in this area include measures for improving health and food safety and making tourism more accessible to the handicapped.

Pacific Asia Travel Asssociation (PATA)

The Pacific Asia Travel Association (PATA) was founded in the year 1951 as a non-profit corporation to stimulate interest in the Pacific region as a vacation land, and to develop, promote and facilitate travel to and among the many Pacific destinations. The association had 44 founder members. The founder, Lorrin Thurston, a leading newspaper publisher in Honolulu, had an idea to organize all travel from the Occident to the Pacific area in a consistent, cohesive and systematic manner so as to ensure maximum benefit from existing opportunities and the creation of fresh opportunities through multimedia publicity. PATA's first conference was held in January 1952 in Honolulu and its headquarters established in San Francisco, USA in 1953. PATA has its own director for Europe who is based in London and works to promote traffic from the European markets into the Pacific region. PATA's first Asian office was opened in Manila, Philippines in 1976.

A Non Profit Organisation

PATA is a non-profit organisation set up with the objective of developing, promoting and facilitating travel to and within the Pacific area and South-East Asian region including India. It primarily operates in the United States market which is the world's biggest travel market. The organisation provides the meeting point for the people involved in all aspects of the travel trade from a large number of countries. It focuses attention on travel opportunities in member countries and builds up awareness and specific contacts among the travel trade in countries from where the tourists originate. The underlying philosophy of PATA is that the entire travel industry must work together to develop an ever-increasing flow of pleasure travel from which each member will derive a fair share of the total business.

Activities

The activities of PATA include assisting small and up and coming destinations to develop their infrastructure, providing expertise, planning group travel schemes, destinations, hotels operations and discounts. It provides up-to-date information and practical and theoretical experience in the field of tourism. The annual conferences of PATA and its workshops provide greater scope to its members to share their ideas and exchange views about promotion of tourism in their respective regions. PATA staff are outstanding experts in their respective fields of marketing and research and regularly exchange information with others on latest techniques and practices in their respective areas. All members benefit directly or indirectly from the continuing programmes of PATA, which include travel research, marketing, training programmes, and the development of visitor plants and services.

Promotion

Promotion occupies a major portion of PATA's total effort. The PATA publication, *Pacific Travel News,* is relied upon by wholesale and retail travel agents as an important source of authoritative material on the Pacific. Recently, PATA has produced the first edition of the *Pacific Area Destination Handbook* which compiles in a single volume all the data that are required for the planning and sale of travel. It is the world's most authoritative and comprehensive handbook on 31 Pacific destinations. PATA also publishes its *Hotel Directory and Travel Guide* listing the hotels, resorts and travel services in the Pacific area.

PATA Membership

PATA has nine categories of membership:

(i) active government
(ii) associate government
(iii) active carrier
(iv) associate carrier
(v) active industry
(vi) allied members
(vii) affiliated allied
(viii) associate members and
(ix) sustaining members

Active government members consist of the primary official organisation designated by the government of any nation, territory, or political division, wholly or partly in the Pacific area. *Associate government* members consist of any organisation charged with the responsibility of the domestic or overseas promotion of tourism as designated by the government of any nation, territory, or political division either situated outside or within the Pacific area but not being the primary official organisation designated for the overseas promotion of travel, or not meeting other criteria as might be required for active government membership. *Active carrier* members consist of any government recognised, registered or certified air or steamship line operating vehicles having individual passenger capacity in excess of twelve passengers and providing regular scheduled common carriage passenger service to and within the Pacific area. *Associate carrier* members consist of any government-recognised passenger-carrier operating vehicles (a) each having a passenger capacity of twelve or fewer passengers and providing regular scheduled common carriage passenger service or (b) having a passenger capacity in excess of twelve passengers but not providing passenger service in the regular common carriage basis as prescribed for active carrier members. *Active industry* members consist of hotel organisation having management authority as distinguished from mere sales, advertising reservations direction, over one or more hotels with a total of one thousand or more guest rooms in one or more Pacific areas, tour operator organisations excluding air or ship transportation. *Allied members* consist of travel agencies, tour operators, hotel representatives and firms serving as general agents of or representing various segments of the Pacific travel industry. *Affiliated allied* members consist of branch offices of an allied member travel agency or tour operator. *Associate members* consist of individual operating organisations and firms such as communication media, media representatives, advertising, public relations and research agencies having definite interest in Pacific travel. *Sustaining members* consist of those organisations, firms or individuals whose commercial or cultural interests, in the judgement of the board of directors, will further contribute to the aims of the association.

The control of PATA is vested in the active government, carrier and industry members. The organisations qualifying for active government or active carrier membership have the right to membership. They require no sponsorship and are requested merely to provide the board of directors with certain pertinent information. Membership in all other categories is at the discretion of the board of directors, and requires not only that the organisation comply with certain guidelines for eligibility, but also that certain categories of PATA members must sponsor the new applicant and vouch for its stability and professionalism.

Presently PATA has a membership drawn from over 50 countries. Besides it has over 50 state and local tourism bodies, 65 airlines and cruise lines, and more than 2,000 travel industry companies. PATA'S chapter membership includes over 17,000 travel professionals in 79 PATA chapters located throughout the world.

India, which was an associate member of PATA since 1957, became a full-fledged active member in 1964.

List of Active Members of PATA

Table 8.4

(i) **Active Governments**

1. American Samoa Office of Tourism
2. Australian Tourist Commission
3. Bangladesh Parjatan Corporation
4. Tourism Bureau of the Republic of China
5. Cook Islands Tourist Authority
6. Fiji Visitors Bureau
7. Guam Visitors Bureau

8. Hawaii, Department of Planning and Economic Development
9. Hong Kong Tourist Association
10. India, Department of Tourism
11. Indonesia, Directorate General of Tourism
12. Japan National Tourist Organisation
13. Kiribati, Ministry of Natural Resource Development
14. Korea National Tourism Corporation
15. Macau, Department of Information and Tourism
16. Tourist Development Corporation of Malaysia
17. Mexican National Tourist Council
18. Micronesia, Department of Development Services
19. Nepal, Department of Tourism
20. New Caledonia, Office du Tourisme
21. New Zealand Government Tourist and Publicity Department
22. Pakistan, Ministry of Culture and Tourism
23. Papua New Guinea, Office of Tourism
24. Philippines, Ministry of Tourism
25. Singapore Tourist Promotion Board
26. Solomon Islands Tourist Authority
27. Sri Lanka, Sri Lanka Tourist Board
28. Tahiti Tourist Development Board
29. Thailand, Tourism Authority Tonga Visitors Bureau
30. United States Travel Service
31. Russia Intourist
32. Vanuatu Tourist Information Bureau
33. Western Samoa, Department of Economic Development

(ii) **Active Industry**

1. American Express Company
2. Hilton International
3. Hotel Indonesia International Corporation Ltd.
4. Unitours

(iii) **Active Carriers**

1. Aeronaves de Mexico
2. Air-India
3. Airlanka
4. Air Nauru
5. Air New Zealand
6. Air Niugini
7. Air Pacific
8. All Nippon Airways

9. Aloha Airlines
10. American Airlines
11. Ansett Airlines of Australia Air Lines
12. Bangladesh Biman
13. Bouraq Indonesia Air Lines
14. British Caledonian Airways Ltd.
15. CP Air
16. Cathay Pacific Airways
17. China Air Lines
18. Condor Flugdienst
19. Continental Air Lines
20. Delta Steamship Lines
21. Deutsche Lufthansa
22. Finnair
23. Garuda Indonesian Airways
24. Gulf Air Company
25. Hawaiian Air
26. Indian Airlines
27. Japan Air Lines
28. KLM Royal Dutch Airlines
29. Korean Air
30. Malaysian Airlines System
31. Merpati Nusantara Airlines
32. Mexicana Airlines
33. Northwest Orient Airlines
34. Pakistan International Airlines
35. Pan American World Airways
36. Philippine Airlines
37. Qantas Airways Ltd.
38. Royal Nepal Airlines
39. Royal Viking Line
40. Scandinavian Airlines System
41. Singapore Airlines Ltd.
42. Sitmar Cruises
43. Thai Airways International
44. Transamerica Airlines
45. Trans-Australia Airlines
46. Trans World Airlines
47. UTA French Airlines
48. United Airlines

49. Western Airlines
50. World Airways

(iv) **Associate Carriers**

1. Ansett-Pioneer Road Passenger Group
2. Japanese National Railways
3. Mid Pacific Air

(v) **Associate Governments**

1. Anaheim Visitor and Convention Bureau
2. Australian Standing Committee of Tourism
3. Bali Government Tourism Office
4. California Office of Tourism
5. Canberra Tourist Bureau (Australia)
6. Central Java Provincial Tourist Office
7. East Java Regional Tourist Development Bureau
8. Gangweon-do Provincial Government (Korea)
9. Hawaii Visitors Bureau
10. India Tourism Development Corporation
11. Jakarta Metropolitan Tourism Board
12. Kementerian Tenaga Rakyat (Malaysia)
13. Long Beach Convention and Tourism Bureau
14. Korea Bureau of Tourism, Ministry of Transportation
15. Marianas Visitors Bureau
16. Melbourne Tourism Authority
17. New South Wales Department of Tourism
18. New Zealand National Travel Association
19. Northern Territory Tourist Commission
20. Pahang State Development Corporation (Malaysia)
21. Penang State Government
22. Philippine Convention Bureau
23. Philippine Tourism Authority
24. Queensland Tourist and Travel Corporation
25. Sabah Tourism Promotion Corporation
26. Sarawak Tourist Development Commission
27. Seoul Metropolitan Government
28. Travel Alberta
29. Victoria Government Travel Authority
30. West Java Regional Tourism Office

PATA Chapters

To assist in the fulfilment of the objectives of the Pacific Asia Travel Association, the board of directors is empowered to encourage and authorise establishment of PATA Chapters at any place in the world. The chapters concept implemented in the year 1960 is unique with PATA among travel organisations. The primary purpose of a chapter is to conduct continuing education programmes to keep PATA members abreast of the changes in Pacific travel. The chapters also do considerable promotional work, and stage social events for the members. The specific objectives of the chapters are as follows:

- (i) To bring together representatives of PATA members at regular intervals to develop a closer working relationship and a better understanding of travel matters relating to the Pacific area.
- (ii) To obtain uniformity and combined action by members in pursuing national and local policies within the framework of PATA.
- (iii) To implement specific PATA objectives and projects.
- (iv) To pass to appropriate government and official organisations such matters approved by PATA, and to obtain action thereon as and when required.
- (v) To process generally and to obtain opinions of members of the chapters on any PATA requirement or objective.
- (vi) To provide a forum which will enable the individual chapter members to conduct their various assigned responsibilities for selling travel, and providing services to visitors to the Pacific in a more effective manner.

There are two types of chapters, namely, (i) area chapters and (ii) promotional chapters. Area chapters were conceived as of the 8th Annual PATA Conference (1959) by a number of allied and associate members as a means of keeping PATA members and their representatives in the Pacific better informed on happenings throughout the Pacific travel industry and on association activities. Some of these chapter activities include programmes involving matters of facilitation, staff training, improving visitor plants and services, and promotions aimed at developing regional tourist traffic and other marketing activities. Promotional chapters were authorised by the 9th Annual PATA Conference (1960) as a means of furthering the promotion of visitors from priority market areas to Pacific destinations. Activities of these Chapters are all designed to increase the sale of travel to the Pacific Asia and include regular meetings of the PATA membership/travel trade with programmes on various Pacific destinations, providing up-to-date information on new developments, facilities, services, tours, educational seminars for travel trade, sales personnel and cooperation with PATA in the overall marketing programme, promotions and other PATA activities.

The chapters are, however, not the branch offices of PATA. They are rather like local civic clubs working for the benefit of their respective communities. A chapter is composed of the highest level of executives representing the local tourism industry who volunteer their services and their expertise to develop a constantly expanding overall business. Presently, PATA has as many as 80 active chapters. Two to three new chapters are organised yearly to help more and more people keep abreast of the changes in Pacific travel.

Finances of the Association

The administration and programmes of the association are financed by way of membership dues and the marketing assessments paid by all members. The amount of dues, however, varies with the category of membership. The marketing assessments of governments and carriers are calculated in accordance with a Stanford Research Institute formula. This formula takes into account, among other things, the growth in visitor arrivals and expenditures at member areas, and the growth in traffic volume of carrier members The association's financial position is reviewed by the board of directors at their monthly meetings, and an annual audit is made by an outside accounting agency. In addition to membership dues and the marketing assessment amounts, there are additional revenues which come from allied and associate members, a portion of which is applied to various marketing programmes.

Functions of PATA

The Pacific Asia Travel Association performs a variety of junctions. These include:

(i) ***Pacific Travel Conference and Workshop***: During the first four months of each year, PATA sponsors and organizes a conference of its members with the objectives of reviewing the progress, exchanging ideas and planning for future programmes. These meetings are held at different areas. The annual conferences attract a large number of delegates from all over the world. The conference also serves as a unique promotional tool for the host government

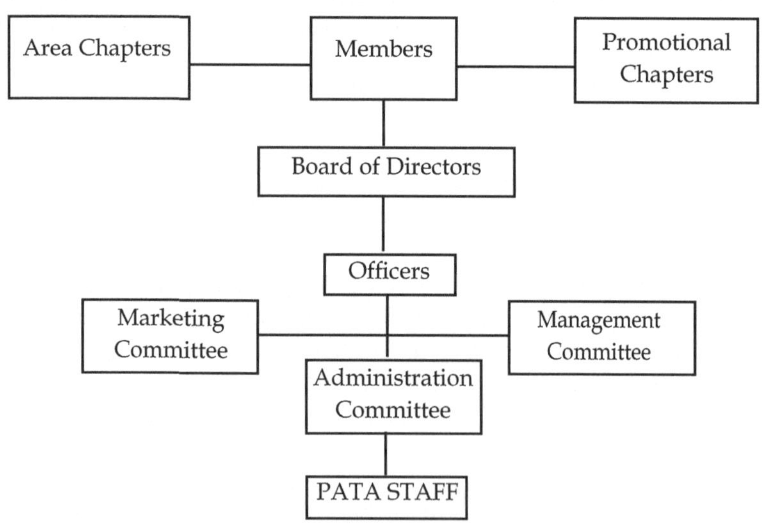

Organisation of the Pacific Asia Travel Association (PATA)

providing it an opportunity to show to the travel industry from abroad what it has to offer in terms of tourist attractions and tourism plant to the foreign visitor.

(ii) ***Marketing***: A long-range marketing programme coordinates all the promotional functions of PATA for a maximum impact in the consumer market and also among sales agents. The marketing programme includes: (a) advertising, publicity and promotion and (b) research and development. An extensive advertising programme schedule is carried in leading national magazines of North America with a view to increase interest in the Pacific region as a major travel area. The association prepares and distributes a wide selection of sales aids and sales promotion materials to travel agents and tour operators throughout the world. A strong trade advertising programme is directed towards travel agents in order to merchandise PATA's consumer advertising and sales promotion efforts. Weekly news releases, special feature stories and photographs are provided to the various newspapers, magazines and radio and television networks by the association's Pacific news service. Members allowed to use the association's various materials including photographs for their own publicity purposes. So far as research and development is concerned, the association's research programme is designed to provide it with the marketing information needed to formulate its own marketing programme as well as to provide its members with information which will assist them in designing their own programmes. The association organizes research seminars, research presentations and technical assistance programmes for its members. Another important facet of the research programme includes the collection, analysis and dissemination of Pacific travel statistics—an effort designed to constantly improve and standardise the tourism statistics of the Pacific region.

PATA and India

India was admitted as an associate government member of Pacific Asia Travel Association in 1957. It was at the specific request of the government that the constitution of the PATA was amended suitably to enable India and other South Asian countries to become associate government members. However, it was only in the year 1964 at Jakarta, Indonesia that India became an active member of the association. Basically, PATA was formed to promote traffic to Pacific countries only. However, the definition of PATA was somewhat enlarged to enable some of the countries bordering on the Pacific to join PATA. India was the first country to enter PATA from among the countries which bordered on the Pacific but were not in the Pacific region. Subsequently, a few other countries also joined the association from this region. Among these countries were Sri Lanka, Nepal and later, Pakistan and Bangladesh.

It was not long before India realised the manifold benefits which this organisation had for promotion of tourism. India realised that PATA was one of the most active travel promotional organisations and that the country's association with it would not only benefit her from getting a share of the world's increasing tourist flow but also from the point of view of exposing it to the modern techniques of tourism marketing and promotion. During the 1964 annual conference at Sydney in Australia, PATA agreed to hold its annual convention in India in 1966. Again, during the 1965 conference in Korea, India's invitation to host the annual convention in 1966 was reaffirmed and accepted by the general body of the PATA Conference. The decision regarding the venue of the conference is generally made three years in advance.

PATA's 1966 conference was the 15th annual conference of the association. The five-day conference and workshop which met in New Delhi was attended by over 500 delegates from a number of countries. India at that time was emerging as a new tourist destination with very little exposure in American and Pacific areas of its tourist attractions. The main objective in inviting PATA conference to Delhi was to expose the facilities to a large segment of foreign tour operators, travel writers, airline executives, etc. The conference was a big success as it resulted in a steady rise in tourist traffic to India during subsequent years. India enjoyed a continuous and uninterrupted growth till 1973 when the steep rise in oil prices followed by initiation in potential tourism markets led to a slight decline in the growth of tourist arrivals. However, during subsequent years the tourist arrivals increased. India after PATA '66 Conference is now a full-fledged member.

India was awarded yet another conference when it was unanimously chosen as the venue of the 1978 conference at the Sydney PATA Conference in 1975. The theme of the conference "Challenge of Change" became particularly significant in view of the fact that tourism was passing into a phase where there were no limits to its growth. The objective of hosting another PATA conference in India after a period of twelve years was to expose tourist facilities to a large segment of tour operators, travel writers, airline executives, etc. The conference was attended by over 1,500 delegates and was the largest conference in the history of PATA. The large number of delegates from all over the world provided an opportunity to India to expose its tourist plant to the international travel world. The conference was responsible for projecting India's image not only as a great tourist destination but also as a great host country. India will host yet another conference in the year 2002.

The PATA (India) Chapter

The PATA (India) Chapter was organised in the year 1969 as one of the area chapters. This chapter has over 130 members with representation from government (Ministry of Tourism), India Tourism Development Corporation, Indian Airlines, Air India and other international carriers, leading travel agencies in India, hotels, tour operators, advertising agencies, etc. The chapter undertakes promotional work specifically for promoting India.

Today, PATA provides it members with an array of programmes and events created to promote the region as the preferred international destination. These activities also aim to develop a sustainable future for the travel industry and to assist members with professional development in a number of fields. Originally oriented towards sending visitors to the Pacific Asia region, PATA has grown to encompass the changing market place and now incorporates intra-regional tourism within the PATA geographic boundaries. The PATA annual conference draws together the top decision makers in the region. The PATA Trade Mart focus on marketing opportunities by matching the buyers and sellers of the region's tourism products. PATA's special-interest marketing seminars and marts are held regularly to help members target new business opportunities and learn the successful techniques for development. PATA also keeps its members up to date on relevant industry trends via the strategic information centre, which provides members with timely research and market intelligence for business planning, product development and marketing.

PATA's office of Environment and Culture and the PATA Foundation coordinate programmes to preserve the region's environmental, heritage and cultural resources. Through targeted marketing and promotional programmes, business networking opportunities, and support and resources services, PATA provides a partnership for their members professional and personal growth. PATA's mission is to enhance the growth, value and quality of Pacific Asia travel and tourism for the benefit of its membership. PATA has long been an advocate of balancing growth with conservation measures.

In recent years there has been rapid and continuous development of both national and international tourism. The international tourism organisations have played and are continuing to play a key role in the tourism development, both national as well as international. India has regularly participated actively in the deliberations of international bodies which afford an opportunity to establish new contacts and renew old ties with persons from all over the world connected with tourism. These organisations also help the member countries to determine the general travel trends for proper channelisation of promotional activities. India's association with these bodies has definitely encouraged the flow of tourist traffic from international tourist generating markets to India.

Present

In 2011 PATA celebrate its 60th anniversary with a series of activities and events focused around the theme 'Building Tourism. Past.Present.Progressive'. On September 6-9, PATA Travel Mart 2011 was held at Pragati Maidan, New Delhi, India.

In 2012, at the Annual General Meeting in Kuala Lumpur, Malaysia, PATA launched PATAmPOWER, which was an enhancement of the Travel Intelligence Graphic Architecture (TIGA) initiative redeveloped in HTML5, to enable use by mobile devices. The objective of PATAmPOWER is to be your one stop for data about the Asia Pacific visitor economy, improving productivity, providing faster insights and enabling smarter decisions.

In 2013, PATA appoints a Corporate Social Responsibility specialist who facilitates signing of MOU with the Global Sustainable Tourism Council, the international body fostering increased knowledge and understanding of sustainable tourism practices by destinations and tourism enterprises.

In 2013 PATA helped to align industry advocacy with other travel and tourism industry bodies, formally launching the Global Travel Association Coalition (GTAC). PATA is a founding member of this global group which also includes Airports Council International (ACI), Cruise Line International Association (CLIA), International Air Transport Association (IATA), International Civil Aviation Organisation (ICAO), World Economic Forum (WEF), World Tourism Organisation (UNWTO) and the World Travel & Tourism Council.

In the same year PATA also launched an interactive training programme PATAcademy-HCD, incorporating intensive classroom interactions led by leading travel industry practitioners with practical activities, group assignments, networking events and field visits in and around Bangkok.

In November, 2014 PATA and Myriad Marketing launched PATA Conversations, a B2B digital publication focusing upon travel and tourism to, from and within the Asia Pacific region.

In December 2014 PATA launched the monthly Connected Visitor Economy Bulletin, making it free to both members and non-members. The Connected Visitor Economy Bulletin is produced on a monthly basis and covers trends and developments across the Asia Pacific region. It aims to monitor the far-reaching impact of travel and tourism across national economies, in order to encourage better and more comprehensive policy responses from governments in support of the sector.

In February 2015, the Tourism Industry Association New Zealand (TIA) and PATA sign a Memorandum of Understanding (MOU) that focuses on four main areas of co-operation: the sharing of information and insight, support for collective policy and advocacy positions, industry connectivity, and collaboration on mutual events.

In March 2015, PATA launched its new microsite, sustain.pata.org. The site, a new online tool for information on sustainable and socially responsible travel and tourism issues, is supported in part by the German Ministry for Economic Cooperation and Development BMZ, implemented by Deutsche Gesellschaft für Internationale Zusammenarbeit (GIZ) GmbH, and by EarthCheck.

In May 2015, in response to the earthquake that killed and injured thousands of people and devastated much of Kathmandu's tourism infrastructure nine days earlier, the PATA Foundation established a Nepal Earthquake Tourism Recovery Fund to assist the PATA Nepal Chapter in its tourism industry recovery efforts.

In May 2015, PATA, in partnership with TripAdvisor, launched the PATA CEO Challenge to help promote uniqueness and diversity of heritage, culture, customs and natural beauty of the world's many diverse destinations. It aims to promote and enhance the number of visitors to emerging destinations and enhances tourism development in the most sustainable manner.

In June 2015 PATA presented Nepal with the PATA Nepal Tourism Rapid Recovery Task Force Report to help the country recover from the devastating earthquake that killed and injured thousands of people and devastated much of Kathmandu's tourism infrastructure.

In June 2015 PATA announced the inaugural PATA Global Insights Conference 2015, to be hosted in Auckland, New Zealand on October 16, 2015 at the SKYCITY Grand Hotel. The conference explored the key influences that will drive and shape future thinking in terms of tourism destination development, design, access and marketing.

In June 2015 PATA and the International Union for Conservation of Nature (IUCN) created a new partnership, in the form of a memorandum of understanding (MoU), recognising the positive impacts that their collaboration can have in the areas of conservation and sustainable development. The specific objectives of the MoU include collaboration in capacity building, knowledge sharing, and networking, both online and in person. PATA members may now increase their knowledge of wider sustainability issues, particularly in relation to Mangroves for the Future (MFF) and coastal tourism, as well as IUCN case studies showcasing positive examples of sustainable tourism on PATA's sustainability website, sustain.pata.org.

In November 2015 PATA forged an organisational partnership with the International Gay and Lesbian Travel Association (IGLTA). The agreement strengthens the bond and shared interests between the two associations. The Memorandum of Understanding (MoU) was signed by PATA CEO and IGLTA President at World Travel Market in London, United Kingdom, November 2015. The agreement commits the two organisations to share knowledge through research and publications, to reciprocate in event participation, to support mutual agreed advocacy positions, and to enhance access for the benefit of members of both organisations

In December 2015, PATA announced an organisational partnership with the Professional Travel Bloggers Association (PTBA) to strengthen the cooperation and shared interests between the two associations. One of the first activities of the newly signed partnership was to combine efforts to encourage buyers, sellers and conference delegates to connect with leading industry travel bloggers at the PATA Adventure Travel and Responsible Tourism Conference and Mart 2016 in Chiang Rai, Thailand in February 2016 at the Dusit Island Resort Chiang Rai.

In April 2016 PATA and the Reef-World Foundation(Reef-World) announced a new organisational partnership that recognises the positive impacts that their mutual support and endorsement can have in the areas of marine conservation and in the sustainable development of marine initiatives and opportunities. The specific objectives of this partnership include the mutual support and endorsement of both organisations as well as collaboration in awareness building and knowledge sharing on related issues.

European Travel Commission (ETC)

European Travel Commission (ETC) was established in the year 1948 as a non-profit making body by the national tourism organisations (NTO) of various European countries. The objectives of the ETC are

- To foster international tourism cooperation in Europe
- To exchange information on tourism development projects and marketing techniques
- To undertake/commission appropriate travel research concerning various issues related to travel and tourism
- To promote tourism within and to Europe from other parts of the world particularly from North America and Europe.

The commission's functions include research, marketing and a range of allied tourism policy issues. The activities of the European Travel Commission are supported by the European Commission, which considers tourism as an industry of great potential and of great economic and social significance within the community.

Indian Ocean Tourism Organisation (IOTO)

Founded in 1995, the Indian Ocean Tourism Organisation's mission is to enhance regional cooperation and understanding through sustainable tourism.

IOTO has stated in its vision statement that every country in the Indian Ocean region has its own unique tourism product, image, strategies and structure and these are tourism issues of common interest and mutual benefit within the region. The vision for the region is that every country around the Indian Ocean Rim will optimise its own potential in a sustainable manner for the benefit of all of its people.

The approach of IOTO is to complement and add value to the strategies and activities of public and private sector tourism organisations around the Indian Ocean Rim by:

- Positioning and marketing the Indian Ocean region as a unique tourism destination area.
- Facilitating cooperation and coordination among IOTO destinations and members.
- Promoting the expansion of appropriate transportation services and facilities to and within the Indian Ocean region.
- Liaising on behalf of its members with governments and authorities towards reducing barriers to travel.
- Encouraging improved service standards and the quality of the visitor experience throughout the destination area.
- Encouraging all members to support sound environmental tourism practices for the long-term benefit of their communities.
- Facilitating information dissemination and skills interchange throughout the region.

The membership of IOTO includes governments, tourism organisations, carriers, major hotel and resort groups, major tour operators and tourism industry entities from the 25 IOTO core countries. The core countries of the IOTO are as follows:

Membership of IOTO

Table 8.5

1. Australia
2. Bangladesh
3. Christmas Island
4. Cocos Island, the
5. Comoros
6. India
7. Indonesia
8. Kenya
9. Madagascar
10. Malaysia
11. Maldives, the
12. Mauritius
13. Mozambique
14. Myanmar

15. Oman
16. Pakistan
17. Réunion
18. Seychelles
19. Singapore
20. Somalia
21. South Africa
22. Sri Lanka
23. Tanzania
24. Thailand
25. Yemen

The Indian Ocean Tourism Organisation secretariat is located at Perth, Australia.

Indian Ocean Tourism Organisation: IOTO Coastal Tourism Resource Centre

The Indian Ocean Tourism Organisation (IOTO) has launched the Indian Ocean Region's first Coastal Tourism Resource Centre, in conjunction with its Foundation Education Member, Edith Cowan University (ECU) of Western Australia.

Designed to create the first comprehensive compilation of Coastal Tourism and Coastal Zone Tourism Management information, the new facility will predominantly focus on destinations whose shores touch, or are surrounded by, the Indian Ocean.

IOTO and ECU's School of Marketing, Tourism and Leisure plan to utilise components of the new information to enhance the Organisation's Web site on the Internet; to make it available to IOTO members - and to include it in future Tourism degree courses at the University.

A major catalyst behind this innovation was the first of five Resolutions from the Organisation's Second Coastal Zone Management Workshop that was held recently in Malaysia. Towards progressing these wide-ranging Resolutions - which were presented to the U.N. Committee for Sustainable Development in April - the regional tourism body has combined with one of the Southern Hemisphere's leading Universities to launch the Region's first such facility. The new Coastal Tourism Resource Centre will be based at Edith Cowan University's Joondalup Campus, north of Perth.

"Since its early days, IOTO has taken a clear leadership and management role in the key area of Coastal Tourism," said IOTO's Secretary General, "Given the Ocean-linked synergy that is shared by the Organisation's member destinations and the particular significance of their coastal tourism products, this is entirely appropriate," he added.

The IOTO CEO stated that the body's key environment programme was its Coastal Zone Initiative - a far-reaching and forward-looking activity that generated both the ten IOTO CZM and Tourism Principles from its First Workshop in Fremantle,

Western Australia in September, 1997 and the five Coastal Tourism Resolutions from the Malaysian Workshop in April, 1999.

"As the momentum grows, IOTO is very confident that the major community and tourism industry issue that sustainable and environmentally sound tourism development and operations in the coastal zone has become, will receive even greater attention, especially by national and state governments, " Graham Hornel predicts. "There are far too many examples of poor planning, negligent regulation and the greed factor dominating all other interests and concerns in coastal tourism development - and IOTO and its members seriously intend that this change before it is too late. It is time that the true interests of the coastal communities was protected," the IOTO CEO stated.

According to the Secretary General, IOTO will expand its Coastal Tourism activities through newly established links with UN-ESCAP, UNEP and WTTC's Green Globe programme. "These potentially productive links - and those which can also be established with PATA - will keep the focus of government, industry and community attention on this vital issue well into the 21st. Century,"

Membership

The Association comprises 21 member states and 7 dialogue partners, the Indian Ocean Tourism Organisation and the Indian Ocean Research Group have observer status.

- Australia
- Bangladesh
- Comoros
- India
- Indonesia
- Iran
- Kenya
- Madagascar
- Malaysia
- Mauritius
- Somalia
- Mozambique
- Oman
- Seychelles
- Singapore
- South Africa
- Sri Lanka
- Tanzania
- Thailand
- United Arab Emirates
- Yemen

Dialogue Partners

Countries with the status of dialogue partners are:

- China
- Egypt
- France
- Germany
- Japan
- United Kingdom
- United States

The Organisation for Economic Co-operation and Development (OECD)

The **Organisation for Economic Co-operation and Development** (**OECD**; French: *Organisation de coopération et de développement économiques, OCDE*) is an intergovernmental economic organisation with 36 member countries, founded in 1961 to stimulate economic progress and world trade. It is a forum of countries describing themselves as committed to democracy and the market economy, providing a platform to compare policy experiences, seeking answers to common problems, identify good practices and coordinate domestic and international policies of its members. Most OECD members are high-income economies with a very high Human Development Index (HDI) and are regarded as developed countries. As of 2017, the OECD member states collectively comprised 62.2% of global nominal GDP (US$49.6 trillion) and 42.8% of global GDP (Int$54.2 trillion) at purchasing power parity. OECD is an official United Nations observer.

In 1948, the OECD originated as the Organisation for European Economic Co-operation (OEEC), led by Robert Marjolin of France, to help administer the Marshall Plan (which was rejected by the Soviet Union and its satellite states). This would be achieved by allocating United States financial aid and implementing economic programs for the reconstruction of Europe after World War II. (Similar reconstruction aid was sent to the war-torn Republic of China and post-war Korea, but not under the name "Marshall Plan".)

In 1961, the OEEC was reformed into the Organisation for Economic Co-operation and Development by the Convention on the Organisation for Economic Co-operation and Development and membership was extended to non-European states. The OECD's headquarters are at the Château de la Muette in Paris, France. The OECD is funded by contributions from member states at varying rates and had a total budget of €374 million in 2017.

Organisation for European Economic Co-operation

The **Organisation for European Economic Co-operation** (**OEEC**) was formed in 1948 to administer American and Canadian aid in the framework of the Marshall Plan for the reconstruction of Europe after World War II. It started its operations on 16 April 1948, and originated from the work done by the Committee of European

Economic Co-operation in 1947 in preparation for the Marshall Plan. Since 1949, it was headquartered in the Château de la Muette in Paris, France. After the Marshall Plan ended, the OEEC focused on economic issues. The OEEC can be seen as a continental planning commission established by the United States following the successful model of their planning commissions of the New Deal. The economic philosophy the commission followed can be characterized as Keynesian.

In the 1950s, the OEEC provided the framework for negotiations aimed at determining conditions for setting up a European Free Trade Area, to bring the European Economic Community of the six and the other OEEC members together on a multilateral basis. In 1958, a European Nuclear Energy Agency was set up under the OEEC.

By the end of the 1950s, with the job of rebuilding Europe effectively done, some leading countries felt that the OEEC had outlived its purpose, but could be adapted to fulfil a more global mission. It would be a hard-fought task, and after several sometimes fractious meetings at the Hotel Majestic in Paris starting in January 1960, a resolution was reached to create a body that would deal not only with European and Atlantic economic issues, but devise policies to assist less developed countries. This reconstituted organisation would bring the US and Canada, who were already OEEC observers, on board as full members. It would also set to work straight away on bringing in Japan.

Structure

The OECD's structure consists of three main elements:

- The OECD member countries, each represented by a delegation led by an ambassador. Together, they form the OECD Council. Member countries act collectively through Council (and its Standing Committees) to provide direction and guidance to the work of Organisation.
- The OECD Substantive Committees, one for each work area of the OECD, plus their variety of subsidiary bodies. Committee members are typically subject-matter experts from member and non-member governments. The Committees oversee all the work on each theme (publications, task forces, conferences, and so on). Committee members then relay the conclusions to their capitals.
- The OECD Secretariat, led by the Secretary-General (currently ÁngelGurría), provides support to Standing and Substantive Committees. It is organised into Directorates, which include about 2,500 staff.

Meetings

Delegates from the member countries attend committees' and other meetings. Former Deputy Secretary-General, estimated in 1997 that the cost borne by the member countries, such as sending their officials to OECD meetings and maintaining permanent delegations, is equivalent to the cost of running the secretariat. This ratio is unique among inter-governmental organisations. In other words, the OECD is more a persistent forum or network of officials and experts than an administration.

The OECD regularly holds minister-level meetings and forums as platforms for a discussion on a broad spectrum of thematic issues relevant to the OECD charter, members and non-member states.

Noteworthy meetings include:

- The yearly Ministerial Council Meeting, with the Ministers of Economy of all member countries and the candidates for enhanced engagement among the countries.
- The annual OECD Forum, which brings together leaders from business, government, labour, civil society and international organisations. Held every year since June 2000, the OECD Forum takes the form of conferences and discussions, is open to public participation and is held in conjunction with the MCM.
- Thematic Ministerial Meetings, held among Ministers of a given domain (i.e., all Ministers of Labour, all Ministers of Environment, etc.)
- The bi-annual World Forum on Statistics, Knowledge and Policies, which does not usually take place in the OECD. This series of meetings has the ambition to measure and foster progress in societies.
- OECD Eurasia Week which includes several high-level policy dialogue discussions to share best practices and experiences in addressing common development and economic challenges in Eurasia.

Secretariat

Exchanges between OECD governments benefit from the information, analysis, and preparation of the OECD Secretariat. The secretariat collects data, monitors trends, and analyses and forecasts economic developments. Under the direction and guidance of member governments, it also researches social changes or evolving patterns in trade, environment, education, agriculture, technology, taxation, and other areas. The secretariat is organised in Directorates:

- Centre for Entrepreneurship, Small and Medium Enterprises (SMEs) and Local Development
- Centre for Tax Policy and Administration
- Development Co-operation Directorate
- Directorate for Education and Skills
- Directorate for Employment, Labour, and Social Affairs
- Directorate for Financial and Enterprise Affairs
- Directorate for Science, Technology, and Innovation
- Economics Department
- Environment Directorate
- Public Governance Directorate
- Statistics Directorate
- Trade and Agriculture Directorate
- General Secretariat
- Executive Directorate
- Public Affairs and Communication Directorate

Various world bodies discussed in the chapter provide a joint platfrom to exchange ides as also resolve problems of mutual interest with a view to facilitating growth and development of global tourism. An organisation is an essential prerequisite prerequisite as it plays a crucial role in its proper planning, development and growth. Various world bodies set up from time to time over the years are elected, representated by experts in various travel and tourism fields whose main purpose is to achieve through action, the objectives for which these have been set up.

PART II

apter

Tourist ccommodation

Tourism is to a great extent dependent on the range and type of accommodation available at the destination. Accommodation is a core area of the tourist industry and plays a distinctive role in the development of this ever-expanding industry. The United Nations Conference on International Travel and Tourism held in Rome in 1963 considered, in particular, issues relating to means of accommodation. The conference acknowledged the importance of means of accommodation, both traditional (hotels, motels) and supplementary (camp, youth hostels, etc.), as incentives to international tourism. The conference recommended that governments should consider the possibility of including tourism projects, and particularly those relating to accommodation, in the list of projects eligible for loans from their industrial or other corporations, and that, where required, they should establish special financial corporations for tourism. It also recommended that governments should give sympathetic consideration to the possibility of granting special facilities and incentives for accommodation projects.

Accommodation is the key element in the tourism product and an essential component of tourism. The World Tourism Organisation's definition of a tourist presupposes that the tourist must spend at least one night in the destination visited. This definition indicates a central role that accommodation plays in tourism. Tourist accommodation, which caters to both domestic and international tourists, is an important input which flows into the overall tourist system. It forms an important feature of the total tourist image of the country. A country which provides adequate accommodation facilities suitably tailored to the requirements of the tourist markets fulfils one of the basic conditions of tourism development.

Many countries have recognised the importance of accommodation industry in relation to tourism and their governments have coordinated their activities with the industry by providing big incentives and concessions to hoteliers, which have resulted in the building up of a large number of hotels and other type of accommodations. For example, availability of hotel sites on liberal repayment terms, special concessions in the form of long-term loans, liberal import licences and taxation reliefs, contributions to the equity capital, cash grants for construction and renovation of building, and similar other concessions are provided to the industry.

Brief History

Historically, accommodation for travellers may be conveniently viewed in two ways. The traveller who left his home on a journey which cannot be completed in a single day required accommodation at his destination. Inns were perhaps the first such accommodation units which catered to the needs of travellers in early times. Innkeeping has been a very ancient profession. In ancient times and during the Roman Empire many such inns were established which provided food, drink and also entertainment to weary travellers. However, with the decline of the Roman Empire by about A.D. 500, the institution of innkeeping lost its importance and for many years there was not much development. Since people travelled very infrequently and there being not much trading activity, there was not much need felt for innkeeping.

Pilgrimage Tourist

Travel subsequently grew again for religious pilgrimage purposes. Travellers in the thousands visited religious centres. Many monasteries and cathedrals welcomed the travellers and made their stay a comfortable experience. The accommodation provided at these places was free. By the fifteenth century, inns had developed in several countries of Europe, especially in England and France. During the seventeenth and the eighteenth centuries, the facilities provided in the inns were expanded. Some of the inns had as many as 30 or more rooms. English common law declared the inn to be a public house and imposed social responsibility on the innkeeper for the well-being of the traveller. Even today large number of old inns still operate in England as hotels. Some of these were built about four hundred years ago.

In the United States another type of accommodation unit known as the tavern was opened in 1634 by a man called Samuel Coles. Coles had come to the New World in search of a fortune in 1630 by a ship. By 1780, taverns were popular meeting places where people used to come for eating, drinking and entertainment. Many important events were associated with taverns. In 1783, General George Washington bid farewell to his top-ranking officers at the Frances Tavern in New York city. The famous Boston Tea Party was planned in a tavern called Green Dragon.

In India the concept of shelter for travellers is not new. In fact, it is as old as its recorded history. The historical records are replete with mention of *viharas; dharamsalas, sarais, musafirkhanas,* etc. These establishments provided a home to all wayfarers, be they pilgrims, scholars, adventurers or merchants. The shelter under various names have always been a part of India's culture as a valuable institution providing a vital service.

Shelters for Pilgrims

The ancient Buddhist monks were probably the first to institutionalise the concept of a shelter in India. The cave temples scattered all over the south-western region of India have both a *chaitya* (sanctuary) for worship and prayer and a *vihara* (monastery). These monks, although living in their quiet retreats, away from towns and villages, were nevertheless mindful of the needs of travellers and pilgrims who found shelter and food at these monasteries. It is interesting to note that these monasteries are located on the ancient trade routes between important deities of the region. It is gathered from some inscriptions that merchants gave liberal donations for the construction and maintenance of these establishments. Mere charity was obviously not the motivation in these displays of generosity. The trader travelled with their merchandise and money on these routes and the *viharas* were their hotels.

In the medieval period this ancient institution gradually assumed a more secular character. Although religious centres invariably had *dharamsalas* and *musafirkhanas* attached to them, the caravanserai appeared as an exclusive traveller's lodge with a *nanbai* or cook attached with it. Sher Shah Suri, the Afghan Emperor and the builder of the Grand Trunk Road, is credited with having built caravanserais at regular intervals all along this highway creating favourable conditions for commerce and travel. However, he was not alone in this venture. The Mughals built such facilities all over their empire. Later kings, rajas, nawabs, rich businessmen and philanthropists built *sarais* making travel less arduous. At approximately the same time, the inn was the Western counterpart of India's *sarais*. With the expansion of commerce, travelling became profitable and with it emerged the business of providing comfortable shelter and good food to the growing number of travellers. The *sarais* in India like inns in Europe or the stagecoach stations in the USA of the eigtheenth and ninetheenth centuries stood all along the well-travelled routes. They provided food and shelter to the travellers and fodder to their horses. The amenities these early hotels offered would seem to us to be primitive but they conformed to the lifestyle of that age.

With the passage of time the age-old institution of the *sarai* or the inn adapted itself to the ever-changing and constantly growing requirements of the market and has evolved into the modern hotel. From the age of the bullock cart and horses through the age of the rail road into the era of the jumbo jet and supersonic aircraft, the hotel industry developed with the simultaneous development of transportation systems. It also reflects the standard of living and the lifestyle of the society in which it operates.

Prototype of Modern Hotel

With the growth of travel in the eighteenth century there appeared in London the prototype of the modern hotel with the opening by one David Low in 1774. The next fifty years saw a gradual increase in the recognizable ancestors of the modern hotel in London and in resorts such as Brighton and Buxton and also certain other places. In the United States of America, hotels emerged from taverns by the simple expedient of a change of name. By about 1800, the terms tavern and hotel were used to describe the same thing. By the year 1820, hotel became the accepted term to describe a place where people stayed for the night and took their meals on payment. In the 1820s the first tourist hotel appeared in Switzerland.

The demand for some kind of accommodation away from home is an important function of travel. It is therefore not surprising that the main influence on the development of accommodation facilities has been developments in the mode of passenger transport. In the field of mass passenger transport, railways could perhaps be credited with being the pioneers. The evolution of the railway system in the eighteenth century greatly affected the quality and the quantity of accommodation used in conjunction with travel. The growth of the railways also brought a speedy network of stage coach services. By the mid-nineteenth century the use of the stage coach as a means of travel had almost ceased. The industrialisation in its wake brought increased urbanisation. The great number of people who flocked to various urban towns in search of employment and also entertainment needed some kind of accommodation. This need for accommodation enabled promising and enterprising people to build hotels and inns in many such urban towns to cater for an increasingly local market and also to serve the large number of travellers carried by the railways.

Until about the middle of the nineteenth century the bulk of the journeys were undertaken for business and vocational reasons, by road and within the boundaries of the individual countries. The volume of travel was relatively small and was confined to a fraction of the rich segments of the population in any country. Inns and similar establishments along the main highways and in the principal towns grew to become the hallmark of the accommodation for the travellers. The traveller could reasonably expect at most inns a clean and comfortable accommodation when he wished to eat or spend the night. It provided the bulk of accommodation en route. This trend continued until the end of the nineteenth century, as most of those who did travel did so by coach.

Hotels

Emergence of Hotel

Although the earliest hotels date to the eighteenth century, their growth on any scale occurred only in the following century when the railways created sufficiently large markets to help make large hotels possible. During this period a large number of hotels grew up at important destinations. The hotels were developed along the main railways and highway routes in major towns. Substantial development of the hotels thus awaited the volume and the type of traffic only the railways could bring. With the development of railway systems in many other countries within and outside Europe, the number of hotels also increased. These hotels catered to the increasing volume of traffic.

The 1860s also saw the introduction of Thomas Cook's railway and hotel coupons. Starting in 1868, Cook arranged regular circular tours of Switzerland and northern Italy from England. By the 1890s, 1,200 hotels throughout the world accepted hotel coupons. Thus we find that railways greatly influenced the development of hotels during the early twentieth century. The demand for accommodation of tourists was thus met by a variety of facilities ranging from inns, taverns, private houses and hotels. The main changes in the demand for tourist accommodation have come about from changes in tourist transportation and in the popularity of different forms of holidays. After the introduction of the motor car and the aircraft, a large number of hotels sprang up at various tourist areas and destinations. The growth of hotels continued until the 1950s. Hotels as a unit of accommodation dominated the scene all over the world.

Definition of Hotel

Hotels provide accommodation, meals and refreshments for irregular periods of time for those who may reserve their accommodation either in advance or on the premises. In broad terms, hotels provide facilities to meet the needs of the modern traveller. The dictionaries define hotel in several ways: 'a place which supplies board and lodging', 'a place for the entertainment of the travellers', 'large city house of distinction', and 'a public building'. The common law states that a hotel is "a place where all who conduct themselves properly, and who, being able and ready to pay for their entertainment, are received, if there be accommodation for them, and who without any stipulated engagement as to the duration of their stay or as to the rate of compensation, are, while there, supplied at a reasonable cost with their meals, lodging, and such services and attention as are necessarily incident to the use of the house as a temporary home."

A definition of the hotel as a business entity was presented by hotel operators during the consideration of the hotel business to authorities of the National Recovery Administration, in Washington in 1933. This definition, as formulated by Stuart McNamara, was:

> Primarily and fundamentally an hotel is an establishment which supplies board and lodging, not engaged in interstate commerce; or in any interstate commerce, competitive with or affecting, interstate commerce (or so related thereto that the regulation of the one involves the control of the other), but is a quasi domestic institution retaining from its ancient origin certain traditional, and acquiring, in its modern development, certain statutory rights and obligations to the public, where all persons, not disqualified by condition or conduct, prepared to pay for their accommodation, are to be received and furnished with a room or place to sleep or occupy if such accommodations are available, and with such services and attention as are incident to their use of the hotel as a home, and/or with food, at stipulated prices, and with or without contract as to duration of visit, and which conducts, within the confines of its physical locations, this business of supplying personal services of individuals for profit. Incidental to such fundamental and principal business, the hotel may furnish quarters and facilities for the assemblage of people for social, business or entertainment purposes, and may engage in renting portions of its premises for shops and business whose contiguity is deemed appropriate to an hotel.

Types of Hotels

Over the years the concept and the format of hotels have changed a great deal. There are various types of hotels catering to the increasing demands of tourists. The size, the façade, architectural features and the facilities and amenities provided differ from one establishment to another. In addition, the landscape in a particular destination area also greatly influences the architectural features of a hotel. The following are the main types of hotels.

International Hotels

International hotels are the modern Western style hotels seen in almost all metropolitan and other large cities as well as principal tourist centres. These hotels are luxury hotels and are classified on the basis of internationally accepted system of classification. The hotels are placed in various star categories. There are five such categories ranging from five star to one star depending upon the facilities and services provided. These hotels provide, in addition to accommodation, all the other facilities which make the stay a very comfortable and interesting experience. Various facilities provided include well-appointed reception and information counter, banquet halls, conference facilities, etc. There are also shops, travel agency, money changer and safe-deposit facilities. Restaurant facilities, bars and banquets are an integral part of the business of a hotel. The various services provided in these hotels include international and local cuisine, food and beverage service and restaurant service. These hotels also provide entertainment for the guests in the form of various dance and music programmes, sports and games.

A number of these hotels belong to the luxury category. There are some international chains which own a large number of such luxury hotels. Hotels belonging to international chains are mostly owned by public companies and controlled by a board of directors. These hotels have various departments which are managed by persons qualified and experienced in the field of hoteliering. The chief of the hotel, designated as general manager, is responsible for the overall management and operation of the hotel through his departmental heads. International hotels are suitable for metropolitan cities and for other large business and commercial towns and principal tourist centres. The potential of these hotels is therefore limited to theses areas. A number of hotels of this type have conference/convention facilities and are suitable for holding meetings, conventions and conferences.

Resort Hotels

Resort hotels cater to the needs of the holidaymaker, the tourist and those who by reasons of health desire a change of atmosphere. Resort hotels are located near the sea, mountain and other areas abounding in natural beauty. Rest, relaxation and entertainment are the key factors around which resorts are built. The primary motive of a person visiting resort hotels is rest and relaxation which he is looking far away from his routine busy work life. Resort hotels are built with a view to provide special services to the visitors and are marked by an atmosphere of informality. The type of services and amenities available in resort property include recreation facilities such as swimming pool, golf course, tennis courts, skiing, boating, surf-riding and various other indoor sports. Other important amenities include coffee shops, restaurants, conference rooms, lounge, shopping arcade and entertainment. The emphasis of resort hotels, however, is on recreational facilities. The clientele of resort hotels is mostly persons with considerable income looking for relaxation and recreation. Resort hotels rarely attract commercial patronage.

Resorts can be of various types and can be classified on the basis of climate and topography. Broadly they fall in the following categories:

(i) summer resorts
(ii) winter resorts
(iii) hill resorts
(iv) all-season resorts and,
(v) health resorts.

A majority of the resort hotels are seasonal establishments which work to capacity during the high tourist season. Generally the high tourist season is the period when there are holidays at educational institutions. However, in recent years many of the resort hotels with a view to extend the season provide certain special facilities and offer various concessions to the guests. The concessions provided include reduced tariffs, free entertainment, sightseeing, gifts, etc.

Commercial Hotels

Commercial hotels direct their appeal primarily to the individual traveller as compared to international or resort hotel where the focus is on group travel. Most of the commercial hotels receive guests who are on business although some have permanent guests. As the hotel caters primarily to people who are visiting a place for commerce or business, these are located in important commercial and industrial centres of large towns and cities. These hotels are generally run by the owners and their success depends on their efficient running and the comforts and facilities they provide. In some of the large industrial towns, fully licensed commercial hotels exist complete with restaurants, grill room, functional accommodation and a garage for those travelling by automobile.

Residential Hotels

Residential hotels can be described as apartment houses complete with hotel service. These are often referred to as apartment hotels. The tariff of rooms in these hotels is charged on monthly, half-yearly or yearly basis and is charged for either furnished or unfurnished accommodation. These hotels which are located mostly in big cities operate exclusively under the European plan where no meals are provided to the guests. These hotels were developed in the United States of America where people discovered that permanent living in hotels offers many advantages. Services and amenities provided in these hotels are comparable to those of an average well-regulated home. These are very popular in the United States and western Europe where these are also known popularly as *pensions*.

Floating Hotels

As the name suggests, floating hotels are located on the surface of the water. It may be on sea water, river water or on a lake. All the facilities and services of a hotel are provided in these hotels. These hotels are very popular in many countries. In some countries old luxury ships have been converted into floating hotels and are proving very popular among tourists. The atmosphere they provide is exclusive and exotic. In India, floating hotels in the form of houseboats are very popular with tourists.

Heritage Hotels

Heritage hotels have unique architectural features used in different periods of time which blend with the culture and tradition of the area. The main idea is to convert these properties which are not being used any more for residential purposes into hotel in order to preserve their uniqueness. Heritage hotels are operating in palaces/castles/forts/hunting lodges/*havelis* (mansions)/residence of any size built several decades ago. The façade, architectural features and the general construction is of distinctive character, quality and ambiance keeping with traditional way of the life of the area. The architecture of the property is normally not interfered and any extension, improvement renovation in the existing structure made is to be with the traditional architectural style. The renovated properties are to maintain general features and ambience conforming to the overall concept of heritage and architectural distinctiveness. The properties so converted have all the facilities of a modern hotel.

Supplementary Accommodation

Although hotels have been and still are the principal form of accommodation, there has been a growth and development of some other forms of accommodation over the years. It can be of various types and can be classified on the basis of its location, type of construction, type of property, type of management, etc. It is therefore difficult to classify the same. Different terms have been used to indicate similar functions of various accommodation units. It is not possible to give a clear-cut definition of various types of accommodation. The various accommodation units differ in a number of respects. A study of the different types of accommodation indicates that their diversity is a reflection of the specific nature of each one and their names simply indicate various ways in which one and the same function can be fulfilled or the need can be satisfied. Hotels, although a very important part of the tourism infrastructure, are not the only type of accommodation available for the tourists. Tourist accommodation need not be viewed from the point of view of hotel industry alone. In addition to hotels, the demand for tourist accommodation is met by a variety of facilities. There are a series of other installations that are able to offer tourists lodging, food and corresponding services. This is popularly known as supplementary accommodation and is, in fact, an important segment of tourism.

Modest Standard of Comfort

Supplementary accommodation consists of various types of accommodation other than the conventional hotel type. It may be described as premises which offer accommodation but not the services of a hotel. All the establishments under the heading of supplementary accommodation are designed to offer accommodation in the broad sense of the term, namely, the possibility of stay overnight and meals in return of payment per day and on the basis of services provided. In supplementary accommodation the standard of comforts is modest compared to that of a hotel. On the other hand, however, there are certain inherent advantages in this type of accommodation. The biggest advantage is that of price. The supplementary accommodation, as compared to the conventional type of accommodation, is moderately priced. In addition, the atmosphere in the accommodation is informal and there is more freedom with regard to manners, dress, etc. There is also more emphasis on entertainment and sports resulting in increased social contact among the guests.

Supplementary accommodation plays a very important role in the total available tourist accommodation in a country. This type of accommodation can cater to both international as well as domestic tourist traffic. In fact, in some countries more tourists utilize this type of accommodation than hotels. In France and Italy, as also in some other countries in Europe and elsewhere, there are more campers than hotel clients. Some of the principal forms of supplementary accommodation are:

(i) motel
(ii) youth hostel
(iii) camping sites
(iv) pension
(v) bed and breakfast establishments
(vi) tourist holiday villages and
(vii) time-share and resort condominiums.

Motel

The concept of motel and motel-hotel originated in the United States of America. Motel was meant for local motorists and foreign tourists travelling by road. Primarily designed to serve the needs of motorists, motels almost exclusively meet the demand for transit accommodation. They serve the function of a transit hotel except that they are geared to accommodate motor-travelling guests for overnight stay.

The services provided by motels include parking, garage facilities, accommodation, restaurant facilities, public catering and recreational facilities. With a view to provide the above services to the motorists, all the motels are equipped with filling stations, repair services, accessories, garages, parking space, elevator service to the automobile entrance, restaurants, etc. There is also equipment and tools available which the guest can use himself if he wishes to repair his vehicle. The price charged for accommodation and meals/refreshments is much cheaper as compared to that in hotels. Motels are mostly located outside the city limits in the countryside along with the main highway and preferably at an important road junction. Since these establishments cater mainly to persons travelling by road, their development is linked with the development of new motorways along which these are necessarily located. Motels are of different types. Some motels provide just the minimum services while others are well furnished with comfortable accommodation and excellent facilities. The accommodation provided in a motel is of chalet type which is furnished having a dining hall with fixed menu. Shopping facilities for travelling public are also provided for in a motel.

In many countries, especially in the United States, motel accommodation is ranked with hotel accommodation and subject to general standards applicable to hotel industry. In countries like Norway, France, Ireland, Turkey, etc., specific legislation has been introduced for motels, which includes requirements for the approval of plans, easy access of cars, provision of restaurant where necessary, minimum standards for facilities and provision of petrol pump or service station where they exist, model classification standards similar to those for hotels. For instance, in France, there are three categories designated by stars, the classification being based on location, sanitary fittings and collective amenities. An increasingly important segment of the accommodation industry, motels are looked upon as distinct asset which has enabled the industry to meet the changes in travel patterns and personal preferences of the modern-day traveller.

Youth Hostel

In the form of a movement, youth hostels made their first appearance in Germany in about 1900. The movement which spread rapidly all over the world was based on the educational principles emphasising the need by youth of large cities to travel on foot throughout the country. In order to provide some sort of accommodation and services, the dormitories in the inns were equipped with cots, mattresses, sheets and blankets. Large rooms in inns were used as dining and living areas providing full board at low cost to the guests. There was also provision of additional kitchen where travellers could themselves prepare their own meals. Since the movement was started with a view to encouraging youth to travel in order to learn and know more about the country and also to socialize, it had an educational value. As such, no service was provided in the inns. The persons staying were themselves required to look after the unit. Subsequently, exclusive youth hostel buildings were constructed to accommodate young travellers.

Youth hostel can be defined as a building which offers clean, moderate and inexpensive shelter to young people exploring their own country or other countries and travelling independently or in groups on holiday or for educational purpose. It is a place where young people of different social backgrounds and nationalities meet together and come to know each other. The objective of youth hostel is therefore not merely to provide accommodation and board, but also to serve as centres which offer opportunity to young people coming from different parts of the country as also young travellers from abroad to know and understand each other. It is a place of friendship, recreation and extra-curricular education. The youth hostels are equipped to accommodate young men and women who travel on foot, by bicycle or other means of locomotion and who, at very little cost, are provided with place to sleep, eat or to make their own meal. The services provided include accommodation, meals and also recreation. The accommodation provided in the hostels is for a limited number of days.

In most of the countries, youth hostels are developed and managed by non-commercial organisations whose main aim is the development of youth tourism. Since World War II, the number of such hostels has increased greatly. These hostels are now planned to provide comfortable accommodation as also such other services and facilities which are required by youth. Also the number of those using these hostels has grown tremendously. Many hostels receive increasing number of groups and organize stays for winter sports or sailing.

The construction of youth hostels is based on certain norms laid down from time to time all over the world. International requirements for these include provision of separate dormitories for men and women, appropriate and clean toilets, washrooms for both men and women, a kitchen where hosteliers can prepare their own meals, common rooms, living accommodation for warden and a left luggage room. There is also a provision of a kitchen where warden and staff can prepare meals for supply to hosteliers, separate small room for instructors, a dining room and classroom for school parties and a warden's office. Some youth hostels have playgrounds attached for the use of hosteliers.

Caravan and Camping Sites

Caravan and camping sites constitute a significant accommodation category in many holiday areas. These are very popular in some European countries as also in the United States. These are also known as open-air hostels, tourist camps or camping grounds. Camping, originally practised by hikers on foot, is increasingly giving way to car camping. The sites are usually located within the large cities in open spaces. Equipped to receive mobile accommodation in the form of caravans, the camping sites provide facilities for parking, tent pitching, water, electricity, toilet, etc. Though the services provided generally include restaurants, recreational rooms, toilets and at certain places a grocer's shop, the type of services often vary from place to place. Some countries have enacted legislation establishing the minimum facilities that must be provided which include health and sanitation standards and prices to be charged for parking and use of various services and facilities.

Pension

Pensions are very popular in certain European countries, particularly in Italy, Austria, Germany and Switzerland. These establishments are used extensively by the tourists. A pension is also described as a private hotel, a guesthouse or a boarding house. Catering facilities are optional and are usually restricted to the residents. Many of them stay for a longer period than a week or a fortnight. The reservation for accommodation is made in advance. Mostly managed by a family, *pension* accommodation is much cheaper than hotel accommodation.

Bed and Breakfast Establishments

Also known in some countries as apartment hotels and *hotel garni*, they represent a growing form of accommodation units catering for holiday as well as business travellers. These establishments provide only accommodation and breakfast and not the principal meals. These are usually located in large towns and cities along commercial and holiday routes and also resort areas and are used by en-route travellers. Some of these establishments are very popular with holidaymakers.

Tourist Holiday Villages

Tourist villages were established in some European countries after World War II. These villages are situated at warm seasides and in the regions which offer certain facilities for the tourists. In some countries like Italy and Spain, tourist villages are located in the regions which are economically not developed thereby helping the region economically. The villages are mostly promoted by important clubs, social organisations and also by tourist organisations.

The village complex is a centre of accommodation providing extensive sports and recreation facilities, riding, swimming, tennis, volleyball, football, sauna, mini-golf, badminton, table tennis and yoga. These provide both board and lodging. The atmosphere in these villages is kept as informal as possible. Telephones, radios, newspapers and TV are banned unless there is an emergency. Wallets and other valuables are locked away at the beginning of one's stay. Instead of money, one uses colourful beads which can be worn anywhere as bracelets, necklaces, etc., The staff are chiefly educated young people who live on an equal basis with the holiday makers. The accommodation provided is usually in multiple units and may provide for self-catering. The furnishing provided in the rooms is minimal. The easy mixing of guests is encouraged by the banning of advance booking of tables in the village restaurants so one rarely finds oneself sitting with the same group twice.

The holiday villages are usually based on family units, each providing a convertible living room, bath/shower and sometimes a kitchen. The villages are self-sufficient providing almost all necessities required by the residents. There is also a small shopping complex where one can buy articles of daily need. The services of a doctor are also available in the village. The accommodation is sold for a week or a fortnight at an all-inclusive price. In Spain and Italy, these are classified into three categories according to the services and amenities provided.

Club Mediterranée (commonly abbreviated as Club Med) can be considered to be pioneers in the development of the concept of tourist villages. The organisation has been consciously built around a philosophy which stresses that people who live and work in cities need holidays in totally different surroundings. The atmosphere of the hundred-odd holiday villages which they operate round the world is kept as informal as possible. When Club Mediterranée started its first "vacation village" on the Spanish island of Majorca in 1950, its initial 2,500 vacationers slept in army-surplus tents, helped cook meals, and washed dishes.

There have been several changes ever since the first holiday village was established. Its hundred-odd vacation villages in about 35 countries are luxurious, upscale complexes that cater to sun-seeking, high-income couples and singles. The modern amenities as are being used in international resort hotels are done away with in order to give a tourist a special feel of living in an atmosphere which is absolutely carefree. The club's staff are known as GOS (gentils organisateurs), who are mainly educated young people who live on an equal basis with the holidaymakers staying in the village. They are trained to act as vacationers' friends and hosts rather than as hotel employees. There are from 90 to 100 GOSs for the average 600-bed village. Accommodation in the basic villages consists of furnished units with all the facilities. The easy mixing of guests is encouraged by the banning of advance booking of tables in camp restaurants so one rarely finds oneself sitting with the same group twice. Each village has a wide range of entertainment and sporting facilities like music, water-skiing, tennis and yoga classes.

The activities in the 'villages' are increasingly being diversified in recent times. There is emphasis on guided tours of countries where resorts are located, along with lectures on local customs, history and language. Business conference and convention sales also are being stressed. Nearly all the activities and services, including lodging, food and wine, are covered by a flat tariff. Club Med now ranks as the 14th largest hotel chain in the world having over 62,000 rooms and 250 hotels.

Time-share and Resort Condominiums

Time-share and condominiums provide a unique range of accommodation to a tourist. This type of accommodation provides on-site fun, flexibility and affordability to a large number of tourists around the world. In the case of condominium, a tourist owns a room or a suite within a condominium or hotel complex and uses the same as required. The same accommodation unit can also be rented out to other tourists. Normally, the owned condominiums are located within a complex of rooms or suites that are rented out as regular hotel or resort rooms.

Time-share holiday, on the other hand, represents a very unique example of both international and domestic accommodation. It is a modification of condominium-ownership concept. In the past, in western Europe the tradition has been for prosperous individuals to buy or build second homes. However, as these properties are often empty for large parts of the year, these are costly to maintain and always run the risk of being vandalised. As an alternative, property developers have thought of an idea of multi-ownership or time-sharing with people who are interested in utilizing these properties as tourists. For a single capital outlay (one-time payment) the buyer gets one or more weeks of fully furnished and equipped holiday accommodation for a given period of years. The cost of purchase varies with the size of accommodation. The term time-share implies that the accommodation unit is shared with others throughout the year.

Resort Condominiums International (RCI) in the world's premier and largest exchange company in the field of time-share resorts. Established in 1974, RCI is widely recognised as a catalyst for the growth of the global time-share industry. RCI is credited with having invented and pioneered the time-share holiday concept worldwide. Today, RCI is the largest time-share exchange company with over 3,300 resorts in 90 countries with more than 2.4 million time-share-owning households. Many hotel properties around the world have benefited from this concept. This concept enables them to tide over low occupancy rates during lean or low seasons. Several hotel chains worldwide have opted for the mixed use concept whereby a certain number of hotel rooms are put into time-share. This enables them to tide over the problem of low occupancy during lean seasons.

Many time-share properties are affiliated with a time-share exchange programme that permit members to trade their weeks for time at another property with which it has an affiliation agreement. RCI exchange programme works like this. When a member asks to make an exchange request, his/her weeks are deposited into the SPACEBANK Pool for someone else to take. The computer searches through its data bank to find a suitable holiday match to the member's request. If a match is found immediately then the member will receive confirmation in writing within 21 days. If a close match is found, the same will be offered to the member. If the member accepts, then the confirmation is made immediately and member's holiday booked. This then is confirmed in writing within 21 days. The reason why a match may not be immediately possible is because sometimes the accommodation which a member is requesting is not immediately available as it has not yet been deposited by another member. The supply of weeks in the SPACEBANK Pool is ever-changing as members deposit their weeks and request exchanges—so the week the members are requesting may only become available at a future date. Vacation exchange programmes have become very popular with the members because it gives them more flexibility.

Classification and Grading Systems

Tourist accommodation is one of the important components of the total tourist product. It is thus an individual component. As an individual product it is intangible, often bought in advance of its use. Thus, the tourist at the time of making purchase cannot inspect or accept or reject. As such, accommodation raises some issues in its development and in its marketing, both as an individual product and as a part of a package. It creates a need for reliable and accurate information for both the tourists and the travel agents and therefore may require supervision and control. An individual operator needs to bring information about his accommodation to the tourist before he sets off on his journey and also when he reaches his destination. Similarly, the tourist, on the other hand, needs to know in detail what accommodation is available at what price in particular destination from which he can make a choice about what and where to stay. Schemes of classification, registration and grading of the tourist accommodation are intended to meet these requirements.

The United Nations Conference on International Travel and Tourism held in Rome in 1963 also emphasised the need for some sort of regulation of the accommodation with a view to safeguard interests of the users. Considering that special attention should be given to relations between the public authorities and the operators of tourist accommodation facilities, the conference advocated the adoption of a hotel trade charter codifying the regulations applicable to the hotel industry and, in particular, giving official tourist organisations powers enabling them to perform the activities devolving on the state in that field.

The conference observed that many states classify tourist hotels or are considering doing so. Acting upon the recommendations put forward by IUOTO and the International Chamber of Commerce, the conference advocated the standardization of methods of classification, and in particular, the subdivision of hotels into five categories, each identified by a conventional sign (stars) in conformity with sets of standards appropriate to different climatic conditions. The conference also considered the question of classifying supplementary means of accommodation such as tourist bungalows and camps.

Classification

Classification separates accommodation into different classes or categories on the basis of certain criteria, for example, by type of accommodation such as hotels, holiday camps and caravan sites. A scheme of classification seeks to present information about tourist accommodation in a form which will enable the user to find information he requires easily and quickly and to be able to compare it with similar types. Apart from having the information classified by location, a tourist needs to know the availability of accommodation which meets his requirements as to type, price and other criteria.

Registration

The aim of registration is to provide a complete list of register of tourist accommodation within a particular definition. A registration scheme results in an inventory of accommodation which can be kept up to date. In order to be comprehensive, it normally has to have statutory legal authority and is administered by a government authority or a statutory body. Because of the wide range of accommodation used by the tourists, a scheme of registration should normally cover all forms of accommodation used by them.

Gradation

Grading separates accommodation into different categories or grades on the basis of judgements on the amenities and facilities of a particular accommodation unit in a form which enables the user to choose the quality of accommodation he requires. This may refer to the physical facilities, food and other services of the establishment, various amenities provided, etc. The establishments are graded individually or collectively by way of giving them numbers, letters or symbols.

The schemes of classification, registration and grading in operation differs in various countries. Some countries incorporate only registration, some others classification and some grading. The standards adopted also differ from country to country.

Volume and Geographical Distribution

The volume of accommodation is determined by the demand. The number and the distribution varies from country to country depending upon the importance of the country as a tourist destination. The demand for accommodation is most pressing near the major tourist attractions, both man-made and natural. The number of international tourist arrivals to a particular country or a region will also determine the volume of accommodation. The share of Europe, for instance, in international tourist arrivals has been over 68 per cent in the early nineties. Similarly, the capacity of hotels and similar establishments in Europe has been the highest (47 per cent). On the other hand, the share of tourist arrivals in South Asia has been the lowest (0.65 per cent). The capacity of hotels and similar establishments in this region also has been the lowest (1.05 per cent).

According to the World Tourism Organisation (WTO) estimates, based on the survey conducted by the secretariat in 1990–91, the total capacity worldwide of hotels and similar establishments like motels, boarding houses, etc., was 11.04 million (number of rooms). The largest accommodation capacity is however available in Europe which is almost 47 per cent of the total room capacity worldwide. This is followed by the Americas.

Source : World Tourism Organisation (WTO)

Table 9.1

Trends in the Capacity of Hotels and Similar Establishments Worldwide

Sub-Regions	*1986*	*1987*	*1988*	*1989*	*1990*
World Total	10,021,752	10,419,914	10,846,967	11,151,886	11,462,239
%	100%	100%	100%	100%	100%
Africa	274,921	280,296	297,975	307,103	327,401
%	2.74%	2.69%	2.74%	2.75%	2.85%
Americas	3,697,038	3,916,202	405,6671	4,175,140	4,308,151
%	36.89%	37.58%	37.39%	37.43%	37.58%
East Asia/Pacific	889,473	953,381	1,031,659	1,108,505	1,199,685
%	8.87%	9.14%	9.51%	9.94%	10.46%
Europe	4,922,171	5,018,600	5,199,305	5,287,452	5,332,545
%	49.11%	48.16%	47.93%	47.41%	46.52%
Middle East	137,306	143,690	148,203	154,343	173,060
%	1.37%	1.37%	1.36%	1.38%	1.50%
South Asia	100,843	1,007,745	113,154	119,343	121,397
%	1.00%	1.03%	1.04%	1.07%	1.05%

Table 9.1 shows the worldwide trends in the capacity of hotels and similar establishments from 1986 to 1990.

In several European countries, hotel development is concentrated in small-and medium-sized hotel constructions. In many countries, within the framework of general expansion of the accommodation sector, the increase in hotel accommodation was outstripped by the increase in supplementary means of accommodation, such as camping and caravanning sites, rented rooms, apartments, etc. This type of accommodation has become the main provider of lodging for domestic tourism and has also started to play a very significant role in international tourism. In the Americas the total capacity of hotels and similar establishments increased significantly in several countries of the region.

In East Asia and the Pacific region, several countries are currently enjoying a hotel boom. In South Asia, the countries of the region are undertaking great efforts to develop the accommodation sector. In the Middle East, hotel construction in the region is mainly concentrated on luxury-class hotels intended chiefly to cater for business travellers. In view of the high profitability, there are many hotel projects which are under construction. In the African region accommodation facilities are concentrated in the northern part of the continent.

Changing Profile

The accommodation sector has undergone substantial changes in recent years. New developments in tourism and transportation, changes in the organisation of travel and technological innovations are some of the factors which are responsible for these changes. In addition, increasing consumer demand among tourists due to the improvement in living standards and economic conditions has also changed the profile of the accommodation sector. All the above factors seem to have influenced the structure of the hotel industry as a whole. The tendency among middle-income groups to take holiday at any time of the year has encouraged accommodation operators to offer novel kinds of arrangements which are now available in addition to traditional hotel accommodation.

New types of accommodation, particularly holiday villages suitable for family type tourists, condominiums and apartment houses, private villas and camping facilities have proved very successful and to a certain degree are replacing traditional hotels and boarding houses. These changes reflect changes in demand with new, often younger groups entering the international travel market and also new approaches to the problem of providing facilities in a very competitive industry with a highly seasonal demand.

The probable future developments in the accommodation sector according to a study undertaken by WTO are as follows:

(a) A significant growth in accommodation supply will continue to be contributed by chain operators, including airlines. This expansion will result mainly from the further development of management contracts and franchise agreements.

(b) There will be a continuing move towards the further diversification of accommodation. The development of budget accommodation, covering budget hotels, and also supplementary means of accommodation, is likely to continue as mass tourism stimulates new demands for competitively priced accommodation.

(c) The standard of accommodation will continue to rise. Demand for recreational and sporting facilities will increase in both business and leisure accommodation.

(d) Rising building and operating costs, growing environment and conservation pressures, as well as the need to keep staffing levels at a minimum, will influence design and construction of accommodation units.

(e) Advances in technology will both influence the traditional construction methods; for example, more frequent use of pre-fabricated building techniques as well as traditional methods of hotel operations.

New and Emerging Hospitality Technology Trends

The hospitality trends for future has seen a new digital wave taking over the hotel industry. While it may not be feasible for you to adopt every hotel industry trend for technology mentioned below, it will empower you to have a greater understanding of what lies ahead.

The Hype Around Data

There are huge amounts of data collection happening via mobile bookings, guest reviews, the internet search engines and even a cloud-based PMS as integrated by the hotel. The key here lies in understanding and prioritising data. Data collected and analysed properly will help a hotel to boost guest experiences and increase revenues. For hoteliers, being able to store and analyse such huge amount of data enables them to have a competitive edge when it comes to taking vital decision pertaining the business.

Predictive Analytics

The use of predictive analytics is one of the most important ways to increase hotel revenue. Before we proceed, let's try to simplify this.

What if you could predict which item on the menu card sells faster during the Christmas vacations/Diwali vacations.

Wouldn't it be great if you could send tailor-made updates via emails, SMSs to customers based on their preferences? For e.g.: A spa coupon can be targeted particularly for guests who have used this service in your hotel earlier. It empowers hoteliers to make informed decisions by understanding what kind of problems they may face tomorrow.

Investing in the right kind of technology in hospitality industry will help one to be prepared and improve a hotel's management in all aspects. For e.g. any hotel that includes multiple POS outlets needs to focus on providing a personalized service to their guests. This will ensure you have a higher chance of getting repeat customers. Any data that helps you to understand a guests' preference is considered to be the best use of data. Guests are interested in knowing about the choices relevant to them rather than looking at a plethora of choices. Technology will be helpful to suggest which guest is suitable for any specific promotion, offers, and discounts. Usage of this information gives a holistic view into the customer's requirements.

Virtual Reality

Hoteliers, marketers, advertisers have been struggling to grab attention of customers in this competitive market. This is when virtual reality brings a massive change to the way properties are advertised and customers are informed. This is going beyond images, text, and audio-visual ads. You can use virtual reality to give the guest a view of the conference room, amenities, guest rooms and even offer a quick trip to interesting locations nearby. Virtual reality for the hotel industry allows guests to make better decisions by knowing what to expect during their stay. It's important to use this technology to tell an engaging story to ensure guests enjoy the experience and give preference to your hotel over others.

Chatbots and Robotics

Chatbots feature as one of the continuing hospitality trends for the future. Chatbots have already taken over the basic tasks that save time and improve efficiency for professionals. Chatbots are helping to enhance communication and provide guests with quick answers to their queries online. The basic questions asked on a hotel's website such as "What is the menu of the day?" can be answered with the use of chatbots. Chatbots help to automate responses and act as an important channel of communication between the guest and the hotel.

Some leading names in the hotel industry have already started deploying robots. These are useful in various departments such as to play the role of a virtual concierge or even at the front desk. The fascination of robotics continues this year as this largely brings down costs and offers service 24X7. The interaction between the robot and the guests assists hoteliers to analyse cognitive behaviour to understand guests' preferences, and more.

Travel and hospitality companies have not stopped at mobile applications and/or accepting digital payments. Startups in this space are experimenting with new cutting-edge technologies like big data analytics, AI/ML to predict patterns, to offer dynamic pricing to customers and thereby increase customer engagement through use of chatbots. Many well known aggregators have hundred of thousand rooms spread over India and overseas markets.

apter

T e ole o T e Travel a ent

A large proportion of both international and domestic travel are arranged by travel worldwide agents. In some countries over 70 per cent of all international travel and 50 per cent of all domestic travel is arranged by them. The important role of the travel agent in the present world is summarised in the *Principles of Professional Conduct and Ethics* of the American Society of Travel Agents (ASTA) as follows: "We live in a world in which travel has become both increasingly important and complex in its variety of modes and choices. Travellers are faced with a myriad of alternatives as to transportation, accommodation and other travel services. They must depend on travel agencies and others in the industry to guide them honestly and competently".

Travel agency business mostly functions in the private sector. The role of the private sector in organisation of travel is therefore very crucial. In most countries, which are in any manner concerned with the tourist industry, the private sector plays a very important role. The private sector's role is not limited merely in selling the tourism product but often also in producing it as many individuals, companies and corporations are involved in promoting, developing and financing tourism. Travel agency is one such organisation in the private sector which plays a key and crucial role in the entire process of developing and promoting tourism. It is the travel agent who packages and processes all the various attractions of the country and sells these to the tourists. In addition, he also sells individual elements of the travel.

Thomas Cook

Thomas Cook (22 November 1808 - 18 July 1892) was an English businessman. He is best known for founding the travel agency Thomas Cook & Son. Thomas Cook was born to John and Elizabeth Cook, who lived at 9 Quick Close in the village of Melbourne, Derbyshire.

At the age of 10, Cook started working as an assistant to a local market gardener for a wage of six pence a week. At the age of 14, he secured an apprenticeship with his uncle John Pegg, and spent five years as a cabinet maker. He was brought up as a strict Baptist. In February 1826, Cook became a Baptist missionary, and toured the region as a village evangelist, distributing pamphlets and occasionally working as a cabinet maker to earn money.

In 1832, Cook moved to Adam and Eve Street in Market Harborough. Influenced by the local Baptist minister Francis Beardsall, he took the temperance pledge on New Year's Day in 1833. As a part of the temperance movement, he organised meetings and held anti-liquor processions.

On 2 March 1833, Cook married Marianne Mason (1807–1884) at Barrowden in Rutland. A son, John Mason Cook, was born on 13 January 1834. Thomas Cook died at Thorncroft, Knighton, Leicester, on 18 July 1892, having been afflicted with blindness in his declining years. He was buried with his wife and daughter at Welford Road Cemetery, Leicester.

Cook's First Excursions

Cook's idea to offer excursions came to him while "walking from Market Harborough to Leicester to attend a meeting of the Temperance Society". With the opening of the extended Midland Counties Railway, he arranged to take a group of temperance campaigners from Leicester Campbell Street railway station to a teetotal rally in Loughborough, eleven miles away. On 5 July 1841, Thomas Cook escorted around 500 people, who paid one shilling each for the return train journey, on his first excursion. During the following three summers he planned and conducted outings for local temperance societies and Sunday school children.

On 4 August 1845 he arranged for a party to travel from Leicester to Liverpool. In 1846, he took 350 people from Leicester on a tour of Scotland. In 1851 he arranged for 150,000 people to travel to the Great Exhibition in London. Four years later, he planned his first excursion abroad, when he took two groups on a 'grand circular tour' of Belgium, Germany and France, ending in Paris for the Exhibition. During the 1860s he took parties to Switzerland, Italy, Egypt and the United States.

The Thomas Cook statue outside Leicester Railway Station, London Road, Leicester (pictured above) was unveiled on 14 January 1994 by his great-great-grandson Thomas Cook. It was sculpted by James Walter Butler RA.

Thomas Cook and Mass Tourism

Thomas Cook was a frontrunner of establishing tourism systems and thus made Mass Tourism possible in Italy. First, the circular tickets could be used on almost all Italian railways. These tickets allowed travel by train for a preset number of days along predetermined routes. Second, Cook designed a series of hotel coupons to complement circular tickets, which could be exchanged for lodging and meals at designated accommodations. Last, he introduced the circular notes which could be changed at designated hotels, banks, and tickets agents for Italian lire at a predetermined exchange rate. Cook's introduction of tourism-specific currency facilitated easier and effective trips within Italy. Also, by introducing a widely dispersed coupon system, Cook "helped to stabilize the burgeoning Italian economy not only by increasing the revenues from tourism but also by expanding the circulation of Italy's new currency, the lira." The coupon system spread rapidly and were well accepted throughout Italian cities. Furthermore, thanks to this system, middle class Italians could afford to travel more frequently and more easily.

Cook had an ultimate goal to put tourism in the service of unifying the Italian state before Italian unification. He became more aware of Italian politics and became particularly concerned with the fate of the newly unified Italian state. He pondered how tourism could ameliorate the economic and political difficulties. He believed that tourism could reinforce the unification of Italy by physical travel from one place to another, connecting different regions of Italy.

In 1880, the Italian government joined Cook's tour company. The Italian economy benefited from additional tourism profits in which Cook programmed and executed as a system. Cook certainly played a key role in not only boosting the Italian economy but also bringing atmosphere and morale of Italian unification. Italians physically felt their country from place to place by travelling.

Thomas Cook and the Organisation of Travel

The organisation and sale of travel, as it is known today, really began in July 1841. A book salesman-cum-Baptist preacher of Derbyshire was on his way to a temperance meeting in Leicester when he was inspired with "the idea of engaging a special train to carry the friends of temperance from Leicester to Loughborough in England and back to attend a quarterly delegate meeting". He thought that it was a sounder proposition to persuade a railway company, then in its infancy, to carry a trainload of passengers at a very cheap fare than to run the train at 'Standard' fares, but possibly only a quarter full. The man was Thomas Cook and his idea was put into operation with characteristic speed and efficiency. A few weeks later 570 travellers made the journey by the Midland Countries Railway at a specially reduced fare. This venture was soon followed by excursions to various other places, and in 1843, 3,000 schoolchildren were taken on a trip from Leicester to Derby in England.

Thomas Cook's real beginning as a 'mass excursionist' however was the Liverpool-Caernaryon trip of 1845. The tourists travelled by rail to Liverpool, from where they took a steamer to Caernaryon. The advertisements for the trip caused a sensation and the response was so overwhelming that a second trip had to be arranged. Cook thought of every detail. He made a preliminary survey of accommodation and facilities and produced a *Handbook of the Trip to Liverpool*. The excursionist's invasion of Scotland soon followed in 1846 and 1847. From 1848 to 1863 Cook conducted circular tours of Scotland, with 5,000 tourists a season. With the citadels of the landed aristocracy falling before him it was no wonder that a man of Cook's humble origins saw ever and more enticing prospects opening before him: "I had become so thoroughly imbued with the Tourist spirit that I began to contemplate Foreign Trips, including the continent of Europe, the United States and the Eastern lands of the Bible."

The Grand Circular Tour

By the mid-nineteenth century holidays away from home had become customary for a larger social group than ever before. Cook's initiative and organising genius provided the final impetus. In the winter of 1850–51 Cook was already negotiating for a tour of America, but his attention was diverted when he was offered the opportunity of conducting excursion trains to the Great Exhibition of 1851. Altogether, Cook conducted 1,65,000 people to and from the Crystal Palace. In 1856 he succeeded in organising his first 'grand circular tour of the continent'. The tour was so successful that it had to be repeated six weeks later.

Cook's conquest of Europe began in 1862 when he made arrangements with Brighton and South Coast Railway for passenger traffic to the continent. His Paris excursions are the first true 'package tours' in that all the details of transport and accommodation were pre-arranged. In 1863 Cook visited Switzerland where his ideas were greeted with enthusiasm by hoteliers and railway proprietors. His next stop was Italy. Cook first made a personal survey of Turin, Milan, Florence and Genoa, to familiarise himself with their touristic attractions and facilities. In 1864 the first guided tour of Italy left England with applications far in excess of the available tickets.

Hotel Coupons

The 1860s also saw the introduction of Cook's railway and hotel coupons. Cook personally examined the system by travelling through Italy to Vienna, down the Danube into Hungary and from there into Switzerland. By the 1890s, 1,200 hotels throughout the world accepted his coupons. Starting in 1868 Cook arranged regular circular tours of Switzerland and Northern Italy.

Thomas Cook and Son had established their first official London office in 1865. John Mason Cook now joined his father as a permanent partner and took charge of the London office. From that year on, the history of Thomas Cook and Son was one of continuous expansion. In the year 1880 John Mason Cook left for India and established offices in Bombay (Mumbai) and Calcutta (Kolkata) and formed the Eastern Princes Department. In 1887 this department arranged the visits of Indian princes to Queen Victoria's jubilee celebrations. By the end of the century, taking advantage of nineteenth-century advances in transport technology, Thomas Cook and Son had effected a revolution in tourism. No longer the preserve of the rich and the aristocrats, tourism was now an industry. Armed with Cook's hotel and rail coupons, the tourist could demand uniform prices and standards of service and accommodation. This new standardisation had distinct advantages. It meant comfort and convenience and less need for decision making on the part of the individual tourist. The tourist was less likely to experience discomfort or embarrassment.

The management of the company passed on to John Mason Cook's three sons in 1898. At the time of John Cook's death, the Cooks business included three main aspects of travel–selling tours, banking and shipping. Soon after the Second World War, the British government acquired the principal interest in the company. In 1972, the British government sold the company to Midland Bank Consortium. Much has happened since that date. The business of the company has now expanded a great deal with abut 700 offices around the world.

The American Express Company

By an interesting coincidence, the two largest worldwide travel agents, Thomas Cook and Son and the American Express Company, may be said to have had their origins in the same year—1841. While Thomas Cook persuaded a railway company to carry a train load of passengers at very cheap fares in the year, Henry Wells started his freight business in the USA at the same time. Henry Wells commenced his business initially as a shipper who later began the well-known company of America known as Wells-Fargo.

The American Express Company, popularly known as Amex, is the world's largest travel agency. It was an offshoot of Wells-Fargo Company. Besides selling tours, the company deals in travellers' cheques. Amex is a major participant in international currency transactions, buying and selling huge amount in foreign currency on each working day. The company has also introduced American Express credit cards. These cards are very popular all over the world and the holder can pay his hotel bills, buy an international air ticket and many more things from places where these are accepted. The company also provides service for life insurance and property insurance.

American Express

The American Express Company, also known as Amex, is an American multinational financial services corporation headquartered in Three World Financial Center in New York City. The company was founded in 1850 and is one of the 30 components of the Dow Jones Industrial Average. The company is best known for its charge card, credit card, and traveller's cheque businesses.

In 2016, credit cards using the American Express network accounted for 22.9% of the total dollar volume of credit card transactions in the US. As of December 31, 2017, the company had 112.8 million cards in force, including 50 million cards in force in the United States, each with an average annual spending of $18,519.

In 2017, Forbes named American Express as the 23rd most valuable brand in the world (and the highest within financial services), estimating the brand to be worth US$24.5 billion. In 2018, Fortune ranked American Express as the 14th most admired company worldwide, and the 23rd best company to work for.

The company's logo, adopted in 1958, is a gladiator or centurion whose image appears on the company's traveller's cheques, charge cards and credit cards.

Early History

In 1850, American Express was started as an express mail business in Buffalo, New York. It was founded as a joint stock corporation by the merger of the express companies owned by Henry Wells (Wells & Company), William G. Fargo (Livingston, Fargo & Company), and John Warren Butterfield (Wells, Butterfield & Company, the successor earlier in 1850 of Butterfield, Wasson & Company). Wells and Fargo also started Wells Fargo & Co. in 1852 when Butterfield and other directors objected to the proposal that American Express extend its operations to California.

American Express initially established its headquarters in a building at the intersection of Jay Street and Hudson Street in what was later called the Tribeca section of Manhattan. For years it enjoyed a virtual monopoly on the movement of express shipments (goods, securities, currency, etc.) throughout New York State. In 1874, American Express moved its headquarters to 65 Broadway in what was becoming the Financial District of Manhattan, a location it was to retain through two buildings.

Introduction of Air Travel

Much has changed since 1841 when Thomas Cook chartered a train to carry 570 travellers from Leicester to Loughborough. Cook, who bought railway tickets in bulk and resold them to members of his group, can be credited with being the first bona fide travel agent to work as a full-time professional. However, neither Thomas Cook and Son nor the American Express Company was then a retail agent as the modern complex distribution chain had not yet evolved in any trade, including tourism. The scope of the roles of these two companies was also limited in the beginning because mass tourism, as we know it now, had not yet begun. It was, however, the introduction of air travel which gave boost to the travel agency business. The introduction of an 'economy class' on aeroplanes crossing the North Atlantic heralded the era of travel agency and was responsible for their growth. This, in effect, was nothing more than a projection of Cook's original idea of adjusting prices to encourage full-capacity use of every means of transport.

Continuing development of transport system, especially the jet travel, improved living standards combined with reduction in working hours. Side by side with the rapid improvements in industry and technology, practically all aspects of life have become more and more complex, particularly during the past half century. This is certainly the case in the travel industry in which, only a century ago, the job consisted almost entirely of arranging a simple reservation for the travellers in some means of transport. Today the functions and duties of a person at the travel agency counter are vastly different and more interesting. He is now called upon to perform a variety of duties rather than just to issue tickets and reserve seats in a train, aeroplane or accommodation in the hotel. Travel today is no longer the privilege of the few, but is sought by millions. No longer does the travel agency exist for the sole purpose of selling tickets from one point to another.

With the worldwide demands on its services, the travel industry developed along certain well-defined lines. The urge to travel became so intense over the years resulting in widespread growth of travel agencies in the world. Most of the travellers wished to have their travel arrangements made in advance and to be relieved of the difficulties of coping with various pre-travel arrangements of which they had only a very limited knowledge.

The Modern Travel Agency

The scope of the functions of a modern travel agency has widened greatly over the years and especially after the introduction of the jet travel. The scope of the activities of the travel agent in the context of modern tourism can be described as follows: "to give advice to the potential tourist on the merits of alternative destination and to make necessary arrangement for a chosen holiday which may involve the booking of accommodation, transport or other relevant services."

As the travel agent has accumulated knowledge, expertise and contacts with providers of services, he is a useful and sometimes invaluable intermediary. The retail travel agent provides a direct link between the consumer (traveller) and the suppliers of tourist services, i.e., airlines, transport companies, hotels, auto-rental companies, etc. The retail travel agent is one who acts on behalf of a principal, i.e., the original provider of tourist services such as hotel company, an airline, a shipping company, railways or a tour operator. The retail travel agent sells the principal's services and is rewarded by a commission.

To deal with the subject of travel agency, the best method of approach is, perhaps, to consider the functions of a travel agency. The function of the travel agency will again depend upon the scope of activities it is involved in and also the size and the location. If the organisation is large, the range of activities will be more wide. In this case the agency will have specialized departments each having to perform different functions. Some of the major functions of a travel agency may be classified as follows.

Provision of Travel Information

One of the primary functions of a retail travel agent from the point of view of the tourist and the general public is to provide necessary information about travel. This information is provided at a convenient location where the intending tourist may ask certain questions and seek clarifications about his proposed travel. This is a very specialized job and the person behind the counter should be a specialist having excellent knowledge of various travel alternate plans. He should be in a position to give up to date and accurate information regarding various services and general information about travel, etc. The presentation to the potential customer must be forceful, and exciting variations must continually be devised to help sell services. A good travel agent is something of a personal counsellor who knows all the details about the travel trade and also the needs and interests of the intending traveller. Communication plays a key role in dissemination of any type of information. This is equally true in case of dissemination of travel information. The person behind the travel counter should be able to communicate with the customer in his language. The knowledge of foreign languages is an essential prerequisite for personnel working in a travel agency.

Preparation of Itineraries

Tourist itinerary is a composition of a series of operations that are a result of the study of the market. A tourist journey is characterised by an itinerary using various means of transport to link one locality with another. Preparation of different types of itineraries is another important function of a travel agency. A travel agent gives advice to intending travellers on the type of programmes which they may choose for their holiday or business travel. The study and the realization of the itineraries calls for a perfect organisation (technical and administrative) as also knowledge of the desires of the public for a holiday and the propensity to receive tourists by the receiving localities.

Liaison with Providers of Services

Before any form of travel can be sold over the counter to a customer, contracts have to be entered into with the providers of various services. These include transportation companies, hotel proprietors, the providers of surface transport like motor cars or coaches for transfers to and from hotels and for sightseeing, etc., and also for general servicing requirements. The work carried out under these headings is usually that of the owners or senior employees of agencies concerned. In the case of a large agency with worldwide ramifications, the liaison work involves a great deal of coordination with the principals.

Planning and Costing Tours

The contracts and arrangements having been entered into, there comes the task of planning and costing tours, both for inclusive programmes and to meet individual requirements. This job is intensely interesting and at the same time challenging. This job calls for a great deal of initiative and drive. The job calls for travel to those places which are to be included in the itineraries. This is essentially a job for a meticulously minded person and calls for considerable training and ability. Many agencies with the cooperation of airlines and other transportation companies take the opportunity of arranging educational tours for such staff to countries with which they deal.

Many large agencies have people who are authorities on particular countries and, in addition to a general programme, many will issue separate programmes dealing with territories. Separate programmes dealing with holiday offers based on specific forms of transportation, e.g., air, rail, road or sea, may also be prepared. Programmes also have to be issued to cover different seasons of the year.

Publicity is an important part of the programme. Having spent considerable time and money on preparing all that goes into the issue of a programme, publicity must feature considerably in the activities of a travel agency and more so if the agency happens to be a large one. The majority of large travel agencies have their own publicity departments under the management of a publicity expert.

Ticketing

Selling tickets to clients using different modes of transport like air, rail and sea is yet another important function of a travel agency. This calls for a thorough knowledge of schedules of various modes of transport. Air carriers, railways and steamship companies have hundreds of schedules and the man behind the counter should be conversant with all these. Ticketing is however not an easy job as the range and diversity of international airfares is very complex and varied. There are nearly 50 different types of fare combinations alone on the North Atlantic route. Changes in international as also in the local air schedules and additions of new flights from time to time makes the job of the travel agent one of constant challenge. An up to date knowledge about various schedules of air companies, steamship companies and railways is very essential.

Computerised reservation system has in the recent years rather revolutionised the reservation system both for air and rail travel. Many large travel agencies are using this system. This system comprises a computer network that can be used by the travel agent to reserve an air or rail accommodation as also accommodation in a hotel. Through a wide network, confirmations of reservations are available in a matter of seconds.

Linked with the function of ticketing and reservation of accommodation in a hotel is the settlement of accounts of the clients. Accountancy plays a great part and is one of the important duties to be performed by the travel agency. Dealing with the settlement of accounts in all parts of the world calls for a thorough knowledge of foreign currencies, their cross values and, above all, the intricacies of exchange control regulations, which vary from country to country.

Provision of Foreign Currencies

Provision of foreign currencies to intending travellers is another specialized activity of a travel agency. Some of the larger travel agencies deal exclusively in the provision of foreign currencies, travellers' cheques, etc. This is an important facility to intending travellers as it saves them a lot of time and energy.

Insurance, both for personal accident risks and baggage, is yet another important activity of travel agency. Some of the larger travel agents maintain sizeable shipping and forwarding departments, aimed at assisting the traveller to transport personal effects and baggage to any part of the world with a minimum of inconvenience.

Looking at the various activities mentioned above, it is clear that the travel agent's range of services in modern times has expanded a great deal. His field of expertise is quite large and is constantly growing with the fast-changing travel needs of the people. The job description of a modern travel agent was summed up in an American magazine in the following words:

(i) Preparation of individual pre-planned itineraries, personally escorted tours and group tours and sale of prepared package tours.

(ii) Making arrangements for hotels, motels, resort accommodation, meals, car rentals, sightseeing, transfer of passengers and luggage between terminals and hotels, and special features such as music festivals and theatre tickets.

(iii) Handling of and advising on the many details involved in modern-day travel, e.g., travel and baggage insurance, language study material, travellers' cheques, foreign currency exchange, documentary requirements (visas and passport) and health requirements (immunisation and inoculations).

(iv) Possession of professional knowledge and experience, as for instance, schedules of train connections, rates of hotels, their quality, whether rooms have baths, etc. All of this is the information on which the traveller, but for the travel agent, will spend days or weeks of phone calls, letters and personal visits.

(v) Arrangement of reservations for special interest activities such as religious pilgrimages, conventions and business meetings and sports events.

Source of Income

The travel agency's source of income is the commission which it receives from various sources. He is also remunerated from certain other sources like: (i) commission on the sales he makes of his principal's service (the main principals include an airline, a hotel company, a shipping company and a tour operator); (ii) commission earned from ancillary services such as travel insurance and charges made for such services as travellers' cheques; (iii) income earned from the short-term investment of money received from his customers and deposits and advance payments; and (iv) profit from the sale of his own tours if he operates as a tour operator.

Setting up of a Travel Agency

Opening a travel agency is not an easy job as it involves lot of planning and organisation. Running a travel agency requires a high degree of specialization and organisational ability. A travel agency may have a very large set-up or a limited scope of activities. This will depend on the extent of people's participation in travel activities. In industrially advanced countries of the world, where a large number of people engage in travel, a large percentage of them utilize the services of a travel agency. In these countries, the travel agencies tend to be large having many specialized departments. On the other hand, the services of travel agencies in developing countries are limited making them smaller in size.

The main divisions or sections which a travel agency or a tour operator would have to include are sales, research and planning, finance and accounts, destination and service and publicity and public relations. All of these departments play an important role in the work of the travel agency. These departments must be staffed with efficient personnel. There is also a need for greater coordination among various departments in order to achieve results. Approval by International Air Transport Association (IATA) is also necessary before starting a travel agency. In addition to approval by IATA, travel agencies also need to have certain other approvals/ recognitions. These, however, differ from country to country.

Organisation of Travel

How does a travel agency organize a travel? We have seen that there are various activities which a travel agency has to perform in order that an intending traveller undertakes his proposed journey and enjoys a holiday of his choice. There are various steps involved from the time a traveller visits a travel agent to buy a ticket until he returns back home after visiting a place of his choice. The various steps involved in organising a travel are discussed in the following paragraphs.

Organised travel by a travel agency can be of two types: (i) single client and (ii) group client. In order to effect the journey, the following main elements (in both types of travel) need to be considered: study of the journey, estimate of expenditure, execution of the journey and presentation of accounts.

Individual or Ordinary Trips

The following steps are involved in organising individual or ordinary trips.

(i) The client turns to the travel agent to organize for him a particular journey (cultural, natural, religious, etc.).

(ii) The agency from this angle will examine as to what will be involved, e.g., scope of journey, when the journey is to take place, various services needed and the accessories required.

(iii) Based on the above evaluation and other elements in his possession, the travel agent will suggest the itinerary and will then communicate to the client the estimated maximum cost, for the client's approval.

(iv) Travel agent will then compile the definite estimates, a total of a series of various costs added up, e.g., transport, accommodation, the services such as those of guides, operative costs (postage, telegrams, telephones, etc.).

(v) Next, the travel agent will present a document in duplicate to the customer of the amount of money to be paid. The client should return one of the debit copies signed for acceptance accompanied by a deposit (in anticipation). The deposit normally is about 25 per cent of the total cost.

(vi) Once the client's approval has been obtained, the travel agent's 'operation' department can now execute the journey.

(vii) The 'operation' department's task now is to book for the established dates the transport and various other services. After confirmations of booking have been received, the travel agent issues the vouchers.

(viii) The travel agent will now prepare the 'tourist itinerary' that will accompany the client through the entire journey. It will indicate the tickets to be used, the hotels and other services booked and will include vouchers, etc. Normally the itinerary is made in triplicate, one for the client, another for the agency and the third for the hotelier or those who will provide the required services paid by means of vouchers.

(ix) The last formality is the delivery to the client of the vouchers, confirmed tickets, the technical itinerary and of all the papers and the necessary guidance about the journey.

(x) On receiving the documents, the client will pay to the agency the remaining amount of money.

Group or Organised Trips

The following steps are involved in organising group or organised trips.

(i) This type of travel is customarily arranged by the travel agent after establishing the estimated number of participants.

(ii) Group travel can be a request from an enterprise (company) or a community and in this case the travel agent should be able to determine in advance the number of participants.

(iii) Even in a group travel, the implementation phases can be identified as (a) study of itinerary, (b) compiling of estimates, (c) execution of the journey, (d) documentation of accounts.

(iv) For the preparation of the itinerary it is necessary to know the type of locality to be visited, means of transport and type of hotel, etc., to be used. An important element regarding group travel is the itinerary planning.

(v) Group travel can also be arranged for certain events, e.g., the Olympic Games, and in this case, there will be a need for launching a certain type of publicity campaign.

(vi) While compiling estimates, the travel agent needs to evaluate various services to be offered (accommodation, entertainments, cost of messages, etc.).

(vii) For hotel bookings, the travel agent uses various means. During 'low season', he uses the allotment system: the hotelier pledges to hold at the disposition of the travel agent a certain number of beds that he will utilize and for which he need not pay a penalty if he is unable to fill them.

(viii) Once the consent has been received, the travel agent will send to the hotel or hotels a tentative rooming list giving names and various types of arrangements needed. Only at the time of group departure, the travel agent transmits a confirmed rooming list to the hotel with last-minute variations, if any.

(ix) When the group is particularly large, e.g., for sports the travel agent needs to take extra care by way of informing public authorities for the purposes of security, etc.

The activities and range of services described above are very wide and comprehensive and are covered by the travel agents in a highly developed market. The role and the activities of the travel agents in any country depend on the extent of economic development of that country. In advanced countries, people, due to higher standards of living and increased leisure time, engage more in travel as compared to developing countries. The services of travel agents are increasingly utilized in developed countries. In some of the advanced countries like USA, Canada and Germany, a very large percentage of tourists use the services of a travel agent.

Need for Legislation

The role of travel agencies was discussed at length by the United Nations Conference on International Travel Tourism held in Rome in 1963. The conference noted that in many cases the responsibilities of the travel agent, both towards his principals (carriers, hotel operators, etc.) and towards general travelling public, are not fully recognised within the community. These responsibilities were of great importance and travel agents should therefore be regarded as having professional status. Some delegates attending the conference were of the view that this could best be brought about by introducing appropriate legislation. The view was also expressed that legislation should be internationally uniform. Some representatives felt that each country should decide on the measure it should take in the light of its own particular problem.

A further view regarding legislation was that travel agents should be "self-regulating" in the sense, for example, of establishing their own code of ethics, should set special training schools, should take such other measures as are likely to enhance their status and provide the travel public with service and protection. It was suggested that it would be a great advantage if the major national and international associations of travel agents were to cooperate in drawing up an international code of ethics. It was also felt that an effort should be made to prepare a draft statute governing agency regulations.

In the conference the point was also strongly made that the rights of principals as well as of agents should be protected if legislation were introduced. In particular, the right of principals to appoint the agents of their choice must be preserved. It was mentioned that in some countries satisfactory bonding arrangements had been made by agreement between principals and travel agents, thus providing some assurance that travel agents were financially sound and efficient and affording principals and the public added protection.

The Tour Operator

The dramatic growth of tourist traffic to the Mediterranean countries of Europe is a principal feature of the history of mass tourism in the last fifteen years. A major contributing factor in this growth of air travel holiday tourism has been the development of the 'inclusive tour', a method of packaging a holiday. The idea of buying a package of travel, accommodation and perhaps some ancillary services such as entertainment became established in Western Europe in the 1960s. Essentially an inclusive tour is a package of transport and accommodation and perhaps some other services, which is sold as a single holiday for an all-inclusive price. This inclusive price is usually significantly lower than could be obtained by conventional methods of booking transport and accommodation separately from individual hotel and transport tariffs. The principal feature of the inclusive tour is that the tourist may buy for a single price a holiday which is much cheaper than would be possible for the holidaymaker if he bought the components of his holiday separately and directly from individual hotels and from transport companies or from a retail travel agent.

The chief functionary or the principal in this system is the tour operator. It is the tour operator who buys aircraft seats and hotel beds and certain other facilities such as surface transport or entertainment and makes up the package. Historically, the tour operator has mostly emerged from retail travel agency. However, today, a clear distinction must be made between tour operator and travel agent. The latter, the retail travel agent, undertakes to sell the travel services of his principal, who will be airline companies and other transport undertakings, hotel groups, shipping lines and the providers of such ancillary services as travellers' cheques.

Unlike the travel agent who is the retailer of the tourism product, the tour operator is a manufacturer of a tourism product. He plans, organizes and sells tours. The tour operator makes all the necessary arrangements—transport, accommodation, sightseeing, insurance, entertainment and other matters—and sells this 'package' for an all-inclusive price. A package tour is designed to fit a particular group of travellers. These may be special-interest tours, e.g., mountain tours, and can be escorted. Escorted tour normally includes transportation, meals, sightseeing, accommodation, guide services, etc. It is the escort or the group leader who is responsible for maintaining the schedule of the tour and for looking after all the arrangements.

Group Inclusive Tour (GIT)

Group inclusive tour is the most popular form of tour in this category where people travel in groups of 15 or more persons. These tours are available for any destination. The terms and conditions for group inclusive tours are laid down by IATA. The escort for such groups normally travels free as the airline provides him with free passage and accommodation. Foreign inclusive tours (FIT), on the other hand, are unescorted package tours. These tours are comparatively more flexible. The traveller can buy a predetermined package with arrangements for sightseeing, hotels and certain meals, where necessary. He does not tour with a group. He can make his own arrangements and programmes according to his liking. The inclusive tour is one of the several devices which enable tourists to enjoy the lower prices.

Lower Unit Costs

How does the tour operator manage to sell the package to the traveller at such a low price? The low price of the package holiday or inclusive tour is made possible by reason of the lower unit costs obtainable both for the air travel and for the hotel accommodation. The tour operator enters into long-term contracts for aircraft and making similar contracts with hotels. By mass producing holidays in the form of package tours, the tour operators are able to procure substantial discounts from carriers, hoteliers, etc., and offer their package deals at much lower rates. The profits of the tour operator and the success of his operations, however, depend on the achieving of very high load factors for the aircraft and very high occupancy rates for the hotel. In this way unit costs can be maintained sufficiently low to enable the tour operator to offer his package at a price which is often less than the cheapest available fare alone. A breakthrough in the business of tour operation came when airlines recognised that tour operation could fill the empty seats and introduced special fares for use exclusively by tour operators for combining into an inclusive tour.

The tour operator has thus emerged as the true manufacturer of the tourist product. The product is the inclusive tour, packaged, standardized and mass produced. The tour operator may sell this product directly to the public or through the channels of the retail travel agencies. It can be marketed successfully in the tourist- generating countries to a mass market just because it is standardized, packaged and quality controlled. The product is therefore susceptible to similar marketing techniques that are applied to the marketing of consumer goods.

Travel Organisations

The American Society of Travel Agents, Inc. (ASTA)

The American Society of Travel Agents (ASTA) is the leading professional society of travel agents in the industry. The world's largest professional travel trade association, ASTA was established in New York in 1931. Originally named the American Steamship and Tourist Agent's Association, its present name was adopted in 1944. The society was set up to foster programmes for the advancement of the travel agency industry, promote ethical practices and provide a public forum for travel agents. It has now over 25,000 members and is the only organisation representing all segments of the travel industry. The membership consists of travel agents, carriers, hotels, etc.

Purpose

The purpose of ASTA is the promotion and advancement of the interests of the travel agency industry and the safeguarding of the travelling public against fraud, misrepresentation and other unethical practices. The society maintains legal representation and also a government affairs office in Washington, D.C. to provide direct contact with the federal government and the regulatory agencies in the travel and transportation field, and to protect the legitimate interests of travel agents.

ASTA's services to travel agents also benefit the general public. Such activities include sponsorship of frequent conferences on travel matters, involving airlines, steamship companies, agents, municipal and government officials, and other interested parties; discussions with airlines on fare structures and travel destinations; research studies into traveller preferences; close cooperation with various city, state and government agencies across the country in travel-oriented matters, assistance to all agencies across the country in travel-oriented matters; and assistance to all levels of government consumerism departments in upgrading standards of service to travellers.

Membership

While ASTA is still primarily the trade association of the travel agency industry, there are more than 25,000 members in the society covering all segments of the travel industry. Out of this, more than 50% are travel agents in the United States and Canada. In addition to travel agents, there are allied members representing airlines, railways, roads, hotels, government tourist offices, etc. The society has a membership in over 130 countries all over the world. In order to qualify for the membership of the society, an applicant must be in the business of travel under its present ownership or control for a minimum period of three years.

There are two basic classifications of membership, active and allied. Active members are year-round travel agents or tour operators; allied members include airlines and steamship companies, railroads, bus lines, car rental firms, hotels, resorts, government tourist offices and other organisations regularly engaged with the travel industry or associated industries.

ASTA has several travel agency members outside the USA and Canada. All are engaged in travel agency operations on a year-round basis and have been in business for at least three consecutive years. The international roster has its own elected governors and actively participates in all phases of society meeting. Membership advantages include education and training in ASTA's comprehensive travel courses and seminars, guidance from ASTA headquarters in resolving many business and trade problems, and a weekly newsletter and monthly magazine containing important reports and articles from the travel front and related information of value to agents, tour operators and other members.

World Travel Congress

The year's foremost meeting place is the ASTA World Travel Congress. The Congress is the single most important meeting held annually in the travel industry and the programme includes workshops, seminars, business meetings, film presentations and social events. Members from throughout the world travel industry participate, give talks, lead discussion groups and conduct sessions. The ASTA World Travel Congress has been the platform for launching many important and beneficial education programmes for agents. The Madrid Congress granted four Travel Hall of Fame awards, an honour given to those whose careers have made long-standing impacts on the development and expansion of the travel industry and tourism.

The Society consists of the following departments policy implementation and administration, industry relations, memberships relations and communications. The members of the Society derive various advantages which include education and training. ASTA has a comprehensive list of travel courses and seminars which are attended by its members. The Society also offers professional training courses to senior travel agency personnel. Various research papers and newsletters are brought out from Society's headquarters for use of its members. The Society also brings out a monthly magazine - ASTA Travel News.

Structure

ASTA has 28 chapters in the United States of America and Canada and another 28 chapters overseas. Each chapter has elected officers and appointed committees. There is a National Board of Directors which establishes policies of the society. Every two years a new president and chairman of the board are elected by active members. Day-to-day activities of the society are looked after by a professional staff which works under the guidance of an executive vice president who, in fact, is the chief operating officer of the society. He makes recommendations on policy matters to the board and executive Board. He directs the headquarters staff in providing a broad programme of services and facilities to ASTA's membership and carrying on the day-to-day business of the society. ASTA world headquarters is located at 711 Fifth Avenue in New York city, USA.

Universal Federation of Travel Agents Association (UFTAA)

The Universal Federation of Travel Agents Association is an important organisation of the travel agents on a worldwide basis. The federation was founded in Rome in November, 1966.

The aims of the federation are as follows:

(i) To act as the negotiating body with the various branches of tourism and travel industries on behalf of travel agents and in the interest of the public.

(ii) To ensure for all travel agents, through their national associations, the maximum degree of cohesion and understanding, prestige and public recognition, advancement of member's interest and protection from legislation and from other legal points of view.

(iii) To offer its members all the necessary material, professional and technical advice and assistance to enable them to take their proper place in the economy of world tourism.

Over the years, the federation has been responsible in improving the professional status and business standing of travel agents. It has a series of achievements to its credit. Prominent among its achievements is its collaboration with the International Rail Union. This collaboration resulted in obtaining increased commission from 7.5 to 8 per cent on several railway networks, creation of professional training courses and introduction of rail inclusive tours. With regard to air transport, the cooperation between the federation and IATA over a number of years has resulted in raising of commission to 8 per cent, introduction of an overriding commission of 4 per cent, 50 per cent reduction for the spouses of travel agents and creation of international correspondence courses for the training of agency sales staff. Regarding hotel industry, the federation, following negotiations with the International Hotel Association, has created an international convention, set down regulations for bookings, cancellations and cancellation fees. A court of arbitration to settle disputes between hotel and travel agents located in different countries has also been created.

The federation consists of the national travel agency association of over 84 countries which in turn represents more than 20,000 travel agencies from all over the world. The membership of the federation is split into nine regions each covering a group of countries. The UFTAA headquarters is located in Brussels, Belgium.

World Travel and Tourism Council

The World Travel & Tourism Council (WTTC) is a forum for the travel and tourism industry. It is made up of members from the global business community and works with governments to raise awareness about the travel and tourism industry. It is known for being the only forum to represent the private sector in all parts of the industry worldwide. Its activities include research on the economic and social impact of the industry and its organisation of global and regional summits focused on issues and developments relevant to the industry.

History

The WTTC began in the 1980s with a group of business executives led by former American Express CEO James D. Robinson III. The group was formed to discuss the travel and tourism industry and the need for more data relating to the importance of what some believed was a non-essential industry. Discussions led to the first meeting of the WTTC in Paris, France in 1989. The first meeting included a speech by former United States Secretary of State Henry Kissinger who suggested that the travel and tourism industry was not widely recognized due to its not having any organisation or structure. The WTTC was officially established in 1990.

The first annual general meeting took place in Washington, DC, in 1991, at which time the council was composed of 32 members. These initial members agreed on the need for a common effort to promote awareness of the economic contribution made by the travel and tourism industry. The founding members provided investment and support to produce economic data that could demonstrate the importance of the industry. They shared an interest in ensuring greater interest from governments and policy-makers in order to ensure the success of travel and tourism.

Robert H Burns took over as chairman of the WTTC in 1993, at which time there were 68 members. It began releasing tourism impact information around the same time, working with Wharton Econometric Forecasting Associates to develop the data. The WTTC formed a group known as the Tourism Satellite Account (TSA) to compile and release the data. The TSA was recognized by the United Nations Statistical Commission in 1999. During the 1990s, the WTTC expanded the activities of the council to include education and training, air transport liberalisation, taxation, and sustainable development. The new activities led to the creation of the World Travel & Tourism Human Resources Centre in Vancouver and the World Travel & Tourism Taxation Policy Centre in the United States.

In 1997, the WTTC organised the first Global Travel and Tourism Summit in Vilamoura, Portugal. Membership in the organisation reached 100 the same year. Two more summits were held in Vilamoura in 2000 and 2003, which were followed with annual meetings held in various locations.

In 2013, the WTTC created the Hotel Carbon Measurement Initiative in partnership with the International Tourism Partnership.

Organisation and Membership

The WTTC is headquartered in London. The staff are led by the president and CEO of WTTC. Seven directors head the different sections of the organisation. The WTTC members are the chief executives, presidents, or chairs of companies from different sectors and regions within the travel and tourism industry. The WTTC has two membership types: global members and regional members. It also has a category for companies that provide services to the industry, referred to as Industry Partnership.

TRAVEL AGENTS IN INDIA

As long back as in the year 1954, the Government of India was aware of the important role which the travel agents were to play in the development of tourism. It was recognised by the Government that tourists who visit a foreign country often prefer to secure the services of travel agents who assist them in order to make best use of time and money at their disposal. The government felt that many a time unauthorised persons offer themselves as agents and in return fail to render satisfactory services, and even exploit the ignorance of the tourists for their personal benefit. With a view to curb this the government evolved a system of granting recognition to travel agents. The rules for recognition were as follows:

(i) No firm shall be granted recognition unless it has been engaged actively in handling tourist traffic for at least one year before the date of the application.

(ii) Firms granted recognition shall be entitled to such right and privileges as may be granted by the government from time to time and shall abide by several terms and conditions of recognition.

(iii) Firms granted recognition shall undertake to maintain an office under the charge of full time members of their staff who should, apart from issuing rail tickets, be in a position to give up to date and accurate information regarding transport and accommodation facilities, currency and customs regulations and general information about travel, etc.

(iv) The recognition may be extended for the whole of the country or be limited to a particular region.

(v) Firms granted recognition shall undertake to employ only guides approved by the Ministry of Tourism.

(vi) All recognised firms shall furnish yearly statement of their activities and such other information in regard to the volume of tourist traffic actually handled and other relevant matters.

(vii) The decision of the government in the matter of recognition shall be final and it reserves the right to cancel or withdraw it at any time.

Subsequently, following clauses were also added:

(i) The recognition to be granted by Ministry of Tourism shall not automatically entitle the firm to be appointed agents for the sale of rail tickets by the Ministry of Railways (Railway Board). The agencies thus recognised shall apply separately to the Railway Board.

(ii) Firms seeking recognition as travel agents should have a minimum paid-up capital of rupees one hundred thousand.

(iii) Applications for grant of recognition by the Ministry of Tourism will be considered only if the firm:

   (a) is approved by the IATA;
   (b) has licence to book foreign passages issued by the Reserve Bank of India;
   (c) has the approval of the Ministry of External Affairs to handle travel documents and to deal with passport offices;
   (d) is registered under the Local Shops and Establishment Act.

The recognition is now granted by the Ministry of Tourism in the Ministry of Tourism and Culture. The application for grant of recognition is to be made in the prescribed form and is to be addressed to the Director General, Ministry of Tourism who is the authority empowered to grant such recognition.

Travel Agents Association of India (TAAI)

The travel agents decided to form an association on all-India basis as long back as in the year 1952, when an All India Travel Agents Association was established. The main objective of the association is to safeguard and protect the interests of its members by way of having a constant dialogue with the concerned government agencies. The annual convention of the association is attended by a large number of representatives from travel trade both government as well as non-government. Important matters related with the promotion of product are discussed in these conventions. The Travel Agents Association of India has its registered office in Mumbai and regional offices in Kolkata, Delhi and Chennai. The association publishes a monthly magazine *Travel News* for of its members.

The vital role played by the travel agents in the growth and development of tourism in the country and its promotion is recognised by all segments of the travel industry. The government works in close collaboration with them not only in India but abroad as well, encouraging them to plan and organize package tours for various destinations in India. In suitable cases, the Ministry of Tourism recommends the foreign exchange to travel agents to enable them to open their branch offices abroad. The ministry has also instituted a special tourism award which is given every year to the agency earning the maximum amount of foreign exchange.

The Travel Agents Association of India (TAAI) was formed towards the end of the year 1951 by a group of twelve leading travel agents, who felt the time had come to create an Association to regulate the travel industry in India along organised lines and in accordance with sound business principles. The primary purpose was to protect the interests of those engaged in the industry, to promote its orderly growth and development and to safeguard the travelling public from exploitation by unscrupulous and unreliable operators. In the following years, the Association's membership has swelled steadily from the original 12 to approximately 2500 members consisting of Active, Associate, Allied, Government and Non-Resident.

Objectives and Aims

- Apply superior technical skills to the jobs on hand.
- Deliver the highest quality of service.
- Act responsibly within sound financial parameters.
- Build trust and credibility in the marketplace.

  The symbol TAAI is an enforcement of reliable and professional service.
- TAAI is conscious of the interest of the travelling public and maintains high ethical standards within the travel trade.
- TAAI aims at the development of the travel and tourism industry in India by constantly improving the standard of service and professionalism in the industry so as to cater to the needs of the travellers and tourists from within India and overseas.
- TAAI is engaged in promoting mutual co-operation among the different segments of the travel and tourism industry, among TAAI members, by contributing to the sound progress and growth of the industry as a whole.

Activities of TAAI

- TAAI functions as a powerful platform for interaction of thoughts and experiences.
- TAAI helps promote, maintain and stimulate the growth of travel and tourism in the industry.
- TAAI educates and equips the members to meet the challenges of tomorrow through conventions and seminars.
- TAAI draws the attention of the controlling and regulatory authorities in the country and discusses with them the problems of the industry and works for the survival and betterment of its members.
- TAAI maintains close contact with world bodies and represents matters affecting the travel and tourism industry of the country.
- TAAI gathers useful information on travel and tourism and disseminates the same to its members for their guidance.
- TAAI helps develop better understanding among the different segments of the travel industry and brings them into its fold by offering membership under different categories.
- TAAI fosters fraternity among its members.

TAAI has signed several MOU's with various Travel Agents Associations in neighbouring countries and around the globe.

The Travel Agents Federation of India (TAFI)

The Travel Agents Federation of India (TAFI) was established in 1986. It is a dynamic organisation that guides the travel industry in India. It is a professional body of Travel Agents coordinating different segments of the travel trade and is a **non-political, non-commercial and not-for-profit body.**

TAFI's membership today comprises of 1400 Active, Associate, Allied and Affiliate (Travel Service Intermediaries - Non IATA) members from all over India. Over 70% of the ticketing business is handled by TAFI members. TAFI is a proud member of World Travel Agents Associations Alliance (WTAAA) and an Affiliate member of the Southern African Tourism Services Association (SATSA). TAFI has signed an Agreement with the Federation of Hoteliers and Restaurant Association of India (FHRAI) for the benefit of its members. TAFI is committed to creating a more evolved and stable environment in the Travel Trade and becoming the cornerstone of the industry.

TAFI represents the travel trade before official bodies of Government, Airlines and other appropriate forums. It ensures healthy growth of the Travel Industry by promoting mutual cooperation among TAFI members and by introducing schemes that would benefit TAFI members as well as provide mutually beneficial alternatives to the airline industry. TAFI augments the development of the travel industry in India by encouraging improvement in the standard of service, inculcating professionalism and spreading awareness and updated information on travel and regulations. It protects the interests of those engaged in the industry by highlighting the need to maintain high ethical standards and ensuring compliance of Rules, Regulations and Guidelines set by the Consulates, Government Authorities and Airlines.

TAFI safeguards the interests of the Travel Agents vis-a-vis service providers such as airlines, consulates, Government authorities and the travelling public from exploitation by unreliable travel agents.

The Travel Agents Federation of India (TAFI) is a dynamic organisation that guides the travel industry in India. A professional body of Travel Agents coordinating different segments of the travel trade, TAFI is a **non-political, non-commercial and not-for-profit body.**

TAFI Today

- TAFI's membership - 1400 Active, Associate, Allied and Affiliate (Travel Service Intermediaries - Non IATA) members from all over India.
- A proud member of World Travel Agents Associations Alliance (WTAAA)
- An Affiliate member of the Southern African Tourism Services Association (SATSA)
- Signed an Agreement with the Federation of Hoteliers and Restaurant Association of India (FHRAI) for the benefit of its members.

Celebrating its silver jubilee, TAFI is committed to creating a more evolved and stable environment in the Travel Trade and becoming the cornerstone of the industry.

Mission

Promote

We ensure the healthy growth of the Travel Industry by promoting

- mutual cooperation among TAFI members
- schemes that would benefit the TAFI members as well as provide mutually beneficial alternatives to the airline industry.

Augment the development of the travel industry in India by

- encouraging improvement in the standard of service
- inculcating professionalism
- spreading awareness and updated information on travel and regulations

Protect the interests of those engaged in the industry by

- highlighting the need to maintain high ethical standards
- ensuring compliance of Rules, Regulations and Guidelines set by the Consulates, Government Authorities and Airlines

TAFI safeguards the interests of the Travel Agents vis-a-vis service providers such as airlines, several consulates, several Government authorities and the travelling public from exploitation by unreliable travel agents.

Association of British Travel Agents (ABTA)

ABTA is a UK travel trade association for tour operators and travel agents.

History

Previously known as Association of British Travel Agents, its name was changed on 1 July 2007 to ABTA, The Travel Association to reflect its wider representation of the travel industry.

On 1 July 2008 it merged with the Federation of Tour Operators (FTO).

It was founded in 1950 by 22 leading travel companies.

Function

ABTA has been around for over 65 years and is the UK's largest travel association, representing travel agents and tour operators that sell around £32 billion of holidays and other travel arrangements each year.

The main functions of ABTA are:

- Raising standards in the industry and by giving guidance on issues from sustainability to health and safety,
- Providing schemes of financial protection,
- Offering holidaymakers a course of redress if something goes wrong,
- Presenting a united voice to government to ensure the industry and the public get a fair deal.

Code of Conduct

ABTA maintains a Code of Conduct which governs the relationship between Members and their customers, between Members and ABTA, and between Members and other Members.

The Code is essentially a guide to good practice, although some of what it contains is also required under UK and European law. Those booking travel arrangements with an ABTA Member can expect to receive:

- Accurate information so one can make an informed choice
- Advice or assistance on passport, visa and health requirements
- An offer of a suitable alternative if there are building works that will seriously impair one's holiday
- A refund of the holiday cost if there's a significant flight delay and one don't want to travel
- A response to any complaint you might have within 28 days
- Resolution of one's complaint as quickly as possible and, if it can't be resolved amicably, the guaranteed option of arbitration to find a settlement.

All ABTA Members have to abide by the Code and those that breach it can face sanctions at ABTA's Code of Conduct Committee.

Consumer Protection

ABTA currently has around 1,200 Members and represents over 5,000 retail outlets and offices. It is estimated that over £32bn is spent on holiday arrangements with ABTA Members every year, 90% of package holidays in the UK are sold through its members.

It has eleven regional divisions. The head office is situated near Vinopolis and Southwark Cathedral, England.

The ATOL scheme of financial protection covers flight-based holidays. If one buys a land- or sea-based holiday such as coach, rail or cruise holiday from an ABTA Member ones monies will be protected by the ABTA scheme of financial protection. This means that if ones travel company fails and ones holiday can no longer go ahead one will be entitled to a refund if he/she are yet to travel and hotel costs and transport home if they are abroad.

In addition to financial protection, ABTA Members are also bound to comply with the ABTA Code of Conduct, which ensures high service standards and fair terms of trading. Booking with an ABTA Member also gives one recourse should one have a problem or complaint with ones travel company.

ATOL

ATOL stands for Air Travel Organisers' Licence. It is a government-run financial protection scheme operated by the Civil Aviation Authority (CAA). All monies one pay for package holidays involving flights and holidays including a flight plus accommodation and/or car hire, must be protected under an ATOL licence. The customer will receive an ATOL Certificate at the time one makes ones payment, and one will need to keep the certificate safe.

ATOL cover means that if your travel company fails and your holiday can no longer go ahead you will be entitled to a refund if you are yet to travel and hotel costs and flights home if you are abroad. Flights booked directly with an airline are not protected under the ATOL scheme.

ATOL is a financial protection scheme, it does not provide other assistance if there are other problems with ones holiday.

apter

Tourism Plannin and Development

Planning is the process of thinking about the activities required to achieve a desired goal. It is the first and foremost activity to achieve desired results. It involves the creation and maintenance of a plan, such as psychological aspects that require conceptual skills. There are even a couple of tests to measure someone's capability of planning well. As such, planning is a fundamental property of intelligent behaviour. An important further meaning, often just called "planning" is the legal context of permitted building developments.

Also, planning has a specific process and is necessary for multiple occupations (particularly in fields such as management, business, etc.). In each field there are different types of plans that help companies achieve efficiency and effectiveness. An important, albeit often ignored aspect of planning, is the relationship it holds to forecasting. Forecasting can be described as predicting what the future will look like, whereas planning predicts what the future should look like for multiple scenarios. Planning combines forecasting with preparation of scenarios and how to react to them. Planning is one of the most important project management and time management techniques. Planning is preparing a sequence of action steps to achieve some specific goal. If a person does it effectively, they can reduce much the necessary time and effort of achieving the goal. A plan is like a map. When following a plan, a person can see how much they have progressed towards their project goal and how far they are from their destination.

Planning Process

Three-step result-oriented process for planning:

1. choosing a destination
2. evaluating alternative routes
3. deciding the specific course of the plan

In organisations, planning can become a management process, concerned with defining goals for a future direction and determining on the missions and resources to achieve those targets. To meet the goals, managers may develop plans such as a business plan or a marketing plan. Planning always has a purpose. The purpose may involve the achievement of certain goals or targets.

Major characteristics of planning in organisations include:

- Planning increases the efficiency of an organisation.
- Planning reduces risks.
- Planning utilizes with maximum efficiency the available time and resources

The concept of planning in organisations involves identifying what an organisation wants to do by using four questions: "where are we today in terms of our business or strategy planning? Where are we going? Where do we want to go? How are we going to get there?

Tourism planning leads to tourism development. In fact, tourism planning is the process for tourism development. In general terms, planning refers to methods and means used in making decisions about the future. Planning not only guides actions to be taken in future but also helps in problem solving and arriving at decisions which help planners in achieving desired objectives. Planning is not static but dynamic and guides future actions. Tourism planning process involves creating a future that is acceptable to the host community as also to others who would be part of the host community as tourists for a short period of time. Since tourism involves hospitality, the planning for various tourism facilities must be based on the needs of the guests.

The Need for Planning

The need for planning arises whenever some rational thinking is required to arrive at a choice among a set of limited means so that certain ends are satisfied especially when the means are substitutable among themselves. In other words, planning essentially attempts to allocate scarce resources between different competing uses with a view to maximising output, income and employment and to ensure the balanced growth of different sectors. Such planning may be at an individual level or at a firm level or at an industry level or for the economy as a whole. There are broadly two economic systems prevailing—planned economy and market economy. Planned economy is one in which each production unit (or a firm) uses only the resources of men, material and equipment allocated to it by quota and disposes of its products to person or firms indicated to it by simple order. On the other hand, a market economy is controlled by the forces of market, like demand, supply, prices, transport, etc. Plan can be applied to any type of economic system, whether centrally structured or built up of many units of purely market economy character. The different institutional frameworks will lead to compulsory planning under the first system and to indicative planning under the second.

Planning for Tourism

In the field of tourism, the need for planned development is of paramount importance. Many countries in the world, especially the developing countries, have lately realised the importance of tourism and the benefits which it brings out. The use of macroeconomic planning techniques for tourism sector are, however, relatively new. The planning methods for national economic development, which have been largely utilized since the end of the World War II, did not always cover tourism development as a particular field. The increasing significance of tourism as a source of income, employment generation, regional development and as a major factor in the balance of payments for many countries has been attracting the attention of many governments as well as others with an interest in economic development. Thus, tourism development became more and more a particular field of research in the economic planning undertaken by many countries. As far back as in the year 1962, the Secretary General of the United Nations had declared: "Impressive unanimity has been achieved regarding the potential value of development planning."

The UN Conference on International Travel and Tourism

The United Nations Conference on International Travel and Tourism held in Rome in 1963 emphasised the need for planning in tourism and made several recommendations. Some of the important recommendations that the United Nations Conferences made in the area of planning in tourism were as follows:

(i) that the governments of developing countries should give high priority to projects concerning the development of tourism in their respective countries.

(ii) that the governments of developing countries should consider the possibility of seeking the assistance of the United Nations Special Fund for regional and subregional surveys of existing and potential tourist resources and for the preparation by experts of tourist traffic estimates and forecasts, with a view to the establishment of short-term and long-term plans for the development of tourist facilities and plant.

The conference endorsed the relevant comments of the group of experts who had pointed out that tourism was expanding swiftly as world economy improved and more and more travellers sought new places to visit. It further stated that to the extent permitted by its economic resources, a country should see a steady growth in the number of new tourist resorts developed. Existing possibilities of attracting tourists—mountaineering, winter sports, fishing, hunting, beaches, spas, national parks, game sanctuaries, national monuments, sites and shrines, folk traditions and customs, pilgrimages, festivals and sporting events—should likewise be developed and protected. Stress was laid on the importance of ensuring protection, not only for monuments, archaeological remains and buildings of historical, cultural or architectural importance, but also for the customs, traditions, art and folklore of indigenous peoples. The conference also agreed that a developing country which proposed to set up a national tourist organisation should consider obtaining a preliminary survey in order to assess clearly what positive tourist attractions the country already had, what potential tourist attractions existed, and how they could most effectively be developed within the limits of the funds available.

The recommendations had far-reaching implications as far as planned development of tourism was concerned. All member states and the specialized agencies of the United Nations were called upon to consider and implement as appropriate the recommendations contained in the report of the conference. The recommendations of the conference were of particular interest to those countries which were just beginning to develop tourism. Until quite recently tourism was principally a feature of, and was largely confined to, the developed countries. Many of the developing countries saw the possibilities in tourism development. Encouraged by the recommendations of the conference, many developing countries introduced tourism development programmes.

UNCTAD

In 1965, the United Nations Conference on Trade and Development (UNCTAD) also emphasised the promise which tourism held out for the developing countries. For some countries, tourism offers a major opportunity since it provides employment for many; it stimulates investment and is an important source of foreign exchange. The third International Union of Official Travel Organisations (IUOTO) Travel Research Seminar held in Prague, the Czech Republic, in 1964, examined in great detail the many problems involved in the development of tourist industry and concluded that planning, whether at national, regional or local level, was indispensable. It concluded that all tourist planning should be based on two types of preliminary surveys: (i) detailed survey of the characteristics of the area being considered for development and, in particular, of its tourist resources; (ii) studies of future customers based on surveys and forecasts.

Careful planning is a prerequisite for complete success of any programme. The haphazard development in many countries had made the planners aware of the need for planning of tourism development based on scientific research. Every country, whether it already has an active flourishing tourist industry or is thinking of developing a tourist industry, has to decide on many crucial issues before launching a tourism development programme. The agencies responsible for tourism development have to consider the various issues. The official government agencies, especially in the developing countries, have to be extra cautious as they cannot afford to waste scarce resources on developmental plans which do not bring benefits. The governments in these countries have to decide on the following issues:

Major Issues

(i) rate of growth of the tourism sector, whether it wishes to encourage mass tourism or develop it more slowly, gradually and selectively;

(ii) the importance of the tourism sector to the national economy and how its development and growth is to fit in with the plans for national, regional and local development;

(iii) the respective roles which it assigns to public and private sector in the development of the industry;

(iv) the respective roles to be played by domestic and foreign capital (whether foreign investments are to be encouraged in case the country's financial resources are limited);

(v) decision as to whether the tourist industry should be treated in the same way as other industries or whether the peculiar character of the industry warrants it being given special treatment; and

(vi) decision as to whether tourist industry is to be developed on a continuous long-term basis or only as a short-term arrangement to overcome the trade deficit.

OECD

The Organisation for Economic Cooperation and Development (OECD) in a seminar held at Estoril focussed its attention on all the above issues. According to the report "much of the discussion turned on the fact that tourism is by its nature somewhat different from other sectors of the economy, since it is an industry based on movement of people rather than goods. For this reason it is particularly susceptible to subjective considerations quite apart from the play of the economic forces. Political and social pressures, psychological attitudes, changes of fashion, may all influence the course of tourism development markedly and unpredictably. It is essential therefore that tourism industry should be as flexible as possible to be able to adapt to changing conditions and requirements." The discussions at the OECD seminar also drew attention to the fact that tourism involves several considerations which are essentially of non-economic nature. The report of the seminar stated: "Tourism often has significant cultural implications (for example, the restoration of ancient monuments); aesthetic (the preservation of beauties of landscape and the safeguarding of the nation's heritage); social (the provision of recreational facilities for the health and welfare of the people); and political (the improvement of international understanding)."

The fact that tourism is by its nature somewhat different from other sectors of the economy necessitates careful planning. This is much more important for the developing countries which cannot afford to waste scarce resources. The various issues involved in the planning and development of tourism show how necessary it is for these countries to adopt growth plans in this specific branch, duly relating to their political and economic institutional framework. Just as a country will adopt a monetary policy, a policy of agriculture, of public works, of health, of transport, and so on as different elements of its national economic plan, so it should on the same grounds, adopt a specific policy of tourism development.

Coordinated Planning

The peculiar characteristics of tourism make it particularly beneficial in terms of general economic development. From this follows the necessity of adopting a development policy, which will take into account all the country's economic sectors which have a direct or indirect interest in its expansion. On the other hand, tourism, as an integral part or specific sector of the general plan of economic development, can only prosper within the context of the country's overall progress even though it calls for its own particular policy. Tourism, like other economic activities, flourishes best when it fits into a context of general economic policies and programmes designed to lead to the optimum growth of the economy of a country as a whole. This calls for coordination. Coordination between tourism planning and the general plan must therefore be based on coordination of effort in all the sectors concerned. Tourism policy must therefore be a global policy of development, taking into account the important implications, affecting the progress of this activity. In addition, the overall tourism development plan must take into account the social and cultural components of the phenomenon, for these also acquire prominence in the development process.

The planning of tourism, whether at the national or the regional level, must be regarded as an integral, and therefore, coordinated part of the country's general economic and social planning. This coordinated approach has a direct bearing on the success of the tourism industry, more so in a developing country. It is also to be remembered that tourism is not one business but involves many industries and a whole range of complex processes. A plan for tourism can only survive and serve its stated purposes if there is coordination among all the processes. A first requisite is the need to ensure that the government organs specifically responsible for the tourist sector play their important role, which is that of cooperating with all those governmental departments responsible for other branches concerned with the expansion of tourism. The essential aim of the tourist plan is to arrive at a balanced growth of demand and supply. In other words, to arrive at an optimum harmonization of the interrelations between the two poles of market while avoiding the creation of serious economic, territorial or social imbalances. Hence, the basis of planning in a sector must be viewed globally and mutually arranged with country's economic and social development and with the overall policy of planning for the territory in which the location of tourist centre assume primary importance.

The Planning Process

A process for tourism planning or the subjects of analysis of a plan of tourism development must be correlated with all the elements noted above, in order that they can achieve an optimum level of expansion without creating serious imbalances of various kinds. If a country, region or an area possesses attractions and provides some hospitality for prospective tourists, tourism will probably develop. If this tourism development is to benefit the host area, a formal forward-looking planning is essential. If tourism planning is to happen in a specific area, someone or some entity must stimulate and enunciate the original idea. This basic inspiration must be shared by some entity which holds controlling interests and responsibility for the resources to be utilized by the tourism industry. This principle holds true for planning a programme of any scope or dimension. For instance, there may be an existing resort, hotel or industry in a region. The stimulus may be realization that there is potential for growth if only existing facilities can be expanded or new ones generated. At the other extreme, an area may have potential but underdeveloped resources. No matter what the situation, for effective tourism planning, there must be active involvement and participation by persons or entities controlling the essential resources.

A description of various planning processes or analysis of a plan of tourism development is very essential. A description given here can only be briefly indicative and is limited to mere suggestions of the topics or the steps without entering into detailed analysis. The plan must take account of these various processes in quantitative terms, if it is to outline the optimum objectives to be attained in a given period of time. The objectives must be related to those of the overall economic development plan. The key steps, or phases in planning, can be as follows: (a) assessment of tourist demand and supply, (b) establishing objectives, (c) territorial planning, (d) basic infrastructure, (e) financial planning, (f) human resource planning, (g) administrative structure, (h) marketing and promotion, (i) monitoring progress, and (j) the time factor.

Assessment of Tourist Demand and Supply

One of the early steps in planning is gathering information on the things the way they are and on the potential available for desirable growth. One of the main problems in investigating the potential of tourism can be the simple lack of information. Recording of information and the development of statistics is therefore of utmost importance. The important initial steps in evaluating a potential for tourism development lies in determining present status. An analysis of the present structure of demand and supply in tourism is a pre-condition of any other estimate. This information base is a prerequisite for initiating tourism planning programme. In the first place, there must be a survey of the tourist attractions of various types which the country has to offer. Without a full study of the attractions a country possesses, it is not possible to plan for future expansion. It is, therefore, of fundamental importance that a very careful assessment be made of all attractions—physical, cultural, historical—that a country possesses.

According to Peters, there are a number of principles on which assessment should be based. First, it is highly desirable that the attractions should be developed progressively throughout the entire country so that tourism is spread as widely as possible. In this way, the benefits which accrue from the industry are also widely spread and most parts of the country benefit. Second, areas and attractions which are singled out for special development should appeal to the widest possible cross-section of tourists over the longest possible season. By adhering to this principle, over-dependence upon a particular season of the year will be avoided. Third, priority should be given to those attractions which can be most easily and most successfully developed. Those attractions which can be based upon the existing infrastructural services should be given priority as these would require less finance. Fourth, since it is very difficult, rather impossible, to develop all the potential attractions at the same time, it is important that similar or competing attractions should not be embarked upon until the volume of visitors can justify them. Finally, it is important to know that the tourist is usually looking for something new: he desires new experiences, different environments, new thrills, etc. Any country possessing attractions which are unique or out of the ordinary should attempt to capitalise on these for they are likely to have a great drawing power.

Demand must then be estimated, for both national and foreign tourists. Both internal and external data on tourism activities affecting the area under consideration should be assembled. This task should use published statistics on travel and tourism which are readily available from international and regional organisations. In addition, travel and accommodation statistics can be assembled from the region under study. Next the tourist supply must include all the different types of facilities additional to various types of accommodation establishments. Special attention must be given to the seasonal factor, i.e., the annual fluctuations in the demand as related to the country's tourist attractions.

Establishing Objectives

The information or the initial data thus gathered should develop a composite picture of what tourism can do for and to a particular area. In order to relate these projected results to a decision on whether to proceed with tourism development, there must be a basis for comparison. This basis is the cumulative set of objectives which should be developed concurrently. Basically, objectives for tourism should be a subset of the overall objectives (either implicit or documented) for the nation, the economy, the people and the social structure within an area. There are, however, no set rules as to what the objectives should be. In general, tourism objectives should deal with growth leading to increased standard of living, employment levels, opportunities for intellectual growth, enhancement of the investment potential in an area or country. Cumulatively, tourism objectives should describe the set of conditions under which a favourable decision should be made.

If the data indicate that reasonable objectives for tourism development can be met, this will generally lead to a decision to proceed with a conceptual planning study. As a basis for moving ahead with a conceptual planning study, a request for proposal (RFP) should be prepared. This is a detailed description and a set of guidelines for the study which will be used by prospective organisations as a uniform basis for submitting proposals. As a first step towards preparation of conceptual plan for tourism development, a market study and resource analysis should be performed. The market study begins with a determination of the type of tourism business which exists and can be expected. Market study provides the basis for conceptual planning. The conceptual plan provides a general view of the future tourism development programme and the steps necessary to achieve targeted results. The various steps involved in conceptual planning, once the market survey has been performed, include (i) statement of objectives; (ii) selection of site, (iii) requirements of various facilities, (iv) supplementary attractions, (v) land use allocation and control, (vi) budgets, and (vii) legislative requirements.

Preparation of a master plan is another important step in planning. Master planning is a process for completing and detailing additional work on the portions of the conceptual plan which are approved for further development. The differences between conceptual and master planning lie largely in the level of details involved. Where conceptual planning, for example, might indicate the need to expand airport runways and terminal facilities, master planning would go into specifics on land and construction.

Territorial Planning

The need will arise of locating each pole of tourism development so as to fit in with the general policy of territorial planning. Particular attention must be given here to natural and cultural assets of the country, while avoiding the damage which results from an unbalanced exploitation of their economic value. The need for tourist territorial planning must be reconciled with the limits in pace of industrialisation and urbanization which, even though complementary to tourism, can constitute a serious danger to it. It will also be necessary to plan further tourism development in the selected zones in order to avoid excessive concentration in one area.

Basic Infrastructure

If a tourism development programme is to succeed, it is necessary to provide life support through a number of infrastructural facilities and services. Infrastructure elements comprise the system of services and utilities which are necessary to the operation of a tourism destination. The estimation of the basic infrastructure required for tourist expansion accordingly becomes a key economic factor in proceeding to the active phase of implementation. This infrastructure will be either specifically tourist in nature, e.g., transport, or more general, such as energy-producing units, and will in any case vary with the type of tourism envisaged. The requirements for infrastructure will vary for different areas. The requirements, for example, will be different for a mountain resort and for a tourist pole adjacent to some cultural attraction. The requirements will be for both tourists and local residents. As various agencies are responsible for development of infrastructure services, coordination is very essential. Without coordination, different elements of infrastructure may infringe upon each other resulting in wasteful expenditure. Specific areas of infrastructure are power, water, communication, sewage and drainage, roads and highways, parks, recreation and health-care facilities.

Financial Planning

Financial planning is very essential for a successful tourism development plan. Before any major attraction, facility or destination gets into full swing, considerable expenses are involved. There follows the study of a vital element in tourist development, that is, the financing of both infrastructure and superstructure. Assessing the cost of the project is relatively easy when compared to assessing benefits. There may be a choice of locations or a choice of techniques. Estimates must be made for each choice within a feasible range. Each proposal must be assessed separately to establish its feasibility, cost–benefit and degree of priority in making a plan. Agencies concerned with the development of an optional national investment programme should compare investments in tourism facilities and related infrastructure with alternative investment opportunities in other sectors. In World Bank Group Operations, this comparison is attempted on the basis of economic rates of return for well-defined investment proposals. In evaluating tourism investments the World Bank Group pays very close attention to the projected financial results. In general, tourism projects financed by the World Bank Group are justified in terms of both their economic impact and their financial viability.

In the case of those countries which already possess an active tourist industry or have potential for increased tourism development, finances for investment will usually be available readily. However, in the case of developing countries, which are anxious to develop tourism, due to financial constraints, the provision of adequate resources of capital may be difficult. The development of tourism sector will be only one of the number of options for development before a government, since government resources will inevitably be inadequate for all the competing claims upon them. In view of this, the proposed investment in tourism must be justified in terms of its anticipated contribution to the economic development of the country.

Except in centrally planned economies, such as in countries like Russia, Poland, Yugoslavia, public investment will be supported by private investment as happens in the mixed economies like France, Italy and India. The government may take the initiative in project development, but it will expect private investment support. If the government is anxious to develop and promote an active tourist industry it will help the private investor to the maximum extent. This can be done, first, by creating a favourable climate for investment and, second, by assisting private investor to consider tourism development as an attractive investment proposition. This could be done by way of offering special financial inducements such as subsidies, tax concessions, preferential rates of interest credits, special facilities for purchase of land, etc. All these investment incentives in some form or the other encourage private investment in tourism sector.

Role of Foreign Capital

In addition to the public and private finance, foreign capital also plays an important role in tourism development programmes. Attention will have to be paid to financial means and facilities designed to attract foreign capital. A basic obligation at this stage will be the calculation of the output capital ratio, which will depend for the most part in the external economies that can be achieved. Foreign investment is usually welcome by many developing countries, largely because of their own acute shortage of capital resources.

Human Resource Planning

Professional and efficient management is an obvious prerequisite to successful tourism development. Of equal importance, however, is the quality of staff training, which is often relatively neglected during the early stages of tourism sector development. Tourism basically being a service business, a developing destination must take the necessary steps to build a pool of efficiently trained people to fill various jobs which will be created subsequently. A variety of jobs will have to be created to look after and manage various tourist services. Special attention, therefore, will have to be given to needs in manpower and personnel to be trained and rendered qualified for the various tourism professions. Special care has to taken to ensure that there will be no shortage of trained manpower in case there is expansion of facilities and services. In the case of a developing country, it will also be appropriate to study at this stage the volume of manpower required for activities complementary to accommodation industry, in particular in the commercial sector.

In planning for human resources development, programme should be established to screen and train prospective employees so that they could acquire both attitudinal as well as technical skills. Attitudinal characteristics contribute to an employee's success in tourism position and include pride, flexibility, adaptability and judgement. Technical skills required include facility and equipment operation and maintenance, financial management, food and beverage production and service, personnel management and administration and system analysis and design. In order to determine the need for various personnel required, a staff planning exercise may be done. This involves a series of steps which include job analysis, preparing job descriptions, job specifications and preparing staff forecasts. This sequence of activities leads to a detailed forecast of exactly what types of persons, with which specific qualifications and skills, will be required at all major facilities within the tourist destination. All this helps in determining the development of requisite education and training programmes within the country for local residents. This will also help in determining whether there is a need for trained personnel from other countries and also whether local people are to be sent for training elsewhere.

Administrative Structure

Next comes the necessity of setting up an adequate administrative organisation to look after various aspects. If a tourism programme is to succeed, the responsibility of success must be assumed by some entity in the form of an organisation. This organisation should have a charter and resources appropriate to carry out various functions. Many countries have established special departments or agencies to manage and coordinate tourism programmes. Depending upon the economic, social and political structure in the country, the tourism organisation may be a governmental department, a semi-governmental agency in the form of corporation supported by government but operating outside its organisational structure. It may also be a private-sector organisation with government support and recognition. Whatever form the tourism organisation takes, it needs to exercise its authority and responsibility in the sphere of tourism development. The administrative organisation looks after the legal aspects, i.e., the preparation of the legislation required for the installation of the various tourism services, dealing with such matters as the classification of hotels or the control of travel agencies, etc. It has various departments for planning, marketing, research, training, and legal and administrative services.

Marketing and Promotion

The final stage of the plan is concerned with the preparation of promotional activities aimed at launching the new tourist industry both within and outside the country. The main concern of tourists is having an enjoyable and pleasant experience rather than details associated with planning their journeys. Most of the tourists leave these details to travel professionals and intermediaries who look after all the details of the travel plans. Contacts with and support of travel professionals and intermediaries are among the most important factors for successful marketing and promotion of tourist destination. Facilities and specialities of travel professionals include national tourist offices, regional travel promotion organisations, airlines including other carriers, tour wholesalers, tour operators, travel agents, travel clubs and convention and conference organizers. The various channels of communication used to inform and stimulate include tourist literature in the form of catalogues, brochures and folders, direct mail, advertising, public relations and publicity. All these media are selected and organised into promotion campaigns aimed at selling to consumers and travel professionals and intermediaries. The media campaigns are timed in such a way that these correspond with the selling effort supporting a destination. It is very important to ensure that these activities match the level of tourist development aimed at.

Monitoring Progress

Monitoring the progress periodically is very crucial to get the best results. Preparation of a plan document is not an end in itself. The task of the planner does not end when a plan for three years, five years or seven years has been prepared. A system of constant revision and monitoring of the plan progress should be a part of the exercise of planning. Targets must be revised continually in the light of changing resources and other circumstances. The error is to mistake a plan for planning. To use a more elegant vocabulary, a plan is static and planning must be dynamic. Plans are interesting mathematical or literary or technical exercises that can be formulated with a great variety of methods and degrees of perfection. Planning, on the other hand, is a diffuse but coherent process of making and revising decisions that must be closely attuned to the implementation of planned action. What is needed is a system of monitoring progress and mechanisms for constantly and rapidly adjusting to the changing conditions and circumstances.

The Time Factor

Time factor is a very important element. The main purpose of development planning is to move towards self-sustaining growth, that is, to create a cadre of trained manpower, to increase knowledge of natural resources and their effective utilization and to create institutions for enterprising investment. All this takes time. The duration of the plan could be for 25 years, 10 years, seven years or five years. Many planners are of the view that the first development plan should be a 10-year plan, as it requires an assessment of long-term perspective. Time is a fundamental factor in the preparation of the plan and in the identification of the objectives to be attained upon its termination. The medium-term plan ranges between three and seven years with five years as the most popular choice. The long-term range upwards from 10 years to 25 years.

The short-term plan on the other hand is an annual plan. The annual plan is the controlling plan as it is the authorised document to check its possible achievements being matched by available resources year by year. It is governed by medium- or long-term plan, which sets its direction. The annual plan in the operative document, while long-term or medium-term plans are merely a set of intentions. Thus the need for orienting the short-term plan budgets with the long-term or medium-term plan budgets is the core of planning process. Time factor is the main element in the planning, including planning of tourism in any nation. It is vital to the prospect of achieving the economic and social expansion which is linked with tourism.

Tourism is receiving ever-increasing attention from national governments and from international development agencies. It can generate much-needed foreign exchange for financing other sectors of the economy of a developing country and also for bridging the trade gap. In its broadest sense, tourism can do more to develop understanding among people, generate employment and raise living standards than any other economic force known. There is unlimited potential for tourism development. If properly conceived and executed, such development will prove not only to be financially viable but will also prove to be of immense benefit to a country. Inadequate planning and development, on the other hand, can increase probabilities of failure resulting in great loss.

Some degree of planning is very essential. It is perhaps much easier to have planned development in countries where there is a potential which is only just beginning to be realised. However, even in those countries having a long established and a highly developed tourist industry, some measure of planning is essential. Planning is essential for three main reasons. First, most countries, to a lesser or greater degree, have planned economies, and if tourism development is to be a part and parcel of national economic development, then this sector of economy also should be subjected to planning. Second, the success of tourism development depends very largely upon appropriate facilities being available in the right place and at the right time, and these can only be provided by adequate research into national tourist assets and markets. Research has a very important part to play in the future planning of tourism development. Third, planning is required to ensure that the natural and man-made assets are conserved and protected to maintain tourist appeal, for lack of care and coordinated development may impair and even ruin those assets upon which the tourist industry is founded.

Environmental Planning

Tourism is the world's largest industry. This fact has now been recognised all over the world. Although a 'smokeless' industry, it has environmental implications. Expanding tourism has the capacity to pollute the environment as would any smoke-ridden industry. A few years back, the United Nations organised a conference in Stockholm on human environment. This conference symbolized the growing importance that the people of the world attach to maintaining and improving the quality of human life and to enrich the human environment. It is a fact that all over the world man has been using the natural resources without any thought for the future. It is the wrong use of these resources which causes problems. Today environmental pollution poses a serious threat to life on earth and this is true not only of the areas where there is a great concentration of industries, but also areas where there is a great concentration of tourists.

The disadvantages of haphazard and unplanned development of tourism are well illustrated by many areas in North America and Western Europe and also to a greater or lesser extent throughout large parts of Asia's tourism circuit. Yugoslavia's Adriatic coast and the Seychelles are other examples. Many of the world's finest resorts have become ugly. Sochi, Russia's popular Black Sea resort, has proclaimed itself the world's first 'no-smoking city'. New laws ban smoking in all restaurants, cinema theatres, public transportation, hospitals and on the beaches. In India, there are many examples of uncontrolled growth of industries, shops and also slums near tourist spots creating problems of environmental pollution. Many of the beaches of North America and Western Europe bear a mute testimony to the havoc that can be wrought by uncontrolled development of tourism. Destinations once noted for their particular character are reduced to unattractive showpieces as many countries endeavour to keep pace with the visitor inflow. Despite a measure of governmental control during the development, the great increase in number of visitors to these areas resulted in rapid, unplanned construction of hotels and dwellings for tourists and for migratory service employees. These expansions threaten to destroy the very environment that is the tourist attraction. A prominent leader in the Seychelles objected to seeing his country become a "nation of maîtres d'hôtel." These examples underline environmental threat, both aesthetic and biological, from overcrowding of particularly attractive areas.

Special Ecological Issues

Tourism development germinates special ecological problems not encountered in other types of economic activity. The environmental resources 'exploited' for tourism attract tourists because of their outstanding beauty, recreational possibilities or educational and cultural interest. Modern tourism's most paradoxical trait is its capacity to destroy those attributes which attracted the visitor in the first place. The well-known economic analyst and futurologist, Herman Kahn, described the rapidly expanding tourism as "next only to atomic power in its potential for environmental destruction." Mass tourism has brought in its wake certain ecological and environmental pollution problems.

The environmental amenities which attract tourists have tended to be taken for granted. Preservation of their quality has only recently begun to concern tourism development planners. For tourism the quality of the environment is the basis for attracting visitors and needs to be conserved. Tourism development can become a positive factor for improving environment if some amount of intelligent planning is done. In fact, the quality of the tourism product depends upon a high quality natural environment. The interrelationship was pointed out by the International Union of Official Travel Organisations (IUOTO), the predecessor of the World Tourism Organisation, as long ago as the 1950s. It was reiterated during the 1960s in the face of growing interest in environmental conservation.

The major social benefits accrue to tourists themselves. But tourism also has valuable spillover benefits for tourist-receiving countries. Notable among these is the contribution of tourism to the preservation of historic and cultural values. Careful maintaining, cleaning and beautifying the monuments, clearing the areas around the monuments, improving them for tourism purposes is a case in point. Through tourism development, the environment is not degraded but, in fact, can be improved. So great has been the national and international demand for tourism and recreational facilities that governments have increasingly to face up to the choice between extending public access and availability of sites and conservation and protection against over-development. Governments are increasingly aware that future growth of the industry will necessitate careful management and avoiding over-development of regions of natural beauty. Moreover, saturation in principal destination areas will require a more active policy diversification and redistribution of tourist flows.

Regional Planning Considerations

The potential of a region for tourism may be so great that its development will be central to economic goals and plans. However, regional planning for tourism more often will be considered as a separate and distinct planning effort, aimed primarily at determining the best location of facilities, hotels, resort facilities and transportation networks. Such planning views tourism primarily as a source of foreign exchange earnings. This approach would recommend development to accommodate maximum possible number of projected visitors and to design facilities to generate the maximum possible spending by the tourists. However, this approach of profit maximising to tourism development can result in deterioration of fragile environment and attractive landscapes through over-building and excessive number of visitors.

Carrying Capacity And Sustainability

Every tourist site has a carrying capacity for the tourists as well as well as for any other type of use. This will vary with the fragility of the area concerned and the nature of the tourist activity contemplated. For instance, an island rainforest is a fragile environment which could be easily endangered by excessive number of people. By contrast a recreational beach is not easily damaged by sunbathers or swimmers. Planning facilities for tourism development in the first case would require limitations on construction of hotels and similar other installations in the region in order not to encourage excessive numbers of tourists. In the second case, high-density accommodations for tourism might well be tolerated.

There have been various attempts to define carrying capacity. Some of these are given below:

> The maximum number of people who can use a site without an unacceptable alteration in the physical environment and without an unacceptable decline in the quality of experience gained by visitors. [Mathieson and Wall, *Tourism: Economic, Physical and Social Impacts*, 1982.]

> The concept of maintaining a level of development and use that will not result in serious environmental deterioration, socio-cultural or economic problems, or be perceived by tourists as depreciating their enjoyment and appreciation of the area. [World Tourism Organisation, *National and Regional Tourism Planning*, (Madrid: WTO) 1994.]

> The level of tourist presence which creates impacts on the host community, environment and economy that are acceptable to both tourists and hosts, and sustainable over future time periods. [Cooper et al., *Tourism: Principles and Practice*, 1993.]

Types of Carrying Capacity

Following are various types of carrying capacity:

Physical

- Acceptable levels of visual impact and congestion.
- Point at which ecological systems are maintained before damage occurs.
- Conservation of wildlife and natural vegetation of both the land and marine environments.
- Acceptable levels of air, water and noise pollution.

Economic

- Extent of tourism that provides optimum overall economic benefits without economic distortions or inflation.
- Level of tourism employment suited to the local community.
- Extent of tourism development that can be absorbed without detriment to the lifestyles and activities of the local community.
- Level of tourism that will help maintain historic and cultural monuments, arts, crafts, belief systems, customs and traditions without detrimental effects.

Socio-cultural

- Extent of tourism development than can be absorbed without detriment to the lifestyles and activities of the local community.
- Level of tourism that will help maintain historic and cultural monuments, arts, crafts, belief systems, customs and traditions without detrimental effects.

Infrastructure

- Adequate availability of transportation facilities and services.
- Adequate availability of utility facilities and services of water supply, electric power, sewage and solid waste disposal and telecommunications.
- Adequate availability of other community facilities and services such as those related to health and safety, and of housing for employees in tourism.

Psychological

- Refers to crowding and the psychological impact of being with too many other people for comfort/enjoyment.
- Congestion

Carrying capacity, however, may change over time. Technological advances, for example, may increase the amount of sewage which may be treated, thereby increasing carrying capacity. Improvements to infrastructure, modes of transport, etc., may also increase carrying capacity over time. An important point to recognise is that the overall carrying capacity of a destination is often determined by just one factor. That is, one factor becomes the limiting factor. For example, there may be enough hotel beds to cater for 10,000 tourists per night, but if the sewage system can only cope with 5,000 then the carrying capacity will be 5,000.

Factors Affecting Carrying Capacity

A wide variety of factors will affect the carrying capacity. These range from the level of technological development to the type of tourist. Any factors which influence physical, economic, socio-cultural, infrastructural and psychological will affect carrying capacity. Major factors usually include.

Alien Factors

- The volume and characteristics of the tourist mass tourism will have a greater impact than independent/explorer type tourism
- The length of stay
- Geographical concentration of visitors
- The degree of seasonality

Local Factors

- The fragility of the local environment: sand dunes, marine environments etc. are more fragile than Trafalgar Square in London or Manhattan in New York.

- The social structure of the host economy: the more developed a country is, the less vulnerable to the influence of the tourist.
- The economic structure: developing countries are less likely to be able to reap the same benefits as a developed country due to the fact that they are likely to have to import more goods to cater for the needs of the tourist because they are not produced locally. They may also be dependent on foreign investment for development-the profits generated from these developments will be repatriated (or at least some will be).
- The political structure: governments may encourage or discourage tourism. This will be reflected in the resources and support made available to cope with the impact of tourism.
- Availability of local resources: the greater the local resources, the lower will be the need for imports and the greater the benefit for the local community. Natural resources will also serve as an attraction for tourists.
- The policies adopted with regard to tourist dispersal.

Combination of factors

- The difference between the tourist and host: the greater the difference the greater the impact. This applies to both differences in wealth and differences in culture.
- The amount of contact: fleeting contact will be less likely to allow hosts/tourists to learn about the other's culture. Segregation of the tourist reduces what is called the demonstration effect.

SUSTAINABILITY

The underlying approach now applied to tourism planning, as well as to other types of development, is that of achieving sustainable development. Sustainability is linked very closely to carrying capacity. Both are related to the concept of maintaining a level of tourism which does not cause irreversible damage and which allows tourism in a given destination to continue into the future. The sustainable development approach implies that the natural, cultural and others resources of tourism are conserved for continuous use in the future, while still bringing benefits to the present society. The concept of sustainable development has received much emphasis internationally since the early 1980's, although tourism plans prepared even before that period often were concerned with conservation of tourism resources.

> The sustainable development approach to planning tourism is acutely important because most tourism development depends on attractions and activities related to the natural environment, historic heritage and cultural patterns of areas. If these resources are degraded or destroyed, then the tourism areas cannot attract tourists and tourism will not be successful. More generally, most tourists seek destinations that have a high level of environmental quality—they like to visit places that are attractive, clean and neither polluted nor congested. It is also essential that residents of the tourism area should not have to suffer from a deteriorated environment and social problems. World Tourism Organisation, *National and Regional Tourism Planning* (Madrid: WTO), 1994.

It is difficult to pinpoint the responsibility to any one particular agency department for achieving sustainable development. Because of the nature of the tourism industry, i.e.., it is fragmented with many players, problems have arisen because of conflicting interests. Venice is a good example of where coordinated overall planning has proved difficult. There is no one government department that has responsibility for planning and conflicts have arisen between the needs of the locals and the needs of the tourists.

It could be argued that everyone involved should take responsibility. The government is usually involved, for instance, in terms of granting planning permission. Developers are involved, but do not always have long-term objectives, particularly if they come from outside the community in which the development is taking place. The local people have a vested interest in ensuring that their "home" is not spoilt, but often there are conflicts between hotel owners (or any one who benefits from tourism) and those who only "suffer" the tourists (e.g., traffic jams). Tour operators and travel agents have started to take a more responsible stance—in their brochures they try and "educate" the tourists to be more aware of local customs and save water. However, their main objective is to make a profit. Tour operators take options for hotel rooms, but if a resort does not prove popular, they can easily 'switch' to another resort and cancel flights. Two approaches to responsible planning for sustainable development are possible—a top-down approach, with plans prepared by a central authority (Central or regional government) or a bottom-up approach, driven by the community. Often a combination of the two approaches achieves the best results.

At Macro Level

- *Creation of "honey pots"*: This is the creation or development of popular resorts in one area, as a way to relieve tourist pressure from another area of a more sensitive nature.
- *Dispersion policy*: The use of "honey-pot" resorts may cause the depletion of resources in one area, and the exclusion of the rest of an area's population from the financial benefits of tourism. To prevent this, a policy of dispersing tourist resorts across a region or country may be adopted.
- *Zoning*: This is the division or categorisation of land permitting only certain kinds of use on it. This may also be applied to lakes. Some lakes may be zoned for water skiing or fishing.
- *Encouragement of green policies*: This is when green policies are adopted to protect and restore the environment or offset an environmental problem, and, at the same time, indirectly improve recreational resources. An example of this is the growth of urban forests which could in turn lead to these sites being used for recreation.
- *Provision of urban tourist facilities* : If there is provision of tourist or recreational facilities like urban farms, water splash parks or access to existing facilities like rivers and lakes, it removes pressure from ecologically sensitive areas as the impact of tourism in urban areas is less. It fulfils the need of the tourists by finding a use for their leisure time and also benefits the local community by retaining income that would have been spent elsewhere. It also reduces the social

and environmental cost of travelling to and from a tourist destination and also in a way substantially removes the need to desire for a holiday by reducing the demand for travel.

- *Create environmental awareness*: Making people aware of the effects of tourism, providing tourists with information on scarcity of natural resources, information relating to cultural differences and advice regarding acceptable behaviour may be considered under this heading.

At Micro Level

- *Restrictive entry*: this is where access is controlled by the use of various means like permits licences, barriers across entry points, and quotas.
- *Use of price mechanism*: To reduce the number of tourists high prices may be charged. This will create an image of "exclusivity" which in turn helps to justify the high price.
- *Signposting*: By providing visitors with information and by the creation of signposted walks, behaviour may be modified and tourists may be kept away from sensitive areas. Signposting can be used in conjunction with information provision.
- *Protecting footpaths*: The sustained use of footpaths can lead to problems such as soil erosion or the widening of paths. In order to prevent this care has to be taken in planning footpaths and also consideration of what materials should be used in order to create a state of naturalness but which also sustains high levels of pedestrian flow.
- *Control of access points*: It is similar to restrictive entry. The location and size of car parks, roads or hotels in relation to areas of sensitive nature can reduce the number and impact of tourists.

All the above steps, however, are to be taken very cautiously as many of these vary from one country to another. In a number of countries, especially in the West, these steps have achieved good results in protecting the environment of the areas and helped in achieving sustainable development. These steps have also helped in conserving natural and cultural resources of tourism for a long- term continuous use. Conserving the environmental amenities of a region and of advancing regional development through tourism are interdependent. The more local people benefit from tourism, the more they will benefit from a commitment to preserve the environmental features which attract tourism. Consideration of the region's ecological characteristics are essential to provide adequate criteria for the development of facilities and viable plans for the use and management of resources for tourism.

Protecting Natural Environment

Of all the modern industries, tourism has the greatest need to protect the environment of the places of natural and cultural importance—be it a monument, a beach resort or a wildlife sanctuary. The planners must consider the environmental process wherever large investments are made in tourism development. The tourist has a strong desire to see and experience places of wonder and beauty in areas where nature remains essentially unspoiled. Destinations noted for their particular character and beauty should not be reduced to innocuous urban jungles in order to keep pace with the visitor inflow. Wildlife, which is deteriorating and vanishing so rapidly, can be safeguarded. The environment in which various animals live can be properly preserved. Similarly, many other tourist areas can be safeguarded against forces which are responsible for their degeneration. Tourism must be used as a positive factor in environmental improvement.

Physical planning and area development are therefore very essential for environmental improvement. Tourism development can become a positive factor for improving the environment if certain amount of basic planning and aesthetics are applied in the entire process. Whenever there is any major tourism development, environmental planning should be made part of that development. Any development without some controls, without any thought given to the environmental factors can, in fact, prove to be disastrous and will ultimately be counterproductive for tourism itself.

As many agencies are involved in tourism development, coordination is necessary among various segments responsible for environmental development and improvement. With a view to preserve the unique character, atmosphere and natural setting of monuments and other places of tourist interest, a coordinated approach needs to be evolved to exercise environmental control of tourist centres. In countries where there are town and country planning acts, these should be made effective enough and their provisions should cover legal protection to control environmental balance in tourist and development areas. In order to ensure that the act is properly enforced, it would be desirable to involve all those agencies which are responsible for tourism development. In countries having federal set-up, the authorities responsible for governing should carefully study the impact that the opening of a new area to tourists is likely to have on the cultural and social environment of the area. Master plans or area development plans should be formulated before permitting the tourists access to these areas. Concerned local authorities should be consulted at the time of working out of the proposals for area development with tourist potential. In order to ensure the implementation of the environmental control, it may be desirable for various regions to appoint coordinating committees consisting of various interests and departments to implement effectively environmental policies.

Conservation Policy

The United Nations Conference on the Human Environment, held few years back in Stockholm, recommended evolving a conservation policy within the framework of the resolution of the World Cultural Heritage. There was a unanimity of opinion that something radical had to be done to save the quality of human life and to enrich human environment. The conference was of the opinion that any development scheme of the particular area should be determined by the absorption capacity of the area; otherwise the environment would deteriorate and may in the long run create more complications than actually serve the purpose. This is true in the case of development of monuments, new tourist areas and resort towns.

A modern concept of conservation is that of science and ecology. The premise is that of man-environmental balance. The only way of striking this balance is to define conservation as protection of natural resources. Conservation means the exercise of rigid controls to prevent habitat destruction, habitat homogenization, reduction of species and natural resources pollution. Conservation, in the sense of preservation of the cultural heritage, is popularly supported today. Many man-made artefacts have a scarcity value that becomes as important to society's well being as do the natural resources. Therefore, conservation means their protection, restoration and interpretation.

Today the relationship between tourism and the environment has been receiving a growing level of attention from both public and private sector organisations all over the world. During the last decade various international bodies have cooperated in the production of great number of studies, programmes, plans and activities on tourism and environment. The degree of importance of the relationship between tourism and environment is cited in the Manila Declaration on World Tourism during World Tourism Conference held in Manila in October, 1980. The declaration states:

> Tourism resources available in various countries consist at the same time of space, facilities and values. These are resources whose use cannot be left uncontrolled without running the risk of their deterioration, or even destruction. The satisfaction of tourism requirements must not be prejudicial to the social and economic interests of the population in tourist areas, to the fundamental attraction of tourism, and historical and cultural sites. All tourism resources are part of the natural heritage of mankind. National communities and the entire international community must take the necessary steps to ensure their preservation. The conservation of historical, cultural and religious sites represents at all times, and notably in time of conflict, one of the fundamental responsibilities of states.

The importance of the relationship between tourism and the environment is also stressed in the letters of agreement exchanged between the United Nations Environment Programme (UNEP) and the World Tourism Organisation. The letters of agreement state:

> The protection, development and improvement of the various constituents of the environment of Man are among the basic conditions for the harmonious development of tourism. Similarly, intelligent tourism management can contribute in large measure to the protection and development of the physical environment and cultural heritage of mankind as well as the improvement of the quality of human life. It is, therefore, advisable that tourism development and sound environmental management should be integral concerns of national development policies.

WTO Environment Committee

The impact of tourism on the environment led the WTO Executive Council to form the Environment Committee. This committee held its first meeting at Madrid in May 1981. The representatives of various countries who attended the meeting attempted to define the relationship between tourism and the environment, and formulate guidelines and activities to be implemented by the World Tourism Organisation in the future in the areas of the environment. Much of the discussion of the Environment Committee meeting centred on the theme "Tourism Development and its Effects on the Environment".

Tourism development can bring positive results to the countries that succeed in establishing an effective programme. It is important that the damage which can be done to the environment through a misuse of natural and cultural resources be avoided through the implementation of proper policies. Possible negative effects such as ecological deterioration in areas of good environmental quality, especially in mountain and coastal regions and in areas surrounding places of historical, architectural or artistic interest; speculative pressure on special sectors with the ensuing destruction of the landscape and wastage of natural environment, destruction of the traditional values of the domestic architecture and deterioration in the latter when the human dimensions of existing localities are exceeded; and saturation and overcrowding of the urban microcosm with consequent deterioration in the quality of the environment in these areas could then be checked.

Various positive steps have been taken with a view to preserve the natural environments. In the national and regional tourism plans compiled by World Tourism Organisation, there is evidence of one or more of the following aspects receiving attention:

(a) Creation of natural reserves and national parks;
(b) Preservation of historical towns;
(c) Alignment of roads and highways so as to minimize environmental nuisance;
(d) Restrictions on the encroachment of the town into the countryside;
(e) Zoning of industry;
(f) Restrictions on dumping at sea, inland and in freshwater of household or industrial residues.

The formation of the Environment Committee by WTO Executive Council is the step in the right direction. The Environment Committee has adopted the following goals:

(a) To identify clusters of closely related touristic environmental issues specifically including: carrying capacity, ecosystem solvency, protection of cultural elements, protection of the built environment;
(b) To systematize field information;
(c) To define ways to involve tourists in the preservation of the environment; and
(d) To develop and disseminate guidelines for use by governments in assessing, controlling and minimizing adverse environmental effects in tourist activities.

With a view to achieve the above-mentioned goals, the Environment Committee recommended a programme of work that includes the evaluation and updating of existing studies and methodology and the general understanding of touristic environmental problems, cooperation between public and private institutions at the national and international levels aimed at developing touristic environmental guidelines and standards and finally, action by WTO and other international organisations to apply guidelines.

Environmental planning therefore is the process of facilitating decision making to carry out land development with the consideration given to the natural environment, social, political, economic and governance factors and provides a holistic framework to achieve sustainable outcomes. A major goal of environmental planning is to create sustainable communities, which aim to conserve and protect undeveloped land.

Environmental planning concerns itself with the decision making processes where they are required for managing relationships that exist within and between natural systems and human systems. Environmental planning endeavours to manage these processes in an effective, orderly, transparent and equitable manner for the benefit of all constituents within such systems for the present and for the future. Present day environmental planning practices are the result of continuous refinement and expansion of the scope of such decision making processes.

Some of the main elements of present-day environmental planning are:

- Social & economic development
- Urban development
- Regional development
- Natural resource management & integrated land use
- Infrastructure systems
- Governance frameworks

The environmental planning assessments encompass areas such as land use, socio-economics, transportation, economic and housing characteristics, air pollution, noise pollution, the wetlands, habitat of the endangered species, flood zones susceptibility, coastal zones erosion, and visual studies among others, and is referred to as an Integrated environmental planning assessment. It is the ability to analyse environmental issues that will facilitate critical decision making.

Sustainability is the process of maintaining change in a balanced fashion, in which the exploitation of resources, the direction of investments, the orientation of technological development and institutional change are all in harmony and enhance both current and future potential to meet human needs and aspirations. For many in the field, sustainability is defined through the following interconnected domains or pillars: environment, economic and social. Sub-domains of sustainable development have been considered also: cultural, technological and political. While sustainable development may be the organising principle for sustainability for some, for others, the two terms are paradoxical (i.e. development is inherently unsustainable). Sustainable development is the development that meets the needs of the present without compromising the ability of future generations to meet their own needs. Brundtland Report for the World Commission on Environment and Development (1987) introduced the term of sustainable development.

Sustainability can also be defined as a socio-ecological process characterized by the pursuit of a common ideal. An ideal is by definition unattainable in a given time and space. However, by persistently and dynamically approaching it, the process results in a sustainable system.

Healthy ecosystems and environments are necessary to the survival of humans and other organisms. Ways of reducing negative human impact are environmentally-friendly chemical engineering, environmental resources management and environmental protection. Information is gained from green computing, green chemistry, earth science, environmental science and conservation biology. Ecological economics studies the fields of academic research that aim to address human economies and natural ecosystems.

Moving towards sustainability is also a social challenge that entails international and national law, urban planning and transport, supply chain management, local and individual lifestyles and ethical consumerism. Ways of living more sustainably can take many forms from reorganising living conditions (e.g., ecovillages, eco-municipalities and sustainable cities), reappraising economic sectors (permaculture, green building, sustainable agriculture), or work practices (sustainable architecture), using science to develop new technologies (green technologies, renewable energy and sustainable fission and fusion power), or designing systems in a flexible and reversible manner, and adjusting individual lifestyles that conserve natural resources.

"The term 'sustainability' should be viewed as humanity's target goal of human-ecosystem equilibrium (homeostasis), while 'sustainable development' refers to the holistic approach and temporal processes that lead us to the end point of sustainability." (305 Despite the increased popularity of the use of the term "sustainability", the possibility that human societies will achieve environmental sustainability has been, and continues to be, questioned—in light of environmental degradation, climate change, overconsumption, population growth and societies' pursuit of unlimited economic growth in a closed system.

National Park Service in the United States

Since 1872 the United States National Park System has grown from a single, public reservation called Yellowstone National Park to embrace over 450 natural, historical, recreational, and cultural areas throughout the United States, its territories, and island possessions. These areas include a diverse varieties of areas —National Parks, National Monuments, National Memorials, National Military Parks, National Historic Sites, National Parkways, National Recreation Areas, National Seashores, National Scenic Riverways, National Scenic Trails, and others.

Beginnings

National Parks 1864–1891

The national park idea has been credited to the artist George Catlin. In 1832 he travelled the northern Great Plains of the United States, where he became concerned about the destruction of the Indian civilization, wildlife, and wilderness as eastern settlements spread westward. He wrote, "by some great protecting policy of government... in a magnificent park... a nation's park, containing man and beast, in all the wild and freshness of their nature's beauty!"

Caitlin's vision had no immediate effect. In the east, romantic portrayals of nature by James Fenimore Cooper and Henry David Thoreau and painters Thomas Cole and Frederick Edwin Church began to compete with prevailing view of wilderness as a challenge to overcome. Slowly unspoiled nature and spectacular natural areas of the West became better known, the idea of saving such places became of interest.

In California, several state leaders sought to protect Yosemite Valley. In 1864, Sen. John Conness of California sponsored an act to transfer the valley and nearby

Mariposa Big Tree Grove to the state so they might be used and preserved for the benefit of mankind. President Abraham Lincoln signed this act of Congress on June 30, 1864. California was granted the valley and the grove on condition that They would be held for public use, resort, and recreation...inalienable for all time."

The Yellowstone country was first "officially" explored by David E. Folsom, Henry D. Washburn, and Ferdinand Hayden in 1869-71. A myth evolved that near the end of the Washburn expedition, discussion around the campfire led several of the members to suggest that the area be set aside for public use and not allow it to be sold to private individuals. This myth was successfully exploited by National Park advocates but eventually was debunked by historians. An early ally in promoting a public reservation was the Northern Pacific Railroad Company. They were seeking major destinations for their route through Montana. In an effort to reduce poaching and other misuse of the park, the U.S. Army established a fort in the area in 1881 and began park protection, establishing a pattern that would be continued by later park rangers.

In 1875, Mackinac National Park was created on a resort island in Lake Huron in Michigan, the second national park. As at Yellowstone, the army garrison at Fort Mackinac were in charge of supervising and improving the park. The fort and the national park were turned over to state control in 1895.

U.S. cavalry units took up a position in California-controlled Yosemite Park in 1891 and took over some management duties. In 1906 the park was completely taken into federal control.

National Parks Conservation Association

The National Parks Conservation Association (NPCA) is the only independent, nonpartisan membership organisation devoted exclusively to advocacy on behalf of the National Parks System. Its mission is "to protect and enhance America's National Park System for present and future generations."

History

Founded in 1919 as the **National Parks Association**, the organisation was designed to be a citizen's watchdog for the National Park Service (NPS) created in 1916. Among the founders of NPA was Stephen Mather, the first director of the National Park Service. Robert Sterling Yard was NPA's first employee. Although Yard received personal financial support from Mather, the two often differed on development issues in the parks. Taking a strong preservationist position, Yard objected to such commercialization of the parks as the jazz bands and bear shows at Yosemite National Park.

The association continued to resist commercial efforts to build dams and promote mining, logging and hunting in the national parks. In 1970, the organisation changed its name to the National Parks and Conservation Association, in response to the national attention to a new range of emerging environmental issues, including air and water pollution. This was shortened to National Parks Conservation Association in 2000.

Activities

In pursuit of its core mission to protect the national parks of the United States, the NPCA "works to educate decision-makers and opinion leaders about the most pressing issues facing national parks". At its headquarters in Washington, DC, and 27 regional offices around the country, it employs 153 staff members, including program and policy experts who work together with committed volunteers, staff lobbyists, community organizers and communications specialists. Under the leadership of President and Chief Executive Officer Theresa Pierno, "the organisation's strategic focus is on ensuring that as the leading advocate for national parks these places continue to be protected and have the resources and infrastructure they need to thrive in their second century."

The NPCA publishes a quarterly magazine, National Parks, the print version of which is distributed primarily to its members, while articles are also available on its website.

Wildlife Tourism

Wildlife tourism is an element of many nations' travel industry centred around observation and interaction with local animal and plant life in their natural habitats. While it can include eco- and animal-friendly tourism, safari hunting and similar high-intervention activities also fall under the umbrella of wildlife tourism. Wildlife tourism, in its simplest sense, is interacting with wild animals in their natural habitat, either by actively (e.g. hunting/collection) or passively (e.g. watching/photography). Wildlife tourism is an important part of the tourism industries in many countries including many African and South American countries, Australia, India, Canada, Indonesia, Bangladesh, Malaysia, Sri Lanka and Maldives among many. It has experienced a dramatic and rapid growth in recent years worldwide and many elements are closely aligned to eco-tourism and sustainable tourism.

As a multimillion-dollar international industry, wildlife tourism is often characterized by the offering of customized tour packages and safaris to allow close access to wildlife.

Description

Wildlife tourism mostly encompasses non-consumptive interactions with wildlife, such as observing and photographing animals in their natural habitats. It also includes viewing of and interacting with captive animals in zoos or wildlife parks, and can also include animal-riding (e.g. elephant riding) and consumptive activities such as fishing and hunting, which will generally not come under the definition of ecotourism and may compromise animal welfare. It has the recreational aspects of adventure travel, and usually supports the values of ecotourism and nature conservation programs.

Negative Impacts

Wildlife tourism can cause significant disturbances to animals in their natural habitats. Even among the tourism practices which boast minimal-to-no direct contact with wildlife, the growing interest in travelling to developing countries has created a boom in resort and hotel construction, particularly on rain forest and mangrove forest lands. Wildlife viewing can scare away animals, disrupt their feeding and nesting sites, or acclimate them to the presence of people. In Kenya, for example, wildlife-observer disruption drives cheetahs off their reserves, increasing the risk of inbreeding and further endangering the species.

The practice of selling slots for tourists to participate in sanctioned hunts and culls, though seemingly innocent, can serve to impact populations negatively through indirect means. Though culls can and do serve a crucial role in the maintenance of several ecosystems' health, the lucrative nature of these operations lends itself to mimicry by unofficial groups and/or groups which are not fully aware of the potential negative impact of their actions. This is especially true of big-game and highly marketable species. Such unofficial organisations can promote the hunting or collecting of wildlife for profit without participating in or being sanctioned by wildlife management authorities while mimicking organised operations to fool unwary tourists. Though not sanctioned by any authority, the fact that these operations are funded by tourists and fueled by wildlife classifies such illicit hunting activity as "wildlife tourism".

Direct impacts wildlife tourism will have on wildlife depends on the scale of tourist development and the behaviour and resilience of wildlife to the presence of humans. When tourists activities occur during sensitive times of the life cycle (for example, during nesting season), and when they involve close approaches to wildlife for the purpose of identification or photography, the potential for disturbance is high. Not all species appear to be disturbed by tourists even within heavily visited areas.

Disturbing Breeding Patterns

The pressures of tourists searching out wildlife to photograph or hunt can adversely affect hunting and feeding patterns, and the breeding success of some species. Some may even have long-term implications for behaviour al and ecological relationships. For example, an increase in boat traffic has disturbed the feeding of giant otters in Manú National Park, Peru. Further disturbance to wildlife occurs when tourist guides dig up turtle nests and chase swimming jaguars, tapirs, and otters to give clients better viewing opportunities. On the shores of Lake Kariba in Zimbabwe, the number of tourist boats and the noise generated has disrupted the feeding and drinking patterns of elephants and the black rhinoceros - it is feared that further increases in boat traffic will affect their reproductive success.

Disturbing Feeding Patterns

Artificial feeding of wildlife by tourists can have severe consequences for social behaviour patterns. Artificial feeding by tourists caused a breakdown of the territorial breeding system of land iguanas on the South Plaza in the Galápagos Islands. Territories were abandoned in favour of sites where food could be begged from tourists, and this has had a negative effect on the breeding success of iguanas. Artificial feeding can also result in a complete loss of normal feeding behaviours. In the Galápagos Islands, overfeeding by tourists was so extreme that, when stopped, some animals were unable to locate their natural food sources. Similarly, until the early 1970s, the diet of some grizzly bears in Yellowstone National Park consisted, to a large extent, of food wastes left by visitors at park refuse sites. When these sites were closed, the bears showed significant decreases in body size, reproductive rate, and litter size.

Positive Impacts

Habitat restoration by eco-lodges and other tourism operations

Many owners of eco-accommodation or wildlife attractions preserve and restore native habitats on their properties.

In a large way, the tourists and travellers visiting the wildlife destinations contribute to the conservation and improvement of the conditions for the animals.

The flow of the people keeps the poachers at bay from killing the valuable animals.

The local tribes have a decent living as the tourism flourishes as it provides opportunities of improved livelihood.

Conservation Breeding

Many wildlife parks (e.g. David Fleay Wildlife Park, Gold Coast, Australia) and zoos breed rare and endangered species as a part of their activities, and release the progeny when possible into suitable habitat.

Financial Donations

Some wildlife tourism contributes monetary donations to conservation efforts e.g. Dreamworld, Gold Coast, has a display of Sumatran tigers, and money from visitor donations and from their 'tiger walk' goes to Sumatra to assist in-situ conservation of wild tigers.

Quality Interpretation

A good wildlife guide will impart a deeper understanding of the local wildlife and its ecological needs, which may give visitors a more informed base on which to subsequently modify their behaviour (e.g. not throw out plastic bags that may be eaten by turtles) and decide what political moves to support.

Culls and Population Maintenance

In order to provide for less invasive wildlife tourism features and maintain ecosystem health, wild populations occasionally require maintenance measures. These measures can include the aforementioned conservation breeding programs to bolster population numbers, or culls to reduce population numbers. Population reduction via culls occurs not only through the obvious means of direct (fatal) removal of individuals, but by implementing an additional selective pressure upon the population. This "harvest selection" can alter allelicfrequency (a measure of genetic diversity, and thus related to genetic health) within a population, allowing the hunters to shape future generations by hunting the current.

Conservation Hunting/Harvest

"Well monitored trophy hunting is inherently self-regulating, because modest off-take is required to ensure high trophy quality and thus marketability of the area and future seasons" . For example in Zimbabwe trophy hunting was largely responsible for the conversion of 27,000 km^2 of livestock ranches to game ranching and a subsequent quadrupling of wildlife populations. In South Africa there are approximately 5000 game ranches and 4000 mixed livestock/game ranches with a population of >1.7 million wild animals, presently 15-25% of ranches are used for wildlife production

Anti-Poaching

Bringing tourists regularly into some areas may make it more difficult for poachers of large animals or those who collect smaller species for the black market. Some examples of tourism having a positive effect towards anti-poaching, are that of non-consumptive wildlife tourism services which in turn provide for economic benefit of rural communities, and also by providing these same local communities with game meat harvested through tourist activities such as hunting. Barrett and Arcese (1998) show that generating money sources from these non-consumptive practices of tourism generate a positive income effect and decrease game meat consumption while lowering illegal hunting (poaching).

Today the relationship between tourism and the environment has been receiving a growing level of attention from both public and private sector organisations all over the world. During the last two decades various international bodies have cooperated in the production of great number of studies, programmes, plans and activities on tourism and environment. Although the most improtant requirement is the financial help required to protect global environment. Various countries and international organisation are making special provision in these area. The degree of importance of the relationship between tourism and environment has been cited as long back in the year 1980 in the Manila Declaration on World Tourism during World Tourism Conference held in that year.

The protection, development and improvement of the various constituents of the environment of Man are among the basic conditions for the harmonious development of tourism. Similarly, intelligent tourism management can contribute in large measure to the protection and development of the physical environment and cultural heritage of mankind as well as the improvement of the quality of human life. It is, therefore, advisable that tourism development and sound environmental management should be integral concerns of national development policies and plans.

apter

Tourism ar etin

Prior to the introduction of price mechanism in the world, the goods and services produced were exchanged through simple barter system. The exchanges have always taken place through various means and it is through these exchanges that some sort of markets were evolved. These exchanges, however, have undergone a great change in the past and particularly since the advent of the industrialized societies first in the West and subsequently all over the world. In the early nineteenth century, most of the country's production was conducted in small manufacturing units and on small scale. The market for the goods produced was also small and limited to the areas surrounding the manufacturing unit. Due to limitation of connectivity to other far- off places in the country it was rare that a particular manufacturer's product were sold in other parts of the country.

Another reason for products not finding wider markets was the absence of distribution channels and non-availability of products in sufficient quantities as required by these channels. The means of transport to carry the goods over to distant areas had not yet been evolved. Limited purchasing power as a result of considerable unemployment was yet another factor responsible for smaller and localised markets. Markets for products other than required as necessary for life was limited. Besides, only a fraction of the total population could afford to indulge in purchase of products other than those which were considered to be essential.

Marketing Evolution

From the times of simple barters to the present-day complex marketing systems, exchanges of goods have always been taking place. These exchanges, however, have undergone many changes since the advent of the industrialized societies first in the West and subsequently all over the world. In the nineteenth century, most of the production of industrialized countries was conducted in small manufacturing units as the market for the goods was limited to the areas surrounding the manufacturing unit. It was seldom that a manufacturer's product found place in other parts of the country.

There were several factors responsible for limiting the sale of products of the manufacturing units within the local areas. The main cause was the lack of efficient and inexpensive transport systems to move the products to other areas. Another important cause was the absence of system of distribution channels as also non-availability of sufficient quantity of products as required by these channels. The absence of quality products due to lack of competition and the means of transport to carry the products to distant areas were yet other inhibiting factors. Besides, large majority of people during this period had limited purchasing power as a result of considerable unemployment. Market for goods other than the necessities was rather limited. Only a fraction of the population could afford to indulge in purchase of products other than those essential for living.

Mass Production and the Markets

The post-industrialisation period witnessed the induction of mass production of goods. A large number of people now had access to the products. Coupled with increase in purchasing power, as a result of higher employment and better wages, more and more people could buy products. Rapid industrialisation placed at the disposal of the consumer a variety of products of improved quality and in abundant quantity from a number of competing manufacturers. More and more manufacturers came in the field as the number of products exceeded the demand. As a result of mass production and competition, the consumers for the first time had a choice to purchase the products from more than one manufacturer.

Consumer choice as a result of competition compelled the manufacturers to give greater consideration to the needs of the consumers. Rapid industrial advancement also witnessed the growth in communication and transport systems. The advent of mechanised transport, first the railways and later road transport, made the physical distribution of products possible over much larger areas. The increasing quantity of production of different manufacturing units found markets in far-off places and was distributed by means of railway and road transport systems enabling more and more people to purchase the same. Subsequently, mass communication means like telephones, telegraphs and newspapers greatly helped the manufacturers in disposing their goods and services. All these developments eventually led to the introduction and adoption of a new concept, i.e., the marketing concept by a large number of progressive and forward-looking manufacturing organisations.

Marketing Concept

Marketing has been variously defined through time, by different people. However, the definition which reflects the nature of marketing most adequately is: "Marketing is a human activity directed at satisfying needs and wants through exchange processes." The British Institute of Marketing has formulated the following definition:

> Marketing is the management function which organizes and directs all those business activities involved in assessing and converting customer purchasing power into effective demand for a specific product or service and in moving the product or service to the final customer or user so as to achieve the profit target or other objectives set by the company.

In essence, the marketing concept is a customer orientation backed by integrated marketing aimed at generating customer satisfaction. The important aspects of marketing concept are:

(i) *Customer orientation*: The companies practising this concept think in terms of the benefits they are selling rather than the products.

(ii) *Dual-core marketing job*: This implies that the first task of the marketer is to identify the customer's needs in order to guide the development of the suitable products and services and the second task is to motivate all the potential customers, through various means, to purchase these products and services.

(iii) *Integrated marketing*: The customer orientation alone on the part of the management is not enough. To be effective it must be backed by an appropriate organisational set-up within the company. Integrated marketing represents such a set-up. It signifies the substitution of a single logic for several different logics of the various departments of the company. It implies the responsibility of the marketing department to ensure coordination of various company actions affecting the buyers.

Application of the marketing concept has certain important benefits. First, the management using this concept realise that customer needs are more basic than particular products. This provides a more reliable and enduring base to the operations of such managements. Second, the focus on the customer needs helps the management to spot new product opportunities more speedily. Third, merchandising becomes more effective under this concept. This is because managements view their tasks as that of supplying want satisfaction rather than creating demand for its products among the customers. The physical product is only a part of the satisfactions sought by the buyer because he wants, in addition, conveniences, service and certain other symbolic values. Fourth, the managements are able to create more harmony between their interests and those of the society because the market orientation under this concept means that the managements build their future profits through seeking better ways to satisfy human needs.

Marketing in Travel and Tourism

It is a well-known fact that as long as the inherent sense of curiosity and adventure dwells in the hearts of human beings, the desire to travel in order to see new sights and experience new things, to live under different environments, will always grow. It may be presumed that such being the case, marketing in tourism industry is greatly simplified as part of the process already been completed by the desire for travel in people. The best example would be that a person may or may not choose a tangible product which has been introduced by a manufacturer in the market, solely depending on his ability to afford it or his likes and dislikes. On the other hand, without exception, all human beings will always nurture a desire to travel in order to see places. The question then arises that if the desire is ever present in people to travel and experience new things, why then would the tourism industry need marketing efforts at all?

Are the marketing problems in tourism so much different from marketing problems in other industries that it is justified to make marketing in tourism a subject for separate and specialized enquiry? To what extent can the concepts and principles, the techniques and methods of marketing which have been applied effectively in other industries be applied to tourism? Answer to both the above questions can be found by identifying and considering the differences between markets for physical, tangible goods on the one hand and the market for tourism on the other. The marketing concept, as the overriding philosophy of any business undertaking, contrasts with the production orientation. Here the emphasis is on producing goods or services whereafter a sales policy has to be devised to sell what has been produced. In tourism, on the other hand, the product, from a destination viewpoint, is an amalgam of various elements or components, some of which are tangible and some are intangible (services). The only open path for the organisation in this case would be to inform itself about the consumer needs, expectations, attitudes of mind, likes and dislikes in order to formulate and constantly develop the tourist supply components or products.

The marketing concept should, therefore, be understood as a reorientation of the business policy and an overhaul of the organisation's or enterprise's management concepts and practices. It helps the tourist organisation or enterprise to establish a consistent and effective communication system with actual and potential tourists in the selected markets or market, and to get to know their wishes, needs, motivations, likes and dislikes in order to be able to condition the tourist supply accordingly. The marketing concept, therefore, facilitates a breakthrough in the tourist system.

Tourism is a very complex industry because of its multifaceted activities which together produce the tourist 'product' and various sub-sectors that are themselves complete industries, if considered independently (lodging industry, transport industry, etc.). Besides, its complexity lies mostly in the fact that tourists are located in different places having different socio-economic structures, different needs, tastes, attitudes, expectations and behaviour patterns. It is therefore necessary to understand the people's tastes and preferences. The understanding that people are different in the same market helps in satisfying their needs in a better way.

Defining Tourism Marketing

Tourism marketing could be defined as the systematic and coordinated efforts exerted by tourist enterprises at international, national and local levels to optimise the satisfaction of tourists, groups and individuals, in view of a sustained tourism growth. According to Krippendorf, "Marketing in tourism is to be understood as the systematic and coordinated execution of business policy by tourist undertakings, whether private or state owned, at local, regional, national or international level to achieve the optimal satisfaction of the needs of identifiable consumer groups, and in doing so to achieve an appropriate return."

Tourist Product

A 'product' may be defined as the sum of the physical and psychological satisfactions it provides to the buyer. Marketing, by definition, is the development of a product to meet the needs of the consumer and then employing the techniques of direct sales, publicity and advertising to bring this product to the consumer. Availability of a product is the prerequisite for any organisation which indulges in the marketing function. Unless there is a certain 'product,' be it tangible or intangible or a service, marketing is not possible.

In the case of tourism, the product is the country's natural beauty, climate, history, culture and the people. Other aspects of the produce would be the existing facilities necessary for comfortable living such as water supply, electricity, roads, transport, communication and other essentials. In other words, the tourist product can be seen as a composite product, as the sum total of a country's tourist attractions, transport, accommodation and of entertainment which hopefully result in consumer satisfaction. The tourist product can be entirely a man-made one or nature's creation improved upon by man. Each of these components of a tourist product is supplied by individual providers of services like hotel companies, airlines or other suppliers, and is offered directly to the tourist by them. A consumer can combine these individual tourist products through a number of ways. There would be many possible destinations, each with a number of hotels, each to be reached by more than one airline. Thus the potential choice of the consumer is very large.

The growing number of tourist destinations have placed at the disposal of a tourist a variety of tourist products in abundant quantity from a large number of competing nations. This eventually has led to the adoption of the new concept, i.e., the marketing concept in tourism by various countries promoting tourism. The important point about modern marketing is that it applies to situations where the choice can be limited to a relatively small number of brands giving the consumer a reasonable choice. The process of selection thus becomes easier. In the field of tourism this process is taking place by the increasing use of 'package tours'. A package tour is a travel plan which includes most elements of a vacation such as transportation, accommodation, sightseeing and entertainment. The tourist product is a composite product, whether it is sold as a package or assembled by the individual tourist himself or his travel agent. The tourist product can therefore be analysed in terms of its attractions, its facilities and its accessibility.

Attractions

Of the three basic components of a tourist product, attractions are very important. Unless these are there, the tourists will not be motivated to go to a particular place. Attractions are those elements in the tourist product which determine the choice of a particular tourist to visit one particular destination rather than another. The attractions could be cultural, like sites and areas of archaeological interest, historical buildings and monuments or scenic like flora and fauna, beach resorts, mountains, national parks, or events like trade fairs, exhibitions, arts and music festivals, games, etc.

Facilities

Facilities are those elements in the tourist product which are a necessary aid to the tourist centre. The facilities complement the attractions. These include accommodation, various types of entertainments, picnic sites, recreation and so on. These are indeed important for every tourist centre.

Accessibility

Accessibility is another important component in the tourist product. It is a means by which a tourist can reach the area where attractions are located. Tourist attractions of whatever type would be of little importance if their locations are inaccessible by the normal means of transport. If the tourist attractions are located at places where no means of transport can reach, or where there are inadequate transport facilities, these become of little value. The tourist attractions, which are located near to the tourist-generating markets and are linked by a network of efficient transport, receive the maximum number of tourists.

Tourist Markets

Identification of markets like that of the product is crucial for any organisation which adopts the marketing concept. In fact, the first step a marketing organisation will have to take is to identify its markets. The term 'market' is used in a number of ways. It may be employed to designate the place where the buyer and seller of a good or service meet and between them the exchange transaction takes place. The buyer of goods or services may be the actual buyer or the potential buyer. It may be used in connection with a particular geographical area or in connection with a particular type of service or product. In the context of marketing and promotion, all of the above aspects are relevant, but especially those related to actual and potential buyers, to product and/or service and to geographical location. Another important additional element to be considered is the time factor. Taking into consideration all these elements, the 'market,' therefore, can be defined as "the totality of actual and/or potential buyer of a given product or service in a specified geographical location at a given point in time or during a given period of time."

MARKET SEGMENTATION

A tourist market may be identified corresponding to each tourist product. The term market may be used to describe the collective actual or potential customers of tourism service or destination. It may apply to the geographical area, country, region or city from which a service or destination draws customers. The identification of tourist market, a segment of the total market, is of crucial importance. With a view to avoid waste, it is essential to reach only that fraction of the total market which is most likely to be attracted. Due to financial constraints, it is not possible for an organisation to reach the entire market. Segmentation of the market is therefore made in order to achieve the most efficient use of marketing resources.

Market segmentation is the process of identifying groups of buyers of the total market with different buying desires or requirements. Most markets are too large for an organisation to provide all the products and services needed by all the buyers in that market. Some delimitation of the market is therefore necessary to ensure efficiency and also to conserve financial resources of the organisations. This leads organisations to select target markets necessitating market segmentation. Market segmentation has certain obvious advantages in that the organisation is (i) better placed to spot and compare marketing opportunities, (ii) makes finer adjustments of the product and marketing appeals possible to cater to the needs of the buyers and (iii) can develop marketing programmes and budgets on the basis of a clearer idea of the response characteristics of specific market segments.

The markets are divided on the basis of several factors. The most commonly used bases of market segmentation include (i) geographic segmentation (the market is divided into different geographic locations such as cities, provinces regions or countries); (ii) demographic segmentation: (on the basis of demographic variables such as age, sex, occupation, income, education, social class, religion, etc.); and (iii) psychographic segmentation (on the basis of psychographic variables which refer to such aspects of an individual as his lifestyle, personality, buying motives and product knowledge and use). In tourism, market segmentation is very important. The strategy of market segmentation in tourism recognises that few vacation areas are universally acceptable and desired. Therefore, rather than waste promotion resources trying to please all travellers, the best market strategy is to isolate those segments of the entire market which are likely prospects and aim at the promotional efforts specifically to the wants and needs of these selected groups. Thus, one of the early steps in marketing tourism is to divide the present and potential market on the basis of meaningful characteristics and then concentrate promotion, supply and pricing efforts on serving these most prominent sections of the market—the target markets. Usually the market segmentation for tourism is in terms of demographic, geographic, psychographic, social and economic criteria. For example the market for a particular area might be largely archaeologists in their mid-years who have an income of over $80,000 per year and who live in mid-eastern United States, or it might be largely businessmen in the age group of, say, 40–60 years who have an income of over $100,000 per year and who live in southern parts of Germany. In tourism marketing, the total tourism market can be divided into the major segments mentioned above. A further segmentation, however, is possible within each of the above major segments for practical marketing purposes. This includes:

(i) ***The vacation tourist***: The vacation or the holiday tourist is the most common and popular tourist. He is immensely affected by changes in price, and is easily influenced by skilled and aggressive marketing effort. This type of tourist is resort oriented (Rome, New York, London, Paris are resorts as much as Venice, Goa, Pattaya, Miami). The vacation tourist market has been regarded as highly seasonal.

(ii) ***The business tourist***: In recent years the market for business tourist has increased greatly. The choice of destination of a business tourist is generally determined by the nature of his business. The marketing efforts will not influence the choice of the business tourist much. Unlike the case of the vacation tourist, who has proved to be very sensitive to price changes, the demand for business tourism is relatively price inelastic. The demand will tend to be big-city oriented. The visits are of shorter duration and relatively frequent. Trade fairs, conventions, exhibitions, conferences and similar events attract this kind of tourism.

(iii) ***The common-interest tourist***: This segment comprises visits to relatives and friends, and visits for the purposes of education, pilgrimages, etc. Demand for this type of tourism will be relatively price elastic. The common-interest tourist will not be very readily influenced by the promotional efforts. The average length of his stay will be relatively longer. Because of his friends and relatives, he will not be a significant user of hotel and other such types of accommodation. The visits will not be frequent and expenditure relatively little on his stay as compared with the other two groups.

Special Features of Tourism Marketing

From the ancient times when travel was a prerogative of a select few who travelled in search of adventure to the present-day jet travel, there have been many changes. Travel in ancient times was a simple affair and could be undertaken without utilizing the services of organisations like travel agents or tour operators. As a result, tourism marketing, as we know it today, was not needed then. The types of facilities which were required by the people for travel were provided to them by a handful of suppliers of such services. It was, however, the introduction of mass travel during the twentieth century that services of travel agents and others were needed. Introduction of air travel, especially jet travel expanded the travel, markets necessitating application of marketing techniques. Marketing in the field of tourism made its formal appearance only in the second half of the twentieth century. As the travel business expanded as a result of the introduction of air travel, it became necessary for managers of travel to use techniques of marketing for selling the tourist product.

Marketing helps to create new customers by way of first identifying their needs and then trying to satisfy these. Customer satisfaction becomes a crucial part of travel sales. The first task of the travel marketer is identification of the customer needs in order to guide the development of suitable products and services. The second task is to motivate all the potential customers, through various means, to purchase those products and services. The objective of marketing in tourism can, therefore, be stated to be as attracting and motivating all the potential customers or users of tourist services to a particular destination and not to another.

Tourism marketing, therefore, begins by a detailed assessment of the actual and potential demand and, on this assessment, development of facilities and services for use by customers. Tourist demand can be divided into 'actual' and 'potential'; 'actual' demand represents those who actually travel to a certain tourist destination while 'potential' demand is the number of persons who fulfil the basic elements of travel and are, therefore, in a position to travel. Marketing of tourist product has certain peculiar characteristics. Although the general principles of marketing, which have proved quite effective in the marketing of products of other industries, could be applicable to marketing of tourist product, there are certain differences in approach. These differences are because of the peculiar character of the tourist product. Among the peculiarities of the tourist product are:

(i) ***Tourism is an intangible, non-material product.*** Unlike a tangible product, say, a motor car, no transfer of ownership of goods is involved in tourism. Instead, certain facilities, installations, items of equipment are made available for a specified time and for a specified use. For instance, a seat in an aeroplane or a train for a journey from one point to another or a booking in a hotel through a travel agent or services such as information and advice are provided to a customer.

(ii) ***Production and consumption of tourist services are closely interrelated.*** The travel agent or tour operator who sells his product cannot store it. Production can only take place or can only be completed if the customer is actually present. There is a close link between production and consumption of tourist services. Most tourist services cannot be consumed incrementally. In other words, consumption, once begun, cannot be stopped, interrupted or modified at all. As a result, risk and uncertainty for the customer are higher, and his need for reliable pre-purchase information is stronger. The potential customer's decision risk and dependence on accurate information is further increased because he cannot see, inspect, compare, or try out tourist services before deciding to use them.

(iii) ***A tourist product is assembled by many producers.*** The tourist product cannot be provided by a single enterprise. Each of the components of a tourist product is highly specialized and together make the final product. This is not so in the case of other tangible products where one manufacturer produces a total product. In tourism, on the other hand, airline considers 'seats flown' or passenger miles to be product; a hotel produces 'guest nights', a travel agent 'bookings', while a theatre, museum or an archaeological site measures its 'production' in number of visitors. In the tourist's view, however, the product he buys covers the complete experience of his visit to a particular place. In other words, the tourist product is not an airline a rail seat, or a hotel bed or a theatre ticket, but rather an amalgam of many components which together make a complete product. Because of these peculiar characteristics, coordination in marketing efforts is very crucial.

(iv) ***Tourism demand is highly unstable*:** Tourism demand is influenced by factors such as seasonal, economic, political, etc. Seasonal changes greatly affect the demand. Seasonality means that tourism plant is frequently used for only a limited part of the year and therefore uneconomic. Many tourist areas have short season—often as little as three months. A corollary of this seasonal usage is the seasonal unemployment, which is a serious problem. Some of the developing countries which have recently established tourist industries suffer particularly from seasonality. It also places strains on the transport system and other services. Thus seasonality presents a problem not only in relation to employment but also in relation to investment. On the other hand, political unrest and economic instability caused by currency fluctuations, inflation, etc., greatly affect tourism demand.

(v) ***Intermediaries play a dominant role.*** In most industries, manufacturers have predominant control over product design, distribution, promotion and the pricing. On the other hand, in tourism, sales intermediaries like tour operators, travel agents, reservation services and hotel brokers play a dominant role and enjoy superior marketing strength. From the standpoint of tourism marketing, this strong position of travel trade has significant implications. The travel trade determines to a large extent which services will be sold and to whom. The type of services to be offered as well as the pricing policies and promotion strategies to be adopted by tourist enterprises, are, therefore, determined not only by the needs and preferences of the customers but also by those expressed by travel sales intermediaries.

(vi) ***Travel motivations are diverse in nature.*** It is comparatively simple to determine why people buy a certain make of refrigerator, smoke certain brands of cigarettes, use certain brand of toothpaste or prefer a certain type of packaged food. The subjective and objective reasons, expectations and desires which influence tourists' choice for certain holiday destination, type of accommodation and vacation activities are far less evident. Very often two people make exactly the same choices for entirely different and sometimes even mutually exclusive reasons. Travel motivations, unlike motivations for buying a tangible article like a refrigerator, are heterogeneous—that is, they are composed of diverse elements. Marketing in tourism, therefore, as compared to marketing in other industries, needs a somewhat different approach.

To a considerable extent, tourism marketing depends on various market factors mentioned above. Unlike the normal consumer product or service, the tourist product is marketed at two levels: (i) The national or regional tourist organisation will be engaged in a marketing campaign to persuade the potential tourist to visit the country or region for which it is responsible. In view of the fragmentation of supply, the complementarity of tourist services, the predominance of many small- and medium-sized enterprises and importance of tourism to an economy, the official tourist organisations have important functions in tourism marketing. The official tourist organisation will, however, not sell a tourist product directly to customers. It will have two major objectives. In the first place, it will seek to create knowledge of its country in tourist- generating markets and persuade visitors in these markets to visit that country. Secondly, it will seek to create an image of its country's tourist attractions in the best possible manner in tourist-generating countries so that the potential visitors are attracted. (ii) The various individual firms providing tourist services can market their own components of the total tourist product after the national tourist organisations have launched marketing campaigns to persuade the potential tourist to visit the country or region for which it is responsible.

Marketing Functions

During the initial days of industrialisation, when the supply was short of demand, the emphasis was on sales management rather than market management function. The rapid industrial advancement subsequently placed at the disposal of the consumer a large variety of goods of improved quality and in abundant quantity from a large number of competing manufacturers resulting in supply exceeding demand. This compelled the manufacturers to give greater consideration to the needs of the consumers. This factor eventually led to the adoption of the marketing concept. Marketing concept in the field of tourism comprises the following major functions:

(a) Market research
(b) Product formulation and development
(c) Product distribution
(d) Advertising
(e) Sales promotion
(f) Public Relations

Market Research

One of the basic considerations for successful marketing is the need for research. It provides the information base for effective marketing. It relates to providing answers to various questions pertaining to the marketing activities. Market research can be defined as the "systematic collection of information relating to supply and demand for a product or a proposed product in such a way that the information may be used by the organisation to formulate informed decisions about its policies and its objectives." The marketing process, in fact, starts by finding out answers to questions like who are the potential tourists where do they come from, what are their likes and dislikes, etc. In order to formulate any marketing strategy, it is very essential for a national tourist organisation and others engaged or marketing a tourist product to know the answers to the following questions:

(i) Who are the persons who engage in tourism and where do they live?
(ii) Who are the potential customers and where do they come from?
(iii) What are their likes and dislikes?
(iv) What are their travel preferences and interests?
(v) What do they buy and where do they stay?
(vi) What mode of transport do they use?
(vii) What are their entertainment preferences?
(viii) What are the trends in competition?
(ix) What type of marketing programmes would be needed?

Market research provides answers to all the above questions. A national tourist organisation's promotion efforts without appropriate answers to the above questions will go waste. To make the overall marketing efforts effective and successful, as in the case of manufacturers of consumer products, the national tourist organisation in a country has to be totally aware of the international trends in the travel habits, vacation habits and, most important of all, the reasons attributed to the better success of a competing destination. A marketing manager cannot visualise successful marketing strategy without having an up to date knowledge of their markets in general. It is very important to have detailed information on all the aspects of a market. Results of such research will work as guidelines for launching a successful marketing programme.

Market research is a continuous process. There are various methods used to collect the data. Among the great variety of methods used, some seem to be widely resorted to because of their advantages over others. Two broad categories of marketing research techniques are (a) desk research and (b) field research.

Desk Research

Desk research includes the collection and analysis of all available data, statistics and published information on tourist trends and markets. In tourism much of the basic information about tourist trends and markets is available from existing sources. There are a number of international organisations like United Nations, UNESCO, IUOTO, WTO, EC, OECD, IATA, ICAO, etc., which publish certain statistical information. Other data and statistics may be obtained from national tourist organisations, trade associations, carriers, hotel companies, etc. This information proves very useful in helping national tourist organisations to identify their markets and determine the objectives. This published information is of a particular use to those countries which do not possess resources enough to undertake independent market research.

Field Research

Field research, on the other hand, is the research work carried out in the tourist-generating markets itself. The special investigations in the field are to be carried out with a view to know more details of the market situation. Field research includes many methods among which the most common are the sample surveys and motivation research.

Sample surveys could be defined as the study of a given population through only a part or a fraction thereof. Much marketing information is obtained through the use of samples. In this method the population or 'universe' for which information is required is defined; for example, all households in a country might be the universe or population under investigation Then, a statistically valid sample of the population is drawn and information is obtained from the sample. Sampling technique consist of personal interviews of tourists, travel agents, carrier and hotel managers, etc., with the help of prepared questionnaires, by mailing questionnaires or through telephonic contacts.

There are certain advantages of this method. Lower cost is the major reason why data are collected by sampling in place of complete enumerations. The actual obtaining of information from the sample units (i.e., households in this case) is done by way of use of interviews and questionnaires. The questionnaire is administered to the sample population and various data obtained. The sampling place could be anywhere. Interview may take place at homes or offices, at the places of arrival/ departure or temporary stay. In many countries there are a number of specialized firms which carry out sample surveys.

The survey investigations can be classified by reference to the kind of information they seek to provide. There are surveys of market behaviour, which record the holiday habits of the population, cross analysed by socio-economic and other characteristics. The trends in holidaymaking over many years may be seen and inferences made about the motives of holidaymakers. Furthermore, surveys may be undertaken to monitor the conduct of marketing campaigns.

Motivation research, on the other hand, attempts to describe and forecast the motives of the population under investigation by use of techniques originally used in psychology. Assuming that every individual knows what he wants, motivation research is oriented to discover the needs of potential tourists in order to adopt the tourist supply accordingly and thus be able to satisfy them. In other words, motivation research is the investigation into the motives behind travel. It concerns itself to answering the 'why' of human behaviour in contrast to answering the 'how', which is subject to sampling surveys. It analyses rather than describes the attitudes of both actual and potential tourists to travelling in general and to the tourist product offered in particular. Motivation research provides answers to very important questions. Research in the past has shown that people from some countries are traditional good travellers (the French, the Germans, the American and the British), while others have become a nation of travellers only recently (the Japanese). One of the most important techniques used in motivation research is the depth-interview method. The questionnaire to be used for this method needs to be carefully designed. As motivation research aims at discovering the deep, subconscious and even unconscious motives of human beings, an ill-designed questionnaire is likely to reach no deeper than the conscious level where rational factors prevail. Other techniques used are the projective methods like word-association tests, sentence-completion tests and pictorial tests, etc., and observations. These means have been devised to record the reactions of a person and to understand his motives.

Market identification through the method of market research leads to the next logical step, which is to develop a sound tourist marketing strategy. It may, however, be mentioned here that the market research, as a continuous process of investigating market conditions, is just a means to an end which is to develop a marketing strategy. This strategy aims at achieving certain objectives which could be an increase in the tourist traffic as well as increase in the foreign exchange receipts. These should be compatible with the characteristics of the market or markets and with the capacity of the tourist plant and facilities available. Realistic assessment of the market—its size, conditions and trends would therefore be the first step in developing the country's tourist marketing strategy.

Tourist Marketing Mix

In general marketing, the term 'mix' has gained prominence in the last few decades. Marketing mix means a mixture of elements which interact and complement each other to achieve the targeted results. Marketing mix can also be defined as "The mixture of controllable marketing variables that the organisation uses to pursue the desired level of sales in the target market".

Marketing mix is a combination of the marketing variables which any organisation uses at a particular time in order to achieve the results. The term 'marketing mix' was first introduced by Professor Neil Bordes in the year 1953. Professor Bordes got the cue from a study of management of marketing costs by Professor James Gulliton who described the marketing executive as a mixer of ingredients. The objective of marketing is to identify, anticipate and satisfy the customer needs in relation to markets. Within the limitations given by the market situation, by the available resources and the general direction provided by the organisation's overall aims, there is a broad range of different activities suitable for achieving the organisation's goals. The organisation or a firm can use a variety of marketing 'instruments' in regard to its products or services, their pricing, their distribution or sale and their promotion. The combination of specific activities is called the marketing mix. Commonly described as the four P's or the four variables, originally used to describe the marketing mix by McCarthy in 1960, these include:

(i) Product
(ii) Price
(iii) Promotion
(iv) Place or distribution

Tourist marketing mix is largely a complex group of several factors intervening to achieve the end product, which is the increased effectiveness in demand output in relation to supply and marketing investment by tourist enterprises. Marketing mix helps the marketing manager or a firm or an official tourism organisation to understand where marketing action can be initiated to improve the acceptability of a tourist product and, at the same time, stimulate the demand. An example of this would be a policy of price reduction of tourist facility or service. This could be substituted either by increasing available facilities and services for the same price or by strengthening promotional activities due to competition and increasing sales output. A policy to combine both reduction of prices and extra facilities or extra advertising campaigns may or may not however achieve desired results.

A tourist enterprise can use a combination of specific activities to achieve the best desired results. An enterprise can decide which of them to use, how, when and where to use and which resources to allocate to them. The various components of the 'mix' may be seen as cooperating with or replacing each other as complements or substitutes. Thus, the tourist marketing mix is largely a complex group of factors intervening to achieve the marketing 'end product', which is increased effectiveness in demand output in relation to supply and marketing investments (input). A balanced mix is necessary to reach this targeted result. The tourist marketing mix can include the following elements:

(i) Product policy,
(ii) Pricing policy,
(iii) Promotion programmes, and
(iv) Channels of distribution and sales.

The use of tour variables in the marketing mix in travel and tourism industry can be described by an example of a well-known luxury train "Palace on Wheels" in India.

The Product

- The characteristics of the product
- Size and facilities offered
- Staff members and their attitudes
- Image, reputation, positioning (upmarket or economical)

The Price

- Normal
- Promoting
- Discounted
- Corporate
- Wholesaler rates
- Seasonal

The Promotion

- Advertising (electronic, press)
- Sales promotion
- Public relations
- Direct mail

The Place (Distribution)

- Channels of distribution
- Reservation systems (CRS)
- Intermediaries (travel agents, tour operators)
- Airlines
- Clubs/Associations

The 'marketing mix' helps in the integrated approach to marketing. It helps the marketing manager, whether an individual or a firm or an official tourist organisation, to understand where marketing action can be initiated to improve the acceptability of the tourist product and stimulate demand. 'Marketing mix' has both short-term as well as long-term aspects. The short-term aspects relate to meeting the immediate moves of competitors and include aspects like price reduction, aggressive promotion, introduction of a new product in the market, etc. Long-term aspects, on the other hand, are based on longer range plans derived from the study of all kinds of trends like natural, economic, social and technological.

apter

ar etin ommunication

Marketing communications uses different marketing channels and tools in combination: Marketing communication channels focuses on any way a business communicates a message to its desired market, or the market in general. A marketing communication tool can be anything from: advertising, personal selling, direct marketing, sponsorship, communication, promotion and public relations.

MC are made up of the marketing mix which is made up of 4P's: Price, Promotion, Place and Product, for a business selling goods, and made up of 7P's: Price, Promotion, Place, Product, People, Physical evidence and Process, for a service based business.

Overview

Marketing communications includes advertising, promotions, sales, branding and online promotion. The process allows the public businesses use to know or understand a brand. Successful branding involves targeting audiences who appreciate the organisation's marketing program.

Advertising is a small but important part of marketing communications; the marketing communications mix is a set of tools that can be used to deliver a clear and consistent message to target audiences. It is also commonly called the promotional mix. Crosier (1990) states that all terms have the same meaning in the context of the 4P's: Product, price, place and promotion. Price can send a message to the target audience. For example, comparing a $50 bag to a $10 bag, the former may be viewed as a luxury or more durable item.

The marketing plan identifies key opportunities, threats, weaknesses and strengths, sets objectives and develops an action plan to achieve marketing goals. Each section of the 4P's sets its own object; for instance, the pricing objective might be to increase sales in a certain geographical market by pricing their own product or service lower than their competitors. This creates a significant change in the market because more people of the target market would aim to do business with your organisation than your competitors, because pricing is one of the most significant aspects of marketing that can change the whole market positively and or negatively.

Definitions

- Communication barriers: Communication barriers are factors that hinder the objectives of a marketing communication. Major communication barriers are:

Noise and clutter, consumer apathy, brand parity and weak creative ideas or strategies. Noise is an unrelated sensory stimulus that distracts a consumer from the marketing message (for example, people talking nearby making it hard to hear a radio advertisement). Clutter is the high number and concentration of advertisements presented to a consumer at any time. As attention cannot be divided, there is a limit to how much can be taken in and processed, which means that a strong marketing communication needs to stand out from the clutter and be heard above the noise.

- Consumer apathy is the tendency of a consumer to avoid marketing communications. The consumer may not be interested, or consider themselves "in the market," and as such attempt to shut out the irrelevant marketing stimuli; this is known as selective attention. Alternatively, a consumer may be "in the market," yet not be aware of the brand or products existence or prevalence. Consumers tend to purchase familiar brands, and will not be inspired to investigate alternatives. One approach marketers use to overcome apathy is to create incentives, such as competitive pricing or loyalty rewards.
- Brand parity means a brand is not significantly different from its competition. Without a distinct value proposition, consumers do not develop brand preference or associations, and instead purchase purely based on price. This is not ideal, as effective marketing communication increases brand equity. One important objective of marketing communications is to develop a strong, unique brand identity that allows the brand to be positioned separate from its competition.
- Marketing mix is the most important part of marketing strategy, which is "the framework to manage marketing and incorporate it within a business context".
- Marketing strategy: how a business achieves their marketing objectives. The initial step to achieve a marketing strategy is to identify the market target and build up a plan that the business can implement.

Communication

Communication is one important aspect of the marketing mix. Marketing communication is often the largest component of communication within a company, which may be to present company values, objectives or specific products and services to investors, customers or the general public. In the 21st century, communications objectives focus on more customized messages, targeting customer groups or individuals to create high responses and greater brand interaction.

As business becomes increasingly global with greater access to Internet, mobile phones and social media, new challenges exist to inform people in targeted foreign markets. Shifts in the global economy and access to new markets lead also to greater demands for product shipping and associated services. To be effective, communication strategies must converge with marketing objectives while also accounting for local languages, dialects and cultural norms.

External communications might involve market research questionnaires, office website, guarantees, company annual report and presentations for investors. Internal communication can be the marketing materials, price list, product catalogues, sales presentations and management communications. On the other hand, each market demands different types of communications. For example, the industrial market demands a more personal communication but the consumer market demands non-personal communication.

There are also 4 different fundamental types of communication.

- **One-to-many:** this kind of communication is the most original communication. It is "generated from a single broadcast point and then available over airwaves or in mass print runs". This type of communication is usually adapted to news distribution that does not specific not even interactive. Such as in an urgent notice play over airwave from broadcast in an industry, it is helpful for the general announcement.
- **Many-to-one:** many-to-one is usually connected to the one-to-many communication. For example, a reply button in your email box, a prepaid number bought from Spark. All the communication techniques proceeded to the public with bi-directional communication from mass communications.
- **One-to-one:** this is the most intensive and interactive communication at a one-to-one level. There are so many examples like a sales presentation; a negotiation in the market or direct delivery is base on the one-to-one communication. Most of this communication is face to face. But in the development of Internet, email and online shopping are taking place the chance to face to face of people. Which is provided the chance to sellers and buyers talk more directly. Another important is instant message 'chat' channel like Wechat and Facebook, which are becoming extremely popular in business.
- **Many-to-many:** on the background of highly developed Internet, the many-to-many communication has been growing up such as online chat rooms, 'blogging' websites. The many-to-many communication stands for the participants are able to exchange their ideas and experiences.

One-to-one is more immediate, while the many-to-may channels tend to be less urgent but with greater longevity.

Communication Process

Communication can be defined as process of using, word, sound or visual cues to supply information to one or more people. A communication process is defined as information that is shared with the intent that the receiver understands the message that the business intended to send. The communication process was once thought of as having the source of the message, which is then encoded, put through the chosen communication channel, which is then decoded by the recipient and then received. Throughout the middle of the channel there is the potential for noise to distort the message being sent. Once the receiver has the message they then give feedback to the original source, where they then find out whether the campaign has been successful or not.

With the prevalent use of technology, customers are seeking out information about brands, products and businesses prior to purchase. This means that there is a need for an additional channel within the communication process, so it is a more accurate representation of the current business environment. Businesses are now having to take into consideration that both opinion leaders and opinion formers who have a great influence over today's society and their perceptions. So they have to be included into the communication process before the recipient of the message receives it.

This model is more effective when there is common ground between the senders and receivers so they can communicate effectively. Choosing the appropriate source helps develop the message and appeal to the targeted audience. The source will be more effective if they are relatable to the target audience. This realm of understanding is represented by the overlapping circles. The more knowledge the source has about who they are targeting, the better they can understand how the receiver may interpret or react to the message.

The components of the transactional model are:

- **Source:** The source is an individual or organisation that has information to share. The source (or sender) creates and sends the information to another person or group of people. The source maybe an individual (e.g. a sales person or spokesperson) or a non-personal identity (e.g. a corporation or organisation). The communication process begins with the source, marketers must carefully choose a source as it affects how the message will be perceived by the target audience.
- **Encoding:** This is transposing the intended meaning of the message with words, symbols or pictures to show a message. Encoding is the development of the message that contains the information the source hopes to convey. It is putting together the thoughts, ideas and information into a symbolic form that can be transmitted and understood by the receiver. Encoding the message is the second step in the communication process. The encoding process leads to development of a message that contains the information or meaning the source hopes to convey. Encoding is extremely important, it is a brain activity that takes effect when the receiver makes sense of a brand message or idea used to convey meaning: words, colour, pictures, signs, symbols or even music. The message may be verbal or nonverbal, oral or written, or symbolic (e.g. the sound of a brass band being redolent of simpler times or heritage). or it can often include 'cues' such as the Nike 'swoosh' which indicates success. Often things can get in the way of the 'correct' encoding and the interpretation of the intended message (decoding). There are methods the sender can use to make sure the receiver interprets the message correctly, these methods include; channels, consumer insights, having similarities with the receiver and frame of reference (e.g. age, values, culture). Finally, it is extremely important for the sender to get to know its receiver and this is accomplished through research for targeting strategy. These concepts help craft the intended message in the minds of the consumer.
- **Message**: The message comes from the encoding process, it is the content, meaning or information the sources hopes to convey. The message can be in many forms such as verbal, non-verbal, oral, written or symbolic.
- **Channel**: The channel is the method by which the communication travels from the source or sender to the receiver. There are two types of channels, personal and non-personal. Personal channels of communication are direct and target

individual groups. Personal communication channels are connected with two or more persons who communicate directly with each other face-to-face, person-to-person through telephone, email or fax. Social channels also fall under the category of personal communications. Friends, neighbours, associates, co-workers, or family members are all means of social channels. Carrying a message without interpersonal contact between sender and receiver is known as non-personal channels of communication. Mass media or mass communications are examples of non-personal channels, since the message is sent to many individuals at one time. Non-personal channels of communication are made up out of two main types, the first being print. Print media includes newspapers, magazines, direct mail, and billboards. The second type is broadcast; broadcast media includes radio and television.

- **Decoding:** The receiver unravels the symbols to interpret what is being communicated. Transforming the sender's message back into thought. This is influenced greatly by the receiver's frame of reference (or realm of understanding) which involves their values, attitudes and state of mind when receiving the message. For the model to be effective the decoding by the receiver would match the encoding by the source, meaning they correctly understand the message that was sent. Decoding is the process of interpreting messages and relies on correct encoding and the ability of the receiver to deconstruct transmitted meaning. Decoding occurs when the message reaches one or more of the receiver's senses. Consumers both hear and see television ads, others consumers handle (touch) and read (see) an advertising offer (e.g. coupon). According to Belch & Belch this process is deeply influenced by the receiver's frame of reference or field of experience, which refers to the experiences, perceptions, attitudes, and values he or she brings to the communication situation. For effective communication to occur, the message decoding process of the receiver must match the encoding of the sender. Over this entire means the receiver comprehends and correctly translates what the source is trying to communicate. Effective communication is more likely to emerge when there is some common ground between the two parties. The more familiarity the sender has about the receivers, the better the sender can understand their needs, commiserate with them, and over all communicate more effectively.
- **Receiver**: The individual (s) that the source shares thoughts or information with. The receiver hears, sees or reads the message and decodes it.
- **Noise:** Noise is any external interference during this communication process. Any external factors that creates unplanned distortion. This distortion can make it difficult for the receiver to interpret or assign meaning to a message as it was intended by the source. Examples of noise in the encoding of the message could be lack of radio or television signal. Noise can also occur when the sender and receivers fields of experience do not overlap, if there is no common ground between them, which may result in a misunderstanding in the meaning of the message. Throughout the communication process, the message is subject to irrelevant factors that can distort or interfere with its reception. Noise is the physical or Psychological fundamentals either from inside or outside of the

process of communication. Noise acts as a barrier as it makes the message less accurate, less productive and unclear. It may even prevent the message from ever reaching the receiver. Physical noise is often triggered by badly made images or messages (e.g. poor print quality) or elements of distraction (e.g. consumer scrolling through TV advertisements). Psychological noise could be mixed meanings, poor credibility of source or the insignificance of the message to the consumer requirements. Not having a connection with the receiver and lacking in common ground usually cause this. This may result in unsuitable encoding of the message such as; using a sign, symbol, or word that is unfamiliar or has different meaning to the receiver (e.g. sending a message in foreign language that is not understood by the receiver). The more common ground there is between the sender and the receiver, the less likely it is for noise and barriers to interrupt a message.

- **Response/Feedback**: The receiver's reaction to the message provides feedback to the sender. This is the set of reactions after seeing, hearing or reading the message. The receiver's response is the feedback and lets the sender know how the message was decoded and received. A form of feedback in an interpersonal selling situation could be questions, comments or any reactions (such as expressions) about the message. In mass media an indication of how the marketing communications were perceived is the amount of sales after the message has been sent. There are many different ways such as attitude change, store visits and inquires that provide feedback in mass media. Feedback can help to improve the communication process and the success of future messages. The receiver's particular type of reactions after seeing, hearing, or reading a message is known as a response. Receivers' responses can range from either non-noticeable actions or noticeable actions. Non-noticeable responses can be storing their information in memory and noticeable responses are immediate action such as dialing the commercials number to order a product advertised on television. One of the main goals of communication is receiving appropriate receiver responses, feedback closes the loop in the communications flow and lets the sender monitor how the intended message is being decoded and received.

To achieve this goal one can ask indirectly or directly for the response, or assist the receiver in giving the response. Receiving feed back can be more difficult for parties that advertise through the channels of mass media, because advertisers are not in direct contact with their customers so other methods must be obtained to determine how their messages have been received. While the critical form of feedback happens through sales, it is often hard to show a direct relationship between advertising and purchase behaviour . So marketers; visit stores, check coupon redemption, use reply cards and listen to customer inquiries to achieve feedback. Once a significant amount of feedback/response study has been gathered advertisers would then have enough information to determine reasons for success or failure in the communication process and from there they can make appropriate adjustments.

Opinion Leaders and Opinion Formers

Opinion leaders are consumers who have large influence over the purchasing behaviour of other consumers. These can be peers or celebrities, and often represent a "desired state" in the eye of the influenced consumer. By following the consumption patterns of opinion leaders, consumers aspire to achieve a similar status or lifestyle, and project a similar image. Because of this, opinion leaders are powerful factors in marketing communications. Having opinion leaders endorse a brand can increase brand awareness and sales. Due to this, large companies pay highly influential celebrities to endorse their products.

You can receive the opinion leaders' thoughts or feeling towards the product/ service through paid advertising, social media, blogs, or any other form of written media. These can be direct, or indirect influences.

Opinion Formers are consumers who are regarded by their peers as being highly knowledgeable and trustworthy. They are considered experts in selecting the highest quality products due to their extensive knowledge, and as such are able to influence the purchasing behaviour of other consumers despite lacking the celebrity status of an opinion leader. They have specialized knowledge about the area which corresponds with the product, service or business. For example, this could be a doctor sponsoring a form of medication, or a personal trainer recommending a sports brand to the customer. This means that both opinion leaders and opinion formers have a large influence on the consumer and their perceived view of the business, product, or service provided. If a brand is specializing in the sale and manufacturing of makeup products, the business would want to look at someone who is both known for their knowledge about makeup and also someone who they know is popular within that community, so that the message is as wide spread throughout their target market as possible. Opinion leaders add another link in the communication process, acting as a "meaning filter" for the receivers of the message (Dahlen, 2010). The message is sent from the sender and the opinion leaders share their opinions with the targeted audience.

Mass Media

Advertising

In today's changing and competitive international marketplace, advertising is important. Advertising is an activity designed to spread information with a view to promoting the sales of marketable goods and services. As such, it operates in two ways: first, by spreading information amongst consumers about the possibilities of consumption, and second, by seeking to influence their judgement in favour of the particular goods which are the subject of the advertisement. Any organisation which uses this promotional instrument has to use certain media space which is paid for. In other words, we can also define advertisement as "paid public messages designed to describe or praise a product". This product in tourism is any destination area which is visited by a tourist. The media space for advertisement can be bought in newspapers, general and specialized magazines, in the form of posters or billboards.

Besides the use of paid media space in the form of newspapers, magazines, etc., use of media time is also made in radio and television in order to transmit a predetermined message to a predetermined audience.

Advertising has several inherent advantages in this method. The biggest advantage is its *wide coverage*. Advertising is especially appropriate for communication with a large number of prospective purchasers of a commodity or a service. A uniform sales message is directed towards all prospective purchasers. An advertisement can be placed before a large number of prospective customers as compared with the efforts of a salesman. *Frequency* is another advantage. It can make its appeal more frequently, whereas the calls of salesmen are usually not so frequent. Another advantage is its *accessibility*. It may reach prospects whom salesmen would find difficult to interview, owing to lack of interest, or inaccessibility to salesmen. Advertisement may reach such prospects through many types of media and under a variety of circumstances, and may thus attract their attention and arouse their interest. *Lower cost* is another major advantage. Large numbers can be reached economically, i.e. at a lower cost per contact than in any other technique available.

Advertising may be used to do a variety of selling tasks. A great deal of advertising attempts to win acceptance for the product. Such advertising may produce few specific demands for the advertised brands, yet when retailers display or show advertised goods they sell more readily than non-advertised ones. Therefore, retailers often hesitate to handle non-advertised goods unless they are obtainable at low prices. Advertising thus directly stimulates sales to retailers. Advertising may at times be used to make the complete sale. Some direct mail and periodical advertising attempts to make sales by requesting readers to forward orders accompanied by the necessary payment. When the number of potential buyers is small and when they are widely scattered, it could be extremely costly to reach them through salesmen. Advertising then becomes the most economical means of doing the entire sales job.

Planning the Advertising

While planning the advertising, the agency must give careful consideration to the actual make-up of the advertisement. This headline copy, illustrations, colour scheme, size, layout, and method of printing or reproducing the advertisement must be planned very carefully. This is necessary in order to gain attention of the customer, maintain his interest in the message, and secure the action desired by the seller. Closely related is the question of periodicity of advertisement. How frequently to advertise? For instance, is it better to use a full-page advertisement once a month or a quarter-page weekly? A frequently presented thought is likely to force itself into our consciousness. People are inclined to believe statements they hear or see repeatedly and hence the logic of frequent repetition of advertisements. In starting a special campaign the advertisements should not be spaced regularly. Early in the campaign they should be used close together, while later on they can be issued at much longer intervals. This is desirable because consumers forget rapidly at first and much more slowly later on. After the facts are retained by the prospects, the advertisements can be presented at much longer intervals.

Media Selection

The advertiser should give careful attention in planning to the selection of the medium or media especially adopted to his needs. The selection will depend upon the factors like the area to be covered, the type of audience to be reached, the appeals to be used and upon the services and facilities of the particular medium in relation to costs. The important factors which influence the media selection are: (i) media habits of the target audience; (ii) product characteristics (for example, TV may be the appropriate medium for those products which may require a demonstration of their operation for effective impact on the target audience); and (iii) cost of the media.

Message Selection

The message selected for use in the advertisement should be such that it retains the interest in the minds of the customers about the product. The customer must maintain his interest in the message, and secure the action desired by the seller of the product. The objective is to present the advertiser's message in such a way that the illustration may lead the reader to favourable considerations of the advertisement. The important characteristics of an effective message are:

(i) *Information*: It should be adequate for a decision;

(ii) *Interest*: It should be able to catch the attention of the target audience;

(iii) *Authenticity*: It should avoid exaggerated claims;

(iv) *Persuasion*: It should be capable of creating a favourable conviction in the target audience; and

(v) *Memory value*: It should have something in it which can help the target audience to remember it.

Cost of Advertising

The agency must relate the estimated cost of the objectives planned and the contribution expected from advertising. Can the advertiser carry on a campaign large enough to make it effective? Are the funds available or will they become available through the sale of the product. How much the agency spends for the advertising? The various methods commonly used are:

(i) *Affordable method*: Here, the advertising budget is set on the basis of what the agency can afford;

(ii) *Percentage of sales method*: In this case, the agency sets the advertising budget on the basis of specific percentage of sales;

(iii) *Competitive parity method*: Here the company sets its budget to match those of its major competitors;

(iv) *Objective and task method*: In this the advertising budget represents the outlay required to perform the various tasks which are necessary to achieve the properly defined advertising objectives of the company. This method is considered the most rational.

Defining Advertising Effectiveness

In today's world, advertisement through any medium has become extremely expensive. Hence, it is important for the agency to ensure that the money spent on it does bring returns by way of increased sales. This could be done by way of evaluating or testing the effectiveness of advertising. Testing methods may be used to evaluate the results of an advertising campaign. By evaluating and analysing the effectiveness of advertisements that have been used, future advertisements may be improved. In addition, tests may be applied before advertisements are run. Pre-testing of an advertisement prevents expenditure that would not be profitable and leads to expenditures that give the best results. In determining advertising effectiveness the commonly used methods are given below.

(i) *Inquiries*: Answer-back coupons, with same inducement, are incorporated in many advertisements. The amount of response is an indication of the effectiveness of the concerned advertisement.

(ii) *Recall tests*: Here the respondents are shown the magazine cover or any other medium in which the concerned advertisement has appeared. They are then asked to tell which advertisements in that publication they remember.

(iii) *Recognition tests*: Here the respondents are shown the advertisements and asked if they have read them.

(iv) *Sales tests*: Here the actual sales results before and after the concerned advertising are examined. The sales results in the selected 'test markets' are also compared to those in some chosen 'control markets', i.e., the markets where the concerned advertising is not done. This is done to eliminate certain factors, other than advertising, which may also have influenced the sales.

In tourism, advertising is used extensively for promotion of various tourist products. This is a far cry from the era when colourful folders and posters were the only apparent form of travel promotion. In the field of tourism, advertising is mainly used to create initial awareness and interest in the tourist service or destination to be promoted and motivates potential tourists to decide to make further enquiries about costs, bookings, facilities, etc. It implies indirect communication with selected target groups—the potential tourists—through paid messages designed to praise a particular destination or an area. For a country which is trying to attract tourists, there can be two principal forms of advertising: (i) consumer advertising and (ii) trade advertising. To reach a wide number of consumers, such media as newspaper advertisements, radio spots, TV prime-time advertising are used. However, this form of advertisement is very expensive. For a developing nation it is extremely difficult to afford such a type of advertisement because of financial constraints. Trade advertising, on the other hand, is an indirect form of advertising and an economical method.

A large number of people today travel in groups. A tourist for various reasons chooses to travel as a member of a group, as opposed to travelling individually. The result, therefore, has been that a number of large tour operators have established their offices in such market areas. While the tour operator puts together inclusive tour packages, the tourist merely pays one package price for all services and is assured of a holiday. Such packages are then sold in retail by numerous smaller travel agents located in various market areas, and the result is that a group is formed. For a country which is trying to market its product, the area towards which these efforts are aimed is thus narrowed down to the important tour operators/wholesalers. The media used to achieve this is large-scale advertising in travel trade journals and newspapers of international repute having travel sections.

Advertising plays a crucial role in marketing a tourist product. If the right combination of conditions is present the effect of advertising would be to increase the demand for the particular country's tourist product. Among the factors favourable to the successful use of advertising are the rising trend of demand in the particular product and an opportunity to stimulate selective demand, i.e., preference for the particular product. This is most likely where, there is a possibility of product differentials, and where consumer satisfaction depends largely on hidden qualities that cannot easily be judged at the time of purchase, or where strong emotional buying motive exists as in the case of tourism.

The American Marketing Association has defined advertising as "any paid form of non-personal presentation and promotion of ideas, goods or services by an identified sponsor". However, there have been several other definitions of advertising. One definition that may be accepted as related to all kinds of advertising is "the planned and controlled communication of persuasive ideas to a defined audience". The question may arise as to the selling function of advertising. The answer to this question is that while advertising will certainly be contributing towards sales, it cannot and does not always complete the sale.

A variety of other factors contribute to this and include pricing, distribution, dealer cooperation, etc., and all these jointly with advertising make up what is today called marketing activity. Mail- order advertising, where readers send in written orders in response to press advertisements or home-delivered catalogues, is perhaps the single instance of directly related advertising selling. In other cases advertising acts as the communication factor contributing to the total selling function. In the case of service products such as tourism, banking and insurance, the direct selling action of advertising is rather limited. It must, however, be stressed that this does not mean that advertising is less important for such products.

Advertising Campaign

Any organisation, in order to promote its product, has to resort to advertising to achieve desired results. Tourism organisations all over the world resort to this communication tool. Launching an advertising campaign for promoting a product is very crucial and has to be done in a planned manner. The term 'product' in the larger sense includes not only tangible products like furniture or a motor car but also service products such as tourism, insurance, etc. There are various stages through which any advertising campaign must evolve.

Stage One: Defining the Product

Before one can develop any communication of advertising for a product it is essential to know what it is that the product offers to consumers. This is very important. When you advertise soap, you are not advertising a cake of compound of alkali and oil in an attractive printed pack, but you may be advertising beauty or deodorant protection or youthfulness. To assess, therefore, what the product means to the prospective users we have to first ascertain the benefits that the users will derive from the product. Here are a few examples of this kind of benefit derivation:

- Car tyre can offer confidence, security or safety;
- Household cleaning can offer convenience, pride or hygienic conditions;
- Cosmetics can offer romance, self-confidence or glamour;
- Cigarettes can offer social status, confidence;
- Travel can offer rest, relaxation glamour, confidence or status.

The above examples show that in most cases the user benefit is not always apparent as a product feature. But it must be remembered that people buy things for the benefits they derive when using them. We must look at the product through the mind and eyes of the user. To do this it is sometimes necessary to conduct research amongst users or prospective users to find out what it is that they get from particular products. One can, at the same time, assess their knowledge, attitude and usage of competitive or substitute products so that the strengths and weaknesses of one's own product are known. This study of consumer assessment is important as in any system of communication the idea existing in the mind of the receiver will affect the interpretation of the message being received. In some cases it may prevent the message from either being noticed or perceived, let alone being received or understood.

Once we have arrived at this product benefit definition, we must then study this in relation to other factors. First, relative importance to the consumer of the several product benefits—the more important the benefit the greater its motivating values. Second, the relative position of one's own brand and substitute brands in regard to these product benefits—to create a unique and memorable message, the main ideas or benefits should be as distinctive and different from others as possible. Let us now assume that we have studied our product and its users and potential users attitude towards the product and have arrived at a definition of product benefits which we feel are most important.

Stage Two: Defining the Market Segments

We have a product. We know what users expect or want from it. Now we must assess how many users we have and where they are located. Most of this information will have been collected through various sources and supplied by the organisation marketing the product. The kind of information that should be available will relate to the following:

(a) Consumer Information

(i) ***Type of consumer***: Number, sex, age, socio-economic profile;

(ii) ***Location of the consumer***: Whether they will be found in cities, small towns or rural areas or in all and in what proportion in each;

(iii) ***Geographic distribution***: Whether there are any regional variations in the market spread and if so, why;

(iv) ***Shopping habits***: The amount or size of individual purchases, the frequency or number of times a product is brought during a month or a year, whether bought on a regular planned basis or through an impulse decision at point of sale;

(v) *Decision making*: Often the person who actually buys the product does not always make the decision. It, therefore, becomes important to find out who it is that makes the decision and also the extent of the actual buyer's role in changing or influencing this decision. The reason for finding this out is to get an idea as to whom the advertising message should be directed. The person who decides is very important and in the case of joint decisions it may well be necessary to direct the advertising to two or more decision makers.

(b) Distribution Information

Types of outlets, number of such outlets and the importance of each type; the location of these outlets in different cities, towns and rural markets; the dealer's part in the selling activity.

(c) Sales Information

The trends over the years and any significant shifts that may have occurred in different geographic areas and the reasons for these changes is very important information. Seasonal variations that may be related to weather, festivals and other local and national reasons are also very important. In giving us all this information the manufacturer will not merely be giving us information about his product but also of competitive and substitute product against which his product will compete. All this information will provide us with a knowledge of the dimension of the market so that we will be in a position to assess which particular markets are of greater importance. This will also assist in creating the media plan to reach each market and also in creating relevant messages for each. In terms of media selection, the statistical information that will be supplied will enable to plan a campaign using media which will provide cover, reach and frequency related to the market definition.

(d) Attitude Segmentation

This relates to segmenting the market by user motivation. For example, it has been shown that certain types of people use certain products in larger quantities and more regularly than others. In the same way, some people travel more often than others. These groups are termed the heavy-user group. And, in most cases, it is not the usual socio-economic categorisation that distinguishes them. This may be termed as attitude segmentation or separation. The problem in such segmenting or separating into two groups is that unlike socio-economic segmentation it is difficult to physically isolate the group. This can, however, be achieved through segmenting as it were the advertising message. It is important to note, however, that this sort of segmentation should not be overdone. Social appeals or segmented campaigns should only be developed if it is found that there are large enough groups of consumers who have attitude which would respond to such appeals. Often, however, it is not only the advertising that is segmented but the product itself is separately produced for each of the segments. At this stage we will have progressed from product definition to a knowledge of the market, its size, location and, different segmentation patterns.

Stage Three: Interpreting the Marketing Objectives

What we have been discussing until now is information of the environment in which the advertising campaign will have to work. As we have discussed earlier, since advertising is only the communication aspect of the total marketing function we have to take into account the marketing plans of the both enterprises in the long-term and short-term, and relate the advertising to these. The marketing objectives that are given by the enterprise will detail the plans that the enterprise has for its product in the coming year and in some cases for a few years ahead. These plans would cover items such as:

(i) The sales targets for the coming years broken down into regional targets or others, as the case may be.

(ii) The distribution, merchandising and sales promotion activities planned to support the sales increase;

(iii) The role that advertising is expected to play in creating consumers;

(iv) The inhibiting factors which will work to prevent the enterprises from achieving the target, competitive products and their advertising, consumer attitudes, etc.

It is important to note that in any marketing operation the product formulation, packaging and pricing, distribution and availability at point of sale are all of vital importance. All that advertising can do is to bring consumer to the point of sale. But if the product is not properly made, packaged or priced or is not well merchandised or promoted at point of sale and, therefore, is not visible, then it is quite possible that the sales effect of the advertising will not fructify. This brings out the importance of integrating these various activities.

Once we have got clearly the marketing objectives of the enterprise and their plans in relation to these objectives, we can see what advertising has to communicate and to whom with a view to provide the maximum relevant support to the agreed marketing plan.

Stage Four: Planning the Advertising Campaign

We now know what we have to sell, to whom we have to sell, where the prospective consumers are located and also how the product will be made available to them. Our object now is to create an advertising campaign which will reach target audience and motivate them to come to ask for and buy the product. We have now processed all the facts that the enterprise has given and have perhaps had a dialogue with the consumer, through research, to ascertain his knowledge, attitude and usage of the product and its competitors. As a result, we have found out the proposition that we feel would be most motivating. We have also found out where the consumer is located, how and when he buys the product. We are now in a position to get down to work on two aspects which make up an advertising plan. These aspects are: (i) the creative strategy and (ii) the media plan

(i) *The creative strategy*: Creativity in advertising is very crucial as on this depends the comprehension of the customer to understand the product. We now have to transform proposition or statement into an idea which is to be communicated to the customer. In converting the proposition into an idea, use of creativity is of paramount importance. Creativity must take into consideration direction and relevance. For the bright idea to be useful, there must be a right idea. It is this idea which has to be communicated to target group. In order to communicate the idea, media personnel, production personnel as well as creative personnel will have to be involved in this area. Finally the idea will have to be channelised into various material that will be required for advertising campaign. This can range from press advertisements to film commercials, to radio spots and TV spots, to posters and other point-of-sale material. All these items will be creative interpretation of the idea.

(ii) ***The media plan***: While creativity is perhaps most closely related in an agency with the development of an idea and its interpretation into advertising material, it also plays a role in the development of a media plan. Let us know briefly the way in which an agency constructs a media plan. Media may be defined as vehicles of mass communication which are used to carry advertising messages. Very rarely, except in the case of direct-mail advertising, are media developed solely as advertising communication vehicles.

One may broadly classify media into two groups:

(a) Media which are read, seen or heard by the consumer for their 'editorial' worth. These are the newspapers, magazines, the radio programmes cinema shows, TV programmes which are read or tuned into or watched by the consumer for the 'editorial' material which they offer. The advertising benefits from the editorial climate of this media.

(b) Media, usually more 'reminder' type of media such as outdoor media, hoarding, transportation signs, posters, kiosks, neon signs, etc., which are noticed in passing only. They obtain consumer exposure due to the fact that the consumer's living habits cause him to pass by them. For instance, commuters in trains and buses, motorists and pedestrians on roads are all exposed to such media.

The above group also includes point-of-sale items. In preparing media plans one has to study the behaviour and exposure of consumer groups with regard to both kinds of media. We have to study both kinds of media. We have to study what media our target consumer looks at for 'editorial' pleasure and when he does so and in what frame of mind. By studying consumers living habits and pattern of movement we can assess which of the second group of media he will be exposed to as a general rule. In the more advanced countries it is possible to get detailed statistics on the kind of audience that each medium has. In advanced countries this information is very detailed indeed and permits one to prepare accurate media plans. In other countries, however, this information is still very scanty and apart from basic circulation information it is rare that one gets much else. However, through experience one gradually builds up a fund of knowledge which enables one to select appropriate media for appropriate markets. Here, apart from the circulation information a study of the quality of the medium in terms of editorial content and style is a very useful method of evaluating reader types.

MEDIA MIX

Media planners have to create what is known as the *media mix,* consisting of various types of mix comprising various types of media. The selection of these media will depend upon the following:

(a) ***The target audience that is to be reached*:** Its reading or media exposure habits and its location and movement and shopping habits will permit us in selecting such media as will reach target consumers most effectively.

(b) ***The product to be promoted and its use by the target audience*:** If one were selling holiday travel to a businessman and one were also selling machinery to the same businessman, it would perhaps be inappropriate to release the former advertising in technical magazines though they might provide adequate coverage of this particular businessman. It would be equally inappropriate to release the latter advertising in a leisure magazine reaching the target audience.

(c) ***The nature of the message*:** Whether it is a persuasive long-copy story, or whether it requires demonstration of the product in action or presentation of the product in colour. All these factors would influence the media planner. Magazines would allow long-copy stories, while film or TV commercials, project demonstrations, posters and colour press advertising would present the product in colour for easy identification. Media mix suggests that a number of different types of media are frequently required to provide total coverage for any campaign. For example, while one might use press or TV to put across the main informative story of a product it may be necessary to utilise some outdoor and point-of-sale media in order to effectively remind the consumer of the product on his way to the market or at the time of buying. This interlinking of different media brings into focus the importance of designing creative material with a unified theme so that the reminder media material can bring back to mind the advertising message conveyed earlier by the informative media.

(d) ***Competitive activity*:** It is considered good media tactics to design a media plan that will let the advertising dominate competitive activity. Often, when the budget is smaller than that of the competitor the media planner recommends heavier use of fewer media so as to achieve this dominance.

(e) ***Budget restraint*:** The media planner has to assess carefully the different buys he can make within budget and then recommend what he feels will give the best impact value for the particular campaign.

At the end of the exercise the media planner will have worked out a list of media detailing the audience that each media offers, the number of insertions or spots to be released in each, the number of times the target audience will be reached and a cost analysis for each media. In order to relate this plan specifically with the targeted sales, separate analysis can also be prepared indicating the amount of coverage or number of contacts that will be exposed to the advertising in each of the sales territories.

We have now a media plan which takes into account the target consumer, the creative requirement, market location and budget limitations. The creative strategy and media plan are then presented to the client. This is what is called an advertising presentation. At this presentation the agency relates their plans to the total marketing effort and indicates how it will fit in.

Stage Five: Implementing the Campaign

Once the advertising campaign has been approved in terms of the creative strategy and the media plan, the agency next has to apply different 'crafts' in order to implement the campaign in the manner in which it was planned. These range from the preparation of press advertisement material to the production of TV and film commercials, recording of radio spots and production of point-of-sale material. On the other hand, the media buyer and scheduler has to implement the media plan in terms of preparing estimates, schedules and release orders for press, cinema, radio and other media. The agency takes on for the advertiser the responsibility of seeing the right time so that the total plan, as envisaged, becomes operative. Once the campaign has been released it becomes necessary to assess its impact. This brings us not only to the final stage of activity on a campaign but also brings us to the first stage of the next campaign.

Stage Six: Assessing the Impact and Value of a Campaign

It is not possible always to evaluate the effect of an advertising campaign in terms of sales as too many other factors are involved. This is particularly so in service advertising. Therefore, the result of a campaign cannot only be shown by way of sales. But there must be some way of measuring the value of campaign. In answer to this question it is felt that the impact of an advertising campaign should be assessed by the extent to which it results in changing the attitude of the selected target consumers. Therefore, having planned, prepared and released the campaign we start after a suitable interval to compile information on its impact value. This study will provide information on the following:

(i) *Awareness*: The extent of shift in the degree of awareness of an agency or product is highly relevant because unless people are aware of something they can neither have an attitude towards it nor act in regard to it.

(ii) *Attitude Dimensions*: It is necessary to measure to what extent the right attitudes have been communicated and accepted. We will have to find out at the time of formulating the proposition what these right attitudes should be.

(iii) *Purchase of the product:* It is vitally important as merely having a favourable attitude towards the product is not enough: it must be one that is motivating enough to cause usage. The measure of users that are created due to the shift in attitude therefore becomes very important.

(iv) *Repurchase of the product*: It is said that advertising can result in a first sale but it is for the product itself to perform and earn the second sale. Of course, by 'perform' one does not only mean preference in visible terms but in satisfaction terms as well (in this case, the amount of satisfaction a traveller has derived from a visit). In other words, the product must live up to the expectation which the advertising has created.

Pre-Testing Advertising

Pre-testing advertising attempts to assess the communication value of an advertisement, whether press advertisement, or TV or radio spot in advance of the actual release or screening. In this way, it is possible to develop advertising material which most effectively conveys the proposition idea. The pre-testing technique can also assist in forecasting the change in attitude, etc., which the campaign can achieve. A set of advertisement commercials, are prepared and these are shown to small groups of representative consumers. The effectiveness of the various approaches in conveying the proposition is then measured. This type of testing assists the agency to judge whether the idea created is in fact correctly communicating the motivating proposition to the target consumer. In this way we are back again at the first stage of the next campaign, and the cycle begins once again.

SALES SUPPORT

In tourism, sales support is all those promotional activities designed to transmit to the public and to the travel trade specific and detailed information on aspects like accommodation, transport, attractions, prices, etc., concerning the tourist services to be promoted. Sales support activities are the measures which establish personal or indirect contact with customers or trade intermediaries. It is also a process of training employees to be proficient salespersons. Sales support has certain distinct, closely related functions which neither advertising nor public relations can be expected to fulfil as effectively. It is a channel of communications between the 'manufacturer' or the 'producer' of a tourist service—accommodation unit, transport company, etc., and the 'distributor' or the 'seller' of that service. Secondly, it aids and assists the seller to do his job more effectively with the support of different techniques. The aim of the sales support activities is:

(a) to inform the customers (tourists—both actual and potential) or trade intermediaries travel agents, tour operators, airlines, etc. about the various services available, their price and quality, etc.;
(b) to assist them in selling these services to the ultimate users;
(c) to motivate them to devote a sufficient level of sales activity to the service promoted.

Sales Support Activities

National and regional tourist organisations as well as tourist service enterprises and tour operators recognise fully well that their sales and profit depend to a very large extent on the support and assistance they provide to retail travel agents and also the way in which they motivate travel agents. This is done by way of sales support activities. In order to be able to sell a service (a room in a hotel, seat in an airline) or a destination to the prospective tourists, travel agents or other sales intermediaries need to be aware of certain factual information which includes:

(i) Country's tourist facilities such as existing as well as new establishments, accommodation capacities, price schedules for various services.
(ii) Various travel regulations and formalities such as visa requirements, foreign exchange rules, health and vaccination regulations including different certificates needed, custom rules, rates of exchange for currency, etc.

(iii) The various transport and communication services available; the schedules of airlines, railways, road transport services, shipping services (where available), their rates.

(iv) Weather conditions at different times of the year, and types of clothing required during different seasons.

(v) The utilization (occupancy rates) of existing tourist facilities at different times of the year.

(vi) Plans for opening of new destinations, hotels, transport routes (railways, airlines, etc.) and also plans for expansion of existing tourist facilities.

Advertising has now created a demand in the form of enquiries made by potential tourists, travel agents and other intermediaries. The potential tourists, travel agents and other intermediaries would now require, in addition to the type of information mentioned above, materials such as brochures, folders, booklets, guide books, directories, maps and illustrations in order to be able to transform demand into definite bookings. Most of the above material is meant for distribution to potential tourists by the travel agents and other sales intermediaries like tour operators, airlines, etc., either directly or through mail. Almost all the tourist organisations and tourist service enterprises produce the material extensively and make use of it by way of distributing it to travel agents, tour operators, etc. Tourist sales intermediaries on their own also produce sales support material for distribution to potential tourists.

Sales Support Techniques

Sales support techniques can be grouped into two main areas—printed material and special offers. Printed material includes brochures, folders, direct-mail material, display material, etc.

Brochure is a pamphlet bound in the form of a booklet. It is a voluminous publication with special emphasis on the quality of paper, the reproduction of illustrations, graphic design of the cover and the layout of the pages. Special emphasis is laid on the quality of the paper and printing. It is mainly used by official travel organisations and tourist service enterprises to inform prospective tourists about the attractions and facilities available in the country. A brochure describes and illustrates a destination or service in more detail. Detailed information on accommodation, prices, travel schedules, etc., is given in a brochure. Travel agents and tour operators use brochures as one of their principal selling aids.

Folder, on the other hand, is a single piece of illustrated paper which can be folded. Folder is less voluminous than the brochure and its production is less time consuming. These are usually printed on a single sheet and then folded. It is perhaps the most widely used advertising media by the official tourist organisations and by tourist service enterprises. It can be used alone or in conjunction with a sales letter. It is relatively inexpensive to produce and can be used in a variety of ways. While producing, special care should be taken about the quality of the paper and printing. Folder, compared to brochure, is short, tastefully illustrated and attractively designed and produced.

Sales letter is a direct-mail material. It is a tool through which an attempt is made to gain agreement or favourable action towards a product. Sales letters offer many opportunities for selling travel services. These could be used alone or in combination with travel brochures or folders. These are sent out to those people whose addresses have been selected according to the likelihood of their being potential users of the services offered. A proper mailing list is a prerequisite for effective use of this tool. Sales letters require very little time to prepare and to distribute. The effectiveness of a sales letter can be measured very rapidly from the response it draws. This is done by way of a reply card which is included with which the recipient can request further information and also travel literature.

Display material includes posters, dispensers for sales literature, cardboard stands, articles of handicrafts, exhibits, etc. This material is used in the agency's office or in travel agent's sales rooms. The material is displayed in such a way that it attracts the attention of a visitor as soon as he enters the office. In many cases, cinema slides are also used, either fixed or on an automatic projector for display purposes.

Special offers like temporary price reductions, free gifts, premiums and various types of contests are being used extensively in competitive industries like cosmetics, packaged foodstuffs, etc. The tourist industry has also started to adopt these techniques as an additional sales support tool. Reduced airfares for students, 'affinity group', special off-season rates at hotels and tourist resorts are the examples of some of the special offers in the tourist industry.

PUBLIC RELATIONS

Public relations is an important promotional technique. It involves measures designed to improve the image of a service, to create a more favourable climate for its advertising and sales support activities. It covers such a wide range of activities and is used for so many different aims that it is not easy to define it. Public relations is the "art and science of planning and implementing communication and understanding between a company and the many different groups with which it is concerned in the course of its operation." Public relations may also be defined as the "continuous and consistent representation of an organisation's policies to the public at large and to sections of the public who have a special interest in the organisation's activities, e.g., to various strata of employees, shareholders, actual and potential customers as well as its local and national government.

A positive attitude to public relations in an organisation's activities is evidence that it recognises a duty to keep the public aware of those activities, and of their impact upon society and its environments. From the definitions of public relations, it is evident that its main function is to inform public about the activities of an organisation. In other words it is a part of a firm's or an organisation's total communication effort. Its purpose is to create best possible reputation for the firm or the organisation by way of presenting facts. In a climate of favourable public opinion, an organisation's or a firm's goals can be achieved more effectively.

In the field of travel and tourism, the need for making information and facts available to both potential and actual tourists assumes special significance. It involves measures designed to create and improve the image of the tourist product, create a more favourable climate for its advertising and sales support activities, especially in regard to travel trade intermediaries and news media. Favourable acceptance of any tourist destination by the public is of utmost importance. In fact, no business is more concerned with human relations than the business of tourism. Public relations in tourism is used to create and maintain a positive image for a country, a tourist destination in the minds of people who are in a position to influence public opinion (journalists, editors, travel writers, etc.), or in the minds of sales intermediaries (travel agents, tour operators, etc.). It is oriented towards creating and maintaining an atmosphere whereby travelling public at large is convinced of the advantages of visiting the country concerned.

Public relations is one of the important functions of the official tourist organisation. In fact, tourist organisations primarily are public relations organisations. The objectives of public relations in the field of tourism may be divided in two parts: the dissemination of information and the creation of a favourable image for the tourist product.

Public Relations Techniques

Public relations consists of a number of interrelated activities oriented towards creating and maintaining a favourable positive image for the tourist product. The main techniques of public relations in the tourist promotion are as follows:

(i) Organising familiarization tours for travel writers, editors, travel agents, photographers and other key personnel from different parts of the world as guests to visit the country and to get first-hand knowledge about it. These persons then write about the country visited in well-known travel and other general interest magazines.

(ii) Organising television and radio contests featuring the destination country.

(iii) Organising press releases and arranging press conferences with key personnel connected with tourism field with a view to disseminate information about the destination.

(iv) Arranging seminars and workshops in the place where the tourist promotion office is located.

(v) Organising cultural programmes, musical and folk shows, TV interviews, exhibitions and national friendship weeks in the country where the national tourist office is located.

(vi) Organising various types of contests about the country.

(vii) Encouraging large departmental stores, organizers of fashion shows and manufacturing companies to project the country or a part of it as a promotion showcase in their premises.

Public relation activities thus range from distributing a simple press release to newspapers to organising familiarization visits for key personnel in the travel trade. It is used to create a favourable climate for sales support and advertising by transmitting facts and information to advertising media and to sales intermediaries. However, to have any prospect of success, public relations planning and organisation should be an integral part of an organisation's management strategy and must be organised on a continuing basis. Public relations function of an organisation cannot be considered as an end in itself or as something which can be introduced at short notice to cope with a crisis situation. An organisation should have a positive and planned public relations policy. It is no coincidence that most of the national tourist organisations devote considerable effort to their public relations programme.

TOURIST PUBLICITY: EVOLUTION AND MODERN TRENDS

In order to round off the total marketing effort, there is need for a well-planned publicity programme. Publicity refers to the dissemination of information without charge for its news value in order to inform the prospect about a particular product. A publicity programme could include regular publicity stories and photographs to newspapers, travel editors, contact with magazines on stories, ideas, and the preparation of story outlines and pictures in order to induce magazines to do feature stories on a particular destination. News releases to travel trade magazines on items of interest to the travel industry, such as opening up of a new area, total expansion, increased transportation facilities, development of a new resort are measures which are adapted together with other publicity through the media of radio, television, lectures, seminars, travel films, etc.

Tourist publicity in the beginning developed in an empirical way under the pressure of the growth of international travel, and to the extent that information had to be supplied to an ever-increasing number of tourists. Thus, at its outset, it was simply informational publicity. With the growth in volume of commercial tourist publicity, particularly in the sphere of transport, and great increase in the number of tourists, various countries realised the importance of tourism in the national life. They recognised it especially in economic terms—earning of foreign exchange. This necessitated the countries to organize their institutional tourist publicity with a new approach and employ experienced commercial publicity technicians to draw up a long-term publicity strategy.

For a successful tourist publicity, one important factor is to be placed at the top of all considerations. In the field of tourism, motive forces and effects lie on different planes. The motive forces of tourism lie mainly on a plane which is outside the scope of economic factors, while the results of tourism are represented in a series of economic processes. Generally speaking, when reference is made to tourism, thoughts go to economic effects of travel and sojourn and an estimate is made of the value of tourism for the national economy in terms of the figures represented by earnings and the influence on the balance of payment of a country. The earnings of foreign exchange become very important. Reference is also made in tourism to supply and demand as market terms and the tourist plant of a country is evaluated according to the place it occupies among the national resources and its potentialities to increase the national income. This purely economic consideration accounts for the striving of every tourist country to obtain the most optimum possible share of the market and tourist publicity is a means of pursuing this effort.

Methods of Tourist Publicity

The methods of tourist publicity in their evolution have lagged behind in comparison with the developments of the publicity methods of other branches of economy which utilize applied psychology and sociology. They are still mainly based on experience, instinct, routine and technique. Publicity still proceeds from the object with a more or less arbitrary combination of rational and emotional appeals and perhaps in consideration of the results obtained by research in publicity media, but in utter disregard of the person to whom the publicity is addressed. So it is not yet clear at all how tourism, whose fluctuating character was proverbial, has now grown into a phenomenon almost impervious to crises, or why the tourist need has undergone a re-classification to other needs in order of importance, as also why, despite the fundamental universality of the tourist need, different human groups have different conceptions about its composition and the urge for experience.

Professor Krapf was the first to undertake a close examination of the tourist consumption. It is of particular importance for tourist publicity when he states that all considerations of tourism must now free themselves from objective facts and institutions and cover the emotional world of man and the conduct of his life. This should be followed up by an examination of tourist behaviour. For the extension and importance assumed by tourism in a particular country or region, the decisive factors are neither the beautiful landscape as a natural assumption, nor the past and contemporary culture of a country, nor the natural medical cures in a region nor the transport and tourist plant in its costs and efficiency relationship, nor the appreciation of the authorities concerned or the favourable measures they may sanction. The determining factors are to be sought elsewhere, as in fashion, opinion, need, interest, which in their turn are to be appealed to as the irrational factors of tourist behaviour. The first named factors constitute the prerequisites of tourism which are publicised; the latter ones can be influenced only with the help of publicity. Considered in market terms, supply in the tourist sector is constantly expanding, its publicity efforts always increasing and getting more intensive and the media it utilises ever more diversified and multifarious.

Coordination of Measures

Rising demand and expanding supply characterise the present-day situation of the travel market with its publicity competition. In this competition, two methods stand out which are quite suitably designated as the methods of the advanced tourist countries and those of the developing tourist countries. The advanced tourist countries show a constantly increasing tendency towards a graded publicity beginning with the publicity of the individual travel trade firms, of resorts, areas, provinces and finally countries, while the developing tourist countries, begin with the country's publicity to which regional and travel trade publicity is added. As yet the differentiation between tourist institutions is too limited for them to enter into competition with each other. However, in the well-known tourist countries this competition takes place inside the country and finally between corresponding tourist resorts and enterprises. This carries in itself the danger of a frittering away of the forces and since the percentage of the ineffective residual part of local publicity is relatively large, it is necessary to undertake campaigns in a manner which is more than proportionate. This has special relevance to publicity abroad, where the desire for the most extensive possible coverage of the demand is somewhat restricted by the available financial means. This reason alone points to the necessity of concentration and coordination of all tourist publicity measures.

The Brand Concepts

Each country is a travel mosaic composed of a variety of distinctive features. These features are not however spread uniformly over the whole country but are very frequently regional or even characteristic of a place. Thus every land has regions which through their distinctive climatic, physical, morphological, cultural or other kind of features, constitute the tourist attractions or can be developed to that end. Notwithstanding these territorial individual distinctions, publicity should satisfy the fundamental principles of clarity of objective and uniformity. Clarity of objective in this case signifies that the entire range of national tourist publicity, despite its multifold ramifications, should not show any contradictions, whereas uniformity serves the purpose of creating the impression abroad that all national tourist publicity campaigns are part of a uniform planning. The central idea of publicity planning should be perceptible. It is very rightly mentioned in the *General Theory of Tourism* of Hunziker-Krapf that "the organisational forms of publicity abroad may differ in detail, but there must be a single goal to put national tourism to the fore and the regional and local features on the second plane. These would come into their own once the foreign tourist has made his choice as to the country to be visited."

The tourist publicity can also make use of the brand concept. This, however assumes a certain guarantee of fulfilment. Professor Lisowski has drawn attention to the possibility of creating brands and consequently to the mutual support between brands in the sequence of enterprise-resort-landscape-region country. This mutual support among brands, which can work in both directions, demonstrates still another method which can be followed, namely, that of the most varied publicity combinations through a coupling of the brands. A tourist publicity programme for a country may be conceived in the following way:

(i) The creation of concepts of satisfaction which, taken together, could form the tourist brand of the country;

(ii) A coordination of all publicity measures of the economic, cultural and tourist institutions of a country in conjunction with a coupling of the brands;

(iii) Constant analysis of satisfactions, market observations and research, as well as publicity effectiveness.

Motivation Publicity

The motivating factors of tourism originate in their preponderant majority from the emotional sphere. Consequently, tourism stands out prominently in the world of experience-seeking ideas and conceptions and it can be said that the holidaymaker lives between imagination and reality and the relationship between the two determines his judgement on the land visited. This will be positive in proportion to the extent that reality corresponds to the world of imagination. It may be inferred from this how very important it is for publicity to steer the formation of imagination towards facts as they really exist. This is easiest in the field of comparable satisfactions whereby guiding information on trends may be obtained through a planned investigation of judgements and criticisms—in other words, public opinion research. This publicity based on motivation forces and influencing the imaginative world of the tourists can be referred to as motivation publicity or the irrational approach.

The most intensive publicity is done for recreation, pleasure and cultural travel, and the publicity campaign for this is aimed mainly in producing the result on the imagination that the existing need would find its maximum satisfaction in a particular tourist offer. It has to contend with the horizontal competition of identical or similar appeals and offers. In the application of this method it is essential to have information beforehand about the market facts and conditions like the income-wise classification of the population of different countries, the mental outlook in respect of the presence or absence of the travel lust, and, above all, information about the national habits and preferences, knowledge about the ideas which the average holidaymakers and pleasure travellers associate with the concept of "holiday travel", the destinations which are in the forefront of tourist interest and the reasons thereof.

Within the framework of this method a relatively larger importance is conceded to landscape publicity for relaxation and pleasure travel. In this connection the importance of this subject, in so far as it does not relate to a particularly beautiful landscape or one especially suited for the practice of certain sports, is too much exaggerated. Each region of the globe has a landscape to offer and every one of these landscapes has a particular charm, especially for those whom its special features make it seem strange and therefore worth the experience. To the primary motivations of holiday and pleasure travel, the pressure of the rhythm of our life has added other factors like the escape from the everyday life, freedom from ties and commitments, the urge to adventure, etc. These psychological factors are not taken sufficiently into account and are inadequately utilised in the service of tourist publicity. Publicity for cultural tourism poses lesser problems. It conforms to realities and appeals to a public with an educational background. On the other hand, however, cultural and tourist publicity are so intimately interconnected that there exists the closest coordination.

The second method of tourist publicity is the "reason why" publicity or the rational approach. It extols in the first place the merits or the arguments in favour of visiting the country on behalf of which the publicity has been undertaken and acts in accordance with the principle of suggestion. The form of expression it assumes is the slogan. It is appreciably more strongly competitive which makes it easily liable to fall into the blunder of superlative forms which we come across constantly in tourist publicity.

Tourist Publicity Media

The publicity itself is carried out through media whose scope is that there are constantly new possibilities. This is of particular relevance in respect of tourist publicity whose new forms and scientifically based planning in publicity media seem to be constructed as a result of the fact that in general their publicity effect is limited to the visual and auditive senses. Illustration, copy and the spoken word are therefore the primary publicity media for tourism. They are multiplied through the media compounded out of them.

The greatest importance appertains to *illustration,* for it can achieve emotional effects in the reproduction of a landscape and its atmosphere and is also universally understood. Even if one is inclined to accept the psychological argument that every human being only projects his own personality in every consideration, the illustration retains from this standpoint also considerable publicity effectiveness because it is viewed and perceived differently by different persons. Given the differences of individual tastes, the illustration motivation plays a decisive role, for the illustration should be bearer of the emotional contents which it should radiate on the viewer. Consequently the best illustration is just good enough for tourist publicity. It depends on the planning and shaping of the publicity media as to whether the illustration is to be employed in the form of a drawing, a painting, or a photograph. Generally, the photograph is adjudged as possessing a greater objectivity in the statement. On the other hand, an artistic representation can be the expression of cultural activity and hence equally effective as publicity. Illustration can be developed through stylisation into a brand and thus create a concept which is derived from the homogeneousness of circumstances or satisfaction.

With *copy* as a publicity factor, the urgent necessity for originality with the object of giving expression to the publicity idea also arises. The purpose of every publicity media is to arouse and sustain attention. Illustration and copy must therefore create desires. In tourist publicity the tendency towards schematisation is extremely strong and counteracts the necessity for publicity originality. The similarity of the printed publicity material of hotels, travel agencies, tourist resorts, areas and even countries furnishes proof of this. The *spoken word* is of decisive importance in the case of personal publicity. The proper use of the spoken word is difficult but effective. "Words are not only conveyors of thoughts and ideas, but also of emotional contents and consequently they reach not only the intellect but also the psychism of the recipient and are expressed to this end." (Walter Hagemann, *On the Myth of the Mass*). Thus the spoken world helps us to approach the imaginative world of person addressed and this accounts for the importance of the information or sales talk as well as of publicity lectures, radio broadcasts, television speeches and publicity receptions. The spoken word is here supported by the appearance and presence of the speaker, as well as by his psychological capacity to adjust himself to the individual as also a group of listeners.

The three primary publicity media mentioned—illustration, copy and the spoken word—form the basis of the composite publicity media which can suitably be arranged in the following groups:

(i) Printed publicity material,
(ii) Advertising publicity,
(iii) Projected publicity,
(iv) Structural forms of publicity,
(v) Personal publicity

Printed Publicity Material

Printed publicity material in the field of tourist publicity is mainly composed of the publicity leaflet, folder, brochure and poster. The publicity *leaflet* is used among others as inset and enclosure in the case of conveying an information or communicating to the knowledge of the largest possible number of persons. The folder is the most commonly used and the most important medium for tourist publicity. It has numerous forms and multiple variations which leaves unsolved the question of the optimum effective folder. The question culminates in the investigation as to what the recipient expects from a folder, what he looks for in it, what he hopes to find in it and whether the folder corresponds to the imaginative conception of the country or region which it should advertise. The logical conclusion would be to the effect that account should be taken of the mental outlook of the recipient at the time of producing the folder. What actually takes place is that different versions of the folder are printed for different countries. This practice is further confirmed by the production of special folders like the cultural folder and those for motor tourists, mountain climbers, fishing and hunting enthusiasts, etc. These folders deal with the special interests of the recipient and are composed for easy comprehension of the client.

The Folder

Production of a general folder which has to advertise for a whole country with its variety of attractions, specialities and circumstances, however, is much more complicated. Here, there exists the danger of "too much" as well as "too little", besides the pitfalls of a dry description, superlative forms, overestimation and misappreciation of the points of attraction. A folder is not a travel guide nor a manual of geography. But it must not also be forgotten that the present-day travellers are very often ignorant in the field of tourism and consequently require directions and help as well as information. This renders the setting and composition of the text of an effective general folder a task which has not yet been satisfactorily solved.

The folder must also possess all the necessary qualities required of a good representative—proper appearance, faultless exterior, an unobtrusive and engaging presence, exact information about everything which is offered, truthfulness in assertions and no fanciful exaggerations. The text should never be long-winded. A concrete and concise description containing exact comprehensive information corresponds to the quick rhythm of our time.

The varied nature of the folder results, however, not only from its conception as a general or special folder, but also from the regional and local publicity arrangements. In most countries, there are of course the central publicity organisations, but there are also regional bodies which deal with the tourist interests of a special province or a department. But only in very few cases do such political territorial divisions constitute self-contained tourist areas as well. Consequently, there arises the possibility of joint publicity associations for the promotion and safeguard of the tourist interests of such areas. A classic example of this kind is the joint publicity association of the European Alpine countries which demonstrates how a geographically scenic homogeneity in the form of a publicity unit can complement rationally in the sphere of publicity the various national publicity campaigns. To be adequately effective, however, the publicity medium of the folder needs not only to be well set up, but should also be produced in a sufficient quantity and have a planned distribution.

The brochure is different from the folder in size as well as in content and detail. The importance of the brochure in tourist publicity has not been adequately appreciated and, on account of financial reasons, it has been insufficiently utilized. The brochure offers greater possibilities than the folder to combine with each other publicity and service, suggestion and information.

The *poster* is another important publicity medium of tourism. The difficulties in respect of the production of the general folder occur especially in the case of the poster. The tourist poster should combine its effectiveness based on psychological factors with the task of expressing the impersonation of a country as a tourist destination working on the limited means at its disposal. The tourist poster further suffers from the fact that there is no well-considered distinction in the production of the poster for application as an interior or outdoor poster. In the majority of cases, there is an interior poster for the premises and show windows of travel agencies and information centres, whose use as an outdoor poster in the streets of large cities is consequently hardly discernible. Nevertheless, it should simultaneously satisfy the imperatives of a good outdoor poster and be designed as an eye-catcher. The problem of publicity is further complicated by the discussion on the pros and cons of graphic and photographic posters.

The publicity journal which is utilized at present by almost every national tourist publicity organisation is more representative than all other forms of printed material. As such, it is expensive and therefore limited in its circulation. For the sake of comprehensive coverage, mention may also be made of the printed publicity material which really belongs to the sphere of customer service, like maps, guide books, directories, inserts, etc.

Advertising Publicity

Advertisements can be considered as the best organised publicity medium, even if they require particularly careful preparation and planning. Two principal mistakes are made in the sphere of advertisements. One, consideration is seldom paid to the fact that as a result of the quality of paper and printing errors, the newspaper advertisement can hardly reproduce illustrations in a manner that they have an emotionally suggestive effect. The original pattern must therefore be contrasted with as few half-tones as possible. Two, the one and same original pattern is used in all the selected newspapers, irrespective of the fact that these newspapers often appeal to different social classes. There exist qualitative as well as quantitative readership analyses. The advertisement has a strong effect on the subconscious and must consequently be designed to catch the eye. But it should also express something and try to win over the reader. It needs to be remarked that tourist publicity is also accountable for its share in the wastage of space in the world press through advertisements which are often only empty boasts and leave the informational aspect absolutely out of consideration. The periodical travel supplements of daily newspapers receive the major portion of such advertisements which frequently contain joint publicity for a region or a country. Individual publicity can be very effective in the form of a series of insertions provided a leading idea clearly establishes the link or connection. The selection of the journal should not be determined only by the circulation figures, but also by the influence of the journal within its social class, which again should be examined in relation to its inclination and potentialities for tourism.

Projected Publicity

Projected publicity media comprise film and slide publicity. Of particular importance is the film which is an outstanding publicity medium, not only on account of its representational potentialities, but also because of its suggestive power. The colour film is assuming increasing significance within the framework of tourist publicity. The central idea of the film should be expressible in terms of motion and this accounts for the cardinal rule of all publicity films: short text but plenty of action which should captivate the attention of the spectators and also aim at influencing memory through emotional factors. Publicity effectiveness is a characteristic not only of the purely publicity film, but also of the feature film as well as the instructional or didactic film. In the United States of America and Western Europe the travel film with a commentary known as the "travelogue" has won extensive popularity. Television is a suitable medium to spread the interest in foreign countries and thus serves tourist publicity. In respect of the colour effect, the 8- and 16- mm films make up the greater portion of travel films. Also in their subject treatment, they are often a sequence of shots without any intrinsic connection, simply filmed scenery. Lectures with slides combine the effect of the spoken word and the illustration for direct emotional influence with a generally satisfactory success.

Structural Publicity

Structural publicity comprise all publicity measures which manifest themselves in constructions and structures, as for example, in the establishment and equipment of a tourist publicity office abroad, in participation in fairs and exhibitions, in the preparation of showcases and window displays, etc. There is also the possibility of publicity combinations whereby tourist publicity can be undertaken in conjunction with business publicity. For example, shops selling sports goods, fashion articles, travel accessories, etc., are willing to have such combinations in their show-windows. Similarly at fairs the joint stands of a country procure publicity advantages for tourism because the exhibition as a whole shows tourism in relation to the country and succeeds in creating lasting impressions.

Personal Publicity

Personal publicity in tourism has various forms of application ranging from the informational and sales talk to publicity travel, which serves the need of maintaining contact with the travel industry and to support it in its sales efforts, and includes the publicity lecture. In all these spheres the personal effort holds sway. Also to this category belong interviews, radio broadcasts, television interviews, receptions, etc.

Mass Media

Television

Television has since its inception dominated the advertising media scene, due to its combination of visual and aural stimulation, allowing for greater attention grabbing and more effective transmission of messages than other forms of media. It has a few disadvantages: television commercials suffer from being "zipped" and zapped". "Zipping" is the term given to fast forwarding commercial break sessions during the pre-recording of programs. Often viewers will record programs purely so they can be viewed without the commercial breaks. "Zapping" is the term given to the habit of many consumers to change channels during commercial breaks. This is also done to avoid watching advertisements. Using television advertisements is beneficial due to its wide reach and the degree to which content can be segmented according to the intended target market. Advertisements are carefully paired with time segments and / or linked with appropriate programming, known as "media vehicles". This helps to ensure the intended audience is being reached with the marketing message.

While initial production costs of a television advertisement are high, it is likely to reach a mass audience and, therefore, maintains a low cost per viewer, making it an efficient communication platform.

Radio

Radio by definition is the broadcasting of sound programmes to the public and today can be live streamed through a broadband connection or digitally transmitted into people's cars or homes. Despite being the oldest form of media transmission still being used, marketing via radio remains a popular and effective choice due to its relatively lower cost and convenience (radio exposure can occur during transit, at work, and during recreational activities). Due to the lack of a visual aspect, radio advertising attempts to create imagery in the consumers mind. Radio advertising is also extremely effective at reinforcing messages encountered in other channels (such as television). A familiar jingle or voice associated with a brand enhances brand and ad awareness, ultimately increasing brand equity. This is an example of "Integrated Marketing Communications", in which multiple marketing channels are simultaneously utilized to increase the strength and reach of the marketing message. Like television, radio marketing benefits from the ability to select specific time slots and programmes (in this case in the form of radio stations and segments within).

Fill et al argue that radio communication promotes "emotional consumer-centric associations" as each listener is forced to construct a visual representation of the words and sounds such as music in their minds. A common technique used by companies is known as imagery transfer, where a complementary visual television advertisement is used alongside a one-dimensional radio advertisement featuring a similar audio track to stimulate a visual association between the two. Research suggests this sub-conscience relational thought process greatly benefits future brand recognition and awareness.

Radio infomercials are often a simple script that is read out by the presenter. This is quick and does not require extensive lead times due to minimal production efforts.

Print

Printed media is the most basic form of media advertising. It is the most challenging to create strong imagery with, due to its lack of sensory stimulation, but can be effective in efficient, clear information communication and message delivery. Where a consumer may miss a message in video or audio (perhaps a loud noise interrupts, or someone blocks their view) in print the message remains visible indefinitely. Aspects such as size, colour and style can be used to increase effectiveness relative to other print advertisements, which is important as despite being a basic media communication channel, print is the second largest medium after television (Ang, 2014. "Principles of Integrated Marketing Communications".

Traditionally, marketing communications practitioners focused on the creation and execution of printed marketing collateral. Traditional media, or as some refer to as old media, has been used within the marketing and advertising world for many years. Traditional media encompasses conventional forms of advertising media, such as television, magazines, newspapers, radio, and direct mail and outdoor. For many decades, these forms of communication have been the main source for marketers to reach both consumers and other companies. In a world with no internet and the vast world of social media, roots of advertising and promotion lie within traditional media, where there is a more direct, physical way of advertising.

Media Mix

Advertising in the form of print is used by businesses in the form of billboards, magazines, newspapers and posters, to get their message across to the target audience. Businesses will usually place a billboard in areas where in can be easily seen and where the target audience will spend their daily activities. Newspaper, magazines and posters are smaller in size and can be found in numerous places allowing the general public availability to read them. Depending on the product or service that is being advertised, marketers may specify where majority of their prints may go to, such as advertisement of a new shampoo may be more common within salons.

Print media are a highly customizable, varying in print size, font, positioning and colour combination. Newspapers commonly use coarse paper and tend to have poor reproduction quality, while magazines can enhance the appearance of a certain product due to the heavy weight gloss paper used which translates colour well and offers a long lasting quality and likeability Magazines function as a frame, a psychological device which manipulates perspective and judgement. For example, Vogue, a leading paid circulation fashion magazine, publishes advertising efforts alongside beautiful imagery and elegant photography, the association of the two communicates respectability and sophistication and promotes the creditability of the brands which appear in the same publication. Due to the high-quality reproduction, magazines tend to last longer and are often found in hair salons and waiting rooms. Consumers often cut out individual images which further prolongs the message and increases potential exposure. Although the relevance of the message may be lost during this extended time, brand awareness may still be raised.

Magazines are often segmented by subject such as women's health, automotive or fashion and therefore effectively reach a particular target market while newspapers focus on geographical regions which tend to appeal to a broad representative population sample and, therefore, offer low impact in selectivity. Newspapers are often run on a weekly schedule offering up to date information and coverage of local events and businesses as a lower coast alternative. Such advertisements in smaller typeface and are black and white.

The quantity and choice of the publicity media is determined in accordance with the market and its publicity characteristics like the mental frame of the population, the estimation made of the offers and, finally, the financial resources available. There results consequently a planning based on economic, sociological, psychological and technical factors. Statistics, market analysis and qualitative market research on the one hand and analysis of the product offered as well as publicity research on the other constitute the fundamentals on which an effective publicity planning must be founded.

apter

Development o Tourism in ndia

The development of tourism in India is a fascinating subject. What makes it fascinating is its history. Tourism thrives on history of the country. In fact, tourism cannot be isolated from history much less in a country like India whose cultural heritage has a wealth of attractions.

India's glorious traditions and rich cultural heritage are closely linked with the development of tourism. Its magnificent monuments attract a large number of visitors from all over the world. The wealth of cultural traditions extending over thousands of years, the natural surroundings, the architectural masterpieces, the music, dance, paintings, customs and languages—all these go to make India a tourist paradise. Few countries in the world provide such varied interests to a visitor.

In the words of Nehru, India is "a land of contrasts", where rural tranquillity rubs shoulders with metropolitan bustle, austerity with pomp and show, and pageantry with simplicity. History has been equally generous in bequeathing a treasure of monuments. There is the immortal Taj, the Dravidian temples of the South, especially those of Madurai, and the world-famous frescoes of Ajanta and Ellora. There is also no dearth of cities that create an impression on the tourist. In the words of Mark Twain, India is "the one country under the sun that is endowed with an imperishable interest for alien prince and alien peasant, for lettered and ignorant, wise and fool, rich and poor, bonded and free and on land that all men desire to have seen and having seen once by even a glimpse would not give that glimpse for the shows of all the globe combined." This sums up the relationship of history with tourism and how these two put together contribute towards the development of the country's economy.

An Ancient Civilization

India's civilization and cultural heritage is not only one of the most ancient, but also one of the most extensive and varied. Throughout the ages, many races and people, who have either temporarily come into contact with India or have permanently settled within her borders have contributed to this richness. "In the long panorama of India's history," wrote Jawaharlal Nehru, "there were men who seemed to know life and understand it, and out of their wisdom they built a structure which gave India a cultural stability which lasted for thousands of years."

The Indus Valley Civilization

The Indus Valley Civilization, which flourished more than four thousand years ago, gives the earliest picture of India's remote past. The invasion of India by the Aryan tribes from the north-west inaugurates the historical period. The oldest literary document of India was composed in the period immediately following this event. The original home of Aryans appears to have been Central Asia from where they spread out in several directions. Sometime in the middle of the third millennium B.C. they started on a great migration which covered portions of Europe and Asia. A section of this migration movement reached the frontiers of India by about 2000 B.C., when large groups of them entered the subcontinent in search of new pastures. When they reached the Indus, they met with well-organised urban communities living in fortified towns. It has been pointed out that when the Aryans entered India, they found there people whose material civilization was in many respects superior to their own. The Aryans were a pastoral and agricultural people living mainly in villages.

Archaeological investigations have shown that great cities flourished along the course of the river Indus as long ago as 3000 B.C. The epoch-making discoveries at the city-sites of Harappa in the Montgomery District of Punjab and Mohenjodaro in the Larkana District of Sind, now both in Pakistan, have revealed that in the third millennium B.C. a full-fledged civilization flourished on the Indian soil based upon a highly developed urban economy and discipline. The dwellings in Mohenjodaro were built of brick and stone with due regard to convenience of accommodation and sanitary amenities. Quite a number of houses had their own wells, which in many cases were accessible to neighbours also. The thoroughfares in the town were more than half a mile and fourteen to thirty feet wide. There was also an underground drainage system.

The inhabitants led a comfortable economic and social life. The household utensils were made of pottery, stone, copper, bronze, silver and ivory. Toilet and cosmetic objects included handled copper mirrors, ivory combs with handle, animal-headed stoppers, toilet sets of copper consisting of piercers, ear-scoops and tweezers. For their daily needs the Indus valley people depended on a variety of tools, implements and weapons mostly of copper or bronze. The inhabitants, besides cultivation of wheat and barley, also cultivated peas. They also depended a great deal on animal food and on river fish. Fine cotton textiles were in use long before they came into vogue in Egypt. The inhabitants were well versed in the arts of writing and sculpture. The Aryans took from the local inhabitants many of their religious beliefs and adopted their urban and village organisations. Their own dominant and enduring contributions were the language of Sanskrit, a literary tradition and adventurous spirit. Mainly urban, the civilization of Indus valley was deeply rooted in the Indian soil and largely influenced the later civilization of the Indo-Aryans.

The Indus Valley Civilization apparently collapsed by the time of the Aryan invasion (roughly 1500 B.C.). The reasons for the breakup of this ancient civilization have partly been attributed to the Aryan invasion and partly to the drying up of the Hakra River and the changes in the course of the Indus River. Gradually tribes of these immigrants moved eastward into the Gangetic valley where they settled down and developed a culture of their own. Many of the newcomers intermingled with the original inhabitants they had conquered. From the Gangetic valley, where the synthesis broadly called Hinduism was evolved, the new social organisation gradually spread to the whole of North India. Consequently, organised states like those of the Bharatas began to make their appearance. The new people soon began to penetrate into the South and the Dravidian States of South India and were accepted within the structure of Hindu life. The political evolution of the Indo-Gangetic valley during the earlier half of the first millennium B.C. was marked by the emergence of a number of States. Though the kingdoms were organised under different dynasties and many communities were republican in character, the social and religious organisations of North India followed a common pattern.

The Origin of the Indo-Aryans

The sacred book of the Hindus, the *Rig Veda,* perhaps the first piece of literature that humanity gave to itself, gives us a clear picture of the social life of the Indo-Aryans. It is by far the most important source of information. The Indo-Aryan society consisted of families which lived in villages on the riverbanks of the Punjab. They were surrounded by their flocks and herds of animals which were their main possession. Their culture was rich. The father was the head of the well-knit patriarchal family and commanded obedience from all the members in the family. The *Rig Veda* mentions a number of deities, the chief among them being Varuna, the benevolent sky god. Other principal gods were Indra, the god of thunder and Mitra, the sun god; Aditi, the goddess of eternity; Prithvi, the earth goddess; and Usha, the beautiful goddess of dawn. Brahma, Vishnu and Rudra, though comparatively later conceptions, also find mention in the *Rig Veda.* The Indo-Aryans of the Vedic period (4000–1000 B.C.) had no temples nor did they build images of their gods.

The early Vedic period may be deemed to have ended around 1100 B.C. During the later Vedic period (1000–600 B.C.) there appeared many sages who probed deeply into the problems of life and its meaning. The ultimate goal of this intense mystical speculation, as embodied in the various Upanishads, was nothing less than realisation of the Infinite. In the words of the celebrated German philosopher Schopenhauer, "There is no study more beneficial and elevating to mankind than the study of the Upanishads (Vedanta). It has been the solace of my life, and it will be the solace of my death." Towards the close of the sixth century B.C. the Vedic period reached its end in the face of the rise of new religions and ideologies which transformed the cultural and intellectual climate of the country. Many religious leaders emerged proclaiming different doctrines and disciplines.

Emergence of Buddhism and Jainism

Gautama Buddha and Mahavira stand out among many such religious leaders and founders of new religious movements. Gautama was born in 566 B.C. in Lumbini on the borders of India within the present Kingdom of Nepal. He was the son of the local chief of the Sakya clan, Suddhodhana. Early in his life he showed a contemplative turn of mind and though his father tried to interest him in worldly affairs, Gautama left his home, his wife and the new-born son, in search of truth and the secrets of human life. He sought knowledge and religious experience from different masters, but failing to obtain satisfaction from their teachings entered on a course of contemplation at the end of which he attained Supreme Enlightenment and came to be known as the Buddha (the enlightened one). For almost forty years, beginning from his sermons near Benaras (present-day Varanasi), the Buddha preached his new religion. The essential feature of this religion was that sorrow was the basic fact of life which could be eliminated only through a discipline meant to eliminate its causes. The sermons were given to all irrespective of caste or social position and were given in popular speech and not in Sanskrit. He established an order known as the Sangha—a monastic organisation to which all ordained monks and nuns belonged. It was the establishment of this Sangha with its rigid discipline which enabled his new doctrine to survive as a great religion. The Buddha attained Nirvana in the year 480 B.C. Though born in Nepal, it was in India that he witnessed his Enlightenment and it was India that was the field of his subsequent activity.

Mahavira was an elder contemporary of Buddha and founder of the Jain religion. Mahavira did not claim to have founded a new religion or to discover new truths but only to explain the teachings of the previous masters. Both Mahavira and the Buddha were contemporaries and preached new doctrines. Their chief contribution was the popularisation of the principle of Ahimsa (non-injury). Both taught the doctrine of Salvation by self-effort; purity of mind, right thought, non-injury and compassion. The teachings of the Buddha and Mahavira also found their way in distant lands.

The Mauryas

Alexander's invasion of India is the first landmark in the authentic political history of India. On his death at Babylon, Chandragupta Maurya led a national rising and expelled the Greek garrison from India. Assisted by Chanakya and allies from north-west India, Chandragupta Maurya established a mighty Indian empire with its capital at Pataliputra (modern Patna) in 321 B.C. Having established his hegemony, he proceeded to expand the empire in every direction. The territories of the north-west conquered by Alexander were recaptured by him. The Mauryan empire of the fourth and the third centuries B.C. not only extended all over the central and northern India up to Afghanistan, but was also well organised and well governed. The administrative system was as good as in any of the most advanced Greek city states of the age.

The Mauryan empire lasted for over a hundred and fifty years and counted among its monarchs, emperor Ashoka, who is recognised as one of the great figures in world history. Ashoka, the grandson of Chandragupta Maurya, was able to build an even greater empire. He was the most celebrated and popular ruler (274–232 B.C.) and brought about many administrative reforms. After an early period of warfare and conquest Ashoka became devoted to non-violence. A convert to the non-violent doctrines of the Buddha, he devoted the rest of his life to the moral elevation of his people, preaching to them a high code of morality and ethics in numerous proclamations which were inscribed on stone. He also embarked on a period of intense missionary activity sending scholars and monks to all parts of the then known world including Syria, Egypt and Macedonia. In the history of Buddhism, Ashoka's place can be said to be only second to that of the founder of the religion. The Mauryan age was also a period of high civilization. Some ideas of the unique artistic achievements of the period can be had from the great stupa (religious mound) at Sanchi near Bhopal and the numerous commemorative pillars erected by Ashoka himself in various parts of the country.

After a glorious reign of over forty years, Ashoka died in 232 B.C. The Mauryan empire faded and with the decay of Mauryan power and the disappearance of a strong central authority, pressures began to develop on the frontiers. There were two major developments in the political history of India. On the one hand, there arose in the Deccan a new imperial power, the Andhras. Northern India, on the other hand, was subjected to a series of invasions from the west by the Greeks and Kushans. Under a notable monarch, Kanishka, the Kushan Empire included vast areas of Central Asia and extended well up to Mathura. Kanishka became an ardent Buddhist. Waves of Indian culture during this period spread to Central Asia and gradually to China.

The Guptas and the Classical Period

The third century may be taken as the beginning of the classical age of Indian civilization. The series of foreign invasions in the preceding period had in no way interfered with the cultural and social life of the country. During this time literature, art, science and philosophy made considerable progress. The foreign rulers were eager to adopt and also patronise the native culture and by doing so contributed materially to its advancement.

Early in the fourth century a new power arose in Magadha. This was the Gupta Empire which marked the revival of the Imperial tradition. The great conqueror of the dynasty was Chandragupta's son Samudragupta. He led an expedition of conquest far into the south and re-established the imperial unity of India. The details of his career were engraved by his minister on an Ashokan pillar at Allahabad. He is described as the main founder of the Gupta Empire. His successors, especially Chandragupta II, Kumaragupta and Skandagupta, were notable rulers under whom India enjoyed a period of prosperity which has led many Indian historians to look upon this period as the golden age of Indian history. The country was well administered by an efficient body of civil servants and big public works like irrigation schemes were undertaken. Trade and commerce flourished greatly. So far as arts and literature were concerned, the age of the Guptas is without doubt India's classical period having great achievements to its credit. Science also progressed a lot. In mathematics, astronomy and medical science, India under the Guptas was far advanced than most countries. Another very significant feature of this period was the growth of important seats of learning. The famous university at Nalanda, where students from all parts of Asia came, and where the great Chinese monk Hiuen Tsang spent many years, was founded by a later Gupta emperor.

The Gupta dynasty was brought to an end by the Hun invasions towards the close of the fifth century A.D. The empire was split up. Northern India was again divided into a large number of separate states. Southern India, on the other hand, witnessed great prosperity under the Chalukyas of Badami. Under their patronage the caves of Ajanta were embellished with beautiful and delicate frescoes. In the beginning of the sixth century the Pallava kings of Kanchipuram became a formidable power in the far south and their King Narasimhavarman Pallava (A.D. 625-645) defeated the Chalukyan king (A.D. 642). A court scene of this event is depicted in one of the great paintings of Ajanta.

During the sixth and eleventh centuries a strong movement arose in the country for the revival of traditional Hinduism. The great rulers of the south carried the new wave of devotional Hinduism by building a number of temples. The period between the seventh century and the eleventh century is one of great development in South India. The period is marked by the rivalry of two strategic areas, the valley of the Godavari and the plains watered by the Kaveri (or Cauvery). The Chalukyas, who ruled over the Godavari area were great builders. The architecture of Ellora is a testimony to their love and passion for art. The Kaveri valley at the time was under the dominion of the great Pallavas who can be called the champions of Aryan culture in the South and could also claim to be the originators of the famous group of temples at Mahabalipuram which constitute one of the glories of Indian architecture. The Pallava power continued till the close of the ninth century, when it was replaced by a new empire of the Cholas. In the far south, the Cholas of Tanjore (A.D. 907–1053) ruled over a vast and powerful empire. The Cholas besides being great administrators were also a great sea power. Their naval power was able to organize expeditions across the seas. Their empire began to show signs of decay by the end of the twelfth century and vanished from history in the century that followed. At the end of the tenth century, northern India was ruled by a number of kings who wasted their energies in continuous warfare. Among them were the Chandelas of Bundelkhand, who immortalised themselves by building the magnificent temples at Khajuraho.

The Muslim Period

The next chapter of Indian history opens with Muslim invasions which began at the close of the tenth century. The Arab conquest of Sind in A.D. 712 was merely an episode in the history of Arab expansion. Sind was conquered by the Arabs by a naval expedition under Muhammad-bin-Qasim. But they could not advance farther east owing to the strong resistance encountered by them. It was not until Islam had been firmly established in the area corresponding to modern Afghanistan that the Muslim conquest of India became possible. A new Islamic State arose in the uplands of Afghanistan with its capital in Ghazni. At the beginning of the eleventh century, Mahmud of Ghazni carried out a number of raids on northern India. Towards the end of the twelfth century Mohammed Ghori succeeded to the throne of Ghazni and invaded India. He undertook an expedition, which may be considered the beginning of the attempt on the part of Muslims to conquer India. The resistance of the Hindu monarchs of the Gangetic valley was easily overcome by Mohammed's General, Qutubuddin, the first Sultan of Delhi, and within a short period of twenty years, about the beginning of the thirteenth century, the whole of the Indo-Gangetic valley, from Lahore to the Bay of Bengal, fell to the power of Islam. Apart from the Sultanate of Delhi, confined to the areas of the Gangetic valley, the power of Islam in North India was represented by local Sultanates like Jaunpur, Malwa, Gujarat and Bengal and in the Deccan by the Bahmani State. The Muslims introduced higher standards in such matters as food, clothing and architecture. Great cities like Delhi, Mandu, Ahmedabad, Bijapur and Golconda with their magnificent forts, mosques, pleasure gardens, etc., based on the Islamic traditions of Central Asia arose in different parts of India.

The Mughal Empire

The founder of the Mughal Empire, Babur, was a descendant of Timur and Chenghiz Khan. Ousted from his ancestral dominions in Central Asia, he was eventually forced to take refuge in the mountains of Kabul, which served as the base for his attack on India. In April 1526, after a series of preliminary raids he routed the forces of Ibrahim Lodi on the historic field of Panipat, where the fate of India has so often been decided. At the time of his death in 1530, he controlled the greater part of northern India. His son, Humayun, succeeded him. Humayun, an opium addict, lacked the energy necessary for the completion of Babur's task. After years of warfare he was defeated by an able Afghan rebel named Sher Shah and was forced to seek asylum in Persia in 1544. He ruled for five years. But Humayun came and tried to recapture his lost dominions. He succeeded in recapturing Delhi and Agra in 1555 but died the following year.

The Mughal Empire, in the real sense, started with Akbar, Humayun's son. Akbar, who ruled from 1556 to 1605, was undoubtedly the greatest of Mughal emperors. He annexed the whole of northern India, Ajmer and Gwalior. Between 1586 and 1601 he extended his rule over Kashmir, Baluchistan, Kandhar and parts of Ahmednagar and Orissa. At his death in 1605 his empire comprised 15 provinces. He was an able administrator and enlisted Hindus in his armies. It was only when his successors departed from the main principles of his rule that the empire began to decline.

His son Jahangir (1605–1627) neglected the administration and was subservient to a selfish junta controlled by his favourite wife, Nur Jahan. He was succeeded by his son Shah Jahan (1628–1666), under whose rule the Mughal Empire reached the zenith of its glory. Shah Jahan had an almost insatiable passion for buildings. Not content with erecting a new capital city at Shahjahanabad, he enriched the world's store of architectural beauties by many other buildings, outstanding among them being the Taj Mahal and Moti Masjid at Agra. His reign was also a period of great activity in the field of arts and literature.

The splendour of the Mughal court under Shah Jahan also set in motion influences which finally led to the decline of the empire. In 1657 Shah Jahan fell ill and in the civil war that ensued between his sons, Aurangzeb defeated Dara in 1658, after which he assumed the imperial title and imprisoned his father in the fort at Agra until his death in 1666. The political and religious intolerance of Aurangzeb (1658–1707) was the chief cause of the decline of the empire.

From the middle of the 17th century there had been a marked deterioration in the character of the Mughal aristocracy. After the death of Aurangzeb, a struggle ensued between his three sons, the eldest of whom being eventually successful. He proclaimed himself emperor by assuming the title of Bahadur Shah. Between the death of Bahadur Shah in 1712 and the accession of Mohammed Shah in 1719 five more persons were successively installed on the throne of Delhi. The Mughal Empire ceased to exist as an effective political force by 1738.

The Marathas

By then the Marathas had come into power in their own right. In Shivaji they had a formidable leader. In 1737 they defeated an imperial army outside the walls of Delhi. In the thirty years that followed, their influence extended upto Lahore in Punjab, to Orissa and the borders of Bengal in the East and to the Gangetic valley in the north. In fact, they had the virtual control of the empire of India. Their expansionist policy, however, was checked at the battle of Panipat when they were defeated by the Afghan king Ahmed Shah Durrani in 1761. However, they were able to stabilise their occupation of Malwa and Central India and exercised effective control over Delhi until the beginning of the nineteenth century when the British, after defeating them, took over North India and became the successor to the Mughals.

There were many achievements in various fields during the Mughal period of Indian history, especially during the period ending with Aurangzeb's reign. There was great activity in the field of art, literature, architecture and economics. Many have proclaimed this period as one of the great creative periods of Indian literature. Architecture found its supreme realisation in great works like the Taj Mahal, the Moti Mosque, the Red Fort in Delhi, the city of Fatehpur Sikri and the beautiful palaces of the Rajput rulers. All these continue to be the great attractions to the people from all over the world.

Travel through the Ages

India can rightly boast of being one of the earliest civilizations of the world. Throughout her history, India has always had a special fascination for the rest of the world. Not only did she attract a series of invaders starting with Alexander, but also great thinkers, scholars and administrators like Buddha, Ashoka and Chandragupta. Unlike today, great many people in the past travelled to India primarily in search of knowledge and spiritual solace. Travellers also came exclusively for trade and commerce purposes. Travel in India in the distant past was not a thing of pleasure as it is the case now. It was, however, the opening of new trade routes which gave a big boost to travel with or without purpose. Travellers from distant lands started coming to India in large numbers. Travel became easier and more regulated. As a result of the opening of the trade routes, early travellers made contacts with India. Trade relations matured into cultural relations and better understanding of each other's way of life.

Travel Facilities in Ancient India

Travel in ancient India was a simple affair. The cumbersome procedures involved in travel today were not to be found in the olden days. No travel formalities existed, for example, in the reign of Chandragupta II, and the famous Chinese pilgrim Fa Hien travelled between A.D. 401 and 410 without a passport. However, as early as the third century B.C. a passport or *mudra* was essential, according to Kautilya's *Arthashastra*, for all travellers, and those not possessing the same were fined 12 *panas*. Each passport had the stamp of a high government official or Mudradhaksha and *mudras* were checked at various points on the way by local officers.

The 'guide', as we know today, also existed during the reign of Chandragupta II. During those days one great threat to tourists came from bandits who used to waylay caravans and loot the travellers. In order to avoid such mishaps, caravans usually hired the services of a brave and experienced guide who was thoroughly familiar with dangerous tracts and the ways to avoid them. Senior officials known as *antapala* were duty bound to protect travellers from bandits and other undesirable elements. The expenditure thus incurred by the state on the safety of travellers was realised by way of toll tax to ward off dangers lurking en route. The ancient traveller religiously practised certain superstitions such as setting off his right foot first, or wearing a boat-shaped amulet round his neck if travelling by river or sea. Each caravan had a *sarthavaha* or leader on whom depended the successful completion of the journey. Generally they travelled by daylight and rested at night, when carts were parked and campfires lit, to cook a meal and at the same time to keep away wild animals. The *sarthavaha* commanded obedience from fellow travellers who were all supposed to move together as a group.

Religion as a Motive

The forerunners of modern-day hotels, the roadside inns known as *serais* and *dharamshalas,* were the ideal place for a night's halt for the travellers of early days. Accommodation in these places was provided either free of cost or at a very nominal rate. In the *serais* and *dharamshalas* of yore, people from different walks of life shared their experiences. The owner of the *serai* offered information to travellers on historical sites in the region. Thus we find that long before travelling for pleasure became one of the great leisure industries of the modern world, the practice of travelling for religious reasons, going on a pilgrimage, for example, was a well- established custom in many parts of the world including India. Nowhere, perhaps, was a pilgrimage as much a part of a people's culture, a sacred duty as it were, to be performed in one's lifetime, as in ancient India. A land of many faiths as it is, pilgrimages continue to be sacred to this day in India.

Going on a journey to holy places to earn spiritual merit or an absolution of sins, goes back in India to the earliest times. The Vedas, the ancient religious texts of the Hindus, enjoined that unless a man went on pilgrimage to the four sacred *dhams* or holy places of the country, he would not attain 'release' and would therefore continue to suffer rebirth for his sins. These four sacred centres were scattered in the far-flung corners of India: the Temple of Lord Jagannath in Puri in eastern India; the Rameshwaram Temple in the deep south, Dwarka on the Gujarat coast in the west and Badrinath in the snow-bound mountains of the Himalayas. These are still India's four great pilgrimage centres and pilgrims flock to them in hundreds and thousands year after year. The rigour of such travel in ancient times can be well imagined. Pilgrimage centres were thousands of miles apart, across the vast continental expanse of India. Roads were mere cart tracks, and even these were non-existent in many places. Forms of transport were slow and primitive. The distances to be covered were enormous, running through thick jungles and across mighty rivers. Hazards from wild animals, thieves and dacoits abounded. And for many pilgrims—specially the old and the infirm—a long arduous journey extending over many months could well turn out to be a journey of no return.

But so deep and so strong was the hold of faith that the ritual of pilgrimage flourished over the centuries. Religion was a great unifying force. Pilgrimages strengthened religious bonds. It provided the impetus for a 'stay-at-home' agrarian society to break out of its narrow geographical confines. It exposed people to new manners and customs, different kinds of food and modes of dress. It encouraged exchange of ideas and fostered trade. It served as a powerful means of forging unity and understanding between people from widely different regions. Interestingly, religious journeys help to evolve what we now call a pilgrimage infrastructure—a unique and efficient system that catered to the simple basic things of all pilgrims, rich and the poor alike. *Serais* and *dharamshalas* were the places where people from different walks of life on their way to various pilgrim centres met and shared experiences.

Trade as Motive

Travel to India was undertaken by people from all over the world for a variety of reasons—the most important among them being trade and commerce. Why trade and commerce particularly? The answer lies in the fact that India from earliest times enjoyed the reputation of being a country of many riches. It is on record that even long before the Christian era, travellers visited India in search of fortune. This trend continued and became more marked in course of time with Europeans heading towards the Indian shores for the sole purpose of trade, until finally the British outwitted all others and entrenched themselves firmly in this country.

Not only did India attract a series of invaders starting with Alexander of Macedonia, but also great travellers like Vasco da Gama. Many foreigners, Arabs and Europeans alike, came here to establish trading posts. The great explorer, Christopher Columbus, set out to find a new route to India and in the process discovered the New World. India throughout had a strange fascination for foreign travellers. Mark Twain described it as a fabulous world of "splendour and rags, the one country under the sun with an imperishable interest, the one land that all men desire to see." The following paragraphs give a brief account of how Europeans travelled to India in search of fortune and eventually settled down in the country to further their main interests.

Portuguese Enterprise

It was nearly twenty-eight years before Babur founded the Mughal Empire that there occurred an incident which rather changed the course of Indian history. In one of the most daring exploits in human history and adventure, the Portuguese explorer, Vasco da Gama, discovered the sea route to India round the Cape of Good Hope, and on May 20, 1498 landed on the harbour of Calicut on the Malabar coast. A man of great adventure and genius, Vasco da Gama won the confidence of the Hindu Raja of Calicut and the Portuguese established themselves as swiftly and surely as any of the earlier invaders of India. In yet another swift and bold exploit, the Portuguese hero destroyed a fleet of Muslim traders which he found off the coast of Calicut, destroying all those who fell into his hands. The expedition, organised under the direct auspices of the King of Portugal, returned to Lisbon in August 1499, where the great explorer was given a hero's welcome. But soon afterwards, in the year I500, another Portuguese fleet came out and landed at Calicut. In his second voyage Vasco da Gama came to Cochin in 1502 and established a factory. Cochin with its excellent harbour became thus the first trading headquarters of the Portugese India. In the year 1505, Francisco de Almedia arrived at Cochin as the first Portuguese Viceroy (1505–1509) and established a number of factories and fortresses.

Discovery of Sea Route

There was a marked increase in the number of travellers coming to India as a result of the discovery of the sea route by Vasco da Gama. This also marked the emergence of a world of new influences. Through Portugal, India first came into contact with Western science—the fruits of Western Renaissance. The immediate result of this was the end of the Arab domination of the Indian Ocean and the Red Sea, built up gradually at the cost of Indian maritime activity. Immediately the Portuguese traders got busy and sent out their ships to monopolise the sea trade of the Asiatic coast. To protect their ships from the Arabs they sent a war fleet under Admiral Albuquerque, who in the year 1510 wrested Goa from the Sultan of Bijapur and made it the capital of Portuguese East India. Under his Viceroyalty the Portuguese became very rich and powerful. Goa became a very popular place with the Portuguese. It was also the first European colony and the centre of Christian propaganda in the East. The Empire of Vijayanagar, with which the Portuguese did an enormous trade, was then at the height of glory and a famous place off the West Coast. Albuquerque also built a fort at Bhatkal, and before long, the Portuguese established settlements at Bombay (now Mumbai), Diu and Daman on the Gujarat coast, at Chittagong and Hooghly in the Bay of Bengal and also in Ceylon (Sri Lanka). Thus within a short period of twenty years of their advent, the Portuguese gained control of many ports of the Indian Ocean. The Portuguese Empire reached its greatest extent in the middle of the sixteenth century. "From Mozambique and Malacca, to their headquarters at Goa on the western shore of India, their power spread so that no vessel could safely sail to or from the Indian ports unless it held a Portuguese permit. The period of this eastern empire of the Portuguese, afloat, corresponds with the first century of Moghal rule, ashore," observes a historian.

The commercial intercourse between India and the West had been going on from time immemorial and reached its height during the Roman Empire. Alexandria and Constantinople were the chief centres where Indian goods were sold and exchanged. These two centres played a great part in publishing India as many potential travellers learnt of India and its riches through the variety of Indian merchandise displayed at these ports. However, the growing power of the Arabs in the Mediterranean and the overthrow of Alexandria in the seventh century almost closed the ancient trade routes to the West. For a time, the Indian trade went on through Constantinople where the Venetians had grown rich in the Middle Ages by supplying Europe with Indian goods, especially spices, pepper, cloves and cinnamon—the items which they required for flavouring their diet and also for medicinal purposes. But when the Turks took Constantinople by storm in 1453, the Europeans realised that the trade route to India was no longer accessible to them. The great achievements of the Portuguese in geography, their mastery over natural forces, adventurism coupled with scientific methods filled the hearts of Europe with a new hope to re-establish the ancient contact between the East and the West for commercial and also for political gains.

The discovery of the sea route to India by the great Portuguese explorer Vasco da Gama and the subsequent control over many seaports by the Portuguese discussed above were great events in Indian history. With the arrival of more powerful Dutch and English fleets in the first half of the seventeenth century, the Portuguese power rapidly declined and Portugal lost its monopoly of eastern trade. The Dutch were the real successors to the Portuguese, and it is they who next established a number of factories on the Coromandal coast, in Gujarat and in Bengal.

The East India Company

On December 31, 1600 A.D. Queen Elizabeth granted a charter to the governor of a company of merchants of London trading with the East Indies. In 1608, a fleet of merchant ships of East India Company, commanded by Captain William Hawkins, arrived at the port of Surat, carrying a letter from the king of England to Jahangir requesting the emperor for trading facilities. Hawkins was anxious to obtain a foothold for the English in India. As it happened the emperor granted all his requests. Thus, in 1612 an English trading centre was established at Surat, the first English settlement in India. By the year 1619 English trading posts were established in Agra, Ahmedabad and Broach (Bharuch). Surat became East India Company's headquarters. The island of Bombay formed part of the dowry of Catherine of Braganza when she married Charles II of England in the year 1661. Seven years later Charles handed it over to the Company. In the year 1687, Bombay replaced Surat as the Company's headquarters. Thus by the end of the seventeenth century the British gained quite a hold in India. The East India Company enjoyed a monopoly of Indian trade until 1813. In course of time the Crown took over the government of India from the East India Company and Lord Canning became the first Viceroy and Governor General. The British rule continued until the year 1947 when they were forced to withdraw under the pressure of national aspirations. What went on during the British period is another matter. That chapter of the history is beyond the scope of this book.

Accounts of Travellers

The various travellers who came to India from time to time recorded interesting accounts of their experiences. These accounts, besides being a valuable source of information, make interesting reading to the extent they reflect the impressions of those who came to India from time to time. The most important of these accounts is the one by Ibn Batutah, who wrote a detailed diary of his travels. He was born at Tangier in A.D. 1304. In 1325, he left his home, and passing through various countries in Africa and West Asia, crossed the Sindhu (Indus) in A.D. 1333. The travels took him as far as Indonesia and China. Out of a total of more than 17,000 miles he covered, more than 14,000 miles in course of his travels through India, Maldives and Ceylon (Sri Lanka). He stayed in India for about fourteen years (A.D. 1333–1347) of which about eight years were spent in Delhi (1334–1342) where he was appointed Qazi by Muhammad bin Tughlak. He was also asked to conduct a royal embassy to China. The travelogue of Ibn Batutah contains abundant information not only on the momentous events of the period but also on the judicial, political and military institutions and social and economic conditions of India during the period of his sojourn. It also throws interesting light on a variety of topics such as postal system and roads, traffic, agricultural products, court ceremonies, trade, shipping, arts, music, etc. When Alexander the Great reached India, he found well-maintained roads lined with trees and provided with wells, police stations, and rest houses. Along one royal highway, 1,920 kms long and about 19 metres wide, man travelled in chariots, palanquins, bullock carts, on donkeys, horses, camels and elephants.

The first medieval traveller to reach the Orient was probably Benjamin of Tudela, a Jewish scholar who left Saragossa in the year 1160. He wrote a detailed account of his thirteen-year journey through Europe, Persia and India, giving information on the Jewish communities, and the geography of the various places he visited.

Young Marco Polo left Venice in the year 1271 with his father and uncle. They travelled through Persia and Afghanistan to the "roof of the world", the then unknown Pamir Plateau. After crossing the windswept Gobi Desert, he reached Kublai Khan's palace and remained in China for twenty years. On his way back home, he stopped in Sumatra, Java, India, Ceylon (Sri Lanka) and returned to Italy with rich jewels sewn in the seams of his tattered clothes. There are also accounts of some European travellers who visited India during the period described above. The Fransciscan friar, John of Monte Corrino visited India on his way to and back from China, during the last decade of the thirteenth century. Mention may also be made here of the famous Portuguese chronicle—the commentaries of the great Alfonso D'Albuquerque. Later in the sixteenth and seventeenth centuries many more European monks, travellers, merchants and adventurers visited India. Also in the early eighteenth century quite a few travellers left valuable accounts of their travels in India.

Opening of Sea Routes

Thus we find that the opening of the sea route and the land routes to India brought in many travellers. These travellers, who came primarily with the intention of excursion or in search of fortune, engaged themselves in trade which ultimately culminated into their forming an empire. The sea and land routes also opened up new markets for Indian raw materials and manufactured goods and for a time India became the largest supplier of a number of commodities to the whole world.

During the days of the British rule in India travelling was more organised. Palanquins were a popular mode of dak travel controlled by the postal department under the East India Company. A person wishing to undertake a journey had to intimate about his plans and itinerary to the post master general about a fortnight in advance. There were dak bungalows on the road for the convenience of dak travellers. In summer, travellers travelled by night and the way was lit by a torchbearer who ran along the road. Besides the four bearers carrying the palanquin, there were an equal number of men to relieve the bearers at regular intervals. Because of limited speed the palanquin proved to be an expensive mode of transport. It was therefore replaced in the year 1850 by the horse carriage dak. This was less expensive and faster than the earlier one. About this time a number transport companies emerged.

India: A Land of all Seasons

India is a land of contrasts—from tropics to snows. It is vast, varied and strikingly beautiful. The second most populous and the seventh largest country in the world, India has the most ancient cultural heritage. More than six hundred million people, diverse in many ways, inhabit over 32,87,782 square kilometres of the Indian soil. It has a land frontier of 15,200 kilometres, and a coastline of about 6,000 kilometres. The variety of its scenery, its intensive and equally varied agriculture, its extremely diversified industry, its big cities and thickly populated areas, its vast open countryside, its ports, its variety of languages and finally its manifold relations with other nations of the world—all of these make India an exciting and fascinating place.

Physically, the mainland comprises four well-defined regions, namely, the great mountain zone, the extensive middle section of Indo-Gangetic plain together with the Brahmaputra Valley of Assam, the desert region and the Southern Peninsula. The Himalayas comprise three almost parallel ranges interspersed with large plateaus and valleys, some of which like the Kashmir and Kulu Valleys are very fertile, extensive and extremely rich in scenic beauty. Some of the highest peaks in the world are found in these ranges.

The extensive middle section of the Indo-Gangetic plain is about 2,400 kilometres long and 240 to 320 kilometres broad and is formed by the basins of three great river systems, the Indus, the Ganga and the Brahmaputra. These are one of the most densely populated areas on earth. The desert regions can be divided into two parts—the 'great desert' and the 'little desert'. The great desert extends from the edge of the Rann of Kutch to beyond the Luni River north-west. The little desert extends from Luni River between Jaisalmer and Jodhpur in Rajasthan up to the northern wastes. Between the great and little deserts lies a zone of absolutely sterile country consisting of rocky land cut up by limestone ridges. Due to the scanty rainfall, this region is almost absolutely sterile.

The great Peninsular plateau is marked off from the Indo- Gangetic plain by a mass of mountain and hill ranges varying from 460 to 1,220 metres in height. Prominent among these are the Aravalli, Vindhya, Satpura and Ajanta. The Peninsula is flanked on one side by the Eastern Ghats, where the average elevation is about 610 metres, and on the other by the Western Ghats, where it is generally from 915 to 1,220 metres, rising in places to over 2,440 metres. Between the Western Ghats and the Arabian Sea lies a narrow coastal strip, while between the Eastern Ghats and the Bay of Bengal there is a broader coastal area. The Southern tip of the plateau is formed by the Nilgiri Hills where the Eastern and Western Ghats meet.

Climate

Climatically, the whole region enjoys a tropical monsoon climate but with extreme ranges of rainfall from under 5 inches in the deserts to the wettest stations in the whole subcontinent. The monsoons (south-west and north-east between June and November) provide 85 per cent of the country's rainfall, with a range of 780 mm to 1,760 mm a year, the extremes being 11,000 mm in Assam Hills and 290 mm a year in parts of Rajasthan.

There are four main seasons in India: (i) winter season (December–February); (ii) hot weather summer season, (March–May); (iii) rainy season, south-west monsoon period (June–September), and (iv) post-monsoon period, known as north-east monsoon period in the Southern peninsula (October–November). Apart from its snow-covered northern fringe, India is generally a hot country. North and Central India experience the two extremes of climate. In December and January, in spite of bright sunshine, it can be extremely cold and frosty. On the other hand, in Western and Eastern India, the cold season is less pronounced, while South India basks under a tropical climate all the year round.

The People

India is the world's second most populous country with more than one billion inhabitants. The inhabitants show an enormous variety of distinct racial and ethnic types. Nowhere else in the world do we find such a fascinating variety of peoples, languages and customs knit together. Corresponding to this complexity of the racial composition is the wealth of equally intricate cultural patterns ranging from the primitiveness of semi-nomadic forest dwellers to the highly advanced stage of civilization represented by the inhabitants of some of the modern industrial cities such as Mumbai, Delhi, Kolkata, Chennai and Bangalore. There are major religions and linguistic divisions, and religion, as it were, is still the principal basis for the delineation of cultural and social divisions of the Indian population. There is something unique about the continuity of this cultural and social heritage through thousands of years of Indian history.

Foreign Influences

Perhaps few other countries in the world can boast of such a continuity of tradition and cultural life. Jawaharlal Nehru in *The Discovery of India* mentions: "There was something living and dynamic about this heritage which showed itself in ways of living and a philosophical attitude to life and its problems. Ancient India, like ancient China, was a world in itself, a culture and a civilisation which gave shape to all things. Foreign influences poured in and often influenced that culture and were absorbed. Some kind of dream of unity has occupied the mind of India since the dawn of civilization." The secret of this dynamic civilization lies in its wonderful capacity for accommodation for absorbing different customs and ways of life that have emerged from the fusion of many races and cultures. People of modern India are a multi-coloured population constituting various religious groups, each fragment with its own peculiar characteristics, customs and ways of life.

The food and dress of the people also vary a great deal. There are hundreds of styles of wearing the graceful multi-coloured saree—a dress of the majority of women in India. The menfolk wear a variety of dresses which differ from region to region. The Western styles of dresses are quite popular with both men and women in cities and towns. With regard to food, India may be considered a 'gourmet's paradise'. Food in India is as varied as the Himalayan peaks, fertile plains and palm-fringed shores that make up so much of the land. There are fifteen and more traditional cuisines in India. Food habits of people differ from one region to another.

Another major characteristic of the people of India is the languages. There are many language groups in India. According to the 1991 census, there are over 800 languages and major dialects in the country. The four major language groups are (i) Indo-Aryan (ii) Dravidian (iii) Tibeto-Burman and (iv) Munda.

Architecture

Indian architecture is essentially of native origin. It has also absorbed many outside influences at different times. During a period extending over many centuries the master builders of the ancient days covered the land with beautiful structures. For the visitor to India it is the numerous and varied buildings—Dravidian, Brahmanical,

Buddhist, Jain, Muslim and Christian deriving from different sources, racial, religious and social, their varying characteristics, that constitute the physical part of the legacy of India. The imposing brick ramparts in the cities of the Gangetic valley such as Kausambi and Vaishali and in other cities like Ujjain belong to the pre-Mauryan period. The remains of Ashoka's capital at Pataliputra (Patna) have rather a special character, and reflect contemporary Persian influences. Numerous foundations of ruined buildings and excavated churches and monasteries prove existence of advanced level of architectural skill of the times.

Cave Temples of Ajanta and Ellora

The famous caves, shrines and monasteries in Orissa, Uttar Pradesh, Madhya Pradesh and Maharashtra are examples not only of the pre-Christian era but also of the beginning of the Christian era. The most important groups of excavated shrines are those of Udayagiri in Madhya Pradesh and the Ellora and Ajanta in Maharashtra. Ajanta and Ellora, India's oldest and most beautiful testimony of religious architecture and painting, are man-made caves hewn out of rocky mountains some 2,000 years ago. The cave-temples at Ajanta were discovered almost 170 years ago by a British army officer who went to the forests near Aurangabad on a tiger hunt. From a vantage point across the scrap of a crescent-shaped hill, he saw the protruding whiteness of a monastery gate shrouded in thick foliage. The first ones were excavated during the second century B.C. to second century A.D. by Buddhist monks. The second phase commenced in the fifth century A.D. and completed in the eighth century A.D. At Ellora, there are 34 caves, all hewn out of the sloping side of a low hill. The most remarkable of the carved shrines at Ellora is the Kailasa temple. This incredible edifice has been scooped out by the ancient master sculptures of India from a single rock with a gateway, pavilion, courtyard, assembly hall, sanctum and a tower. Besides these places, there are many more magnificent temples and a wealth of sculpture in which the spiritual and material history of three millenniums is visibly recorded.

Architectural skill as it developed during the Muslim period needs no introduction. The great wonders like the Taj Mahal, the Qutab Minar and Fatehpur Sikri are living testimony of India's genius in the field. The impressive buildings and churches which were constructed all over the country during the British period are another example of Indian craftsmanship.

Arts, Literature, Music and Dance

Indian art can be described as traditional since it was dedicated to reveal the divine nature and enchanting dignity of places of worship. The function of art was to present or recreate the objects of worship in different forms. The ancient Indian artist was trained to produce images in different shapes and sizes which in their abstract perfection would reflect the divine nature of the original. Indian images are abstractions of the human form, the handiwork of the creator. Thus Indian art is essentially an art devoted to the exposition of the personality and deeds of deities.

By and large modern Indian literature, particularly the literature in the regional languages of the country, continue to draw their inspiration from the old ancient classics. Epics like the *Mahabharata* and the *Ramayana*, and the Krishna story as told in the *Bhagwata Purana* constitute the core of Indian heritage of ancient wisdom, philosophy and literary traditions. Indian literature had its golden period during the reign of the Guptas, as also during the Mughal rule. Even when Indian men of letters came under the influence of the West, the content of their outpourings, whether in prose, poetry, or drama, remained intrinsically true to the soil.

Music and Arts

Music has been greatly influenced by religious traditions of the country. Chanting of hymns and prayers has been in vogue since the beginning of the Aryan civilization. Some of the early musical literature is in the nature of minor scriptures. Early songs embody philosophical concepts, ethical and moral precepts and discussions and social criticism. Music can be thus said to have developed as an adjunct of worship and that temples have always been the biggest repositories of music and dance. A great many singers in India were saints. The *raga* (mode) is the glory of Indian music and is the basis of melody. It consists of the use of certain notes and microtones at the exclusion of others. Indian music can be identified into two main divisions—the Hindustani or the Northern School and Carnatic or the Southern School. However, the spiritual basis and the fundamental features of both the schools are the same. Both the systems are governed by the same principles of *raga* and melody. The Hindustani music, however, contains many traces of foreign influence.

There is a large variety of musical instruments in India, which reflect the varying stages of Indian life and culture beginning from the stage of primitive nature worship. Between the drums and primitive musical instruments of the remote past and the intricate and many-toned mandolins of the present day, there is a large variety of musical instruments which have evolved with varying degrees of culture in India. The more famous instruments like *sitar* and *veena,* which have been in use for hundreds of years, still continue to be the most popular. The melody of these instruments has won the hearts of people not only in India but in many countries of the world.

Another type of music which is very popular in India and especially in the countryside is the folk music. This category of music flourishes in the villages and has a pronounced agricultural background. In almost all parts of the country people recite folk music during the harvesting season. Some of the folk songs are very popular in appeal and have therefore been adopted by the composers of modern music. A variety of instruments are used in folk music. These musical instruments have been devised locally, taking into consideration the tradition and culture of the area.

Dance Forms

Like music, Indian dance form has also been predominantly influenced by religion. Together with music, it formed an inseparable part of aesthetic perfection for the worship of God. The origin of all the classical systems has been the Hindu temple. It was in the temples that Indian dance styles, were conceived and nourished to attain their full stature. Essentially devotional in character, Indian classical dance is a highly perfected art. The performing artist is expected to acquire complete control over the movements of his body. The dancer conveys abstract ideas through his dance. The dance was an integral part of Vedic rituals and the dancer worshipped the Lord by dancing before him. Many a dance has stories to tell. The stories are conveyed through different postures of the body and gestures, through the spoken word, through costumes and through facial expressions.

There are various types of dance forms. One of the famous dance forms is the Bharat Natyam, a highly perfected devotional dance prevalent mainly in South India. This form is an art which had royal and religious patronage for centuries. Dancers were attached to well-known temples and participated in the offering of worship. Bharat Natyam unravels a story through a language of gestures and facial expressions set to the rhythm and melody of background music. Another major dance form is Kathakali which is also popular in South India. This dance evolved from earlier forms of mono-acting, a characteristic tradition of the Sanskrit stage. The dancer wears colourful and elaborate costumes and make-up. The differences in costume and make-up are according to the characters represented. The performance, which often lasts until the early morning hours, opens with loud beat of drums to take the spectators to the mythical world of the Hindu gods, goddesses, and sages. The theme is usually derived from the great epic stories of *Ramayana* and *Mahabharata*. Unlike Bharat Natyam, the Kathakali dancers are all male.

Another major dance form popular in North India is Kathak. This dance was patronised by the Muslim rulers. Consequently, Persian influences affected this dance form to a great extent. Originally a temple dance, it became a court dance. The dance is performed skilfully and gracefully by the artist. The dancers can reproduce the exact sounds made by the drums in their footwork. The musical accompaniment consists of a singer, who not only sings but also reproduces the drum syllables.

Manipuri is yet another famous dance form performed in Manipur in Eastern India. This dance form is again purely religious in character. The dance items re-enact the love story of Radha and Krishna. A highly devotional dance form, it depicts the separation and reunion of Radha and Krishna in an enchanting romantic style. Faces of the dancers remain immobile and the meaning is conveyed through the swaying body and the graceful movement of arms. The costumes are extremely gay and colourful. The accompanying music and chorus are typical of the region.

Indian Paintings

Like music and dance, Indian painting was also a widely practised art in ancient India. Evidence of early existence of paintings can be found in many places. Frescoes of Ajanta caves painted by the Buddhist monks between the second century B.C. and the seventh century A.D. are the examples of the rich styles of paintings as practised in ancient times. Paintings in the Ellora caves are yet another proof of the richness of Indian art. Between the eighth and the twelfth century, miniature paintings came into vogue and a great volume of palm leaf manuscripts of Buddhist scriptures were illustrated. Later, Jain scriptures were illustrated. In the Middle Ages, mural paintings in South India became very popular when temples and palaces were decorated with elaborate paintings. In the sixteenth century, Rajput miniature paintings made their appearance. During the same period under the patronage of the Mughals, an exquisite school of Mughal miniature paintings developed. It presented a rich pageant of court scenes, war episodes, and birds and flowers combining both the

Persian and Indian styles. During the eighteenth century, paintings developed in the remote states of Himalayas, such as the Kangra school of painting. This school has the distinction of creating some of the most charming paintings till the end of the nineteenth century. The paintings of Kangra proper exhibit finer workmanship in delicacy of line, brightness of colour and minuteness of decorative detail. All the types of paintings mentioned above are very popular today. Even modern Indian painting, which has come under the influence of modern art concepts, is equally distinctive.

Indian dance, music, literature, painting and architecture have all been intimately connected with Indian religion and philosophy. The finer points of Indian arts have earned worldwide fame. This is quite apparent from the reception with which India's well-known performing artists of dance and music of today are greeted by large audiences in Western countries. Artists like Ravi Shankar, Ali Akbar, M. S. Subbalaxmi, Lata Mangeshkar, Bismillah Khan, Yamini Krishnamurti, Indrani Rehman and Uma Sharma are now familiar names in the West. In short, few countries in the world provide such a varied feast of interests to match the taste of any visitor. The beautiful countryside, the exotic panorama of bright snow-capped Himalayas, the bewildering variety of races and customs, golden beaches, vast desert lands, lush green valleys, tropical jungles, lakes and waterfalls—it's all here in addition to the pleasures of sights and sounds which the arts and crafts of this country provide.

The great German Orientalist, Max Muller, had this to say about India: "If we were to look over the whole world to find out the country most richly endowed with all the wealth, power and beauty that nature can bestow—in some parts a very paradise on earth—I should point to India. If I were asked under what sky the human mind has most fully developed some of its choicest gifts, has most deeply pondered over the greatest problems of life, and has found solutions of some of them which well deserve the attention even of those who have studied Plato and Kant—I should point to India."

Development of Tourism in India—Historical Perspectives

Travel has always been and continues to be one of the important means of social intercourse between the nations of the world. Throughout the ages, men have always had the urge to see distant lands and learn about the customs and manners of people in other countries. Thus travel has been aptly called the best part of one's education. The world would have been poorer today but for the records and impressions of travels and journeys undertaken by great travellers in the past. With the modern advances in technology and development of faster and comfortable means of communication, the urge to travel and to see far-off and distant lands is now finding greater scope for satisfaction. The modern- day travellers have now become tourists and tourism is regarded as one of the important industries. What was tourism like on the eve of Independence? How did India receive a visitor who came to see the astounding beauty and variety of the country and the glory of the ancient past? What were the early efforts of the Government to promote tourism in India? What were the various facilities and infrastructure available?

Sargent Committee

In India, the importance of tourism had been recognised even before the Second World War. The intervention of War, however, put a stop to the tourist promotion activities of the Government. The first conscious and organised efforts to promote tourism in India was made in the year 1945, when a Committee was set up by the Government of India under the Chairmanship of Sir John Sargent, the then Educational Adviser to the Government of India. The main objective of the Committee was to survey the potentialities of developing tourist traffic in the country. Following were the terms of reference of the Committee:

(i) After reviewing the nature and extent of tourist (and pilgrim) traffic in India both from within the country and from overseas which existed before the war, to examine what scope there is for increasing such traffic or for developing other like traffic during the post-war period.

(ii) To suggest ways and means of creating, both in India and overseas, the desire for touring, including visits to holiday resorts, good climate stations, scenic places, places of pilgrimage, of historical and of archaeological interest in India.

(iii) To suggest what facilities should be provided at places to be developed and advertised (a) Indian visitors; and (b) foreign visitors. The facilities to be considered should include means of travel from nearest railway station, residential accommodation, supply of literature and guide books, provision of authorised guides, etc.

(iv) To recommend what action should be taken for providing the necessary facilities by (a) Indian States and/or local government; (b) various departments of the Central government.

(v) To deal with other aspects of tourist traffic not covered by the above terms of reference.

The Sargent Committee which submitted their interim report in October 1946 was of the opinion that it would be in the interest of India to encourage and develop tourist traffic both internal and external by all possible means. The Committee was of the opinion that successful steps in the promotion of tourism would result in a substantial addition, both direct and indirect, to India's revenue and that, if properly organised, every aspect of business could benefit greatly by an influx of tourists. One of the major recommendations of the Committee related to the setting up of a separate representative organisation of semi-officials. The Committee recommended that the question of promoting and developing tourist traffic was a matter of great national importance and, therefore, it deserves the whole-time attention of a separate organisation which should take initiative in such matters as:

(i) Publicity both in India and abroad.

(ii) Production of suitable literature such as guide books, folders, posters, etc.

(iii) Provision for training of guides.

(iv) Liaison with other government departments responsible for providing facilities required by tourists, including information in regard to industries and commercial matters.

(v) Liaison with the travel agencies which would necessarily remain responsible for the detailed arrangements of tourists.

(vi) Liaison with hotels and catering establishments.

(vii) Collection of tourist statistics.

Some of the other major recommendations of the Committee were:

(a) Coordination with air and train services with a view to facilitate both air and train journey and to make it comfortable in India.

(b) Provision of a chain of first-class hotels of international standard for the convenience and comfort of foreign tourists.

(c) Starting of publicity bureaus in London and New York and in the capitals of other countries from where substantial number of tourists might be forthcoming.

On careful examination of the terms of reference of the Committee it is evident that all the major aspects of tourism as we see them now have been covered. The major areas like provision of infrastructure, publicity both overseas as well as domestic, facilitation, coordination of agencies dealing with tourism at all levels were covered. The recommendations of the Committee had far-reaching effects on tourism as it developed during the subsequent years specially after India attained Independence. The recommendations were the guidelines for the establishment of tourist organisation in the country soon after Independence.

On the eve of Independence, India had a fairly large infrastructure available for tourism. There was a large network of all types of hotels catering to the needs of both foreigners as well as Indian. There was an adequate transport and communication system operating in the country. Almost all the major tourist spots were easily accessible by rail or by road, some even by air. The country's many airports were in a position to receive international carriers. However, in the absence of a central tourist organisation there was no coordination between the various services. Tourism in India developed properly only after a central tourist organisation was set up as a result of the recommendation of the Sargent Committee. It was only after the creation of a separate tourist traffic branch in the year 1949 that whole-time attention was paid to the development of tourist traffic in India. (See the section Ad hoc Tourist Traffic Committee in Chapter 6.)

Advisory Bodies

In order to establish liaison with various Ministries, and coordinate various activities pertaining to tourism, the Department was represented on the following Committees and Advisory bodies.

1. Standing Facilitation Committee of the DGCA.
2. Civil Aviation Development Fund Committee.
3. Advisory Committee on the Indian Airlines.
4. Export-Import Advisory Council.
5. Indian Board for Wild Life.
6. Central Advisory Board of Archaeology.
7. Aerodrome Planning Group.

8. Hotel Industry Study Groups of the Ministry of Labour.
9. Governing Body of the Institute of Hotel Management, Catering Technology and Nutrition, New Delhi, Calcutta, Bombay and Madras.
10. Ad hoc Committee to review statutory rules regarding the use of protected monuments and sites for holding public functions sponsored by the government and non-government organisations.
11. Central Post and Telegraph Advisory Council.
12. India Tourism Development Corporation.

In order to reflect on the growth of tourism over the years, it will be necessary to know the role of the various officials as well as non-official bodies constituted and attached to tourism. During the early years the Department of Tourism had constituted high level advisory bodies in the form of boards, councils and committees. The bodies both official as well as non-official have played a very vital role in the development of tourism in the country. But before we discuss in detail the constitution and working of these high level bodies, let us understand what actually these are.

Tourist Boards

Boards consist of an odd number of members, neither too many nor too few appointed by the executive head of the government department for overlapping terms. The Boards constituted by a resolution serve for a specific period of time. The members constituting the Board are generally experts in this specific and allied fields and represent both the government as well as private organisations. The members are appointed by the government. Boards have certain specified responsibilities and functions. The rules and procedures for the conduct of business are specified. The members of the Board are free to advise the Chairman either on his request or on their own initiative on matters relevant to the objectives of the Board. They are entitled to be kept informed and have access to all records. Their suggestions and recommendations are generally followed.

Councils are an assembly of experts summoned or convened for consultation, deliberation and advice. The Councils are appointed by a resolution and are represented by both official and non-official members who are experts in the field or in allied fields. The Council members who meet at regular intervals give suggestions and recommendations which are generally followed. The decisions of the Council as far as possible are unanimous in nature. In case this is not so, the decision is reached by a simple majority of the votes cast and in the event of votes being equally divided, the Chairman has an additional or casting vote. The Chairman has all the necessary powers to supplement the rules and to give rulings for the orderly and prompt despatch of the business of the Council. The minutes or proceedings of each meeting are prepared as soon as possible by the Secretary of the Council and are authenticated by the Chairman. Copies of the minutes are furnished to all the members. The Councils are constituted for a fixed period of time after expiry of which, they are reconstituted.

Advisory Committees are of two general types—constituent and technical. Members of the Constituent Advisory Committees may be chosen for their personal qualifications or because they represent social, professional or other groups in the community. Technical Advisory Committees, on the other hand, are designed to assist the administrative officers in the formulation of plans and in the development and application of various techniques of value in the particular programme. The advisory committees are established on a temporary basis. The members who constitute the committee are both official as well as non-official and are experts in the given field or in allied fields. The head of the committee is a Chairman. The committees meet at regular intervals and their suggestions and recommendations are generally followed.

The Department of Tourism since its inception has had the following top level expert bodies: (i) The Tourist Traffic Advisory Committee, (ii) Regional Tourist Advisory Committees, (iii) National Tourism Board, (iv) Tourist Development Council. In the following paragraphs details of these high level expert bodies have been discussed.

Tourist Traffic Advisory Committee

In order to associate the public and the travel trade with their tourist promotional activities, the Ministry of Transport, Government of India, set up a Central Tourist Traffic Advisory Committee at New Delhi in the year 1950. The Committee was reconstituted in February 1953. The Committee which included representatives of the various Ministries concerned and of tourist trade as also public men was set up with the objective of coordinating the work at the Centre and advising the Government on tourist problems. Regional Advisory Committees were also formed at Delhi, Bombay, Madras and Calcutta with a view to assist the Regional Tourist Officers. The Committees provided a common forum to the various elements of tourist trade to meet together and exchange their views with their assistance and in cooperation with the Central Ministries and State Governments concerned.

Composition

Following was the composition of the Central Tourist Traffic Advisory Committee.
Minister for Transport and Railways-Chairman.
Deputy Minister for Transport and Railways-Vice-Chairman

Official Members

- Secretary, Ministry of Transport
- Chairman, Railway Board
- Secretary, Ministry of Home Affairs
- Secretary, Ministry of Commerce and Industry
- Secretary, Ministry of Information and Broadcasting
- Director General of Archaeology
- Director General of Civil Aviation

- Representative of the Ministry of External Affairs (External Publicity Division)
- Representative of the Ministry of Finance (Revenue Division)
- Deputy Secretary, Ministry of Transport-Secretary, of the Committee
- Representatives of various State Governments/ Regional Tourist Officers.

Non-Official Members

- Representative of Airlines
- Representative of Hotel Association
- Representative of Travel Agents.
- Chairman or any other non-official representative of each of the Regional Tourist Advisory Committees.

The Regional Tourist Traffic Advisory Committees were represented by both official as well as non-official members. Official members included representatives of various concerned authorities like police, customs, municipal corporations, transport and railways. Non-official members included representatives of travel agents, hotel associations, airlines, shipping companies (on the Regional Tourist Traffic Advisory Committees-Bombay, Calcutta and Madras), taxi owners, and automobile associations. The Regional Tourist Officer in each region was either Convenor or Secretary of the Committee.

In a meeting of a Central Advisory Committee held in December 1954, the representatives of the State Governments were asked to establish State Tourist Advisory Committees as well as Local Committees in the important places of tourist interest within their respective jurisdiction. It was decided that each State government should establish a Tourist Advisory Committee to advise them in regard to the development of tourist centres in that State. The Local Committees were to send representatives to the State Advisory Committee who, in turn were to serve representatives on the Regional Advisory Committees concerned. As a result of this decision, several States formed the State Tourist Advisory Committees.

Functions

The main function of the Central Tourist Traffic Advisory Committee was to associate the public and the travel trade with the tourist promotional activities of the Government. This was ultimately to result in the growth of tourism in the country. Another important function of this Committee was to have a proper liaison between various Government departments concerned with tourism as it was felt that coordination was very essential for proper growth and development of tourist traffic.

The function of the Regional Advisory Committee was to advise the State Governments within their respective regions about the deficiencies at important tourist places in the region and in regard to the improvement of roads, transport, hotel accommodation etc. Looking after the infrastructure was its main concern. The Regional Committee was also to keep in touch with the State Governments, the local tourist agencies, the railway authorities, the airlines, shipping agencies and hotels and was to bring to the notice of the Ministry of Transport or the local authorities as the case may be, such complaints made by tourists as well as tourist agencies regarding lack of amenities which cannot be resolved by local officers. One of its sub-committees known as the 'Cultural and Hospitality Sub-Committee' had an important function. This sub-committee was to arrange for cultural programmes for visiting tourists by way of dances or music performances by artists of repute. Opportunities were also afforded to visiting tourists to get to know local people in the cities by arranging for visits to the homes of private local families.

The State Tourist Advisory Committees were responsible for taking care of the development and publicity of all the important places in the State concerned. They were also to make suggestions for the improvement of tourist traffic facilities in their respective States. Development of domestic tourism was to be the main responsibility of the State committee. The Chairman of each of the State Tourist Advisory Committees was generally the Minister in charge of Tourism in the State.

The Local Committees were intended to look after the improvement of the local tourist centres and to bring the deficiencies to the notice of the State Governments with a view to their removal. They were also expected to look into the complaints of the tourists.

A close look at the functions of various committees will show that the scope of these was very wide, covering a wide range of subjects of tourist interest. It is, however, difficult to quantify the achievements of these committees but it can be definitely said that as a result of their deliberations tourist traffic did receive a lot of encouragement. Considerable progress was made in the relaxation of various governmental regulations regarding registration and custom formalities, currency exchange, recognition of travel agents, improvements in hotels, etc. Other important matters considered by these committees were guide services, collection of tourist statistics and revival of internal tourist traffic to hill stations.

In the eleventh meeting of the Central Tourist Traffic Advisory Committee held in Shimla on June 22, 1957, a recommendation was made that the existing Central Tourist Traffic Advisory Committee should be reconstituted into a Tourist Development Council so as to make it more influential and representative. This meeting was also attended by the representatives of State Governments dealing with tourism as well as heads of the tourist offices and representatives of Regional Advisory Committees. The recommendation was accepted and also implemented. Thus was born Tourist Development Council.

Tourist Development Council

The Tourist Development Council was set up in February 1958 under the then Department of Tourism, Ministry of Transport and Communication. This was the principal advisory body at the national level. The Council consisted of 64 members, including the State Ministers of Tourism, Central Government officials connected with tourism, archaeology and forests, representatives of railways, shipping, transport and airlines, 9 members of Parliament, representatives of the Federation of Hotel and Restaurant Association of India, Wild Life Association of India, and 9 members of the public. The Tourist Development Council met once a year and the deliberations generally lasted for two to three days. Matters relating to tourism were discussed at length and resolutions passed for implementation by the various tourism authorities at the Centre and in the States.

Composition

The Council which was reconstituted in October 1971 composed of the following members :

Minister of Tourism and Civil Aviation in the Central, Government-Chairman

Minister of State or Deputy Minister of Tourism and Civil Aviation in the Central Government-Vice-Chairman

Members

- Member (Industry), Planning Commission.
- Ministers-Incharge of Tourism in each State and Union Territory.
- Secretary-Ministry of Tourism and Civil Aviation.
- Director General, Department of Tourism.
- Director General, Department of Civil Aviation.
- Director General, Archaeological Survey of India.
- Inspector General of Forests, Ministry of Food and Agriculture.
- Representative of Ministry of Finance, Department of Expenditure.
- Representative of Ministry of Works and Housing.
- Representative of Ministry of Railways.
- Representative of Ministry of Transport and Shipping.
- Chief Secretary of a Union Territory
  (where there is no legislature).

Members of Parliament (Nine). They shall be nominated by the Government of India in the Ministry dealing with Tourism.

Functions

The main function of the Council is to recommend various measures necessary for the promotion of tourist traffic to India from other countries and from one part of the country to another. Development of both foreign as well as domestic tourism is thus its main objective. The recommendations of the Council relate to augmentation of accommodation transport and communication of plans and schemes, minimising of nuisance created by touts, beggars, hawkers by setting up a tourist police force and encouragement of youth travel. Construction of holiday homes, declaration of tourism as an export industry with incentives to be taken as in the case of other export industries are some of the other important recommendations. While the recommendations of the Council are generally in respect of matters concerning the country as whole, it is not debarred from making the same in respect of measures for the development of tourist traffic to a particular place.

The recommendations of the Council are advisory in character, but in view of the high level representation on the Council, its recommendations assist in uniformity of approach at the levels of the Centre and the States.

It is difficult to quantify the achievements of the Council as no review or assessment of its achievements is made and it is achievements, however, can be noted in terms of the recommendations it makes and the resolutions it adopts when it meets once a year. Several important developments in the field of tourism in India have, however, been the result of the Council's recommendations.

Regional Tourist Advisory Committees

In order to ensure that the resolutions of the Tourist Development Council were implemented by the member States, four Regional Tourist Advisory Committees were constituted in February 1970. Another objective of setting up these advisory committees was to establish closer coordination among the States on a regional basis. The States represented on each Regional Committee were as follows :

1. Northern Region
   Jammu and Kashmir, Punjab, Haryana,
   Rajasthan, Uttar Pradesh, Himachal Pradesh,
   Delhi and Chandigarh.
2. Western Region
   Maharashtra, Gujarat, Madhya Pradesh and Goa.
3. Southern Region
   Tamil Nadu, Kerala, Karnataka, Andhra Pradesh and Pondicherry.
4. Eastern Region
   West Bengal, Assam, Bihar, Orissa, Nagaland, Tripura,
   Manipur, Andaman and Nicobar Islands.

Composition

The composition of the committees was as follows :

Regional Director, Government of India Tourist Office
Convenor
Secretary Tourism, State Government.
Director of State Tourism Boards.
Concerned officers deputed by the State Governments.
Regional representatives of Customs,
Indian Airlines, Travel Agents, Hotel and Restaurants.

Functions

The primary function of the Regional Committees comprises coordination between Central and State Governments as well as the essential segments of the tourist industry. The committees were set up primarily for implementing the Tourist Development Councils' recommendations, ensuring regular regional consultation and better coordination between the Centre and the States.

The meetings of these committees took place in the respective State of the region by rotation. The Minister of Tourism in the State where the meeting takes place is requested to preside over the meeting. The Committees which started with initial enthusiasm have rather lost their momentum because all State Governments have now their own Tourism Advisory Committees.

National Tourism Board

The formation of the National Tourism Board was announced by the Minister of Tourism and Civil Aviation in Parliament on 11 May I972. The Board which consists of official and 6 non-official members is an apex body. The official members represent the various government departments including undertakings with which the Department of Tourism is closely connected. The non-official members belong to the travel trade and also include some prominent figures in the field of tourism. The Board was created as part of the partial implementation of the recommendations of United Nations Development Programme (UNDP), experts and the report of the Indian Institute of Public Administration. The recommendations contained in these reports related to the merger of the Department of Tourism and Indian Tourism Development Corporation in a National Tourism Authority for unified and concerted tourism promotional policy. However, this proposal was not accepted. Instead, the Government decided to set up the highest policy-making body in the sphere of tourism and gave it the name National Tourism Board.

Setting up of the National Tourism Board was one of the major institutional changes brought about in an effort to make the national tourist organisation more responsive and capable of meeting the requirements of the growing industry. The objectives of the Board were to advise the Minister in the matters of policy and to provide fresh impetus to the development of tourism in the country.

Functions

The Board which was been set up as a standing body was to deal with specific programmes and plans of tourism development in the country touching all aspects of tourism industry. The Board will have the task of preparing the overall national plan for tourism covering both the public and private sectors. The Board which is expected to meet once in three months, will be serviced by the Department of Tourism and India Tourism Development Corporation for implementation of its recommendations. It was not considered necessary to delegate any executive or financial powers to the Board as implementation would be the responsibility of the Department of Tourism and the India Tourism Development Corporation. Its functions will, therefore, be distinct from those of the Tourist Development Council which is a deliberative body on matters of policy and overall programmes. The Council has also a very large membership in order to enable adequate thinking on issues of policy. The Board is, on the other hand, a smaller body with distinct functions in relation to plans and physical targets. The Board was set up to advise the Minister on the directions in which Tourism should be developed in the Fifth Five-Year Plan when a large increase in investment was expected.

Composition

The composition of the National Tourism Board was as follows :

Minister of Tourism and Civil Aviation-Chairman

Minister of State for Tourism and Civil Aviation-Vice-Chairman

Official Members

- Secretary, Ministry of Tourism and Civil Aviation.
- Financial Adviser (Tourism),
- Ministry of Finance.
- Chairman-cum-Managing Director, India Tourism Development Corporation.
- Member (Traffic), Railway Board.
- Managing Director, Air-India.
- Managing Director, Indian Airlines,
- Director General, Archaeological Survey of India.
- Chairman, Inter-State Transport Commission.
- Director General Department of Tourism

Non-Official Members

- Representative of Hotels
- Representative of Travel Trade Press
- Representative of Travel Agents.

The official members of the Board representing various government departments were to provide the coordination necessary for the implementation of various tourism schemes. The non-official members on the other hand were expected to contribute vital new ideas and give the Department of Tourism the benefit of their expertise in the field of tourism. With regard to achievements of the Board so far, it can be stated that some of the recommendations made by its members in various meetings held so far had some impact on the industry. In its meetings held so far, the Board has discussed the following matters and made specific recommendations:

1. Various facilitation measures at International Airports primarily to help the incoming tourists.
2. Directions for the Fifth Plan on tourism. Recommendations about development of various schemes during the Fifth Plan.
3. Undertaking a Cost Benefit Study on tourism and its impact on Indian economy. The assignment of the above study to the National Council of Applied Economic Research.
4. Restructuring of India Tourism Development Corporation.

The various government bodies appointed for the development of tourism have played a crucial role in making tourism an important industry. Besides these, the Government also appointed some other important expert committees to look into various facets of tourism. These were :

Ad Hoc Committee on Tourism

The Ad Hoc Committee on Tourism set up in March 1963 can be considered a landmark in the history of development of tourism in India. The Committee appointed by the Ministry of Transport and Communication was set up to enquire into the causes of the decline in the rate of growth of tourist traffic which began slowing down in 1960-62 and to suggest ways and means of expanding tourist traffic. The terms of reference of the Committee were as follows:

(i) Examine, generally, the conditions prevailing in the country from the point of view of promoting tourist traffic and to suggest ways and means of improving those conditions with a view to achieving an expansion in the traffic by at least 20 per cent a year in the next three years, and thereafter at a progressive rate of increase.

(ii) In particular to

  (a) assess the requirements of tourism in respect of hotel accommodation and transport arrangements and suggest necessary measures for the speedy provision and improvement of these facilities;

  (b) examine the present rules and procedure regarding visa, customs and other formalities with a view to facilitating entry and exit of tourists; and,

  (c) recommend necessary reorganisation of publicity programmes and other steps required to bring about the desired expansion of traffic.

(iii) Suggest measures necessary to ensure that the foreign exchange earned from tourism and resulting from its expansion is protected against leakage.

The Committee consisted of the following :

Secretary, Department of Economic Affairs-Chairman.

Joint Secretary, Department of Economic Affairs.

General Manager, Indian Airlines Corporation.

Joint Secretary, Ministry of Home Affairs.

Officer on Special Duty, Central Board of Revenue.

Director General and ex-officio Joint Secretary,

Department of Tourism-Member Secretary.

The Committee which held its first meeting on March 13, 1963 subsequently met eighteen times between March 28 and August 12, 1963. The report was submitted on August 23, 1963. The Committee covered a large number of areas. A number of important recommendations were made by the Committee. The recommendation made related to areas like value of tourism, frontier formalities, provision of facilities at airports, transport facilities, hotels, publicity and promotion, development of tourist centres, shopping and entertainment, training of personnel for tourism, leakage of foreign exchange and building up of a tourism organisation.

Tourist Promotion Committee (1957)

With a view to coordinating and increasing promotional activities, a committee called Tourist Promotion Committee consisting of the Cabinet Secretary and heads of Departments of the Government of India whose functions related to tourist promotion was set up in December 1957. The Committee was set up to consider various aspects of tourist developmental activities such as tourist publicity, provision of amenities at airports, management of rest houses, modernisation of airports, establishment of duty- free shops at airports, etc.

Hotel Standards and Rate Structure Committee (1957)

The Hotel Standards and Rate Structure Committee was constituted by the Government of India on September 18, 1957. Following were its terms of reference :

(i) To frame criteria for the classification of hotels keeping in view the criteria laid down by existing international organisations dealing with the hotel industry.

(ii) To recommend the number and type of classifications that should be applicable, e.g. whether to introduce the Star system as is prevalent in some countries or any other suitable system of classification.

(iii) Taking into account the price level obtaining in India, the cost of hotel keeping and other relevant factors, to recommend a rational rate structure for each category of hotels and other establishments.

(iv) For the purpose of promoting tourist traffic, to consider any other aspect of the hotel industry including the desirability or otherwise of legislation and/ or of assistance.

The Committee met in Delhi and prepared a questionnaire which was widely circulated, in the hotel industry. The questionnaire, elicited over 350 replies. The Committee also examined about 400 witnesses from the Chief Ministers of States to the least paid worker in the hotel. The Committee decided that its members should visit some of the important places of tourist importance in order that a quick survey should be made of existing conditions in hotels. A fairly large and comprehensive inspection was undertaken by the Committee of the hotel facilities available in different parts of India.

The main objectives the Committee set before itself can be summarised as follows :

(a) To lay down the criteria for the purpose of classification of the hotels in India keeping in view international standards that apply to similar establishments elsewhere;

(b) To suggest ways and means of promoting tourist traffic to and in India;

(c) To suggest what arrangements or improvements on existing arrangements are desirable for the purpose of promoting, internal and external tourism;

(d) Whether legislation, and if so of what type and/or assistance and if so of what kind are necessary for the purposes of the hotel industry generally; and

(e) Keeping in view the price structure prevailing in India to suggest a suitable rate structure for the hotel industry.

The Committee visited as many centres as it was possible in the short time available to it. The result of these visits confirmed the Committee in its opinion that it had become undoubtedly a matter of great national urgency to promote the influx of foreign tourists into India in the context of progressively expanding development plans envisaged by the Government of India. The members of the Committee were of the opinion that time had come for the rapid expansion of the hotel industry and suggested that this should be done under a proper and planned scheme of development. According to the Committee the hotel industry did not figure in the first and second Five-Year Plans. They were of the opinion that they would urge the Planning Commission and all the interests involved, including the Ministry of Transport, that no time should be lost for the purpose of planning the development of the hotel industry on a rapid but rational and scientific basis keeping in view the requirements of the country in this behalf for the next 15 years or so. The above Committee was formed under the Chairmanship of Rajya Sabha members. The Committee had ten members and a Member Secretary.

Hotel Classification Committee (1962)

Tourists in general, and the travel agents in particular, always welcome an authentic guide, indicating the categories of the various hotel establishments in a country, hotels which have been inspected and categorised by an impartial, authoritative and representative body. Almost all the tourist-minded countries in the world engaged in international tourism have some form or the other of categorisation of their hotel establishments. The need for classification is all the more urgent in countries where there is shortage of hotel accommodation, or countries which have, comparatively speaking, entered the tourist field only recently.

It is for this reason that the Hotel Standards and Rate Structure Committee headed by M.P., had strongly recommended in its report submitted to the Government of India in 1958, that the classification of hotels in the country should be undertaken as early as possible. That Committee which went into this question in great detail, recommended that the classification of hotels should be on the "Star" system which has been adopted in several important countries in Europe. According to this system, hotels are classified into five categories, i.e., from the minimum of One Star to the maximum of Five Star. One and Two Star hotels can be considered as of economy class, the Three Star ones as of medium class, and the Four and Five Star ones as hotels of luxury class. The Hotel Standards and Rate Structure Committee had also suggested some broad criteria for classifying hotels in India and even indicated the number of marks to be allotted to each of them.

The Government of India accepted the recommendation regarding classification made by the Hotel Standards and Rate Structure Committee and appointed the Hotel Classification Committee on June 15, 1962 under the Chairmanship of Deputy Director General, Department of Tourism. There were two other members of the Committee. The Committee was asked to associate representatives of the four Regional Hotel Associations when they inspected the establishments in their respective regions. The State Governments were also requested to nominate their representatives to be associated with this Committee during its sojourn in the respective States. The local health authorities also assisted the Committee in many of the places visited by the Committee. Following were the terms of reference:

(i) To invite applications from hotels which are interested in getting Government's recognition and which fulfil the minimum criteria laid down by the Hotel Standards and Rate Structure Committee for being categorised as "Starred" hotel.

(ii) To inspect those hotels among the applicant establishments which in the opinion of the Committee prima facie fulfil the minimum conditions.

(iii) To assess the relative standards of the establishments so inspected and to classify them according to the Star system recommended by the Hotel Standards and Rate Structure Committee.

(iv) To formulate criteria for recognising restaurants which are of sufficiently high standard for purpose of catering to tourist traffic and to inspect those that fulfil such criteria and recommend for Government's consideration the recognition of those establishments which actually fulfil the stipulated criteria.

The response from hotels and restaurants for classification/ recognition was wide and enthusiastic. In all, 324 hotels and 123 restaurants submitted their applications. Of the hotels/ restaurants which were on the Government of India's ad hoc list of recognised hotels and restaurants, only a few failed to apply. The Committee was impressed by the immense improvements effected by most of the hotels prior to the Committee's visit and to note that its visit had helped to raise the standard of the hotels and restaurants to a higher level. The Committee's inspections were quite detailed. All the areas, like public rooms, cloak rooms, private rooms and bath rooms, kitchen, pantry, store rooms, bakery, etc. were inspected by the Committee. The persons incharge of these departments and individual workers were also interviewed by the members of the Committee.

Hotel Review and Survey Committee (1967)

One of the 29 recommendations made by the Hotel Classification Committee was that the classification of hotels should be reviewed at least once in three years. All the recommendations of this Committee were accepted by the Government including the one that the classification of hotels be reviewed once in three years. At the meeting of the Tourist Development Council in Simla in 1967, it was suggested that an assessment should be made of the economics of the rates charged by the hotels in different categories with a view to determine whether a rational basis could be evolved in standardising the rates.

The Hotel Review and Survey Committee was accordingly appointed in November 1967 under the Chairmanship of Deputy Director General, Department of Tourism. The following were the terms of reference of the Committee :

(i) To invite applications afresh from all such hotels as are interested in being placed on the approved list of the Department of Tourism; are desirous of being classified on the basis of criteria evolved by the Hotel Standards and Rate Structure Committee and subsequently amended by the Hotel Classification Committee, 1963 and agree to abide by the regulatory conditions laid down by the Department of Tourism from time to time.

(ii) To survey the requirements of additional hotel bed capacity at the important tourist centres, as given below, to be provided by both public and private sectors by the end of the Fourth Plan period i.e., March 1974; and also to recommend the type of hotels suited for each place :

Agra, Ahmedabad, Ajanta-Ellora, Aurangabad, Bombay, Bangalore, Bhubaneswar, Calcutta, Cochin-Ernakulam, Darjeeling, Delhi, Gulmarg, Goa, Hyderabad, Jaipur, Jammu, Khajuraho, Kanchipuram, Konark, Madurai, Madras, Mahabalipuram, Mysore, Puri, Srinagar, Tanjore, Trivandrum, Udaipur, Varanasi, and such other places as the Committee may unanimously agree to add to this list.

(iii) To review the rates charged by hotels which are classified on the star-system with the object of determining a rational basis for standardising the rates in each category.

(iv) To inspect restaurants with the purpose of according approval to those which are of the requisite standard in catering to the needs of international tourists, on the basis of the criteria evolved by the Hotel Classification Committee in its report submitted in 1963.

Besides the Chairman who was an official of the Department of Tourism, the Committee was constituted of one representative of the hotels in the private sector, one representative of the hotels in the public sector, one representative of recognised travel agents in India, one representative of international airlines, and a representative each of the State Governments of the areas which the Committee visited.

Travel has always been and continues to be one of the important means of social intercourse between the nations of the world. Throughout the ages, human beings have always had the urge to see distant lands and learn about the customs, manners and way of living of people in other countries across the globe. Thus travel has been aptly called the best part of one's education. The world would have been poorer today but for the records and impressions of travels and journeys undertaken by great travellers in the past. With the modern advances in technology and development of faster and comfortable means of communication, the urge to travel and to see far-off and distant lands is now finding greater scope for satisfaction. The modern- day travellers have now become tourists and tourism is regarded as one of the important major industries.

lossar o Terms

Over the years, several publishers both in India and abroad have published books written by authors. These books give the reader a global perspective of travel and tourism industry in its various manifestations. The books also try to cover the structure, nature, organisational set -up, marketing and promotion of global tourist industry, planning and its impacts on various social, economic and cultural aspects on visitors themselves as also the host community.

These publication are useful not only for those pursuing tourism studies but also those working in tourism field. These publications in addition also provide useful information to tourism organisations, transport and hospitality firms, travel agencies, tour operating companies and others engaged in travel and tourism business.

Although the tourism publications referred to above explain the tourism phenomenon in simple and comprehensive manner, yet at time it becomes difficult for the reader to find correct and appropriate meaning of a particular term and are rather a loss. For example while reading a chapter on ' Travel Agency Management 'they come across the term 'affinity group'. Many of the readers who do not have the prior knowledge of the subject will get stuck at that point and will require assistance before proceeding further. Another example could be a term 'carrying capacity 'often used in 'planning and environment 'material. This difficulty is encountered not only by students alone but also by teachers and other professionals.

Like in most industries, travel and tourism is full of terms, acronyms and jargon. Confusion arises when different people use terms to mean different things. Different authors may provide different interpretations. What is therefore important is that the definitions of terms used in various publications will found to be consistent and well defined set which will aid value by encouraging for reader same terms with same interpretation.

The listing contains over 170 definitions used throughout the world. It covers all aspects of tourism industry including hospitality, transport as also ancillary services. It also decodes important abbreviations often used in the travel and tourism industry. The entries may vary from one line definitions to 100 word write-up.

The listing is an essential reference tool for anyone involved in tourism studies including hospitality, travel agency, tour operating management, airlines and would be of value to the students as also working professionals.

Advertising
Any activity designed to spread information with a view to promoting the sales of marketable goods and services.

Add-on
Any additional components of a package tour that is not included in the package price.

Affinity Group
A group bound together by a common interest or affinity. Where charters are concerned, this common bond makes the members eligible for charter flights. One must have been a member of the group for six months or longer. They must travel together, on the departure and return flight but they can travel independently where ground arrangements are concerned.

Accessibility
The degree to which a market segment can be reaced or served.

Adventure Tourism
The nature based tourism in an unusual, remote and exciting environment. A type of tourism which presents a challenge to the tourist as it requires testing of the tourist's skills and physical fitness.

Airline
Any air transport enterprise offering or operating a scheduled international air service.

Airway Bill
Equivalent to the term 'air consignment note', meaning the document entitled "Airway bill consignment note" made out by or on behalf of the shipper which evidences contract between the shipper and carrier(s) for carriage of goods over routes of the carrier(s).

Alternative Tourism
A form of tourism that advocates smaller scale and limited tourism in terms of numbers of tourists involved and the dimension of tourism development. It is also called green tourism or responsible tourism.

Amenities
Features which enable a visitor to enjoy various attractions and which draw him to a country and for the use of which he normally has to pay. These refer to recreational and entertainment programmes, cultural and art centres, hotels, restaurants, transport services, etc,

Antiquities
Art objects which are more than one hundred years old and which cannot be traded.

Attractions
Natural or man-made features which collectively or singly create the appeal of a country.

Baggage
Personal property of passengers or crew carried on an aircraft by agreement with the operator.

Baggage Accompanied
The baggage carried on the same aircraft as that on which the passenger is carried.

Baggage Check
Those portion of the decade which relate to the carriage of passengers checked baggage.

Baggage Excess
That part of the baggage which is in excess of the free baggage allowance and for which the passenger has to pay extra freight charges.

Baggage Tag

A document issued by the carrier solely for identification of checked baggage, the baggage (strap) tag portion of which is attached by carrier to a particular article of checked baggage and the baggage (claim) tag portion of which is given to the passenger.

Brochure

A pamphlet bound in the form of a booklet.

Bulletin

Brief, periodically-issued mailing or promotion piece, often devoted to trade news. Painted outdoor display.

Campaign

A connected, integrated and organised series of advertising and promotional efforts.

Camping Site

A place providing simple and inexpensive shelter to travellers. The site provides wayside amenities for tourists travelling by long distance coach tours and self-driven cars.

Cargo

Equivalent to the term "goods", meaning anything carried or to be carried in an aircraft, other than mail or baggage, provided that unaccompanied baggage moving under an airway bill is also Cargo.

Cargo Transfer

Cargo arriving at a point by one flight and continuing its journey by another flight of the same or a connecting carrier.

Cargo Transit

Cargo arriving at a point and departing therefrom by the same through flight.

Carrier

A public transportation company such as air or steamship line, railroad, bus, etc.

Carriage

Equivalent to the term transportation, meaning carriage of passengers and/or baggage by air.

Carrying Capacity

The maximum number of people that a resort site or other area can sustain before there is reduction in the quality of visitor experience or advers effect on environment of host community.

Carriage Domestic

Carriage in which, according to the contract of carriage, the place of departure, the place of destination or stopover and the entire transportation are within one nation or its territories.

Carriage International

Carriage in which, according to the contract of carriage, the place of departure and any place of landing are situated in more than one nation. As used in this definition, the term national includes all territory subject to the sovereignty, mandate, authority, or trusteeship thereof.

Charter

The bulk purchase of any carrier's equipment (or part thereof) for passenger or freight. Legally, charter transportation is arranged for time, voyage or mileage.

Charter Flight

A flight booked exclusively for the use of a specific group of people who generally belong to the same organisation or who are being 'treated' to the flight by a single host. Charter flights are generally much cheaper than regularly scheduled line services but are not open for sale to the general public. These may be carried out by the regularly scheduled or supplemental carries.

Coach Tour

A guided bus tour for a group of holiday makers that follows a secheduled itirnerary visitors purchased all arrangements from the in-bound tour operator prior to arrival at the destination.

Conducted Tour

A pre-paid, pre-arranged vacation in which a group of people travel together under the guidance of tour leader who stays with them from the start to the end of the trip. Also referred to as an "escorted tour".

Coupons

Documents issued by tour operators in exchange for which travellers receive pre-paid accommodation, meals, sightseeing trips etc. Also referred to as vouchers.

Courier

A professional travel escort who accompanies carriers.

Cultural Impact

The effect of tourism activity or tourism development on the culture of the region or locality.

Cultural Tourism

A form of tourism in which the culture and traditions of the region is the main attraction.

Day Visitor

A tourist who does not stay overnight at the destination. Also known as Excursionist.

Destination

The place at which a traveller terminates his journey. The ultimate stopping place according to contract of carriage.

Destination Facilities

All plant and infrastructure available in a country, an area of local destination.

Destinational Tourist

A tourist who terminates his journey at a particular country for the purpose of making a tour travelling from place to place for pleasure in that country.

Destinational Traffic

Persons (tourists) carried by transportation lines and terminating their journey at one particular place.

Disembarkation

The leaving of an aircraft after a landing, except by crew or passengers continuing on the next stage of the same through-flight.

Display
In general, whatever attracts.

Domestic Independent Travel
A tour constructed to meet the specific desire of a client within a single country.

Domestic Tourism
A form of tourism where people of a country travel within the boundaries of their country.

Domestic Tourist
A local person who makes a tour travelling from place to place for pleasure, business, family, mission, meeting etc., within the country.

Ecotourism
Ecology oriented green tourism in which tourists seek out environmentally sensitive travel or vacations which help improve the knowledge of an environment of the area.

Embarkation
The boarding of an aircraft for the purpose of commencing a flight, except by such crew or passengers as have embarked on a previous stage the same through-flight.

Immigration
Going out of the country to another country.

Escort
A professional tour escort often called Tour Manager or Courier.

Exchange Voucher
A document issued by a carrier or its agents requesting issue of an appropriate passenger ticket and baggage check or provision of services to the person named in such document.

Excursionist
A temporary visitor staying less than twenty-four hours in the country visited.

Facilitation
The act of assisting progress or helping to move forward. To make easier or less difficult. Promoting any measure which will facilitate international travel with prime emphasis on achieving minimum entry and exit formalities for temporary visitor.

Facilities
Services which enable tourists to enter and move around the country with the maximum of ease and the minimum of obstacles and to secure maximum enjoyment of their visit.

Familiarisation Tours
Complimentary or discounted tours offered to travel agents or wholesalers to introduce them to destination or product.

Flycruising
A travel plan wherein the travellers fly to a port of embarkation and then board a cruise ship for most of the tour. Fly cruise are generally part of the tour package.

Fly/drive tour
An independent tour that allows travellers to visit multiple destinations during their trip and usually includes air transport, a carrental and lodging at several hotels.

FN/cruise Tour
A tour where travellers fly to a port of embarkation and then board a cruise ship for most of the tour.

Folder
One piece of illustrated paper which can be folded. It is usually printed on a single sheet and then folded for easy handling.

Ground Arrangements
All services provided for the traveller by his tour operator after the traveller reaches his first foreign destination. Also referred to as Land Arrangements.

Group Inclusive Tour
A tour which includes group air and ground arrangements for a minimum of 15 persons. They may or may not stay together as a group for both the land and air portion of the trip.

Guaranteed Tour
A tour which is guaranteed to operate unless cancelled 60 days prior to departure. In the event of cancellation within 60 days of the departure date, full commission is paid to agents of sold clients.

Guide
A person who is licensed to take paying guests on local sightseeing excursions.

Guided Tour
A tour conducted only by local city guides.

High Season
Time of the year when tourist traffic and rates are usually the highest becasue the demand is highest.

Hosted Tours
A tour where participants have an opportunity to travel independently, but also to receive guidance and assistance from a host at each of the tour's destinations.

Hotelier
A person, firm or corporation which provides hotel accommodation and/or meals, refreshments etc., to visitors.

Inbound Travel
Inbound travel comprises short term arrivals into a country by nationals/residence of other countries.

Inclusive Tour
A tour which includes all elements of an itinerary, making it unnecessary for a passenger to spend money for anything except personal extras during the course of the tour.

Independent Tour
A tour where participants travel independently without a group or a guide.

Infrastructure
The basic public services needed for the successful operation of tourism enterprises and for optimising the comfort of the visitors. It includes such services as roads, electricity, water, security, sanitation and health services, telephone and postal communication, railways and airports.

Interline
Between two or more transportation lines.

Itinerary
Pertaining to a journey. A tourist itinerary is a composition of a series of operations that are a result of the study of the market.

Joint Agent
A person having authority to transact business for two or more transportation lines.

Land Arrangements
All services provided for the traveller by his tour operator after the traveller reaches his first foreign destination. Does not apply to overseas travel. Also referred to as Ground Arrangements.

Market
The totality of actual and/or potential buyers of a given product or service in a specified geographical location at a given point in time or during a given period of time.

Marketing Mix
A mixture of elements which interact and complement each other to achieve the targeted results. It is the combination of marketing variable that the firm uses to pursue the sought level of sales in the target market.

Market Segmentation
Process of identifying groups of buyers of the total market with different buying desires or requirements.

Market Segmentation
The process of indentifying or defining smaller distinct groups into 'segments' with the larger market place; 'beach resort travellers' for example, as segment of 'resort travellers'

Marketing
A total activity which includes an evaluation of market and the requirements of individuals within that market, together with an evaluation of a service, facility or visitor plant, separately or jointly, its cost or accessibility, and the total facilities to provide visitor satisfaction. It includes a merchandising programme aimed at a particular type of customer to convert him to a user or purchaser of the service.

Mass Tourism
Large scale movement of travellers and the development of a standardized product.

Media
Non-personal communication channels, including print media, a newspaper, magazines, direct mail, broadcast media (radio, television) and display media (billborads, sings, posters).

Motel
A place which provides wayside amenities for tourists travelling by road, by automobiles. It provides under one roof all usual facilities expected by the tourist including attached bath.

Motivators
The factors which motivate consumers to buy a particular type of holiday.

Multiplier

The numerical coefficient showing how great an increase in income results from each increase in such investment spending.

Multiplier Effect

The money spent by the tourist circulates through the economy and stimulates it, as it changes hands and is spent and respent a number of times. There is a chain reaction of spending, triggered off by the "injection" of the tourist dollar into a destination economy. This constant turnover of tourist expenditure is known as the 'Multiplier Effect'.

Multimedia

Multiple forms of information i.e. text, audio, graphics, animation, vedio, inter activity, internet.

National Park

An area which is strictly reserved for wildlife and where activities such as forestry, grazing and cultivation are not permitted.

National Tourist Organisation

The body responsible for the formulation and implementation of national tourist policy. It is the agency and the instrument for the execution of the national government's responsibilities for the control, direction and promotion of tourism.

Niche Tourism

Tourism that combines elements designed to appeal to those with certain narrow or special interest.

Optional

In travel literature the word means that the traveller has a choice of taking or not taking the service mentioned. If he takes it, there is always an additional charge which is not included in the basic tour price.

Package

A travel plan which includes most elements of a vacation, such as transportation, accommodations and sightseeing.

Passenger, Transfer

A passenger arriving on one flight and continuing his journey on another.

Packaging

The practice of combining different elements of products and services (often from different firms) into a single package for one price. Travel package for example often include airfare, hotel, meals, sightseeing for a single price.

Passenger, Transit

A passenger continuing his journey on the same through-flight.

Passport

A document issued by national governments to their own citizens as verification of their citizenship. It is also a permit to leave one's own country and return.

Pension

A French word, widely used throughout Europe, meaning guest house or boarding house.

Poster
A pictorial representation of an idea. It is intended to attract attention rapidly to a single word or idea.

Potential Tourist
A person who is likely to purchase a tourist product or can became a tourist at a later date. He may be with holding the purchase in the present time because of certain personal reasons and not because he cannot afford to pay.

Promotion
All activities in producing and increasing sales, including advertising, publicity, personal selling. The activities that supplement and make more effective advertising and personal selling. Special events individually treated to bring public attention to specific products.

Public Relations
Continuous and consistent representation of an organisation's policies to the public at large and to sections of the public who have a special interest in the organisation's activities.

Rack Rate
The official rate advertised by a hotel company, or other tourism provider. This is the rate across the counter, the one offered to the public before any discont are applied.

Resort, Resort Complex
A self contained site which provides all or most of the products and services required by a tourist. They tend to combine attractions with support services such as accommodation and catering.

Rest and Recreation
Specified time usually included in most planned tours to allow the traveller time to relax and/or shop and visit places of interest not included in the tour.

Rest House
Semi-hotel establishments situated in out-of the-way places. The Rest Houses are popular establishments in India and most of these are owned by the State governments. These establishments at certain places are also called Circuit Houses and Dak Bungalows and are scattered all over India close to National Highways. Primarily meant for Government officials on tour, foreign tourists can also stay under certain conditions. These are convenient for tourists travelling by road.

Retailing
The sale directed to the ultimate consumer, distinguished from wholesaling-the selling of relatively large quantities of products to those who resell (the retailers).

Sample Survey
Study of a given population through only a part or a fraction thereof.

Sales Letter
A direct mail material through which an attempt is made to gain agreement or favourable action towards a product.

Sales Promotion
All activities in producing and increasing, sales, including advertising, publicity, personal selling. The activities that supplement and make advertising and personal selling more effective.

Social Tourism

All the relations and phenomenon resulting from the accession to tourism of low income groups made possible or facilitated by specific social measures. It is the type of tourism practised by those who, otherwise, would not be able to meet the cost without social intervention, i.e., without the assistance of an association to which the individual belongs.

Scheduled Flights

Typically take place using predetermined routes according to a planned time table.

Stopover

A point, between origin and destination of an itinerary at which passenger remains for a period of time.

Statistics

That branch of science which deals with the frequency of occurrence of different kinds of things or with the frequency of occurrence of different attributes.

Suggested Itinerary

A preliminary itinerary provided by tour operators for the traveller's consideration. This generally shows routings and approximate times as well as recommended hotels and suggested sightseeing excursions, and spells out the conditions under which these services will be provided.

Supplementary Accommodation

Various types of accommodation other than the conventional hotel type. It includes accommodation for travellers in youth hostels, motels, camping sites and guest houses, etc.

Tariffs

The published fares, rates, charges and or related conditions of carriage of a carrier.

Tele Marketing

Using Telephone to sell directly to the consumer.

Tour Conductor

A professional employee of a tour operator who accompanies a group on tour. Not to be compared with Guide.

Tour Manager

One who controls, directs, and manages an enterprise with judicious economy and care.

Tour Operator

A company which specialises in the planning and operation of pre-paid, pre-planned vacations, and which makes these available to the general public through travel agents.

Tour Organiser

A person who organises a group of passengers to participate in a specially prepared itinerary.

Tour Package

A travel plan which includes most elements of a vacation, such as transportation, accommodation and sightseeing.

Tour Wholesaler

The company that combines various components of travel industry such as hotels, airlines and local attractions, into a "package" for sale by retailers.

Tourism
The practice of touring or travelling for pleasure or recreation and the guidance or management of tourists as a business.

Tour Retailer
A person or business entity that buys the tour products from the tour wholesaler either at a net cost or on a commission basis, and sells these products to the general public.

Tourism Facilities
Facilities which include accommodation like hotels, boarding houses, guest houses, youth hostels etc. They also include recreational and sport facilities of great variety and also all the necessary infrastructure like transportation and utilities.

Tourism Policy
Guidelines and decisions designed to assist the tourism industry in meeting objectives and goals. Tourism policy usually result from the actions of the government's various agencies and organisations.

Tourism Research
Investigation relating with various aspects of tourism. The main objective of tourism research is to find out how people travel, where they travel and why they travel. The areas like travel, demand, domestic and international tourism, accommodation, transport, planning etc., are covered in the research. The findings of the research become the base for planning and implementation of various programmes connected with tourism.

Tourist
A temporary visitor staying at least twenty-four hours in the country visited and the purpose of whose journey can be classified under one of the following headings: (i) leisure (recreation, holiday; health, study, religion and sport); (ii) business, family, mission, meeting.

Tourist Centre
A village or town with a definite concentration of tourist resources, material base and infrastructure of tourism development.

Tourist Charter
A flight booked exclusively for the use of a specific group of tourists who generally belong to the same organisation or who are being 'treated', to the flight by a single host.

Tourist Complex
A massive architectural installation specifically meant for the, infrastructure of tourism.

Tourist, Domestic
A local person who makes a tour, travelling from place to place for pleasure, business, family mission, meeting etc., within the country.

Tourist Flow
Undisturbed and even movement of tourists from one country to another for the purpose of travelling for pleasure.

Tourist, International
A person who makes a tour travelling from place to place for pleasure to areas foreign to his residence.

Tourist Lodge

A small house providing temporary accommodation to a tourist. The accommodation provided is inexpensive as compared to a conventional hotel. The lodge also offers meals.

Tour Escort

A tour accompained by a professional Tour Escort also called Tour Manager.

Tour Hosted

A tour where participants have an opportunity to travel independently but also to receive guidence and assitance from a host at each of the tourist destination.

Tour Guided

A tour conducted only by a local city guides.

Tourist Object

Any object from a natural, socio-economic or cultural-historical viewpoint-which has some specific attractions for the tourists.

Tourist Product

A sum total of a country's tourist attraction, infrastructure and tourist services which hopefully result in consumer satisfaction.

Tourist Region

A branch of economic region with specific high dependence on natural and man-made tourist attractions.

Tourist Visa

A document issued under the authority of the Government to a person visiting a particular country as a tourist.

Transfer

The service provided to travellers when they arrive in and leave a given city-taking them from the airport, air terminal, pier or railway station to their hotel and vice versa, generally accompanied by the local representative of the other operator who planned the tour.

Transit Traffic

Persons (Tourists) carried by transportation lines and passing through a country enroute to some other destination.

Transit Visitor

A visitor who is passing over or through a country enroute to some other destination. Unlike Destination Tourist, he spends limited time and visits few places of tourist interest.

Travel Agent

A person, firm or corporation qualified to provide tours, cruises, transportation, hotel accommodation, meals, transfers, sightseeing and all other elements of travel to the public as a service.

Travel Kit

A sort of container which contains accessories or tools. Travel kit contains various type of materials like folders, pamphlets, exhibits, presentation items, give-aways etc., which helps travel manager in promotional activities. It is an aid which helps in promoting and projecting a product. The contents of a kit, however, vary depending on the area where it is to be used and also amount set aside for the purpose.

Travel Magazine

A magazine which contains articles and other reading material devoted to all types of travel and tourism. The main objective of a travel magazine is promotion of tourism.

Travel Markets

Travel markets are areas which exist in populated localities whose individuals possess leisure, money and desire to visit areas foreign to their residence.

Vacationer

A person staying away form home for at least four nights on any one trip and may in some instances include tourists travelling for a combination of business and pleasure.

Visa

An endorsement on the passport issued by the representative of a Government. The endorsement enables a person to travel to a country for which it is issued.

Visa, Entry

An endorsement on passport issued to persons who wish to visit a country for purposes of business, employment, permanent residence, profession, etc. Initially issued for a period of three months these are extendable to a further period of three months.

Visa, Tourist

An endorsement on passport issued to a person who wishes to visit a country as a tourist. The visa is effective for a period of three months. Tourists must arrive within six months of the date of the issue of visa. The tourist can extend his stay for a further period of three months if he applies to the concerned authorities. .

Visa, Transit

An endorsement on passport which is issued to a tourist whose destination is somewhere else and is passing across. Such visitors passing through a country enroute to some other destination are granted Transit Visa on production of through tickets for the onward journey.

Visitor

Any person visiting a country other than that in which he has his usual place of residence, for any reason other than following an occupation remunerated from within the country visited.

Visitor-Plant

All accommodation, transport etc., parks, points of interest in a destination area.

Vouchers

Documents issued by the tour operators in exchange for which travellers receive pre-paid accommodation meals, sightseeing trips etc. Also referred to as Coupons.

Wholesaler

A travel oriented organisation that creates and presents ready-made travel package or tailor-made travel programmes exclusively at the request of a travel retailer (travel agent). The travel agent communicates with the prospective traveller, and discusses with him whether he needs a readymade or tailor-made itinerary.

Wildlife Sanctuary

An area where protection is given only to the fauna, and the operations like harvesting of timber, collection of minor forest products and private ownership rights are permitted, so long as they do not interfere with the well-being of animals.

Youth Hostel

A building which offers clean, simple and inexpensive shelter to young people exploring their own country or the world, travelling independently or in groups for holiday or educational purposes.

Zoning

Zoning is the process of applying different management objectives and regulations to different parts or zones of a specific area. It is important tool in the site planing and design process.

nternational Tourism r anisations

UN ORGANISATIONS

United Nations Environment Programme (UNEP): C.P. 30552 Nairobi, Kenya.

United Nations Development Programme (UNDP): 1 United Nations Plaza New York, N.Y. 10017 U.S.A.

United Nations Conference on Trade and Development (UNCTAD): Palais des Nations 1211 Geneve 10, Switzerland.

Department of Economic and Social Affairs: (Statistical Office, Centre for Housing, Building and Planning) 1 United Nations New York, N.Y. 10017 U.S.A.

UN ECONOMIC COMMISSIONS

Economic Commission for Europe (ECE): Palais des Nations 1211 Geneve 10, Switzerland.

Economic and Social Commission for Asia and the Pacific (ESCAP): United Nations Building, Rajdamern Avenue, Bangkok, Thailand.

Economic Commission for Africa (ECA): P.O. Box 3001 Addis Ababa, Ethiopia.

SPECIALIZED AGENCIES

International Labour Organisation (ILO): 4, route des Morillons 1211, Geneve 22, Switzerland.

International Bank for Reconstruction and Development (IBRD): 1818 H. Street, N.W. Washington D.C. 20431 U.S.A.

International Monetary Fund (IMF): 700 19th Street, N.W. Washington D.C. 20431 U.S.A.

International Development Association (IDA): 1818 H Street, N.W. Washington D.C., 20431 U.S.A.

International Finance Corporation (IFC): 1818 H Street, N.W. Washington D.C., 20431 U.S.A.

Food and Agriculture Organisation (FAO): Via delle Terme di Caracalla, 00100, Rome, Italy.

United Nations Education, Scientific and Cultural Organisation (UNESCO): 7, Place de Fontenoy 75700 Paris, France

World Health Organisation (WHO) : 1211 Geneve, Switzerland.

Inter-Governmental Maritime Consultative Organisation (IMCO): 101-104 Picadilly, London, WIY UAE England.

International Civil Aviation Organisation (ICAO) : 1000 Sherbrooke Street, West Montreal Quebec, Canada.

NON-GOVERNMENTAL ORGANISATIONS

International Air Transport Association (IATA): 800 Place Victoria, Po Box 113 Montreal, Quebec Canada, H 42 IMI E-mail : atdi@iata.org

American Society of Travel Agents (ASTA): 711 Fifth Avenue, New York, N.Y. 10017 USA.

Universal Federation of Travel Agents Association (UFTAA): 30, Avenue Marnix, 1050 Bruxelles, Belgium.

Conference of Government Tourism Organisations and Travel Agencies 01 Litewska 200-581, Warsaw, Poland.

International Federation of Tour Operators (IFTO): Amaliegade 37, 2 TR, 1256, Copenhagen K, Denmark.

International Congress and Convention Association (ICCA): 15, rue de L' Arcade, 75008 Paris, France. WWW.ICCA.NL.

International Centre for Conservation (ICC): 13 Via di San Michele 00153, Rome, Italy.

International Youth Hostel Federation (IYHF): Midland Bank Chambers, Howardsgate, Welwyn, Garden City, Hertfordshire, England.

International Association of Convention and Visitors Bureaus: 1390 Market Street, San Francisco, California 94102 USA.

Pacific Asia Travel Association (PATA): 228 Grant Avenue, San Francisco, California 94108, USA.

The Travel Research Association (TRA): P.O. Box 8066 Foothill Station, Salt Lake City, Utah 84108, USA.

International Federation of Tourism Journalists and Writers (IFTJR): rue de L' Autumne 32, 1050, Bruxelles, Belgium.

International Social Travel Federation : 99-101 rue de la Loi, 1040, Bruxells, Belgium.

Inter-American Federation of Journalists and Writers in the Tourist Trade : Calle Rivadavia 755, Buenos Aires, Argentina.

International Federation of Tourist Centres : Schrutkagassell, 1130 WIEN, Austria.

International Federation of Camping and Caravanning: Rue d'Arenberg 44-B.P. 955, Bruxelles, Belgium.

Federation of International Youth Travel Organisations (FIYTO): 81 Islande Brygge 2300, Copenhagen 5, Denmark.

European Travel Commission (ETC): P.O. Box 536 Dublin, Ireland.

East Asia Travel Association: 2-10-1 Yurakucho, Chiyodaku Tokyo, Japan.

American Hotel and Motel Association (AHMA), 888 Seventh Avenue, N.Y. 10010, USA.

International Bureau of Social Tourism: 7, Boulevard de I'lmperatrice, Gare Centrale, Bruxelles 1, Belgium.

International Bureau for Tourism and Youth Exchanges, P.O. Box 147, 1389 Budapest, Hungary.

World Association for Professional Training in Tourism: 105 rue-St-Lazare 75009 Paris, France.

International Association of Scientific Experts in Tourism (AIEST): C.P. 2728, 3001 Berne, Switzerland.

International Academy of Tourism: 4 rule des Iris Monte Carlo, Monaco.

International Touring Alliance (ITA): 2, Quai Gustave Ador 1207, Geneva, Switzerland.

International Union for Conservation of Nature and Natural Resources : 1110 Morges, Switzerland.

World Association of Travel Agencies (WATA): 37 Quai Wilson 1211, Geneva 1, Switzerland.

World Tourism Organisation (WTO): Calle Captain Haya, 42, Madrid-20, Spain.

International Centre for Advanced Tourism Studies (CIEST): Coronel Porfirio Diqz, 50 San Jeronimo Lidice,Mexico 20 D.F. Mexico.

Discover America Travel Organisation (DATO): 1899 L Street N.W-Washington, D.C. 20036, U.S.A.

International Airline Passenger Association (IAPA) www.IAPA.COM

International Hotel and Restaurant Association (IH&RA) www.IH-RA.COM

American Society of Travel Agents (ASTA) www.ASTA.COM

World Travel and Tourism Council (WTTC) 20, Grosvenor Place, London SWIX 7TT United Kingdom, E-mail: creatingjobs@www.wttc.org.

Universal Federation of Travel Agent's Association UFTAA www.UFTAA.COM

Pu lications o nternational r anisations

World Tourism Organisation (WTO)

WTO, Publications Section, Calle Captain Haya, 42, Madrid 20, Spain.

- Domestic Tourism
- Economic Review of World Tourism
- Hand book on Tourism Forecasting Methods
- Integrated Planning
- International Travel Statistics
- Marketing of Tourist Products of Developing Countries
- Physical Planning and Area Development
- Testing the Effectiveness of Promotional Campaigns in International Travel Marketing
- Technical Bulletins
- The Impact of International Tourism on the Economic Development of the Developing Countries
- The role of Tourist Administration concerning the Environment and Folklore
- The Changing World of Travel Marketing
- Tourism Compendium
- Tourism Latest Trends
- Tourism Surveys and Research
- Tourism Vocational Training in Africa
- Economic Effects of Tourism
- Evaluating Tourism Resources
- Travel Abroad-Frontier Formalities
- Travel Research Journal
- World Travel
- World Travel Statistics
- WTO-What it is, What it does, How it Functions
- Aims, Activities and Fields of Competence of National Tourist Organisations
- Compendium of Financial and Fiscal Schemes for Development

- Economic Review of the World Tourism
- International Travel Statistics
- Survey of Africa's Tourism Prospects
- Relations between the National Tourist Office and the Travel Agencies
- Resolutions and Recommendations of the UN Conference on International Travel and Tourism (Rome, 1963)
- Study on the Economic Impact of Tourism on National Economics and International Trade
- Technical Bulletins
- Travel Abroad-Frontier Formalities
- Travel Research Journal
- Tourist Bibliography
- World Travel
- World Travel and Tourism Review
- Compendium of Tourist Statistics
- Travel and Tourism Fairs
- Shining in the Media Spotlight
- What Good Tourism Managers Need to Know
- Tourism 2020 Vision-Executive Summary
- Role and Structure of National Tourism Administration
- Manila Declaration on World Tourism
- Economic Effects of Tourism
- Physical Planning and Area Development for Tourism in the six WTO Regions
- Tourism Forecasting
- Development of Leisure Time and Right to Holidays
- Determination of the importance of Tourism as an Economic Activity within the framework of the National Accounting System.
- Domestic and International Tourism's Contribution to State Revenue
- Study of Tourism's Contribution to State Revenue
- Concept, Production and Innovations of the Tourism Product
- Tourist Carrying Capacity
- Economic Review of World Tourism

Organisation for Economic Cooperation and Development (OECD)

OECD-Publications Office, 2 rue Andre Pascal, 75775 Paris Cedex 16, France.

- Evolution of Tourism in Mediterranean Countries
- International Tourism and Tourism Policy
- Measures of Leisure
- Equality and Welfare

- Tourism Development and Economic Growth
- Tourism Development and Economic Growth-Estoril Seminar
- Tourism Policy and International Tourism in OECD Member Countries
- Consumer Protection Concerning Air Package Tours
- Tourism Development and Economic Growth
- Impact of Tourism on Environment
- Tourism Policy and International Tourism in OECD Member Countries.
- Case Studies of the Impact of Tourism on the Environment

International Labour Organisation (ILO)

ILO Publications, International Labour Office CH-1211 Geneva 22 Switzerland

- Activities of the International Labour Organisation in the Field of Tourism
- Careers in Hotel and Tourism Sector
- Study on the Training of Travel Agency Personnel
- Training of Tourist Office Personnel
- Vocational Training for Hotel and Tourist industry

Pacific Asia Travel Association (PATA)

228 Grant Avenue, San Francisco California 94108, USA www.PATA.ORG.

- Pacific Travel News
- Annual Statistical Report
- Pacific Hotel Directory
- Pacific Area Destination Handbook
- Glossary of Travel and Marketing Terms
- The Pacific: Your Log of Exploration
- Inside PATA
- Meetings Pacific
- Events in the Pacific.

International Civil Aviation Organisation (ICAO)

P.O. Box 400, Place de L'Aviation Internationale, 1000 Sherbrooke Street West, Montreal, Quebec, Canada H3 A 2 R2.

- ICAO Bulletin
- International Standards and Recommended Practices on Facilitation
- Council Statements
- Digests of Statistics
- Manual Circulars
- Journal of Travel Research
- Tourism Recreation Research

- Annual of Tourism Research
- Cornell Hotel and Restaurant Administration
- Hospitality Research Journal
- Journal of Leisure and Research
- Journal of Travel and Tourism Marketing
- Travel and Tourism Analysis

World Travel and Tourism Council (WTTC)

20 Grosvenor Place, London SWIX 7TT United Kingdom, E-mail: creatingjobs@ www.wttc.org.

Travel and Tourism in India : The Economic Impact and Potential
South Africa's Travel and Tourism-The Economic Impact of Travel and Tourism
China and Hong Kong: The Economic Impact of Travel and Tourism
Steps to Success-Global Good Practices in Travel and Tourism

Business International Limited. The Economic Intelligent Unit (EIU)

P. O. Box 154, 151 Dartford Trade Park Hawley Road, Dartford DAI IQB, Kent United Kingdom

- Competitive Strategies for the International Hotel Industry.
- European Car Hire Industry
- The European Long Haul Travel Market
- European Railways
- Far East and Pacific Travel In the 1990s.
- The Japanese Overseas Travel Market in the 1990s.
- Tourism in Eastern Europe
- The World Cruise Ship Industry
- Tourism and the Environment
- International Tourism Forecasts to 2005

Federation of Hotel and Restaurant Association of India (FHRAI)

B-82, 8th Floor, Himalaya House, Kasturba Gandhi Marg, New Delhi-110001 INDIA

- Hotel and Restaurant Guide
- Guidelines and Incentives for the hotel industry in India
- Indian Hotel Industry Survey
- Market Research on Franchising opportunities in the Budget Hotel Sector in India

Tourism Periodicals

OVERSEAS

Asia Travel Trade : Interasia Publications Ltd., 200 Lockhart Road, 13th Floor, Hong Kong.

Asia Travel News : American Society of Travel Agents, 488 Madison Avenue, New York, N.Y. 10022, USA.

Asian Hotelkeeper and Catering Times : Media Transasia 3/F Sarasin Building 14, Surasat Road, Bangkok, Thailand.

British Travel News : British Travel News, 239 Old Marylebone Road, London N.W.I., England.

Canada Tourism News : Canadian Govt. Office of Tourism, Ottawa, Canada KIA OH6.

Canadian Travel Courier : 481 University Avenue, Toronto, Ontario, Canada.

Canadian Travel News : 1450 Don Mills Road, Ontario, Canada.

Congressi : Centro International dei Congress Palazzo dei Congressi, Firenze, Italy.

Digest of Tourist Statistics : British Tourist Authority, London, England.

Far East Traveller : 1350 Avenue of the Americas, New, York, USA.

Far East Traveller : 28-4-1, Motoasabu, Minato-ku, Tokyo, Japan.

Future Tourist : P. O. Box 138, Balmain, Sydney, Australia 2041.

Gourmet : Gourmet Incorporated, 777 Third Avenue, New York, N.Y. 10017, USA.

Hungarian Travel : Hungarian Tourism Board, P.O. Box 223 H-1906, Budapest, Hungary.

In Britain: British Tourist Authority, 64 St. Jame's St., London SWIA, England

Incentive Travel Manager : Barrington Publication Inc; 825 South Barrington Avenue, Los Angeles, California 90049 USA.

Index : Centro Per La Statistica Aziendale, Via A, Baldes, 20, 50131 Firenze, Italy

International Tourist Quarterly : The Economist Intelligence Unit Ltd., Spencer House, 27 St. James' Place, London SWI, England.

Journal of Leisure Research : US Department of Commerce,Washington D.C., USA.

Journal of Travel Research : Business Research Division, University of Colorado, Colorado, USA.

Look East : Ruang Seang Publishing Ltd. Partnership 987-989- New Road, Bangkok, Thailand.

Marco Polo : Cathay Pacific Airways, 17 Thomson Road, 13th Floor Hong Kong.

National Geographic : National Geographic Incorporated, (2) Century Plaza, 2049, Century Park East, Los Angeles, California, USA.

Orientations : Pacific Magazines Ltd. 13th Floor, 200 Lockhart Road, Hong Kong.

Pacific : Fuji Incorporated, Ginza Chuo Building, 1-20, Tsukiji, 4-Chome, Chuo-ku, Tokyo, Japan.

Pacific Magazine : Pacific Magazine Emphasis Inc. Central Roppongi Building, 1-4-27 Roppongi, Minato-ku, Tokyo, Japan.

Pacific Travel : Pacific Asia Travel Association, 274 Brannan St., San Francisco, California, 94107, USA.

Pacific Travel News : Pacific Asia Travel Association, 288 Avenue, San Francisco, California, 94108, USA.

Recreation and Tourism : SRI International, 333 Ravenswood Avenue, Melano Park, California, USA

Service World International : Cahnes Publication, 55, Wabash Avenue, Chicago, 911, 60603, USA.

Singapore Travel News : Singapore Tourist Promotion Board, 131, Tudor Court, Tanglin Road, Singapore.

South Asia Travel Review : Thomson Press Hong Kong Ltd., Media Transasia, 3/F Sarasin Building, 14 Surasak Road, Bangkok, Thailand.

Sunset : Lane Publishing Company, 3055 Wilshire Boulevard Los Angeles, California 90010, USA.

Tourism International : 136, Gloucester Place, London N.W.I., England

Tourism International Air Letter : Tourism International Press, 154, Cromwell Road, London SW7, England

Touristiques Internationale : 40, rue du Colisee, Paris 75014, France.

Tourist Review : Organe official del L'Association International d'Experts Scientifiques du Turisme AIEST Case Potale 2728, 3001, Berne, Switzerland.

Travel : Travel Magazine, Inc; Travel Building 5 Floral Park, New York-11001, USA

Travel Agent : World Travel Inc. 730 SW Fifth Avenue, Portland, Oregon, USA

Tourism Journal : Asian Institute of Tourism, University of Philippines, Diliman, Quezon City 3004 Philippines.

The Travel Agent : American Traveller Incorporated, 2 West 46th Street, New York, NY 10036 USA

Travel Holiday : Travel Magzine Incorporated, Travel Building, Flora Park,New York 10036 USA.

Travel Holiday Inc. P.O. Box 49692 Los Angeles, California 90049, USA.

Travel and Leisure : 1750 Avenue of the Americas, New York,USA

Travel Asia Pacific : 306, Temple Chambers, Temple Avenue, Fleet Street, London E.C.4, England.

Travel Journal : Moritani Travel Enterprise, Inc., Izumiya Tokoten Building, 1,3-Chome Kojimachi, Chiyoda-Ku, Tokyo 102, Japan.

Travel Holiday Magazine : 51 Atlantic Avenue, Floral Park, New York, U.S.A.

Travel Review : Media Transasia, 3/F Sarasin Building, 14 Surasak Road, Bangkok, Thailand.

Travel News Asia : Travel News Asia, 1911 Hanglung Centre, Peterson Street, Hong Kong.

Travel Research Journal : World Tourism Organisation, Avenida Del Generalisimo, 59, Madrid, Spain.

Travel Trade Reporter : Orient Pacific Enterprises Ltd., 526 Ploenchit Road, Bangkok, Thailand.

Travel Trade Reporter : Orient Pacific Enterprises, Penthouse Six, Aman Hotel, 526 Ploenchit Road, Bangkok, Thailand.

Travel Journal International : Moritani Travel Enterprise, Inc. 1, Kojimachi 3-Chome, Chiyoda-ku, Tokyo 102, Japan.

Travel Post : Intergroup Communications, Inc. Katigbak Building, 1000 A Mabini Street, Ermita, Manila, Philippines.

Travel Trade Le Repertuire Des Voyages : 40, rue de colisee Paris 75008, France

Travel Trade : Box M-204, Sydney Mail Exchange, N.S.W. 2010, Australia.

Travel Trade : 605 Fifth Avenue, New York, NY:10017, USA.

Travel Trade Gazette Europa : 11, Blot Court, Fleet Street, London, England.

Travel Trade Gazette : 30 Calderwood Street, London, England

Travel Trade Gazette Asia : 5 B, 5th Floor, 9 Comfort Terrace, Hong Kong.

Travel Week : 73, Commonwealth Street, Sydney, Australia.

Travel Management Daily : 888 7th Avenue, 29th Floor, New York, USA.

Travel Weekly : 1, Park Avenue, New York, U.S.A.

Viaggi Vacanze : Via A. Manzoni 37 Milan, Italy.

Voyages : 59, rue du Rocher, Paris 75008, France

Vue Touristique : Centre International de Documentation de la F.I.J.E.T. 1060 Bruxelles, Belgium.

World Travel : Shimru Building, 17, Shiba, Nishikubohiramachi, Minato-ku, Tokyo, Japan.

Hospitality and Tourism, University of Surrey, Oxford, England.

Leisure Recreation and Tourism. Abstract CAB, Oxford, England

IN INDIA

Air Observer : Air Observer Publications, Warsha House, 6, Zakharia Bunder Road, Sewri, Bombay 400 015 INDIA.

Destination India : Cross section Publications, 7 Dwarka Sadan, C/42 Connaught Place, New Delhi-110001, INDIA

Indian Hotelkeeper and Traveller : Oberoi Intercontinetal, 90-91, Maidens Hotel, Delhi-110006, INDIA

Indrama : Sita World Travel (India) Pvt. Ltd. F-12, Connaught Place, New Delhi-110001.

Indian Magazine : Wadia Building, 17/19 Dalal Street, Bombay 400 023 INDIA.

India-Best of the Best : Durga Das Publications Pvt. Ltd. 72 Todarmal Road, New Delhi-110001, INDIA

Explore India : Durga Das Publications Pvt. Ltd. 72 Todar Mal Road, New Delhi-110001

Travel and Tourism : Indian Express Newspapers (Bombay) Ltd. 1st Floor, Express Towers, Nariman Point, Mumbai-400021, E-mail: ehc@vsnl.com

Hotelier and Caterer : Indian Express Newspapers (Bombay) Ltd. 1st Floor, Express Towers, Nariman Point, Mumbai-400021, E-mail: ehc@vsnl.com

Indian Travel Guide : Post Box No. 423, 72 Big Street, Triplicane, Madras, 600 005, INDIA.

Magic Carpet : Air India, Air India Building, 218, Nariman Point, Bombay-400021.

Namaskaar : Air India (Inflight Magazine) Media Transasia, 3rd Floor Sarasin, Building, 14 Surasak Road, Bangkok, Thailand.

Namaste : Welcomegroup Publication, The Hotels Division of ITC Ltd., 28, Community Centre, Basant Lok, Vasant Vihar, New Delhi-110057 INDIA

Safari India : Young Asia Publications, 7, Ansari Road, New Delhi-110002 INDIA

Soma : East India Hotels Ltd., 7, Alipur Road, Delhi-110054, INDIA

The Taj : The Indian Hotels Company Ltd; Apollo Bunder Road, Bombay-400039.

Travel News : Travel Agents Association of India, 35, Anjali, 1st Floor, Arthur Bunder Road, Colaba, Bombay-400005, INDIA

TCI News : Travel Corporation (India) Private Limted, Chander Mukhi, Nariman Point, Bombay 400 021, INDIA.

Travel World : 160, Chittaranjan Avenue, Calcutta 700 007, INDIA

Signature : Diners Club of India Pvt. Ltd., RahejaChambers 213 Nariman Point, Bombay 400021, INDIA.

Tourism and Wildlife : 24, Gole Market, Netaji Subhash Marg, New Delhi-110002, INDIA

Tourism and Travel : National Press Agency, 182, Jor Bagh, New Delhi-110003, INDIA

Youth Hosteller : Youth Hostel Association of India, 5 Nyaya Marg, Chanakyapuri, New Delhi-110021, INDIA.

Trav Talk : Durga Das Publications Pvt. Limited, 72 Todar Mal Road, New Delhi-110001.

Travel Trends Today : Cross Section Publications Pvt. Ltd., F-74, Bhagat Singh Market, New Delhi-110001 INDIA

Outlook Traveller, AB-10, S.J. Enclave, New Delhi-110029, INDIA

TRAVEL GUIDES ON INDIA

Biswas, Sukumar : Traveller's Guide to India; Rupak Publishers Calcutta

British Airways BA : Explorer 2-A London/Threshold Guide: Guide to the Orient and Pacific; Threshold Books Ltd.

Chellani, Ramesh A : Look India-Tourist Guide; R.A. Chellani

Chatterjee, D: Handbook of India (Vol. I and II); Calcutta, Print and Publication Sales.

Fodor E & Curtis, W. (Editor) : Fodor's Guide to India; New York, Fodor's Modern Guides, Inc.

George, A.Simon: India-Simon's Handbook on; Ernakulam, International Advisers and Publishers.

Gupta, S.P. and Krishna Lal : Tourism Museums and Monuments in India ; Delhi, Oriental Publishers.

Publications Division : Handbook of India ; New Delhi, Publications Division, Ministry of Information & Broadcasting.

Roy, P.B. : India-Handbook of Travel; Calcutta

Rushbrook Williams, L.F. (Editor) : Handbook of Travellers in India, Pakistan, Burma and Sri Lanka; London, John Murray.

Waldo, Myra: Travel Guide to the Orient and the Pacific; London, Macmillan and Co.

Insight Guides : India, APA Productions (HK) Ltd., P. O. Box 219 Orchard Point Singapore 9123.

PATA, Asia Pacific Business Travel Guide, Priory Publications Ltd., Brackley, Northants NN 13, 5HH, UK

ducation and Trainin in Travel Tourism

OVERSEAS

I. Higher Degree in Tourism

Centre D'Etudes du Tourisme, Universite D'Aix en Provence, 3 Agenue Robert Schuman, 13-100 Aix 'en Province, France.

Doctorate of 3rd Cycle Speciality in Economy and Law of Tourism, Duration: 2-3 years.

The Scottish Hotel School, University of Strathclyde, Ross Hall, Crookston Road, Glasgow G 52 3NQ, United Kingdom.

Master of Science M.Sc. in Tourism.

Duration: One year.

Department of Hotel and Catering Management, University of Surrey, Guildford, Survey, United Kingdom.

Post Graduate Diploma in Tourism with possible extension to M.Sc. Duration: 1-2 years.

Universita delgi Studi di Firenze, via Curtatone, Florence, Italy.

Higher Diploma Courses

Duration: 1-2 years.

George Washington University, Washington, D.C., USA.

Master's Degree in Tourism Administration

Doctor of Education with a concentration in Tourism.

Duration : 2-4 years

University of Calgary, Canada.

Advance Master's Degree in Tourism Administration.

Duration : 2 years

University of Surrey, Guildford, Surrey England

Post Graduate Diploma in Tourism.

Duration : One year

University of Simon Bolivar Caracas, Venezuela

Post graduate Courses in Tourism.

Duration : One year

University of Sorbonne, Paris, France
Post graduate courses in Tourism.
Duration : One year
University of Zagreb, Yugoslavia.
Advance Courses in Tourism Administration
Duration : 2 years
University of Lincolnshire and Humberside UK
Bachelor of Business Administration
B.B.A. Hons. with specialisation in Tourism
Duration : 3 years
Edith Crown University, Perth, Western, Australia, E-mail : business@cowan.edu.au
Degree Course in Tourism Management
Duration : 3 years.
The Netherlands Institute of Tourism and Transport Studies, Sibeliuslaan 13 4837 CA Breda. The Netherlands
Graduate Course in Tourism Management
Duration : 4 years
Centre International De Glion, CH 1823 Glion Sur Montreux Switzerland
Graduate course in Hospitality and Tourism Management
Diploma Course in Hospitality and Tourism Management
Duration : 1-3 Years

II. Diploma and Short Courses in Tourism

Department of Hotel and Catering Management University of Surrey, Gvildford, Surrey, United Kingdom.
University certificate.
Duration: 1 year.
Centre D'Etudes Superieures du Tourisme, Universite de Paris l, 13, Rue de Santeuil, Paris 5e, France.
Higher Diploma,
Duration: 1 year.
Institute Technici per il Tourismo, Via Della Badia dei Roccettini 1l, San Domenico di Fiesole, Florence, Italy.
Certificate of Profession.
Duration: 1 year.
Scuola International di Scienze Turistiche, Via Cavalier,d'Arpino 5/A 00197 Rome, Italy.
Post Graduate Diploma.
Duration: One year
Hochschule Fur Welthandel, Institut Fur Fremdenverkhresforschung, Fraz-Kleingasse 1, 1190 Vienna, Austria.
University Course in Tourism leading to the University Certificate,
Duration: 1 year.

Adelaide College of TAFE Adelaide, South Australia, Australia.
Diploma in Tourism Management,
Advanced
Certificate in Tourism.
Duration : 1-2 years

Univeristy of Hawaii, School of Travel Industry Management, Honolulu Hawaii, Advanced Course in Travel and Tourism.
Duration : 2 years

III. Technical Courses in Tourism

Technical courses in tourism are directed at the development of technical and practical skills in tourism with the direct objective of a career in the industry. The main emphasis in these courses is on vocational orientation. The course contents are suitably structured to equip students with at least the basic techniques of practice in one or other section of the industry. These courses are below University level. In practice however, they attract students with a wide variety of educational background and qualifications.

Institute Professionale Alberghiero, Via di Tor Corbone 53, Rome, Italy.

Courses in specialist training such as agriculture, catering and tourism. Diploma di Qualifica is awarded on completion.
Duration: Three years.

Ecole Nationale de Commerce, 70 Boulvard Bessiers, 75017
Paris, France.
Diploma Course,
Duration: Two years.

Lycee Technique D'Hotellerie et de Tourisme, 144 Rue de France, 06048 Nice, France.
Diploma Course
Duration : 2 years

Hosta Hotel and Tourism School CH-1854 Leysin, Swtizerland
Diploma in Travel and Tourism
Duration : 9 months

Lycee Technique D'Hotellerie et de Tourisme, 144 Rue de Lucerne, 67085 Strasbourg, France.
Diploma in Tourism
Duration : Two years

Instituto Technici per il Turismo, Via delle Terme di Diocleziano 23, Rome, Italy.
State Diploma
Duration: Five Years.

Provinciaal Institut Voor voedings-industrieen en Toerisme 1070 Brussel-Emile Gryzonlaan l, Anderlecht, Brussels, Belgium.
Graduate in Tourism,
Duration: Two years.

Coloma Instituut Malines, Belgium
Diploma Course.
Duration: Two years.
Hoger Technisch Instituut, Spoorwegstreat 12, 8200 Bruges, Belgium.
Diploma Course.
Duration: Two years.
Institute International de Glion, 1823 Glion-sur-Montreux, Switzerland.
Diploma in Tourism.
Duration: Two years (Full time).
Durham Technical College, Framwellgate Moor, Durham, United Kingdom.
Diploma in Travel and Tourism.
Duration: Two years (Full time).
Henley College of Further Education, Coventry; United Kingdom.
Diploma in Tourism Studies.
Duration: Two years (Full time).

IV. Business Studies Courses in Tourism

Department of Hotel and Institutional Management, Sheffield Polytechnic, Pond Street Sheffield S/ 1 1 WB, United Kingdom.
Higher National Diploma in Business Studies (Tourism)
Duration: Two years
School of Hotel Keeping and Catering, Ealing Technical College, St. Mary's Road, Ealing, London W 5 5RF, United Kingdom.
Higher National Diploma in Business Studies (Tourism)
Duration: Two years
Faculty of Tourism, Catering and Hotel Administration, Bournemouth College of Technology, Landsdowne, Bournemouth BHI 3 JJ, United Kingdom.
Higher National Diploma in Business Studies (Tourism)
Duration: Two years (Full time).
Fachhochschule Munchen, Studienrichtung Fremdenverkehr, Lothstrasse 34, 8 Munich 2. West Germany.
Management Studies and Business Administration with a tourism option.
Duration: 4 years:
Netherlands Wetenschappelijk Instituut Voor Toerisme en Rekreatie;Haagweg 21, Breda, Holland.
Business and Tourism Studies.
Duration: Three years.
Blackpool Technical College, Courfled Hornby Road, Lance, United Kingdom.
Courses in Tourism Studies.
Duration: l-2 years.
Higbury Technical College, Dovercourt Road, Gesham Portsmouth, United Kingdom.
Technical Course in Tourism:
Duration: 1-3 years.

V. Tourism Courses for Students from Developing Countries

International Centre for Advanced Technical and Vocational Training, International Labour Organisation (ILO), Palazzo del Lavore, Corso Unita D'Italia, 10127 Turin, Itlay.

Three Certificate Courses a year.

Duration: 3 months.

Institute of Tourism and Hotel Management, Salzburger Unterrichtsanstalten Fur Fremdenverkehrsberufe, Schloss Klesheim, A 5071 Siezenheim bei Salzburg, Austria.

Diploma Course.

Duration: 8 months (Full time)

Scuola Internazionale Di Scienze Turistiche, Via Cavalier d Arpino 5 A 00197 Rome, Italy.

Post graduate Course.

Duration: 7 months (Full time).

International Centre for Advanced Tourism Studies (CIEST) World Tourism Organisation (WTO) Calle Humboldt, 49, Mexico, D.F. Mexico.

Correspondence Courses on:

(i) Introduction to Tourism
(ii) Tourism Marketing
(iii) Promotion of Tourist Services
(iv) Forecasting, Distribution, Promotion
(v) Distribution and Sales of Tourist Services

Post graduate Certificate Courses.

Duration: 6-9 months.

Bournemouth College of Technology, Lansdowne, Bournemouth BHI, 3 JJ United Kingdom.

Diploma Course.

Duration: 8 months

Commissariat General au Tourisme de Belgique, Central Station, Brussels, Belgium. (The Belgian National Tourist Office).

Certificate Course,

Duration: Three months.

Deutsches Wirtschaftswissenschaftiliches Institut Fur Fremdenverkehr an der Universitat Munchen, HermannSack-Strasse 2, 8 Munich 2 West Germany.

(The courses are under the sponsorship of the German Ministry of Economic Co-operation and are conducted in association with the University of Munich).

Graduate level course.

Duration: Three years.

VI. Courses Sponsored by the Tourist Industry.

With a view to improving the technical skills and managerial qualities of the existing staff, the tourist industry in recent years has evolved certain training programmes: A number of courses and seminars are conceived or sponsored by the tourist industry. These include the following:

IATA Aviation Training and Development Institute, 800 Place Victoria. P. O. Box 113, Montreal Quebec, Canada H4Z IMI E-mail : atdi@iata.org

IATA/UFTAA Courses on :

Senior Management Level Diploma

Management Level Diploma

Consultant Level Certificate

Foundation Level Certificate

The above career development courses in travel and tourism are convenient self teach, home study as also class room courses.

Duration : 3 months to 2 years.

Algemene Vakschool Voor het Reisbureaubedrif, Leidse Dreef 2 Leiderdo Holland: (A.N.V.R. Courses). The Dutch Association of Travel Agents and Tour Operators, the A.N.V.R. started the course for the initial training of prospective travel industry personnel.

Certificate Course.

Duration: 10 months.

American Hotel and Motel Association 1407, South Harrison Road, P. O. Box 1240 East Lansing, Michigan 48826 (Professional Training Courses of 3-6 months)

Universal Federation of Travel Agents Association (UFTAA) 30, Avenue Marnix 1050, Brussels, Belgium.

Professional training courses (Correspondence).

Duration : 6-12 months

American Society of Travel Agents (ASTA) 711 Fifth Avenue, New York, N.Y. 10017, USA.

Professional Training course.

Duration : 3 -12 months

International Union of Official Travel Organisations (IUOTO), Palazzo del Lavero, Corso Unita D'Italia, 10127, Turin, Italy.

General Correspondence Course.

Duration : 9 months

TOURISM COURSES IN INDIA

University of Delhi, College of Vocational Studies, Sheikh Sarai, New Delhi-110007.

(a) Degree Course

Duration : 3 years (Full time)

(b) Post-graduate Diploma Course

Duration : 2 years (Part time)

University of Garhwal, Faculty of Tourism, Srinagar, Garhwal, Uttar Pradesh

Post-graduate Diploma Course

Duration : 2 Years (Full time)

Marathwada University, Marathwada, Maharashtra

Post-graduate Diploma

Duration : 2 years (Full time)

University of Madras, Department of Audit and continuing Education, Madras.
Post-graduate Diploma
Duration : 1 year

University of Rajasthan, Institute of Correspondence Studies and Continuing Education, Jaipur, Rajasthan.
Post-graduate Certificate
Duration : 1 year (Correspondence Course)

Kurukshetra Univeristy, Kurukshetra, Haryana
Department of Ancient Indian History, Culture and Archaeology
a) Paper in Tourism in Graduate Course
Duration : 3 years
b) Post-graduate course in Tourism Administration (MTA)
Duration : 2 years

Annamalai University, Faculty of Professional Management Courses, Annamalai Nagar, 608101 Tamil Nadu.
a) B.A. (Tourism)
Duration : 3 years
b) Post-graduate Diploma
Duration : 1 year (Part time)

Academy of Management Science and Studies, 5 Padmanabha Nagar, Adyar, Tri Junction, Chennai, 600 020, Tamil Nadu.
Diploma Course in Travel and Tourism Management.
Duration : 6 months

University of Lucknow, Isabella Thoburn College, Lucknow, U.P.
Diploma in Travel Counselling and Tourism
Duration : 6 months

University of Agra, Agra, UP.
Post-graduate course in Tourism
Duration : 1 year

Lady Amritbal Daga College for Women, Nagpur, Maharashtra, Bombay.
Post-graduate Diploma
Duration : 1year

K.C. College of Management Studies, Mumbai
Diploma Course
Duration : 1 year

Sophia College, Shri Sasant Kumar Somani Memorial Polytechnic, Bombay.
Post-graduate Diploma
Duration : 1 year

Godavarish College of Vocational Studies, Department of Travel, Tourism and Hotel Management, Nageswar Tangi, Bhubaneshwar 751 014 Orissa.
Degree Course (Specialising in Tourism)
Duration : 3 years

Madurai-Kamraj University, University Building, Palkalai Nagar, Madurai 625021
Master's Degree in Tourism Management
Duration : 2 years

Alagappa University, Directorate of Distance Education, Alagappa Nagar, Karaikudi 623003
Post-Graduate Diploma in Tourism Management
Duration : One year

Devara College, St. Patricks Complex, Opposite Opera Theatre, Residency Road, Bangalore 560 001, Karnataka.
Diploma Course
Duration : 1 year (Full time)
Similar Courses available in Mumbai and Chennai.

YMCA School of Commerce and Management, 12-N Parekh Marg, Mumbai-400 039, Maharashtra.
Diploma Course in Travel and Tourism
Duration : 6 months

YWCA Women's Technical Training Institute, Bangla Sahib Lane, Off Jai Singh Road, New Delhi-110 001.
P.G. Diploma Course in Travel and Tourism Management
Duration : 1 year

South Delhi Polytechnic for Women, N-9 South Extension, Part-I, New Delhi 110 049.
Diploma in Tourism
Duration : 1 year

India International Trade Centre, (IITC) 105 Nirmal Towers, New Delhi-110 001.
Diploma in International Travel and Tourism Management
Duration : 6 months
(Similar Courses available in Mumbai, Chennai, Bangalore and Secundrabad)

Bhartiya Vidya Bhavan, Rajendra Prasad Institute of Communication Studies, New Delhi and Mumbai.
Post-graduate Diploma
Duration : 1 year

Institute of Management Studies H.P. University, Shimla-171005
Master of Tourism Administration
Duration : 2 years

Indian Institute of Travel and Travel Management, Gwalior, Madhya Pradesh
Basic and Advanced Management Courses leading to award of PG Diploma in Tourism Management
Duration : 14 months

Indira Gandhi National Open University IGNOU, New Delhi
Correspondence courses leading to
Master's Level (MTA) in Tourism Administration
Bachelor's Level (BBA) in Tourism Administration
Diploma in Travel and Tourism
Duration : 1-3 years

elect i lio rap

Addison, William, *English Spas* (London: Batsford, 1951).

Aerni, M.J., "The Social Effects of Tourism". *Current Anthropology*, 13 (1972).

Alastair, M. Morrison, *Hospitality and Travel Marketing* (New York: Delemar 1989).

Aldous, *T. Battle for the Environment* (London: Fontana/Collins, 1972).

Anand, M.M. *Tourism and Hotel Industry in India* (New Delhi: Prentice-Hall of India, 1976).

Anderson, N. *Work and Leisure* (London: Routledge and Kegan Faul, 1961).

Archer, B.H. "Tourist Research in the United Kingdom". *Journal of Travel Research.* 10; 4 (March 1972).

Archer, B.H. *Demand Forecasting in Tourism* (Cardiff : University of Wales Press, 1974).

Archer, B.H. *The Impact of Domestic Tourism* (Cardiff: University of Wales Press, 1973).

Ashworth, G. J. *Marketing in the Tourism Industry* (London : Routledge 1990).

Ashworth, G. *Recreation and Tourism* (London : Bell and Hyman 1984).

Avvill, R. *Man and Environment* (London: Penguin, 1967).

Balsdon, J.P.V.D. *Life and Leisure in Ancient Rome* (London: Bodley Head, 1966).

Beazely, E. *Designed for Recreation* (London: Faber, 1970).

Bernecker, Paul. *Methods and Media of Tourist Publicity* (Vienna: Austrian National Tourist Office, 1961).

Bhatia, A. K. *International Tourism-Fundamentals and Practices* (New Delhi: Sterling, 1991).

Bhatia, A. K. *Tourism Management and Marketing* (New Delhi: Sterling, 1997).

Bhatia, A.K. *Tourism in India-History and Development* (New Delhi: Sterling, 1978).

Boniface, B and Cooper, C. *The Geography of Travel and Tourism* (London : Heinemann, 1987).

Brunner, E. *Holiday Making and the Holiday Trades* (London: Oxford University Press, 1945).

Bryden, John M. *Tourism and Development* (Cambridge: Cambridge University Press, 1973).

Bull, A. *The Economics of Travel and Tourism* (London: Pitman, 1991).

Burkart, A.J. and Medlik, S. *Tourism: Past, Present and Future* (London: Heinemann, 1976).

Burkart, A.J. *The Management of Tourism* (London: Heinemann, I975).

Burton, R. *Travel Geography* (London : Pitman, 1995).

Burton, T.L. (Ed.) *Recreation Research and Planning* (London: Allen and Unwin, 1970).

Butler, R.W. "The Social Implication of Tourism Development"; *Tourism Research* 2, 2 (1974).

Calder, N. *The Environment Game* (London: Panther, I969).

Checchi and Co. *The Future of Tourism in the Far East* (1961).
Cherry, G.E. *Town Planning and its Social Context* (London: Hill, 1970).
Chuck, Y. Gee. *The Travel Industry* (New York :Van National Reinhold 1989).
Clare, A. Gunn *Tourism Planning* (Washington DC: Taylor & Francis, 1993).
Clare, Gunn. *Tourism Planning* (New York : Taylor and Francis, 1988).
Clayne, R. Jensen. *Leisure and Recreation-Introduction and Overview* (Philadelphia: Lea and Febiger, 1977).
Cleverdon, Robert. *The Economic and Social Impact of International Tourism on Developing Countries* (London: The Economic Intelligence Unit Ltd., 1979).
Cohen, Eric. "Towards a Sociology of International Tourism", *Social Research* 39, 1 (1972).
Colley, G. *International Tourism Today* (London: Lloyds Bank Review, 1967).
Cooper, C. *Tourism Principles and Practices* (London : Pitman, 1993).
Cosgrove, Isabel and Jackson; R. *The Geography of Recreation and Leisure* (London: Hutchinson, 1972).
Crampon, L.T. *An Analysis of Tourist Markets* (Colorado: University of Colorado Press, 1963).
Crampon, L.T. *The Development of Tourism* (Colorado: University of Colorado Press; 1963).
Dale, E. *Management Theory and Practice* (New York: McGraw-Hill, I973).
Davidson, R. *Business Travel* (London : Pitman, 1994).
Davidson, R. *Tourism in Europe* (London : Pitman, 1992).
Davis, H.D. *Potentials for Tourism of Developing Countries* (London: Finance and Development, 1968).
Donald, E. Hawking (Eds.) *Tourism Planning and Development Issues* (Washington: George Washington University, 1980).
Donald, E. *Tourism Marketing and Management Issues* (Washington: George Washington University, 1980).
Douglas Pearce. *Tourist Development* (Longman, 1989).
Douglas, Pearce. *Tourism Today : A Geographical-Analysis* (New York : Longman, 1987).
Dower, M. *The Challenge of Leisure* (London: Civic Trust, 1965).
Dumazedier, J. *Towards a Society of Leisure* (New York: Free Press, 1967).
Ed Gell, D. L. *International Tourism Policy* (New York : Van Nostrand Reinhold 1990).
Edmunds. *Environmental Administration* (New York: McGraw-Hill, 1973).
Edward, J Mayo. *The Psychology of Leisure Travel* (Boston : CBI Publishing Company, 1981).
Edwards, Francis, G. *How to Focus Your Marketing Efforts* (London: Louis A. Allen Associates, I976).
Engel, James F. (Eds). *Market Segmentation: Concepts and applications* (New York: Holt, Rinehart and Winston 1962).
Feiffer, M. *Giving Places* (London : MacMillan, 1985).
Forster, John. "The Sociological Consequences of Tourism", *International Journal of Comparative Sociology*, (1964).
Foster, D. *Travel and Tourism Management* (London : MacMillan, 1985).
Frank, R.E. *Market Segmentation* (New Jersey : Prentice-Hall, Inc; 1972).
Gearing Charles, E. *Planning for Tourism Development* (New York: Praeger Publishers, 1976).

Glasser, R. *Leisure: Penalty or Prize?* (London: Macmillan, 1970).
Gray, H. Peter. *International Travel-International Trade* (Lexington: Health Lexington Books, 1970).
Gunn, C. *Tourism Planning* (New York : Taylor and Francis, 1988).
Hammarskjold, K. "Economics of Air Transport and Tourism" (Montreal: I.C.A.O., 1972).
Heath, E. *Marketing Tourism Destinations* (New York : Wiley 1992).
Hibbert, Christopher. *The Grand Tour* (London:Weidenfel and Nicolson, 1969).
Hiller, Herbet L. "The Development of Tourism in the Caribbean Region." *Air Travel and Tourism* (August 1972).
Hodyson, A. *The Travel and Tourism Industry* (Oxford: Pergamon, 1987).
Hollander, S. *Passenger Transportation* (Michigan: Michigan State University, 1968).
Holloway, J. C. *Marketing for Tourism* (Harlow:Longman, 1995).
Holloway, J.C. *Marketing for Tourism* (London : Pitman 1988).
Howard. *Marketing Made Simple* (London: W.H. Allen, 1972).
Hudson, E. "Vertical Integration in Travel and Leisure Industry." *Institute of Air Transport* (Paris, 1972).
Hunziker, W. *Social Tourism, Its Nature and Problems* (Geneva: Aliance International de Turisme, 1951).
Hurdman, L.E. *Tourism : A Shrinking World* (New York : Viley, 1980).
Ian M. Matley. *The Geography of International Tourism* (Washington : Association of American Geographers, 1976).
Inskeep, E. *Tourism Planning* (New York : Van Nostrand Reinhold, 1991).
Jefferson, A. *Marketing Tourism* (Harlow : Longman, 1988).
Jefferson, A. *Marketing Tourism-A Practical Guide* (Harlow, Longman 1991).
Jenkins, J. R. Zif, J.J. *Planning the Advertising Campaign* (New York : MacMillan, 1973).
John M. Bryden. *Tourism and Development* (London:Cambridge University Press, 1973).
John, Lea. *Tourism Development in the Third World* (New York : Routledge 1988).
Joseph, D. Firdgen, *Dimensions of Tourism* (East Lansing, Michigan : American Hotel and Motel Association 1991).
Kaiser, Charles Jr. and Larry E. Helber. *Tourism Planning and Development* (Boston: CBI Publishing Company, Inc., 1978).
Katler, P. *Introduction to Marketing Management, Analysis, Planning and Control* (London: Prentice-Hall, 1975).
Kernan, J. B. *Promotion* (New York: McGraw-Hill, 1970).
Kerry Godrey and Jackie Clarke. *The Tourism Development Handbook* (London: Cassell, 2000).
Kotler P. *Principles of Marketing* (New York : Prentice-Hall, 1999)
Krippendorf, J. *The Holiday Makers. Understanding the Impact of Leisure and Travel* (Oxford : Heinemann 1987).
Lansing, J.B. Blood, D.M. *The Changing Travel Market* (Michigan: University of Michigan, 1964).
Law, C. *Urban Tourism : Attracting Visitors to Large Cities* (London: Mansell, 1993).
Laws, E.C. *Tourist Destination Management: Issues, Analysis and Policies.* (London : Routledge, 1995).
Lawson, Malcom. *Teaching Tourism-Education and Training in Western Europe-A Comparative Study* (London : Tourism International Press, 1975).

Leadley, P. *Leisure Marketing* (Harlow: Longman, 1992).

Lickorish, L. J. *Tourism and International Balance of Payments* (Geneva: International Institute of Scientific Travel Research, 1953).

Lickorish, L. J. *Tourist Promotion and Publicity Media* (Geneva: National Institute of Scientific Travel Research, 1955).

Lickorish, L.J. and Kershaw, A.G. *The Travel Trade* (London Practical Press, 1974).

Loughlin, Carleen. "Tourism in the Tropics: Lessons from the West Indies" *Insight and Opinion.* (1970).

Lundberg, D.E. *The Tourist Business* (New York : Van Nostrand Rheinold 1990).

Lundberg, Donald. *The Tourist Business* (Boston: Cahners Books, 1974).

Lundberg, *International Travel and Tourism* (New York: Institute of Certified Travel Agents, 1970).

Mathieson, A, *Tourism: Economic, Physical and Social Impacts* (London : Longman, 1982).

McIntosh, R.W. *Tourism Principles, Practices and Philosophies* (Ohio: Grid; 1977).

Medlik, S. and Middleton V.T.C., "The tourist product and its marketing implications", *International Tourism Quarterly* (1973).

Medlik, S. *Economic Importance of Tourism* (Surrey: University of Surrey, 1972).

Medlik, S. *Higher Education and Research in Tourism in Western Europe* (London: University of Surrey 1966).

Medlik, S. *Profile of the Hotel and Catering Industry* (London: Heinemann, 1972).

Middleton, V.T.C. *Marketing in Travel and Tourism* (London : Heinemann, 1988).

Middleton, V.T.C. *Marketing in Travel and Tourism* (Oxford : Heinemann, 1988).

Mill, R.C. *The Tourism Business: an Introductory Text* (London : Prentice-Hall, 1985).

Mill, R.C. *The Tourism System* (London : Prentice-Hall International, 1985).

Mill,R.C.*Tourism-The International Business* (New Jersey : Prentice-Hall, 1990).

Mitchell, Frank "The Value of Tourism in East Africa", *East African Economic Review.* 2, (June 1970).

Morisson, A. M. *Hospitality and Travel Marketing* (New York : Delmar, 1989).

Murphy, Peter E, Tourism : A Community Approach (New York : Methuen 1985).

Neulinger, John. *The Psychology of Leisure* (Springfield: Charles C. Thomas, 1974).

Nicholson, M. *The Environmental Revolution* (London: Penguin, 1972).

Norval, A.J. *The Tourist Industry* (London: Issac Pitman and Sons Ltd., 1936).

Ogilvie, F.W. *The Tourist Movement: An Economic Study* (London: Staples Press, 1933).

Page, S. *Urban Tourism* (London : Routledge, 1995).

Parker, S. The *Future of Work and Leisure* (London: Mac Gibbon and Kee, 1971).

Patmore, J. A. *Land and Leisure* (London: David and Charles, 1970).

Peaker, A. "Holiday Spending by the British at Home and Abroad", *National Westminster Bank Quarterly Review* (August 1973).

Pearce, D. *Tourism Organisations* (Harlow : Longman, 1992).

Pearce, D. *Tourism Today* (Harlow : Longman, 1987).

Pearce, D. *Tourist Development* (Harlow: Longman, 1989).

Pearce, Sales, J. *Travel and Tourism Encyclopedia* (London: Blandford, 1959).

Peters, Michael. *International Tourism*: "The economics and Development of the International Tourist Trade" (London: Hutchinson, 1969).

Pigram, J. *Outdoor Recreation and Resource Management* (London:Croom Helm 1993).

Pimlott, J.A.R. *The Englishman's Holiday* (London: Faber, 1947).

Pudney, John. *The Thomas Cook Story* (London: Michael Joseph, 1953).

Rae, W.F. *The Business of Travel* (London: Thomas Cook and Son, 1891).

Ram Acharya. *Civil Aviation and Tourism Administration in India* (New Delhi: National Publishing House, 1978).

Raymond, F. *Ecological Principles for Economic Development*, (London: John Wiley, 1978).

Reilly, R. T. *Travel and Tourism Marketing Techniques* (New York: Delmar 1988).

Richards, G. *Tourism and the Economy* (Surrey: University of Surrey, 1972).

Roberts, K. *Leisure* (London: Longman, 1970).

Robinson, G.W.S. 'The Recreation Geography of South Asia," *Geographical Review* (October 1972).

Robinson. H. *A Geography of Tourism* (London: MacDonald and Evans, 1976).

Ross, G. F. *The Psychology of Tourism* (Melbourne : Hospitality Press, 1994).

Rothfield, Crampon, Wahab, *Tourism Marketing* (London: Tourism International Press, 1975).

Ryan, C. *Recreational Tourism : A Social Science Perspective* (London : Routledge, 1991).

Schmoll; G:A *Tourism Promotion* (London: Tourism International Press, 1977).

Sessa, Alberto. *Tourism in Developing Countries* (Paris: Reprint from Manual on the Conservation, UNESCO, 1970).

Sigaux, G. *History of Tourism* (London: Leisure Arts, 1966).

Smith, S. *Tourism Analysis* (New York: Longman, 1989).

Smith, S.J. *Tourism Analysis* (Harlow : Longman 1995).

Smith, S.L.J. *Recreation Geography* (Harlow : Longman, 1983).

Smith, S.L.J. *Tourism Analysis* (Harlow : Longman, 1989).

Susan Horner, *Marketing Tourism Hospitality and Leisure in Europe* (London: International Thomson Business Press, 1996).

Sutton, Geoffrey. *How to Sell Travel* (London: Travel Topics, 1959).

Sutton, W.A. "Travel and Understanding notes on the Social Structure of Touring". *International Journal of Comparative Sociology*. (1967).

Tata, J.R.D. "The Story of Indian Air Transport". *Journal of Royal Aeronautical Society* (London: 1961).

Trease, Geoffrey. *The Grand Tour* (London: Heinemann, 1967).

Tull, D.S. *Marketing Research: Measurements and Methods* (London : Prentice-Hall 1993).

Turner, Louis and Ash John. *The Golden Hordes-International Tourism and the Pleasure Periphery* (London: Constable and Company, 1975).

Wahab, Crampon Rothfield. *Tourism Marketing* (London Tourism International Press, 1976).

Wahab, Salah. *Tourism Management* (London: Tourism International Press, 1975).

Walter, Pasini, *Tourist Health : A New Branch of Public Health* (Rimini : WHO 1988).

Waters, Somerset R. "The American Tourist", *Annals of the American Academy of Political and Social Sciences*: (1966).

White, J. *History of Tourism* (London: Leisure Art, 1967).

Young, George. *Tourism: Blessing or Blight?* (London: Penguin, 1973).

Yukic, T.S. Fundamentals of Recreation (London: Harper Row, 1963).

Zeithaml, V.A. *Services Marketing (London: McGraw-Hill, 1996).*

nde